Mourning into Joy

Mourning into Joy

Music, Raphael, and Saint Cecilia

Thomas Connolly

Yale University Press   New Haven and London

Designed by Sonia L. Scanlon
Set in Berkeley type by Tseng Information Systems,
Inc., Durham, North Carolina.
Printed in the United States of America by Edwards
Brothers, Inc., Ann Arbor, Michigan.

Library of Congress Cataloging-in-Publication Data
Connolly, Thomas, 1931–
Mourning into joy : music, Raphael, and Saint Cecilia /
Thomas Connolly.
p.   cm.
Includes bibliographical references and index.
ISBN 0-300-05901-9
1. Music in art.   2. Cecilia, Saint—Art.   3. Raphael,
1483–1520. Ecstasy of Saint Cecilia.   I. Title.
ML85.C66   1995
272'.1'092—dc20   94-5325
                                    CIP
                                    MN

A catalogue record for this book is available from the
British Library.

For Margaret and Stephen

Contents

8

"My eyes are always upon the lord"

Raphael and St. Cecilia   238

Appendix 1

Selected Scripture Texts of Mourning and Joy   263

Appendix 2

Books of Hours with Miniatures before Each
of the Seven Penitential Psalms   268

Illustrations

Acknowledgments

The research out of which this book grew had its beginnings in the observation of a colleague in classical studies that the basilica of S. Cecilia in Trastevere stood on the site of a shrine of a pagan goddess who cured eye disease and his further suggestion that the name of the saint derived not from the Roman clan of the Caecilii but from the Latin word for blindness, *caecitas*. My realization shortly thereafter that, unbeknown to liturgiologists, there were unmistakeable hidden references to this goddess in St. Cecilia's liturgy diverted my attention from the chant manuscripts of the basilica to the saint herself and awakened an entirely unexpected interest in the problems surrounding her. And so I gratefully acknowledge that whatever light my work may shed stems from that observation of Robert E. A. Palmer. Without it, this study would never have been undertaken and the intervening years would have been filled in far different and, I believe, less absorbing and productive ways.

But my debts of gratitude are legion. I am especially grateful to friends and colleagues in the United States who have offered so much helpful advice and comment and who have assisted in practical ways. Siegfried Wenzel responded readily to questions about sermons and paleography. Craig Wright, one of the first to express an interest in this research, was especially helpful in bringing it to publication. A most particular word of thanks must go to John Shearman, who read the manuscript in one of its later forms. His vast learning and generous advice smoothed away a number of the gaucheries that an amateur art historian almost made; if any remain or have entered since then, they should most emphatically not be laid at his door. Nigel Morgan was most helpful during his years at the Index of Christian Art, Princeton; and John Griffiths Pedley, director of the Kelsey Museum of Ancient and Medieval Archaeology at the University of Michigan, promptly answered questions about his work on the Bona Dea at Paestum and elsewhere. Many others merit thanks for their frequent and generous encouragement and comment, as well as for practical help. Among them I should especially mention Lawrence Bernstein, John Boe,

Joseph Dyer, Paul Elkin, Thomas Kelly, Ellen Klein, Jeanne Krochalis, Ann Matter, John McCoubrey, William Melczer, Charles Minott, Craig Monson, Helen North, James O'Donnell, Edward Peters, Homer Rudolf, Tilman Seebass, Colin Slim, Norman Smith, Leo Steinberg, Nancy Van Deusen, and Paul Watson.

A difficulty, but also a delight, of carrying out this work has been the need to spend so much time in Europe. My way there was eased by many friends and colleagues, with advice and help in all manner of situations. Carla Bernardini in Bologna must head this list. Monsignore Angelo Magognoli, pastor of San Giovanni in Monte, Bologna, responded courteously to several requests. I am enormously grateful also to Gabriella Zarri, Mario Pazzaglia, Lorenzo Bianconi, Nicoletta Bonafè, Carlo Delcorno, Vera Fortunati, and many other Bolognese friends too numerous to mention. Nino and Lea Pirrotta, Roberto Rusconi, and Pierluigi Petrobelli were also of great help, especially on my visits to Rome. Jean-Louis Biget, distinguished historian of Albi, responded promptly and efficiently to my appeal for assistance with illustrations. My nephew, Christopher Connolly, and his wife, Dominique, helped with hospitality and transport on my visits to Toulouse and Albi. Curtis Price and Rhian Samuel, Lindsay and John Northover, and Jonathan Liebenau did the same repeatedly when I went to London. The Padri Dehoniani of Marechiaro, Naples, were many times my hosts; to them and to their longtime fellow worker and my good friend, the late Father John Emanuel, I shall always be deeply grateful.

From yet further afield, Jehoash Hirshberg, of Hebrew University, was an encouraging and helpful reader of my manuscript. And Christoph Stroux, of the University of South Africa, gave early advice of the discovery of manuscripts from S. Cecilia in Trastevere at the Cape of Good Hope.

Many librarians have been particularly helpful: Marjorie Hassen and the staff of the University of Pennsylvania libraries; Don Faustino Avagliano at Montecassino; Don G. Zivelonghi at the Biblioteca Capitolare, Verona; M. J. Pons and staff at the Bibliothèque Rochegude in Albi; Jean Lefebvre of the Bibliothèque Municipale, Laon; Janet Backhouse and C. M. Hall of the Department of Manuscripts of the British Library; William Voelkle at the Pierpont Morgan Library, New York; Maureen Pemberton, who helped with slides from the Bodleian Library, Oxford; Elizabeth Burin and Elise Calvi of the Walters Art Gallery, Baltimore; and above all Father Leonard

Boyle, prefect of the Vatican Library. No visit to any library gave me more pleasure than B. S. Cron's gracious introduction to his collection, and especially to his eleventh-century lectionary from Trastevere.

Many graduate students have read and discussed parts of this book in recent years, and I have benefitted from their insights. I especially thank Lloyd Frank for his work on the symbolism of unplayed instruments and Morton Olsen for his research on Gerson's discussions of the spiritual senses.

Several fellowships enabled me to spend the time and make the journeys without which little could have been achieved. The National Endowment for the Humanities and the American Council of Learned Societes provided fellowships, each for a year of research in Europe. Other generous support came from the American Philosophical Society and from the Research Foundation of the University of Pennsylvania. Funding for publication was provided by the American Musicological Society, by the School of Arts and Sciences of the University of Pennsylvania (my special thanks for this go to Dean Rosemary Stevens), and once again by the Research Foundation of that institution.

I have often asked myself what other work of scholarship would allow one to spend as many joy-filled hours as I spent in the Pinacoteca Nazionale, Bologna, before the masterpiece of Raphael that is so central to my book. When I acknowledge my debt to the director, Andrea Emiliani, I only echo the thanks of so many for the skillful care and deep learning and love he has brought to bear on Raphael's work and the whole of that splendid collection. My deep thanks go to him and his staff, most especially to Giampiero Cammarota for his assistance with the illustrations.

My concluding thanks go to those who have helped with the editing and final shape of this book. Harry Haskell, Laura Jones Dooley, and Emily Boochever of Yale University Press showed remarkable skill, tact, and at times forbearance in bringing this work into production. Of all my editors, in learning as in life, my wife, Margaret, has been the most consistent and the most effective. Whatever *claritas* is engendered by my work must in large measure be attributed to her; any *confusio* that remains is entirely my own.

Acknowledgments

Introduction

"The most tangled question in all Roman hagiography" was how Hippolyte Delehaye described the case of St. Cecilia, that figure whom we commonly know as the patron saint of music. When he wrote this, the great Bollandist was thinking only of the obscurity of the saint's origins—indeed of the doubts about her very existence—and not at all of the many other mysteries with which her story is replete. Her musical character is itself one such mystery, regarded by scholars as a late interpolation into her cult, the result of a simple-minded medieval mistake. Yet when we know Cecilia only in this familiar guise as music's patroness, we behold, as it were, the last surviving shard of some ancient ritual vessel whose purpose has been long forgotten. Could we but find the lost fragments and reconstruct the vessel, we would go far toward answering that "most tangled question"—not just the question of her origins and identity, but the whole baffling complex of problems that surround her.

What lies before us, then, is a painstaking work of restoration, not unlike what occurs at an archaeological dig. If we could reconstruct the relevant motifs of the culture in which the legend of St. Cecilia arose and developed, we would understand more of what she signified to those who established and elaborated her cult. Like the archaeologist sifting the debris in hope of finding some hint to the wholeness and design of the vessel whose single shard is in his hands, we, too, must be alert for any clue that would help us draw a more complete picture of the ancient and medieval view of St. Cecilia. Such a clue has, fortunately, come to light and has given this book its title. Elucidating it will be our principal task in the pages that follow.

And so the subject of this study is precisely what the title declares it to be, a concept that I have labeled "mourning into joy." It is best described as a figure or theme that was prominent in the visual and literary arts from antiquity through the Renaissance and that expressed the soul's passages between vice and virtue as a flux of the contrary passions of joy and sadness. For reasons that will become clear, it strongly influenced the legend

1

and developing cult of St. Cecilia. Though the figure seems to have gone unstudied by modern scholarship, many instances of its use can be cited, from a poem of Prudentius in the late fourth century, for example, to a painting by Raphael at the beginning of the sixteenth.

Of necessity, the study addresses a variety of disciplines and covers a broad historical spectrum. It will have much to say to the art historian, for it begins and ends with a discussion of Raphael's famous altarpiece in Bologna, *L'Estasi di Santa Cecilia*—settling definitively, I believe, the problem of the work's strange musical iconography—and treats at length of musical symbolism in the visual arts. The student of the saints, too, will be engaged by a probing of the case of St. Cecilia. Cecilia's legend and liturgy, we will find, even at their inception at around A.D. 500 made significant use of the figure of mourning-into-joy. Her liturgy's use of it would exercise a decisive influence on the development of her musical character and of the musical iconography that would later distinguish her. By linking the stational liturgy at S. Cecilia in Trastevere, on the Wednesday after the second Sunday of Lent, to Trastevere's cult of Bona Dea Oclata, the study opens a new set of considerations for the liturgiologist about the way the early mass formularies were fashioned and the stational liturgy created. Scriptural texts embodying the theme of mourning-into-joy became commonplaces of the medieval pulpit, perhaps particularly so among the mendicant orders and in sermons preached on Cecilia's station day. In the later Middle Ages, further contemplation of mourning-into-joy shaped the cult of Cecilia in such a way that she became a symbol and exemplar of deep spiritual change, both for those at the beginning of this passage and for those venturing into the higher reaches of the spiritual life. The literary scholar will find that this fact illuminates Chaucer's retelling of Cecilia's legend in *The Canterbury Tales,* and that Dante weaves the theme, though not in its alliance with St. Cecilia, into the fabric of his cosmography in *The Divine Comedy.* This study addresses the musicologist, too, for it is concerned with the way the people of earlier times thought about music, in particular with how they conceived its laws as underpinning their cosmos; and by this route the study offers a completely new explanation for Cecilia's becoming linked to music as its patroness.

"Mourning-into-joy" describes a habit of the medieval mind that synthesizes a view inherited from pagan antiquity with a mode of thought drawn from the Bible. The Aristotelian passions of the soul were held to be summarized in just two of their number, sadness and joy, a reduction the Middle Ages justified principally from a passage in Boethius (*Consolation of Philosophy* I, m.7). This reduction was meant not simply as a description of static states of happiness and sadness but as a representation of all mutability, of all that could and did change in the universe that existed between the fixed realms of divine joy and damned woe. For sadness and joy, like all the passions (except wrath), are a pair of contraries, and it was on the flux of contraries (and of sadness and joy above all), according to much ancient and medieval thought, that all change in the created universe depended. In this sense the fluctuations of sadness and joy stood for all change—within the individual, within the material world, and within the working out of the divine scheme of redemption. The best-known example, and one to which the study will make some reference, is the cosmography Dante employed in *The Divine Comedy,* in which the poet's progress from the Woeful Kingdom to the Empyrean is marked by symbols of ever-growing joy and fading sadness.

Music is one such symbol, and one of peculiar power. As Dante and Beatrice rise through the spheres, they seem to encounter more joyous strains at every step in their ascent. Dante's linking of this signifier, joyful music, with this signified, progression from sadness to joy, is more than a felicitous poetic device. It renders concrete an abstract concept that underlies the ancient and medieval world views, so different from the modern: that the universe is governed by the same laws that govern music. Pythagoras and Plato both thought in this way and indeed spelled out their views in great detail. Medieval thinkers adopted this outlook without question, basing their vision especially on what they read in Macrobius. As with so many other things, Christian thinkers found a reflection of this concept in the Bible, in texts that describe the flux of sadness and joy in terms of music. There are a number of such texts, forming a distinct group within the larger group of scriptural references to changing sadness and joy. Many of the larger group (gathered in appendix 1) are exceedingly familiar today, commonplaces of pulpit and spiritual discourse like John 16:20 ("you will be saddened, but your sorrow will be turned into joy"). Others are less well known, including several that use musical imagery and became chief vehicles for giving a Christian expression, and a Christian interpretation, to the idea that the Middle Ages had inherited from Plato and Pythagoras and Macrobius.

The texts from this smaller group—and they have given this study its title—are, in the view espoused here, the basis for the strange musical iconography employed by Raphael in the painting of St. Cecilia that forms the beginning and the end of our inquiry. Job 30:31 ("my harp is turned into mourning, my organ into the voice of those who weep"), Lamentations 5:15–16 ("the joy of our heart is fled, our singing is turned into mourning: the crown is fallen from our head, woe unto us, for we have sinned!"), and Esther 13:17 ("turn our mourning into joy . . . and do not close the mouths of those who sing your praises") are the three that will most engage us, but there are others.

The concern of the study will be not just to show that these texts explain Raphael's iconography, not just to show how they can be linked to the cult of the saint he was painting, but also to come to grips with their implications for the medieval mind. And they were employed in a great number of contexts: in theological treatises, in sermons, in discussions of the philosophy of change, in poetry, in moral discourse, in painting, to name but a few. The common thread that binds them all is in fact the notion of change, or, to use a more accurate and useful term that thinkers in antiquity and the Middle Ages would have preferred, of motion. The word *motion* is used a great deal throughout this work, and the reader should be sensitive to its complex technical meanings in the thought of earlier times. More often than not, it carries the sense of change in general rather than of movement from place to place.

But within this whole area of change, of mutability, one kind of change —change in the heart—seems to have been Cecilia's particular domain. As her legend tells us in its two best-known phrases, she "sang in her heart to God alone" and "kept the gospel always within her heart." The failure to appreciate the significance of the phrase "in the heart," employed so often in her liturgy and set so many times to music in her honor by Renaissance composers, underlies our larger failure to understand how and why Cecilia was a musical figure much earlier than is today recognized. Most who have written about her have mentioned the phrase, but usually only to point out that her singing was internal, not audible, and for this reason irrelevant to any connection between the saint and "real" music.

The import of the phrase "singing in the heart" is not simply that Cecilia's song was inward, but precisely that her song was located "in the heart." "Heart" had a much wider meaning for earlier times than it does for our own, even if we discount the present-day emphasis on the romantic heart. In this study I shall not attempt to define the abundant meanings and implications the word had in the Middle Ages; rather I shall demonstrate in a general way that it extended to a much greater range of human faculties than it does in the modern era. The popularity in Christian tradition of the phrase "in the heart" stems from common biblical usage, but chiefly from St. Paul, and particularly from the Epistle to the Ephesians, which had great influence on Cecilia's legend. The heart, in this broad sense, became a focal point in the Christian mystical tradition as writers like Origen and Gregory of Nyssa struggled for language to express a knowing that seemed far deeper than ordinary intellectual experience. A fundamental part of this vocabulary was concerned with the dwelling of the divine word "in the heart" and with a range of spiritual capacities that paralleled the five physical senses and were commonly described as the "spiritual senses." When medieval philosophers discussed the workings of the human person, their writing was always tinged with the awareness of such spiritual activity and of the operation of the heart in this broader sense. They were concerned also, as they sought to assign various human functions to their proper seat of operation, to distinguish the roles played by "the head" and "the heart."

If sadness and joy, following Boethius, could signify all the passions, indeed all change, this was doubly true of spiritual change, of change "in the heart," the kind of change with which Cecilia was so closely associated. The association is readily apparent in later writers, especially certain late medieval mystics, but given the references to *luctus* and *gaudium* in the saint's legend and liturgy, there is reason to suspect that it goes back to the very inception of her cult.

In examining later manifestations of the theme, we labor under the disparities of modern and medieval usage. The word *conversion* will likely seem an equivalent of what is conveyed by mourning turning into joy as an expression of change in the heart. But conversion has a narrower sense for the modern mind—a decision taken, an altered way of acting. To the medieval mind, conversion suggested real changes within the soul. Beyond this more complex notion of conversion, medieval teaching on progress in

Introduction

the spiritual life was intensely concerned with, and quite specific in describing, the successive stages in this progress, the best-known analysis being that of St. Bonaventure in his doctrine of the three ways. Here we approach the center of our argument, for the medieval mystics' references to Cecilia and to mourning and joy were often made in the course of describing such spiritual progress. Further, the mystics made frequent use of musical symbolism to describe their inner experience, the spiritual sensation that resulted from their divine communing. "Going to nuptials while instruments played" was how the fifteenth-century mystic Camilla Battista da Varano (citing a phrase from the legend of Cecilia) described the intense experience that preceded her passage from the night of the soul (sadness, mourning) to divine union (joy). Neither her experience nor her musical description of it is unique.

Cecilia's association with mourning-into-joy, understood as a musical motion of the heart, is at any rate the closest approach that could be made to a simple statement of the subject of this book. The book uncovers the centuries-long consciousness that explored the path of spiritual development, the conversion and growth that proceed in complex ways from mourning to joy; that viewed music as intimately expressing these experiences; and that crystallized the conjunction of spirit and music in the elaboration over time of the figure of St. Cecilia.

This book constitutes a search for a lost tradition. That search must be conducted with as much awareness as possible of the tendency of earlier minds toward allegory and symbol, toward imbuing all manner of events, objects, and expressions with significances not at once apparent to the modern reader and viewer. In chapter 1, I define the problems that Cecilia's strange musical iconography presents, taking Raphael's famous altarpiece in Bologna as my point of departure. In chapter 2, I examine her identity and origins, the beginnings of her peculiar cult in Trastevere, and its character in later times and places, while at the same time looking deeply into liturgical texts and formulations that gave the cult its earliest expression. The singular *Passio,* largely if not totally fictitious, and itself the source of significant texts in the saint's later liturgy, is the subject of chapter 3.

In chapter 4 we turn our attention to an exceedingly common medieval miniature that provides powerful evidence for Cecilia's links to the idea of conversion, or radical spiritual change: the penitent David commonly called the David-in-Prayer or David-in-Penitence. How and why David achieved such prominence in both the early and medieval Church, how and why he came to be the medieval exemplar of penitence, how and why the discarding of musical instruments became a characteristic detail of these miniatures—these questions prepare the way for an extensive analysis of the type's symbolism and its position in missals, psalters, and books of hours. In this connection, I investigate the scriptural texts of mourning and joy—not just Job 30:31 and Lamentations 5:15–16, but many others that express the same thought and were common currency in medieval discourse.

A critical part of our search is directed, in chapter 5, at the commissioning of Raphael's painting. Here I draw on the studies of a number of other scholars, but from a different perspective, for evidence of the tradition being revealed. In particular I retrace the path of Gabriella Zarri in her reading of the works of Pietro da Lucca, spiritual director of Elena Duglioli dall'Olio, Raphael's principal commissioner. I go further than Zarri (though along a path whose promise she was aware of) by reading pertinent works of the spiritual master cited more than any other by Pietro da Lucca, that is, Jean Gerson. Gerson's works are thoroughly imbued with the symbolism of mourning and joy and provide the clearest insight into the tradition we are seeking in the form in which it reached Raphael himself.

The insights gained from Gerson enable us to pursue the tradition of mourning-into-joy, in chapter 6, in the broader cultural context of medieval literature and of spiritual writing and preaching. We find it in the late fourth century in Prudentius, and a century and a half later in Boethius. Dante's *Divine Comedy* and Chaucer's retelling of Cecilia's legend draw on this current as well. It finds its most evocative expression in the writings of certain medieval mystics who take Cecilia as a model and use the scriptural texts of mourning and joy to describe the spiritual change that accompanied their progress through the ways of perfection to perfect union with God.

One might reasonably ask, as did some readers of this book when it was still in manuscript, whether the notion of profound spiritual change that is embedded in the cult of Cecilia in the centuries leading up to Raphael's painting, and indeed also in the years that follow, is reflected in the texts of the music that was then being composed in her honor. This was after all the age of Dufay and Josquin, of Gombert and Palestrina, and of all the other masters of Renaissance polyphony. Upon further thought, however, the question's relevance fades. For the texts that the great Renaissance masters set in Cecilia's honor were almost without exception those that her liturgy had taken, hundreds of years before, from her legend: *Cantantibus organis, Dum aurora, Biduanis ac triduanis,* and numerous others. As antiphons and responsories, they had already provided the grist of symbol for the artistic mill throughout the centuries when chant held sway. It is for this reason that the texts that were set in the polyphonic era receive no special attention here; they will have been amply treated in my discussion of the texts of the *Passio* and of the liturgy.

Having established the breadth of the mourning-into-joy tradition over the course of the fourth to the fifteenth centuries, I extend the search, in chapter 7, into the long history of artistic representation of Cecilia that preceded Raphael. In so doing, I argue that the ideas behind his vision were not at all as novel as critics of his painting have held. Artists had already captured the sense of profound spiritual change in the cult of Cecilia, most particularly by having her adopt the organ as a symbol at about the same time that instruments began to appear discarded in miniatures of David. With this, the identification of the tradition that links Cecilia, David, and the texts of mourning and joy will be complete, and I return in chapter 8 to a painting that remains, even if we shall see it in a somewhat different light, one of Raphael's loveliest, yet most profound and erudite, accomplishments.

"but who can make anything of four saints?"

One   Raphael's Painting of St. Cecilia

"I have seen a quantity of things here—churches palaces statues fountains pictures, and my brain is at this moment like a portfolio of an architect or a printshop or a connoisseurs common place book. I will try to recollect something of what I have seen for indeed it requires, if it will obey, an act of volition."[1] If the words sound like lines from a letter home by a tourist newly arrived in one of the more picturesque Italian cities, it is because they are, the beginning of a letter that the poet Shelley, traveling south from Venice in the autumn of 1818, addressed to his friend Thomas Love Peacock, to describe his first impressions of Bologna. Continuing to read, one finds that it was the pictures, more than the buildings or statues or fountains, that most fired the writer's imagination; almost the whole letter is devoted to them, and even when he cries "Enough!" he returns immediately to the same subject.

Shelley is an enthusiastic viewer of paintings. He is moved by what he sees, yet what he sees is much what one would expect from a person of his time, his opinions, and his sensibilities. He complains of the visual engorgement he suffers in a great picture gallery, but retains clear impressions of a number of its treasures and records them for his friend. "Of course in a picture gallery you see three hundred pictures you forget for one you remember. I remember however an interesting picture by Guido of the rape of Proserpine, in which Proserpine casts back her languid & half unwilling eyes as it were to the flowers she had left ungathered in the fields of Enna—and there was an exquisitely executed piece of Correggio's—about four saints one of whom seemed to have a pet dragon on a leash. I was told it was the Devil who was bound in that style, but who can make anything of four saints, for what can they be supposed to be about?"[2]

Shelley's question is a revealing one, and many modern-day viewers will sympathize with it. What, indeed, can one make of these four saints, to say nothing of those countless other saints with their conventional emblems, in their conventional poses, repeated from picture to picture, in

9

gallery after gallery and church after church? What, indeed, can they be supposed to be about? Shelley did not give, and did not need to give, a direct answer, for the question was clearly rhetorical and his aversion to the religious viewpoint was well known to Peacock.

Other religious paintings that he saw, however, led him to acknowledge, and to describe more directly, his incomprehension, even as he declared his admiration: "I saw many more of Guido—one a Samson drinking water out of an ass's jawbone in the midst of the slaughtered Philistines. Why he is supposed to do this God who gave him this jawbone alone knows, but certain it is that the painting is a very fine one." Yet others provoke his revulsion, like Guido's *Slaughter of the Innocents* ("finely coloured & with much expression, but the subject is very horrible"); or like a Crucifixion by the same artist, which prompts him to decry all depictions of the subject: "One gets tired indeed whatever may be the conception and execution of it of seeing that monotonous & agonized form forever exhibited in the one prescriptive attitude of torture—but the Maddalena clinging to the cross with the look of passive & gentle despair beaming from under her bright flaxen hair, & the figure of St. John, with his looks uplifted in passionate compassion . . . & the whole of this arrayed in the colours of a diviner nature, yet most like natures self—of the contemplation of this one wd. never be weary."

Romantic and platonist, Shelley saw and responded to the successful pursuit of an ideal beauty, to the perfect artistic expression of an imagined passion. Whether the subject was Proserpine seized by Pluto or St. Margaret accompanied by her dragon, his reaction was of the same kind. Proserpine's "languid and half unwilling" glance was viewed from the same stance as the countenance of a Christ by Correggio, "heavy as it were with the weight of the rapture of the spirit, the lips parted but scarcely parted with the breath of intense but regulated passion." Beyond comments of this kind Shelley did not go, nor did it seem to occur to him that he *might* go. The figures he had seen in Italian religious paintings belonged to a world view that had, for him, dwindled to a myth just as surely as had Pluto and Proserpine, with the result that he could make nothing of four saints nor remotely suppose what it was they might be about.

What paintings are "about" is a question as tortured as any baroque Crucifixion, and one that will suffer no further affliction here than the observation that different kinds of paintings are "about" their subjects in vastly different ways. A sunflower of Van Gogh and the Madonna in Piero della Francesca's *Misericordia* altarpiece, for instance, are totally unalike in the way they are "about" what it is they portray, the altarpiece springing from a world whose cultural lifeblood was still myth, allegory, and symbol. That a painting should carry such a freight of allusion says nothing, of course, of its worth as art, but simply what kind of a work of art it is, something that should be kept in mind throughout the discussion that follows. Shelley's attitude toward religion anticipates a view more common in our own times. In this way he is a very satisfactory representative of the critical view of painting's relation to religion from the early nineteenth century to our own day.

Among the paintings Shelley saw in Bologna was one whose content— whose "aboutness," if you will—has always been something of an enigma, though the painting itself has been greatly admired and praised, as it was indeed by Shelley. That this work impressed him more deeply than any other in all that overabundance of viewing is made plain not only by his description of it but also by the fact that he returned to the Accademia the next day to see it again.[3]

We saw[,] besides[,] one picture of Raphael—St. Caecilia—this is in another and a higher style. You forget that it is a picture as you look at it, and yet it is unlike any of those things which we call reality. It is of the inspired and ideal kind, and seems to have been conceived & executed in a similar state of feeling to that which produced among the antients those perfect specimens of poetry & sculpture which are the baffling models of suc[c]eeding generations. There is an unity and perfection in it of an incommunicable kind. The central figure St. Caecilia seems rapt in such inspiration as produced her image in the painters mind, her deep dark eloquent eyes lifted up, her chestnut hair flung back from her forehead, one hand upon her bosom, her countenance as it were calmed by the depth of its passion & rapture, & penetrated throughout with the warm & radiant light of life. She is listening to the music of Heaven, & I imagine has just ceased to sing[,] for the three [sic] figures that surround her evidently point by their attitudes towards [her], particularly St. John who with a tender yet impassioned gesture bends his countenance towards her languid with the depth of his emotion. At her feet lie instruments of music broken and unstrung. Of the colouring I do not speak, it eclipses nature, yet it has all its truth and softness.

What Shelley saw in November 1818 was not quite what previous critics had seen. When the French took the work, created by Raphael as an altarpiece on wood, to Paris (along with much else) in 1796, they found it had deteriorated so badly that they had it not only cleaned and repaired, but transferred to canvas as well.[4] By 1818, the year of Shelley's letter to Peacock, it had been restored in a double sense: to Bologna in 1815 (though to the Pinacoteca, not to its original home at S. Giovanni in Monte) and to the state of lifelike color that so entranced the poet (plate 1).

Raphael had painted Cecilia standing in an open landscape among four other saints. She is richly clothed, though beneath her outer garments there can be seen the hair shirt which, her legend tells us, she wore next to her skin. Her head is thrown back, her ecstatic gaze bent on a point just forward of six angels who appear in the guise of boy singers through a rent in the darkened clouds above and behind her. They are grouped about two choirbooks, and it seems that their heavenly music has suddenly seized all of Cecilia's attention. In her hands, held carelessly upside down as if she had just ceased to play it at the moment when the celestial strains enthralled her and were now about to discard it without further thought, is a portative organ from which the pipes are beginning to slide to the ground. This organ, like many other representations of the instrument in medieval and Renaissance times, is reversed; that is to say, its longer, lower-pitched pipes are to the right, and its shorter, higher-pitched pipes to the left, an arrangement opposite to that of an actual organ.[5] Other instruments, all broken and discarded, lie scattered at her feet.[6] Her companion saints are St. Paul and St. John the Evangelist to the left, St. Augustine and St. Mary Magdalene to the right. The male saints are bareheaded, the two women wear light head-coverings: Cecilia a kind of turban, and Mary Magdalene a veil of lace wrapped around her shoulders and over her head. On a low hill in the background there is a round, domed building, beside which stands a tower surrounded by scaffolding.

The attendant saints are remarkable for their contrasting gazes, contrasting not only among themselves, but also as a group with the upturned gaze of Cecilia, who alone seems aware of the music of the angels. Paul stands pensive, looking down at the broken instruments; his right hand supports his bearded chin, his left holds two sheets of paper and the handle of a sword, the point of which rests just within the discarded triangle. John, pictured as a youth of great beauty, stands between Paul and Cecilia but a little beyond them and looks across toward either Augustine or, perhaps, Mary Magdalene. A large eagle, his traditional symbol, stands on a book on the ground before him. On Cecilia's other side, Augustine is pictured as a vigorous man of middle age; the strongly profiled head, bearded and balding, seems to gaze directly at John. He wears a cope richly embroidered with human figures[7] and holds a crozier in his right hand, while his left is raised as if in discourse. But it is Magdalene, at the extreme right, who is the most arresting of the four. Elegant, clad in a silvery-white robe, and carrying her traditional vessel of perfume, she gazes frankly, boldly even, at the viewer, while her slightly bent left knee, which suggests to some that she has just arrived on the scene, is the only hint of movement in an otherwise static scene.[8] That she seems somewhat apart from the rest of the group (though the disjunction of the group as a whole has been a common criticism of the painting) is due principally to the candor of her gaze and to the sense of slight movement in her figure.

Shelley's unreserved admiration for the painting, his sense of its unique beauty, may fairly be called general; certainly its technical excellence has never been questioned. The legend that Francesco Francia sickened and died upon seeing it, recognizing in its perfection his own artistic inferiority, is no more than legend, but the early acceptance of the story offers evidence of the powerful effect the work had on its first viewers.[9] Yet it has had its detractors, too, beginning with the seventeenth-century historian of the Bolognese painters, Carlo Malvasia, who was bold enough to call Raphael the *boccalaio Urbinate* (literally, a maker or vendor of ceramic from Urbino) and who was the first to raise, though obliquely, the problem of the iconographic scheme by suggesting that the artist's hands had been tied by the commissioners.[10]

The problem is really twofold, embracing not only Raphael's strange iconography but the whole question of Cecilia's association with music. This association, according to all I know who have written about it, is described as a fairly recent development in Raphael's day, an opinion which makes the saint's assumption of a musical instrument as her emblem a novelty even in the Bologna painting. Raphael is thus seen as having em-

Raphael's St. Cecilia

ployed a double novelty: first, by painting Cecilia with instruments at all and, second, (and more daringly, because it was unique) by having her abandon them.

This widely held opinion would have it that there is nothing in Cecilia's legend or early cult that can explain her association with music, nor any evidence at all for that association before the first representations of her holding an instrument. It used to be thought that Raphael was the first to depict her thus, though more recently it has been allowed that some such pictures are known from the late fifteenth century, while a few writers have realized, correctly, that examples from the early part of the century are also to be found.[11] What is not in question is that the instrument she holds, in all the earliest representations, is the organ.[12] There is, to be sure, a reference in the *Passio,* around A.D. 495–500, to *organa* at her wedding (strictly instruments of any kind, though often interpreted as the organ), but it is not Cecilia who plays them.[13] She might even be understood to have turned a deaf ear to them as representing the allurements of fleshly delights. "There came the day on which the bridal chamber was prepared," goes the passage, "and while *organa* played [*cantantibus organis*] she sang in her heart to the Lord alone the words: 'May my heart and my body be kept stainless lest I be confounded [*ne confundar*].'"[14] Cecilia is here said to have sung, but it was a "singing in the heart," a metaphor evidently for her interior prayer, and hardly grounds, it seems, for the extreme music-centered cult that later grew up around her.

A connection between the *organa* of her legend and the organs of her iconography was suggested at the very beginning of the seventeenth century by Antonio Bosio, the first great investigator of the Roman catacombs, who was present at the opening of Cecilia's tomb in S. Cecilia in Trastevere in 1599.[15] Writing about the *cantantibus organis* passage, Bosio stated that the word *organa* was used of instruments in general by the ancient world, that many kinds were played at weddings, and that it was this passage that gave rise to the custom of painting her with an organ in her hands. Others repeated Bosio's opinion, eventually adding to it the assertion that her musical role was due to a misunderstanding of the passage as it was used, in abbreviated form, in her office. The misunderstanding was alleged to have come about as follows. Although the legend appears in its entirety in medieval sources as readings at matins and the unabbreviated *cantan-*

tibus organis passage was sung—also at matins—as a great responsory, at vespers and lauds the passage was used as an antiphon, but now shortened by omitting the words "in her heart" (and also "and my body," though this is never remarked on). The resulting sentence could easily have given the impression that Cecilia actually sang, even to the accompaniment of an organ: "While an organ played Cecilia sang to the Lord the words: 'May my heart be kept stainless lest I be confounded.'"[16] It is not certain who first made the suggestion that Cecilia's association with music was due to a medieval misunderstanding of this antiphon, but its present almost universal acceptance is probably due to its having been championed in 1910 by Dom Henri Quentin.[17] So widespread has the opinion become that it is now repeated as if it were a well-established fact, although there has never been any real evidence for it beyond its surface plausibility.

It is precisely this willingness to attribute little beyond "misunderstanding" to medieval thinkers, to proceed oblivious of their categories of thought, and to impose modern categories on their works, that has led to ignorance about why Cecilia is associated with music and to a simplistic and unmedieval contrast, in discussing her cult, between earthly and heavenly music. These misconceptions inevitably obscure our understanding of Raphael's painting. Indeed, the distorting lens began to be imposed early in modern times, not so very long after the creation of the painting itself.

The tone of future discussions of the musical content of the painting was set in 1609 by Adriano Banchieri, Olivetan monk and organist of S. Michele in Bosco, on the outskirts of Bologna.[18] He is well aware of the problems surrounding both Cecilia's association with music and the use of the organ as her emblem. Yet while he denies that Cecilia played the instrument and explains the true significance of *cantantibus organis,* he is nonetheless ready to call her the heavenly organist and singer, and seems to blur the distinction, so important in later criticism of the painting, between audible singing and her "singing in the heart." He attaches an explicit symbolic meaning to the painting, which he describes at some length, by putting into Cecilia's mouth the words: "Away with you, sounds, songs, and all you worldly pleasures! Away with you, to your primeval mother! Let me desire nothing else, but only to have a place in that holiest of choirs, among those elect and victorious musicians and organists who make music eternally before my most sweet spouse, Jesus: 'Holy! holy! holy!'"[19]

The sounds and songs of worldly music that lie broken at Cecilia's feet are here aligned with "worldly pleasures"—the "vanities" condemned by preachers and spiritual writers—and all are consigned to their "primeval mother," that is, to the world that is synonymous with the kingdom of Satan. If this symbolic reading of the painting's musical iconography seems fairly obvious, it is nonetheless worth emphasizing, especially in contrast to those modern critics who see the painting as making a statement about music itself: about the superiority of sacred music over secular, or of vocal music over instrumental. Banchieri's commentary also conveys us into that symbolic country whose language, it will be shown, this work of Raphael's so eloquently speaks, a country whose borders Banchieri has already skirted in the two texts of Scripture he has cited at the beginning of his preface. Psalm 136:2, "on the willow-trees that grow there, there we hung up our instruments," is his theme, and he follows it shortly with a phrase from Job 30:31, "my organ [is changed] into the voice of those who weep."[20] Both texts, but especially the second, will be seen to have had a place in the development, many centuries before Banchieri, of the singular symbolism that grew up around the figure of Cecilia and that has given this book its title. Banchieri, indeed, adumbrates this trend by juxtaposing the ideas of "song of joy" (*carmen laetitiae*), which, he says, he draws from Nicholas of Lyra's and Alexander of Hales' comments on Psalm 136:2, and of "song of mourning" (*carmen luctus*), which permeates that same psalm.

Not for some three hundred years would critics pursue the question of the painting's musical content further than Banchieri had done, even though the long list of relevant studies that appeared during those years includes works of great significance from other points of view. San Giovanni in Monte and its famous altarpiece became a small stop on the grand tour, with the result that travelers, savants, and literati from the north of Europe—among them Richardson, Addison, Winckelmann, Reynolds, de Brosses, Burney, Goethe, Wackenroder, Stendhal, Liszt, Balzac, Schopenhauer, Mommsen, Ruskin, the Goncourts, and Nietzsche—have left their impressions and reflections, alongside those of Italians, in a variety of essays, books, memoirs, and letters.[21] Diverting in themselves, these reports of encounters with the Bologna *St. Cecilia* are at one with Shelley's in their lack of interest in what these saints, and the strange musical debris amid which they stand, might be about.[22] None of the writers, though he might discuss the iconographic scheme at greater length than did Banchieri, makes any more of it than a preference for heavenly over earthly music, with the sole exception of the Romantics, who tended to see in the painting confirmation of their belief in the divine superiority of music over the other arts.[23]

As criticism, the references take on a certain sameness, leading one to suspect that the authors read one another seriatim as the years went by. Generally they admire the color, the drawing and expression of the heads, the naturalness of the draperies. If they find fault, it is with the artist's arranging the five heads in a straight line, or with his having brought together people who, as a matter of history, could never have met. When they refer to the musical content, it is to repeat that Cecilia has abandoned her instruments because the heavenly concert has made her realize the poverty, by comparison, of earthly music, or to rhapsodize about the power of music or its primacy among the arts.

Karl Justi's essay of 1904, "Raphaels Heilige Cäcilia," was the first of a group of studies that sought to examine the painting within its own historical context by taking into account the spirituality of the age in which it was created. These studies, in particular those of Karl Justi, Walter Gurlitt, André Chastel, Stanislaw Mossakowski, Daniel Arasse, Gabriella Zarri, and Wolfgang Osthoff, were concerned with such things as the motives for and circumstances of the commissioning; the character of the principal commissioner, an evident mystic; the strong movement for religious reform in Italy around 1500—the *preriforma cattolica*—and its effect on Raphael and the commission; and the Christian Neoplatonism of the time, especially within the circle of the papal court of which Raphael was part.[24]

Important though these studies are to an understanding of the painting, they all share a set of fundamentally mistaken assumptions. All seem to accept without question that the musical iconography was a novelty, that Cecilia's association with music was relatively new in the early cinquecento, that she had only recently begun to be depicted with musical instruments as emblems, and that by painting her amid abandoned instruments Raphael had accomplished a masterstroke (albeit a baffling masterstroke!) of originality. In questioning these assumptions, I maintain that Raphael, though he introduced a new element into the iconography of Cecilia by showing discarded instruments about her, was in fact making reference to one of the most common, most eloquent, and at the time best understood Christian images of the later Middle Ages and the Renaissance. I further maintain that Cecilia's association with music was much more venerable than commonly supposed, and in no way due to a misunderstanding of the *cantantibus organis* passage, and that the organ had been among her emblems at least since the early trecento.[25]

But Raphael's musical iconography does not derive merely from earlier depictions of Cecilia. The image to which he made reference by painting Cecilia as he did was one that Christianity had absorbed long before from Judaism and that had been developed over many centuries through the meditations and reflections of saints, scholars, mystics, and preachers: the image of David kneeling in penitence for his adultery with Bathsheba and for the contrived death in battle of her husband, Uriah. The story had become, as it remains, a story for all time, of the heart rebellious against God recognizing instantly and without reservation its sin, and becoming by its humility, by its turning away from its own will to accept the will of God, the embodiment of the attitude that was seen as the only foundation of spirituality and the sine qua non of all growth therein.

Around the type of the kneeling David, commonly referred to nowadays as the David-in-Prayer or the David-in-Penitence, the Middle Ages developed an iconography of astonishing richness and complexity that reached its most intricate elaborations in miniatures of the late fifteenth and early sixteenth centuries, just prior to and contemporary with Raphael's Bologna altarpiece. Something of this development will be considered in chapter 4. For now I draw attention only to two pieces of evidence that suggest that the type was a point of reference for Raphael's *Cecilia*. The first is an iconographic detail—a harp on the ground beside the kneeling king—that is found frequently within the type in the fifteenth century and that signals to an alert viewer that there is a compositional similarity between the common image of David-in-Penitence and Raphael's uncommon image of Cecilia. The second is a group of scriptural texts—some of which accompany the David-in-Penitence in manuscripts, while others are the source for the detail of the abandoned instrument—that the type shares with the liturgy of Cecilia and that tell us much about the meaning of musical instruments in the iconography both of the king and of the virgin-martyr. Both these pieces of evidence require careful explanation.

Representations of David playing or holding musical instruments, most often the harp or the psaltery, are among the most common of all medieval images, known perhaps as early as the sixth century.[26] But within the type of the kneeling royal penitent, the harp, together with the royal crown, commonly rests on the ground near him and is rarely seen in his hands. Though other texts are not without bearing, these images are almost certainly a reference to Lamentations 5:15–16, "The joy of our heart is fled away, our singing is turned into mourning. The crown is fallen from our head: woe unto us, for we have sinned," and to Job 30:31, "My harp is turned into mourning, and my organ into the voice of those who weep."[27] Plate 2, a David-in-Penitence from a northern French book of hours of the late fifteenth century, which in fact shows two instruments beside the king, is an apt example.[28] The fact that these instruments are the harp—the most common visual translation of the biblical *cithara*—and the organ, and that the king's crown lies nearby, renders exact the reference to the two passages cited: "the crown is fallen from our head," "my harp is turned into mourning, and my organ into the voice of those who weep."

The same example shows the strong compositional similarity to Raphael's Cecilia. David kneels, instruments on the ground beside him, and gazes up at a vision of God in the heavens above; Cecilia stands, instruments about her feet, and gazes up at a vision of choiring angels. Considered alone, this similarity would be no more than mildly suggestive. But (and the point must be stressed, for it is a cornerstone of my argument) the texts that the David-in-Penitence miniature almost exclusively accompanies in medieval books, and the texts I have cited, are closely entwined in the liturgy of Cecilia. Let us consider both groups of texts in order.

The David-in-Penitence occurs commonly at three places in medieval liturgical books, and all three are important beginnings: the beginning of the seven penitential psalms (to the medieval mind these were David's prayer of repentance) in books of hours; the beginning of the liturgical year in mass books, where it heads the introit of the first Sunday of Advent—the first chant of the first day of the Church year; and the beginning of the psalter, which gives it a significant place not only in psalters as such but in bibles and breviaries as well. Two of the texts found at these beginnings may be called Cecilian. One is Psalm 24:1–3, which is the offertory for the ancient station day at the "home church" of the saint, S. Cecilia in

Trastevere, as well as the introit of the first Sunday of Advent.[29] It has an obvious aptness for the image of the kneeling David: "To Thee I have lifted up my soul. My God, I put my trust in Thee; let me not know shame."[30] The other text is the opening words of Psalm 6, the first of the seven penitential psalms, which are also the first words of Psalm 37. Psalm 37 is not only the third penitential psalm, but also the entrance psalm (introit) for the Trastevere station day: "Lord, do not reproach me in your wrath, nor chastise me in your anger."[31] The Cecilian reference of these texts would have been obvious to the medieval mind, which was as deeply steeped in the liturgy and the lives of the saints as it was in the Bible.

If this concurrence of Cecilian and Davidic psalm texts makes it less likely that the compositional similarity of Raphael's Cecilia to the David-in-Penitence is due to mere chance, such likelihood recedes even further when one considers the "intertwining," as I have called it, with Cecilia's liturgy of Job 30:31 and Lamentations 5:15–16, the texts that refer directly to the casting down of David's harp and crown. This matter, however, calls for a seeming digression.

The stational liturgy at S. Cecilia in Trastevere, on the Wednesday after the second Sunday of Lent, may well be the most curious of all sets of early Roman mass texts, for reasons having to do with its origins at the site, in Trastevere, of a shrine of a Roman goddess, the Bona Dea, who cured eye disease there under the names *Oclata* (the Good Goddess with the Eye) and *Restitutrix* or *Restituta* (the Restorer).[32]

This mysterious divinity was a goddess of women, especially in their domestic concerns, and was considered a guardian of married female chastity. For this reason both men and the plant myrtle, which was sacred to Venus, were banned from her secret rites in early December, as well as from her temple on the Aventine. When the liturgical compilers selected and composed texts for the stational liturgy at S. Cecilia, some time in the fourth or fifth century, they did so with an eye to the nearby pagan cult or its remnants, for these texts make a number of oblique references to it. They include orations that use symbolic language of vision and sightlessness, even one that addresses God as "Restorer," an epithet of Bona Dea at the Trastevere shrine. But none of them is stranger than the text that provides the intertwining of St. Cecilia's liturgical texts with the texts from Job and Lamentations that speak of the turning of joy into mourning: that is the day's lesson, which is from Esther 13:9–11, 15–17, the only passage from Esther that was used as a lesson in the early Roman mass liturgy.

This passage, which contains the words of Mordecai's prayer to the Lord to save Israel from the plotting of Haman, is unusual for two reasons. First, the Hebrew form of Esther's name is Hadassah, which means myrtle, the plant banned from the rites of the Bona Dea. Second, all the most ancient records of the liturgical form of this text, and all medieval manuscript versions of it known to me, are alike in that they alter the scriptural attribution of the words to Mordecai and place them instead on the lips of Esther. The compilers thus selected a reading about a woman whose very name spelled hostility to the pagan rite; and they altered the scriptural attribution of the text in order to have a woman, not a man, speak them, as if in mimicry of the exclusion of the male from Bona Dea's rites and temple.

Toward the conclusion of this singular lesson, at verse 17, are words that even on the surface seem to be a possible early source for Cecilia's association with music: "Hear our prayer, and look kindly on the people you claim as your own; turn our mourning into joy, so that we may live and praise your name, O Lord; and do not close the mouths of those who sing your praises." [33] A plea to God not to close the mouths of those who sing his praises seems an apt enough sentiment in a liturgy with such close links to the saint who was to become music's patroness. Most likely it has gone unnoticed for so long because attention has been paid only to Cecilia's feast, on November 22, and not at all to the equally significant station day. Yet the words preceding this plea are more remarkable still, for they exactly reverse the sense of the texts from Job and Lamentations, which explain the instruments cast down in the David-in-Penitence: Where these declare that music has turned into mourning, the harp into sorrow and the organ into the voice of those who weep, Esther now pleads that the mourning of her people be turned into joy and that they be allowed to sing God's praises. Thus, if the words from Job and Lamentations are the scriptural source for the instruments cast aside in the David-in-Penitence, it seems likely that the reversal of these words in the lesson for the Trastevere station day will link music in Cecilia's iconography to music in the iconography of the kneeling, penitent king, and in so doing will cast a penetrating light on her association with music.

This curious linking raises a great many questions and intimations.

Why should there be any link between David and Cecilia, between the adulterous, murderous king grieving bitterly for his sin and the Christian virgin who epitomized chastity triumphant? Why and how did the musician-king, the sweet singer of Israel and the creator of the Psalms, come to be depicted with his instruments cast down, and thus to be described visually as having turned his joy into sadness? Why and how did a Scripture text that describes the opposite situation, the turning of sadness back into joy, come to be applied to Cecilia? What, if anything, does all of this have to do with Cecilia's assumption of musical instruments as an emblem? And what, finally, did Raphael mean to convey when he painted her as he did, standing ecstatic between the discarded instruments and the singing angels, and holding so distractedly the upturned *organetto*?

Whatever the answers to these questions, they already suggest a view of Cecilia and music so radically different from previous modern interpretations that we can only think in terms of a tradition largely lost after Raphael painted his altarpiece. Only Banchieri, the Bolognese monk and organist, writing some one hundred years later, betrays any familiarity with such a tradition, when he quotes Job 30:31, "my organ into the voice of those who weep." Yet he says nothing of the reversed text of Esther 13:17, "turn our mourning into joy," nor does he suggest that these texts about mourning and joy have any bearing on Cecilia's association with music. Indeed, he seems to find that association something of a puzzle, just as later scholars would. But Banchieri's lines yield other signs that he is in touch with an earlier tradition, even if he does not seem fully to understand it, and I shall return to these as my argument develops.[34] Our next step is to address the complex questions of Cecilia's origins and identity. From the very beginning of the historical record of her cult, and deeply involved in that cult, there are clear indications of the theme I have labeled mourning-into-joy and hints of the reasons for her association with music as well.

the origins of the legend

Two *Caecilia Restituta*

The scholar perplexed by Cecilia's *Passio,* the art historian baffled by the musical debris in Raphael's painting: how far removed from each other their problems seem! But the apparent distance is greater in time than in concept. Indeed, it has become evident that the several scholarly problems revolving about Cecilia in diverse disciplines (I think especially of the Chaucerians' difficulties with the *Second Nun's Tale,* Chaucer's retelling of the saint's legend, as well as of the art historians' puzzlement over Raphael's painting) might not have presented themselves at all if scholars had faced up to the question of just who Cecilia was. It is not a question that can be solved simply by reading her story in the *Golden Legend.* This would be to adopt a modern view—that medieval devotion to the saints, though quaint and not without antiquarian interest, need not be approached with the seriousness reserved for, say, medieval philosophy—and to disregard a medieval one—the deeply ingrained conviction that saints have succeeded in life's inescapable struggle, and are our models and advocates in making those gravest of choices that determine our eternal fate. It is true that in the Middle Ages the saints' lives were often represented in ways that are amusing, or grotesque, to modern taste. But they were also the subject of deeply contemplative thought and discourse. Later scholarship has, unfortunately, been more concerned with the former. This is not to say that there is not excellent scholarship in hagiology. There is, but it tends to be disregarded in interdisciplinary work.

My search for the lost tradition behind Raphael's painting must begin, as it actually did begin some eighteen years ago, by asking who Cecilia was, and by coming to grips with the foundation of the complex spiritual thought relating to her cult that is encountered in the later Middle Ages. My first focus is upon the two bodies of texts with which her story commences and which for so many centuries were the sole source of contemplative thought from which those later and more luxuriant growths of Cecilian spirituality took their nourishment. These are her legend and the texts of her early liturgy. The legend has a clear priority, for the liturgy that formed about her did so in response to the understanding of her life that her legend had already ingrained in early Christian consciousness.

It is a demanding task, for the case of St. Cecilia was rightly characterized by the most eminent of twentieth-century students of the saints, Hippolyte Delehaye, as "the most tangled question in all Roman hagiography."[1] In a shrewd analysis of the evidence, Delehaye advanced the only theory that, at least up to that point, did not encounter insuperable difficulties. Yet he also warned that "the last word has still not been said on the subject in the big books." While I advance new evidence and propose new conclusions in this chapter, my argument builds on Delehaye's hypothesis rather than rebuts it, and if anything strengthens its central point. But it will still not be the last word to be said in the big books.

So tangled is the array of evidence that we shall do better to consider the case in outline before becoming caught up in its intricate details. At the heart of the problem is this, that around the end of the fifth century, suddenly and for the first time, a saint appears who receives all the cult due to one of the most revered of the Roman virgin-martyrs yet seems to have been unknown to previous generations. She is listed in the Canon of the Mass alongside other saints of irreproachable historical credentials; she is depicted in the earliest mosaics in Ravenna; her tomb, in the most honored crypt of the catacombs, is pointed out; and she is being celebrated at a basilica in Trastevere with obvious enthusiasm by the Roman populace.[2] But her story, related in a *Passio* reliably dated about A.D. 495–500, is an obvious fiction, and there is practically no evidence that she was venerated much earlier than this date—no evidence, indeed, beyond what seems to have been a deeply ingrained popular cult, that she ever existed.[3] This is all the more puzzling in that the age of martyrs had ended with Galerius's edict of toleration in 311 almost two centuries earlier. How different she is, then, from those other martyrs who were so well known to earlier Christian writers, even though fanciful details may have been added to their legends! Augustine, Ambrose, Prudentius, and others, who knew so much about Agnes and Eulalia and Agatha, do not even breathe Cecilia's name, nor is she mentioned in the fourth-century list of Roman martyrs known as the *Depositio martyrum*. More telling yet is the absence of her name and image from gold-glasses, those little devotional objects found so commonly in early Christian Rome. Such an absence shows rather conclusively that she had no public cult in the fourth or early fifth centuries. This total silence of earlier generations, contrasted with the sudden burgeoning of devotion to her in about 500, is what makes it so difficult either to accept her as a historical figure or to explain how her popular cult came into being.

The evidence in the case is in part literary and historical, in part archaeological. It centers on her legend, as known from the *Passio* (the Roman Martyrology mentions no more than a name); and on the two Roman sites traditionally connected with her story, the basilica in Trastevere and a chamber in the Catacomb of St. Callistus that is believed to have been her burial place. The *Passio* tells of a noble Christian maiden, vowed to virginity, who was constrained by her parents to marry a young pagan nobleman named Valerian. She told him on their wedding night of her vow, and he was converted, along with his brother, Tiburtius. Eventually all three were martyred, Cecilia being condemned to suffocation in an overheated Roman bath, then beheaded when she was miraculously preserved from the first sentence. The *Passio* tells how Cecilia, in her last hours, willed her house to the Church, though it does not say that it was in Trastevere. And it tells how, after her death, the pope had her buried "amongst his fellow bishops," a phrase that has been taken to mean the hallowed crypt in St. Callistus where several popes of the third century were laid to rest.

Yet there is a good deal of evidence outside the *Passio* to connect the name of Cecilia both with the basilica in Trastevere and with the papal crypt in St. Callistus, though it is all later in date than the *Passio*. There is excellent evidence, for instance, that a Cecilia was venerated in a crypt adjacent to the papal tombs in St. Callistus in the century after the *Passio;* but, in contradiction of earlier archaeologists, it was shown in 1935 that this crypt was constructed after, not during, the age of persecutions, thus making it unlikely that it was built for a martyr.[4] It is equally clear that a feast in honor of St. Cecilia was being celebrated at the Trastevere basilica by 545 on the day that is still observed as her feast, November 22, for the *Liber pontificalis* reports that on that date in that year troops sent by Justinian seized Pope Vigilius in the basilica as he was finishing mass and hurried him aboard a ship in the Tiber to be transported to Constantinople.

Caecilia Restituta

Evidently, then, the author of the *Passio* wrote for Romans who knew of a Cecilia buried in the catacomb and of a Roman basilica that bore the same name, but who knew so little about this person (or these persons, if they were not one and the same) that he was able, around the years 495–500, to present a fictitious story about her as the truth. Considering this, Delehaye suggested that the Cecilia of St. Callistus was no martyr, but rather a pious Roman lady who, because of her illustrious family, its long connection with the catacomb, and perhaps her own generosity to the Church (she might, for instance, have paid for the decoration in marble and mosaic that Pope Damasus is thought to have carried out in the papal crypt in the second half of the fourth century), was given the privilege of burial near the tombs of the popes. Later generations, believing that a sarcophagus thus honored must hold the remains of a great martyr, began to venerate her as such, and went on to include the Trastevere basilica, which also bore the name of a Cecilia, within this same cult.

There is much to support Father Delehaye's hypothesis. It takes into account the conclusions of archaeologists that the crypt next to the crypt of the popes in St. Callistus was built after the persecutions and that a Cecilia buried there could hardly have been a martyr; and it supposes something that is known to have happened in other cases, the "canonization" of a pious person or donor by the attachment of the epithet *saint* to a name that previously lacked it.[5] Yet there are problems. The greatest is the spread of this cult from the catacomb, where it could not have begun much before the end of the fourth century at the earliest, to the basilica in Trastevere, about the origins of which so little is known. Father Delehaye himself foresaw this difficulty by pointing out that his theory depended on one supposition: that the Cecilia of the catacomb and the Cecilia of Trastevere were one and the same. He saw no reason to doubt it, since the identity seemed to have been accepted since at least the fifth century.[6]

The problems of Fr. Delehaye's hypothesis become apparent if we follow it to logical conclusions. If we suppose that the lady Cecilia buried in the catacomb was in actual fact the donor of the house in Trastevere, we must wonder how the fact of her donation was so clearly remembered or recorded, while at the same time a false story of her martyrdom could be given credence. Otherwise, and more logically from Fr. Delehaye's standpoint, we must suppose that the Trastevere property indeed bore the name

of Cecilia but that she was a different Cecilia from the Cecilia of the catacomb and that her true identity had simply been forgotten. When the lady
of the catacomb came to be labeled a saint, popular belief simply accepted
that she was the same person as the one whose name was attached to the
church in Trastevere.[7] One wonders, however, whether an identification in
the catacomb could have led so quickly to the cult that developed in Trastevere. And another and graver problem arises from the *Passio* itself, one that
Delehaye called attention to but did not pursue.

When the author of the *Passio* describes Cecilia's donation of her house
to the Church, he writes that she had the property registered under the
name of a certain Gordianus so as to hide its true ownership from the authorities and thus prevent its confiscation. In an invented story, such as
we know the *Passio* to be, this episode seems quite gratuitous. Delehaye
himself pointed out the likely explanation.[8] The Trastevere property had
actually belonged to a certain Gordianus and still bore his name at law; that
is, the property was still known, to some at least, as the "title of Gordianus." The author of the *Passio*, needing to give legitimacy to the appellation
"title of Cecilia" (which could have been a totally new name but was more
likely an existing alternative), took care of the problem by inventing the
story of Cecilia's hiding her ownership under the name of Gordianus. Thus
it seems that the future basilica was known, in late fifth-century Rome,
under two names: the title of Gordianus and the title of Cecilia. This is a
crucial point in the search for St. Cecilia, for I contend that the name of
Cecilia became attached to the basilica not because a Cecilia had owned it
and given it to the church but for another reason having to do with popular
local usage. But this point takes us a little further into the argument than
we are yet ready to go. It is time to step back from what has so far been
a summary of the evidence in our "tangled question" and to look at that
evidence in more detail.

One might expect the so-called Hieronymian, or Roman, Martyrology
to shed some light on Cecilia's identity. This compilation of martyr-lists
received its final form during the fifth century (though numerous inter-
polations were added later) and is thought to represent a complete list of
all the feasts that were celebrated at that time without any reference to
their liturgical ranking or solemnity. But this fundamental source introduces further complications. It shows four separate entries for Cecilia: on

August 11, September 16, November 17, and November 22.[9] The first of these is clearly the result of a late redactor's having confused the Tiburtius who is celebrated on August 11 (a martyr buried on the via Labicana) with the Tiburtius who, according to the *Passio,* was St. Cecilia's brother-in-law. This second Tiburtius is celebrated, along with a Valerian and a Maximus (whom the *Passio* describes as the officer appointed to guard the brothers and as having been converted by them and then martyred with them), on April 14. They are thus authentic martyrs, of whom nothing is known except that they were buried in the cemetery of Praetextatus, and who were evidently "borrowed" by the author of the *Passio* for his story.

The other three entries differ not only in their dates, but also in their treatment of Cecilia's name, which on November 17 is given a masculine form: "At Rome, in Trastevere, [the feast] of Caecilius [*Romae Transtibere Caecilii*]." Almost all students of the matter have simply regarded this as a copyist's error. Delehaye, however, expressed a distaste for corrections of this kind, corrections for which there is no warrant other than the avoidance of an extraneous difficulty. For him it was but "another problem waiting for a solution."[10] This entry for November 17 is, in addition, the only entry that mentions Trastevere, the others simply stating that the memorial is observed in Rome.

Giovanni Battista de Rossi, the great nineteenth-century archaeologist who rediscovered the crypt of the popes and the adjacent chamber of Cecilia, suggested that September 16, with its reading "At Rome the passion of Saint Cecilia," was the actual date of her martyrdom.[11] Delehaye surmises that perhaps some "vague Cecilia, lost in a list of names, drew the attention of one of those interpolaters whose touch is evident on so many pages of the Hieronymian Martyrology, and he introduced the rubric 'at Rome' before the name of this Cecilia."[12] But what of the two dates in November, and of the fact that the entry for November 17 specifies Trastevere, while that for the traditional date of St. Cecilia's feast day, November 22, does not? November 22 is the date given in the first true Roman liturgical book, the so-called Gelasian Sacramentary; but one notes that the earlier Verona mass book, though it does not specify a date, places St. Cecilia between the celebrations of the Four Crowned Martyrs and St. Clement, a position that could imply November 17 as easily as November 22.[13] If the diversity of dates still confuses us, considerable light has been shed by recent archaeology on the problems surrounding the crypt of Cecilia in the catacomb of St. Callistus, though its effect on the problem of her historicity is wholly negative. The nineteenth-century's rediscovery of the catacombs, initiated by the Jesuit Giuseppe Marchi and Giovanni Battista de Rossi, began at this very place.[14] In 1849 the twenty-seven-year-old De Rossi, already well-versed in the written history of the catacombs, found a broken fragment of marble inscribed with the letters "—NELIUS MARTYR" in an ancient but long-abandoned chapel along the via Appia. He surmised correctly that it was the tombstone of Pope Cornelius, who had been martyred in 253 and buried in the papal crypt in St. Callistus. Aware that such fragments usually do not migrate far from their place of origin, and that there was an unidentified and unexplored cemetery beneath the vineyard on which the chapel stood (this was evident because a light shaft descended into the ground there and corridors could be seen leading away from it), he persuaded Pope Pius IX to buy the property for the Church. His excavations led him almost at once to the papal crypt, now sadly decayed, and to the other part of Pope Cornelius's marble slab.[15] De Rossi knew that the *Passio Caeciliae* told of her being buried by Pope Urban "among his fellow bishops" and that other evidence of the sixth and seventh centuries—the lists of martyrs compiled by the Abbot John when he gathered oil from the lamps at their graves under Gregory the Great, and the pilgrims' itineraries of the seventh century—linked her burial place to the cemetery of St. Callistus.[16] When he found that the crypt dug behind the papal crypt (it is entered through the door at the left rear of the papal crypt; see figs. 2.1 and 2.2) was ornamented with paintings of St. Cecilia, he concluded, reasonably enough, that he had found her actual resting place, indeed the very tomb in which Pope Urban buried her, just as the *Passio* described it (fig. 2.3).[17] Her remains had of course been removed long before and had found their way, it was believed, to a final resting place beneath the high altar of the Trastevere basilica. But of that more will be said shortly.

Yet De Rossi's great discovery, which was to cast such brilliant light on the Roman cemeteries in general, served only to obscure even further the case of St. Cecilia, when Paul Styger realized in 1935 that her crypt in St. Callistus had been constructed in its entirety after the Peace of the Church and not, as De Rossi and others thought, during the persecutions. The

Figure 2.1. The crypt of the popes in the catacomb of St. Callistus as discovered by De Rossi

(From De Rossi, *Roma sotterranea*)

Modern exploration of the catacombs began when De Rossi rediscovered this crypt in 1854. Because several martyred third-century popes were buried here, it was one of the most sacred sites in early Christian Rome. At the left rear, a door leads to the crypt of St. Cecilia.

papal crypt, begun probably during the fourth decade of the third century, was itself completed in stages over a long period. Some time after it was finished, and after the persecutions had ended, a narrow passage was dug through the left rear wall and a small chamber was opened up, just large enough for a niche in which a sarcophagus was evidently placed. Some time later still, and again in stages rather than all at once, this space was enlarged, the huge light shaft was dug, and walls, niche, and passageway were adorned with marbles and mosaics. Part of this work may have been done under Pope Damasus (366–84), whose zeal for the cemeteries and especially for the crypt of the popes is well known, but there is no certainty

Figure 2.2. De Rossi's hypothetical restoration of the crypt of the popes

(From De Rossi, *Roma sotterranea*)

De Rossi envisioned the crypt as it might have been before the tombs were broken and the relics taken. His discovery on the ground above of a broken slab reading simply -NELIUS MARTYR had led him to suspect that he was close to the tomb of Pope Cornelius, who he knew had been buried in the lost crypt in 253.

about this. Nor is there anything to show that the initial embellishment of this crypt had any relation to Cecilia. There is in fact no evidence whatsoever to suggest that the crypt was built for a martyr, nor any evidence for the cult of a martyr there until very much later. The *Passio*, about 495; the lists of Abbot John, about 600; the seventh-century pilgrim lists; and the artwork in the crypt, all of it even later still—this is the sum total of such evidence.[18]

A historical meditation about Cecilia made at her crypt in St. Callistus is thus hardly likely to be the peaceful reflection one might wish: doubts and questions simply will intrude. The situation is no better at the

Figure 2.3. The crypt of St. Cecilia in the catacomb of St. Callistus

(From De Rossi, *Roma sotterranea*)

The *Passio* of Cecilia of c. 495 says she was buried near the tombs of the popes, and other evidence confirms her cult here at that time. De Rossi found two wall-paintings of the saint, one to the left of the niche in which he believed she had been entombed, the other in the light-shaft. Yet later evidence has shown that this whole crypt was built after the age of persecutions. The door to the left of the niche leads to the crypt of the popes.

Trastevere basilica, the reputed site of her house and of the scene of her martyrdom. Recent archaeological judgment has allowed not a single stone from these two monuments, the catacomb and the basilica, to be advanced as evidence for the saint's existence. "The monuments have shed no light whatsoever on the historicity of a martyr named Cecilia," wrote the archaeologist Pasquale Testini in 1966, ". . . the answer that was expected from the archaeologist must be sought again in the domain of the hagiographer."[19] And excavations carried out even more recently do nothing to alter this state of affairs. Yet new considerations of an archaeological kind with bearing on the case have come to light since Testini's trenchant judgment. These have to do with Cecilia's monument in Trastevere and its obscure origins, and they are best considered within the context of the evidence that the basilica itself has furnished in the case.

The entrance to S. Cecilia in Trastevere is still enchanting: a sudden leaving behind of the bustling street and the little piazza crammed with parked cars, a passage through the ochred portal into a courtyard graced with hedges and flowerbeds, graveled paths, and an ancient cantharus fountain. But the frequent rebuilding the church has undergone soon becomes apparent, even from the outside, in the façade and the medieval brick bell tower, an impression confirmed as soon as one enters the church itself. The present interior (see fig. 2.4) is the result of a number of restorations, largely demanded by the structural problems that beset the basilica.

Figure 2.4. The interior of the basilica of S. Cecilia in Trastevere

(Photo: Thomas Connolly)

Built by Pope Paschal I about 820 and much altered since then, this church replaced an earlier church dedicated to St. Cecilia that had been fashioned from a conglomeration of ancient Roman buildings.

Figure 2.5. The apsidal mosaic of S. Cecilia in Trastevere

(Photo: Thomas Connolly)

In this mosaic erected by Pope Paschal I c. 820, an example of the well-known *Adventus in gloria* composition, Christ stands in the clouds of heaven beyond the heavenly Jordan, his hand raised in blessing. On the left are Pope Paschal with a model of the basilica, St. Cecilia, and St. Paul. To the right are Sts. Peter, Agatha, and Valerian. A phoenix sits in the palm tree to the far left.

In 1823, when Giorgio Doria Pamphili was titular cardinal, heavy pilasters were built around the collapsing pillars of the nave, and the interior was stuccoed.[20] But the church's medieval aspect already had been largely lost a century before, when, under Cardinal Troiano Acquaviva in 1725, the ceiling of the nave was covered with wood and adorned with Sebastiano Conca's painting *The Apotheosis of St. Cecilia.* At the same time, the mosaics of the triumphal arch were removed and the cosmatesque pavement of the nave was covered with the present geometric design in marble.

Isolated but magnificent indications remain, however, of the building's medieval origins. The apsidal mosaic, executed when the present basilica was built by Pope Paschal I around 820, looms imposingly over the sanctuary. It is an example of the scene known as the *Adventus in gloria,* and shows Christ in the clouds of heaven with Sts. Paul, Cecilia, and Pope Paschal to his right, and Sts. Peter, Valerian, and Agatha to his left (see fig. 2.5).[21] There is, besides, the superb ciborium by Arnolfo di Cambio, securely dated 1293 when an inscription to that effect was uncovered during

the restorations that began in 1978. And in the choir of the attached convent, abutting and overlooking the nave of the church, is the most beautiful
fresco in the world, Pietro Cavallini's *Last Judgment,* painted in the same
year that Arnolfo built his ciborium. Other medieval remains came to light
in the recent restorations, remains that had been covered by the work on
the ceiling in 1725: two large mosaics, of the cities of Bethlehem and Jerusalem, on either side of the vault of the apse; large remains of frescoes,
thought to be by Cavallini, along the central nave; and in the tympanum at
the rear a fresco of the Annunciation.

As one stands in the nave and surveys this not unpleasing architectural
amalgam, one's gaze is soon and inevitably drawn to an artwork of singular beauty, designed and positioned so as to draw all eyes to itself and
to focus the viewers' minds on the person, the events, the legend that are
the whole raison d'être of all that surrounds them. Stefano Maderno was
only twenty-five when he carved the gleaming white statue of the martyred
Cecilia that lies before and below the high altar, at the level of the pavement
(see fig. 2.6).[22] It shows her reclining, in death, her face turned downward
and away from the viewer, and her neck marked with the stroke of the executioner's sword. The gentle folds of her simple vesture and of the cloth
that covers her head are carved with an exquisite verisimilitude. The knees
are slightly bent, and the straightened arms, held a little before and away
from her body, lead the gaze down to hands that touch but are not joined
and to fingers folded in a gesture that is alleged to symbolize her faith in
the unity and trinity of God.

Maderno's statue has gathered to itself a puzzling and persistent legend
that seems to recapitulate the whole story of Cecilia. It was carved following the excavations and restructuring carried out at the basilica by
Cardinal Paolo Sfondrati in 1599, when the sarcophagus believed to contain Cecilia's body was discovered beneath the sanctuary. The legend soon
took root, and has since flourished, that the saint's body was found incorrupt when the sarcophagus was opened; and that Maderno's sculpture is
an exact record of what the witnesses at the opening saw. Antonio Bosio,
who was one of these witnesses, has left a meticulously detailed account
both of what he saw and of what he was told by Cardinal Sfondrati and
others.[23] His description of the body's position is indeed very close to what
we see today in Maderno's statue: it "lay resting on its right side, the legs

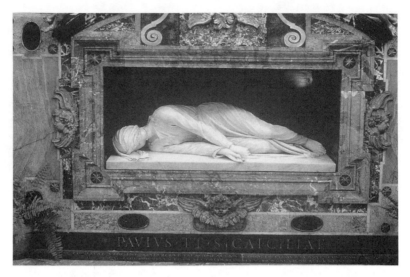

Figure 2.6. Stefano Maderno's statue of St. Cecilia

(Photo: Thomas Connolly)

Maderno was present when the tomb beneath the high altar of the basilica was opened during excavations by Cardinal Paolo Sfondrati in 1599. Legend has long maintained that he carved the saint's body exactly as he saw it, but careful reading of the reports casts serious doubt on the story.

slightly bent, the arms held forward, the head somewhat twisted, the face turned towards the ground, like someone asleep." But his verbal sketch goes somewhat beyond his evidence, for he also reports that the remains were covered with a silken veil, much darkened by age and obscuring the body from view, which, out of a sense of delicacy, no one dared remove.[24]

Delehaye shines a clear and unrelenting light on this point. The plain fact is that no one saw the remains, that none of Bosio's statements about their condition can be accepted apart from those that the covering veil allows us to accept. Delehaye has no qualms in styling the body a "mummy," noting moreover that its small size ("five and a half palms long," something under four feet) suggested that this was the body of a child, not that of a mature woman who had founded a Roman *titulus*. This is so even if we add in the height of the head, which had been removed by Pope Paschal I before the body was deposited in the basilica, something that Bosio knew of but forgot to take into account.

Even as we doubt the popular legend surrounding Maderno's statue, the reader is surely asking the question raised above: How did these remains, which (if our analysis of the record has been correct) were once present in the crypt in the catacomb of St. Callistus, find their way to the Trastevere basilica? It was in fact Pope Paschal I who placed them there when he built the present basilica on the site of the original structure in about 820. But the report of the event, in the biography of that pontiff in the Book of the Popes, raises more difficulties than it solves. Nonetheless the account will help us to understand better the character of the present basilica and will provide a proper context for a discussion of the original *titulus Caeciliae* and of the Christian cult that developed there.

Dismayed by the ruinous state of the ancient structure, Paschal set about building the basilica that still stands, greatly modified, in Trastevere. He adorned and furnished it munificently, and made generous provision for its musical service.[25] He wished above all to enrich his foundation with the relics of its patron, and set inquiries afoot to that end. But his efforts came to nothing, and he was persuaded to accept the common report that the Lombards, under King Astolph, had seized Cecilia's body during their siege of Rome in 754 and carried it off to Pavia. One day, overcome with fatigue as he was taking part in the choir services, he drifted into sleep and had a dream in which Cecilia herself appeared. Her relics had not been taken away by the invaders, she told him, nor even discovered by them, for all their efforts: he must begin his quest anew, find her remains, and set them in their proper resting place. Paschal searched once more, with great diligence. This time, the Book of the Popes tells us,

> by God's grace he discovered [her body] in the cemetery of Praetexta-
> tus, which is situated outside the Appian Gate. It was clad in golden
> vesture, and was with the body of her venerable spouse, Valerian. There,
> too, were the linens, filled with the blood of her martyrdom when the
> martyr of the Lord Christ, who reigns for ever, was struck by the im-
> pious executioner. . . . He gathered all these things with his own hands,
> and with great ceremony placed the body of the holy virgin under the
> high altar in the church, within the city of Rome, that is dedicated in
> her name, along with Valerian her beloved spouse, with the martyrs
> Tiburtius and Maximus, and with the popes Urban and Lucius.[26]

The salient point is that Paschal found Cecilia's body in the catacomb of Praetextatus, whereas all previous mentions of it had placed it in Callistus. Praetextatus, its entrance just a few hundred yards from and on the other side of the via Appia from Callistus, was, as has been noted, the burial site of the authentic martyrs Valerian, Tiburtius, and Maximus, borrowed by the author of the *Passio* to serve his purposes in the story he wove about Cecilia. It was evidently the burial place of Pope Urban as well, the "Bishop Urban" of the cemetery of St. Callistus being most probably an unknown bishop, not a pope, of the same name.[27] Many explanations have been offered for this sudden appearance of Cecilia's remains in a different catacomb, but Father Delehaye's hypothesis remains the most persuasive. He considered it most likely that the Lombards had indeed stolen the body of the Cecilia venerated in St. Callistus: she was, in the eighth century, among the most honored of all Roman saints, and Astolph was a renowned pillager of such relics. Pope Paschal found the remains of a young girl in a tomb very near that of the St. Valerian honored in Praetextatus, a body still clad in gold vesture, with a folded cloth that seemed steeped in blood lying nearby. It would have been easy for him to conclude that these were the remains of the martyred wife of this St. Valerian, removed for safekeeping during the Lombard incursions to a spot near her husband. As for the bloodstained cloth, Delehaye points to an incident reported by De Rossi, in which he and Father Marchi opened a sarcophagus during their explorations and found exactly such a scene: a body clad in gold, stuff of purple lying with it. The truth was (as Delehaye goes on to suggest) that this kind of burial was not uncommon, and it is likely that Paschal found such remains somewhere near those of St. Valerian and concluded that the purple stuff was blood-soaked linen.

These remains, in any event, along with those of the Valerian, Tiburtius, and Maximus, the Urban and Lucius, of Praetextatus, were removed solemnly by Pope Paschal I to Trastevere and buried there beneath the high altar of the new basilica. The pope believed that he was returning the body of the saint to the site of her house and to the scene of her martyrdom. There the relics lay undisturbed until their second invention by Cardinal Sfondrati some 780 years later. With this interment, the basilica's prestige as a place of special cult was enlarged and solidified, and it remained one of the most venerated of Roman churches throughout the Middle Ages. Yet in building as he did, Paschal obscured for us the origins of the ancient *titulus,* for he destroyed (or at best masked) the character of what had been there before.

This question, of what was at the site in the years before Pope Paschal's work, along with the allied questions of what he actually preserved and of how he arranged the site as the cult place of the saint, has received considerable attention from archaeologists, even in quite recent times.[28] Following the extensive excavations at the end of the nineteenth century, under Cardinal Rampolla, G. B. Giovenale asserted that there had been an earlier basilical church, dating from the sixth century, at the site before Pope Paschal's intervention. Richard Krautheimer ruled this out, however, and his opinion has been sustained by later research. Krautheimer similarly found no positive evidence that the structure superseded by Paschal's church was a so-called *domus ecclesia,* or house-church, a private home turned into a church, something that has been alleged about the earlier building and that is known to have happened in other instances. He would say no more than that the earlier church had been formed from a conglomeration of Roman buildings of indeterminate character. One can surely conclude, however, that whatever building was there at the time the *Passio* was composed, in about 500, was not inconsistent with a private dwelling, for this was a detail the Romans knew at first hand and about which the author could hardly have been inventive.

More intriguing is the relation of the complex to the Roman bath in which, according to popular belief, an attempt was made to suffocate or burn Cecilia. The *Passio* is quite explicit that this bath was in her house, and that her death by the sword took place in the same bath when the flames left her unharmed.[29] Remnants of such a bath were evidently incorporated by Pope Paschal I into the ninth-century basilica, a circumstance that surely indicates that this chamber had formed part of the complex that the basilica replaced. The chamber seems always to have served as the particular chapel or oratory of St. Cecilia. It lies on the epistle side, or liturgical south (in actual fact the north, because the apse of the basilica is to the west), and is entered about halfway along the side nave. Its function seems to have been forgotten in the Middle Ages, and to have come to light again only during the restructuring carried out by Cardinal Sfondrati, when the pipes and Roman floor mosaics were uncovered.[30] Investigations some fifteen years ago suggest that there may have been a larger Roman bath here, perhaps of the public kind, extending to the north of the present basilica.[31] If the suggestion can be sustained (and this must wait on further excavations that may never be carried out), it may hold interesting implications for the view I shall now advance about the origins of the cult of Cecilia, a view whose explanation forms a principal goal of this chapter. For the area just to the north of the basilica was the site of the little pagan shrine from which this view has taken shape.

Most pilgrims and visitors to S. Cecilia in Trastevere approach the basilica from the west. They have perhaps been first to S. Maria in Trastevere and savored the bustling life that goes on about its famous piazza and in the northern parts of the district; or, coming from other parts of the city, they may have alighted from buses or trams on the heavily traveled viale Trastevere. Their way will lead them along the via dei Genovesi, and their first sight of the basilica of S. Cecilia will be of the exterior of its apse, just to their right where the street intersects with the via Anicia. High on the wall of the building to their left, at the northwest corner of the intersection, they will see, if they look up, one of those numberless pieces of ancient Roman debris that have come to light at various times and have been immured close to the place they were discovered lest all contact be lost with their original site and significance (see fig. 2.7).[32] This stone was part of a little shrine that was dug up here in 1744 when workmen were laying the foundations of the building to which the stone is now attached. It tells us that "M. Vettius Bolanus ordered the shrine of the Good Goddess to be restored":

65. BONAE DEAE / SACRUM / M. VETTIUS BOLANUS / RESTITUI IUSSIT [33]

A well, no doubt used for ritual purposes, was also dug up, along with two other inscriptions. Though the stones themselves seem to have been lost the content of the inscriptions is recorded:

66. B[ONAE] D[EAE] R[ESTITUTAE *or* ESTITUTRICI] / CLADUS / D[ONUM] D[EDIT]

67. BON[AE] DEAE RESTITUT[AE *or* RICI] SIMULACR[UM] IN TUT[ELA] INSUL[AE] / BOLAN[I] POSUIT ITEM AED[ICULAM] / DEDIT CLADUS L[IBENS] M[ERITO]

Yet two more inscriptions, both clearly from the same cult-place as these first three, have since been recovered nearby. One (no. 75), a marble base, was found beneath the garden of S. Maria dell'Orto, a church just a few steps south of S. Cecilia along the via Anicia, the other (no. 813) beneath S. Cecilia itself:

75. ANTEROS / VALERI BONAE / DEAE OCLATAE / D[ONO] D[EDIT] L[IBENS] A[NIMO] // C. PAE——— / NIUS ET——— .

813. ———SPETUS MAG[ISTER] D[ONUM] D[EDIT] / [———N]OMINA SCRIPTA SUNT QUI IN HOC / [———]T C. ATEIO CAPITONE C. VIBIO POSTUMO CO[N]S[ULIBUS]

The general significance of the inscriptions is clear enough. From no. 65 it appears that M. Vettius Bolanus (consul in A.D. 66), who owned an apartment house, an *insula,* adjoining the shrine (thus no. 67, which tells us that Cladus's gift of a statue was for the safekeeping of Bolanus's property), ordered the restoration of the shrine after it had fallen into disrepair. That it had been in existence since A.D. 5 is learned from no. 813, which marks a gift by a priest (*magister*), for that is the year of the consular listing it bears ("in the consulate of C. Ateius Capito and C. Vibius Postumus"). Numbers 66 and 67 both record the gift of a cult statue by Cladus some time after Bolanus had the shrine repaired.

The cult of the Good Goddess surrounding this shrine, I contend, was intimately bound up with the early cult of St. Cecilia that developed at this same spot, and their common bond was a concern for the restoration of vision, of light. As has already been intimated in the titles given her in the inscriptions, and as I shall explain at greater length, Romans appealed to the Good Goddess here for help in curing eye disease. I shall further suggest that the name Cecilia was applied to the Christian cult that grew up here not from any association with the Roman *gens* of that name but because the cult concern of the goddess for *caecitas,* blindness, interacted in some way with that same Christian cult. Hypotheses will be presented about this interaction, but it must be stressed that they are no more than hypotheses. Of the fact of interaction, however, there can be no doubt. The proof lies in certain early Roman liturgical texts that were formulated for use at the *titulus* and that show a remarkable awareness of the pagan cult of the Good Goddess. But first we should survey what is known of the cult of the Good Goddess herself.

This curious figure was one of the more mysterious Roman divinities, very likely a goddess of old Rome, worshiped in the days when the city was

Figure 2.7. Stone from the Shrine of Bona Dea Oclata in Trastevere

(Photo: Thomas Connolly)

In 1744 workmen digging the foundations of a new building immediately behind S. Cecilia in Trastevere unearthed an ancient shrine of which this stone, now immured just behind the basilica, was part. The shrine was dedicated to Bona Dea, to whom believers appealed at this site for cure of eye-disease (*caecitas*). The name of the Christian saint derived from links to blindness, not because she belonged to the Roman *gens Caecilia*.

ruled by kings and its power extended no further than the lower reaches of the Tiber. Such at least was the opinion of Cicero, who declared before the senate that her rites had been received from the kings and were as old as the city itself.[34]

Most recent scholarship has interpreted her cult in Cicero's time as a result of the fusion of the Greek Damia, introduced after the capture of Tarentum in 272 B.C., with an ancient Italic earth-goddess.[35] Though we have information about her from many writers, from republican to early medieval times, the exact nature of her cult remains uncertain, chiefly because of the secrecy that surrounded it, and that extended even to her true name, the use of which was avoided by calling her simply *Bona Dea*, the Good Goddess. The unused name was reported to have been Fauna, linking her with the ancient rustic divinity Faunus as either his wife or his daughter.[36] A model of chastity in one form of the legend, Fauna is said to have kept company exclusively with women and to have been beaten to death with rods of myrtle when, though plied by Faunus with wine, she would not yield to his sexual advances. Another version has it that she was slain when she offended Faunus by drinking wine against his wishes.[37]

Yet whatever the uncertainty about her cult, the fundamental characteristics of Bona Dea are clear enough. They are beneficence, especially through healing, and fecundity, both of the earth and of women. She was in fact a particular goddess of women, men being excluded from her temple and her rites, and was identified as Theos gynaikeia.[38] Her principal rites, at least in late republican times, were celebrated each year on a night in early December, at the house of a magistrate who held the *imperium*. His wife or mother presided, assisted by the Vestal Virgins, in the presence of women from the rich and powerful families of the city. Much of our knowledge of these rites comes from the reports of their profanation by P. Clodius in 62 B.C., when they were held at the house of Julius Caesar. Clodius was in love with Caesar's wife, Pompeia, and thought to gain access to her disguised as a female musician, a *psaltria,* but was discovered. There was a great scandal and eventually a trial, at which Clodius was acquitted through evident bribery. The pontiffs ordered the rites to be repeated. Caesar divorced Pompeia and made his celebrated remark that Caesar's wife must be above suspicion.[39] It was a festive occasion, with much music (as at all Roman religious celebrations), and the house was decorated with vines and flowers of all kinds, myrtle alone excepted. This last detail stemmed from the legend of Fauna's death, as did the subterfuge of calling the wine that was used milk, and the vessel in which it was kept a honey jar, *mellarium.* Everything male was banished from the house for the night, animals as well as men, and even the pictures of men were covered. Legend had it that the man who looked upon the rites would be struck blind, but this seems to have been the common penalty for illicitly observing any sacred rite.[40]

Juvenal, in scathing and explicit lines, describes the rites of Bona Dea as occasions of extreme sexual licentiousness. Corrupted by wealth and power, the degenerate women of Roman society joined in these rites, he says, and defiled the religious institutions that had formerly bound them together in the pursuit of the Roman feminine ideal.[41] He, too, mentions the music, which incited the participants to passion, and the wine, which rendered them completely shameless. His description has no support from other writers, although Arnobius places the mysteries of Bona Dea at the head of his catalogue of vicious rites, with emphasis on the drunkenness they encouraged;[42] and Tibullus and Ovid describe the visits of wives to these rites as excuses for assignation.[43]

That a sacrifice was offered to Bona Dea we know from Plutarch's description of the conspiracy of Catiline, where Cicero's wife, Terentia, is said to have interpreted a sudden flaring up of the sacrificial fires (Cicero was consul, and the rites were being held at his house) as an omen that he should execute the conspirators he had taken into custody.[44] The sacrifice was of a sow, as for Ceres and Proserpine, with whom Bona Dea was sometimes identified.[45]

Though much of his material is gathered from earlier writers and is thus not contemporary, and though almost certainly he himself was not Italian, Macrobius (whose dates are unknown, but who flourished around the beginning of the fifth century) remains our best witness to Roman customs at the time of the final decline of paganism—the time when the liturgical formularies of the Roman Church were being assembled. When he treats the month of May in his discussion of the calendar, he cites Cornelius Labeo (who composed a history, since lost, of Roman-Etruscan religion) as asserting that on the kalends of May a temple had been dedicated to Maia as the Earth, Terra, under the name of the Good Goddess.[46] Cornelius, he says, affirms that the secret ritual shows Bona Dea and Terra to be the same, and that the pontifical books (*libri pontificum*) invoke this goddess as Bona Dea, Fauna, Ops, and Fatua for the following reasons: she is called Bona Dea because she is the source of all that is needed for life ("quod omnium nobis ad victum bonorum causa est"), Fauna because she looks favorably (*favet*) on everything that serves the needs of living creatures, Ops because it is on her help that life depends ("ipsius auxilio vita constat"), and Fatua (from *fando*) because infants at birth cannot utter a sound until they touch the earth. Other identifications are made, he adds, with Proserpine and Hecate, and by the Boeotians with Semele. The banning of myrtle from her temple, the use there of the names *lac* and *mellarium* for the offered wine and the wine jar, and the exclusion of men are all stressed, as well

Figure 2.8. Altar of Bona Dea at Glanum

(Photo: Thomas Connolly)

Bona Dea was a mysterious figure, a goddess
especially of women. Honored as a bearer of
beneficence and fertility, she was sought out for
special healing powers at some shrines. A healer of
eye-disease in Trastevere, she perhaps cured problems
of hearing here at Glanum, near St. Rémy-de-
Provence, as the ears carved upon her altar
suggest.

as the character of the temple as a place of healing. Herbs were kept there,
he says, from which the priestesses made medicines, and serpents (sacred
to Aesculapius) moved about freely, "neither frightening nor fearful [*nec
terrentes nec timentes*]."[47]

The Roman temple of Bona Dea stood at the northern end of the eastern part of the Aventine, directly south of the eastern part of the Circus
Maximus, close to where the church of St. Balbina now stands.[48] Founded
probably in the third century B.C., and restored by both Livia and Hadrian,
it was still standing in the fourth century, but no trace of it remains today.
Its location, just below the rock (*saxum*) from which Remus was said to
have taken the auspices, gave it the name Aedes Subsaxana.

Caecilia Restituta

Such was the general cult, as we know it, of this mysterious goddess, who received a particular veneration for her specialist's healing power—the curing of eye disease—at the little shrine that formerly existed at the present site of S. Cecilia in Trastevere and that is known to us from the inscriptions dug up there in the eighteenth century. The two epithets applied to the Good Goddess in these inscriptions help define the special aspect of her cult there: she was called *oclata* (no. 75), the goddess with the eye, and she was also referred to by a title abbreviated as *restitut* (no. 67). This could be *restituta,* a name that some claim was given to her following the restoration of the Aedes Subsaxana on the Aventine by Livia,[49] or it could be—and this is perhaps more likely—*restitutrix,* "restorer," because she was the restorer of health, especially of the eyes. This view of her as the restorer is perfectly compatible with either supplement and is supported by another inscription, found at the third milestone on the via Ostia, which thanks her "for lights restored [*ob luminibus restitutis*]" with the offering of a white heifer.[50] When the doctors had been unable to heal the patient, a complete cure had been wrought by the Good Goddess ("per eam restituta omnia") through the ministry of Cannia Fortunata, one of her priestesses (a *ministra*). In the same sense in which she was here called the restorer of light or sight, Bona Dea was elsewhere known as *lucifera,* the light-bearer.

The evidence these inscriptions furnish for the existence of a special cult of the Good Goddess who cured eye disease at the shrine in Trastevere is both clear and firm. It comes, however, from early imperial times, roughly four hundred years before the first indication that a Christian liturgical celebration of a Cecilia was held at the same spot. That the pagan cult could have survived so long is not at all hard to accept, given what we know of the persistence of such cults, especially those that held out promise of the healing of terrible afflictions. That it did indeed survive seems probable, given the survival of the pagan shrine itself, along with its inscriptions; and is proven beyond doubt by the references to the cult of the Good Goddess and the restoration of light that were made in liturgical texts formulated for worship surrounding the figure of St. Cecilia at the Christian *titulus.* It will be best to present the evidence these texts furnish in its entirety before dealing with its implications.

Two sets of such texts were developed for Christian celebration at S. Cecilia in Trastevere. One was for the saint's *dies natalis* (literally "birthday," but birth into divine life at her martyrdom is meant), which is to say her traditional feast day on November 22.[51] The other was for the station day that was observed there every year on the Wednesday after the second Sunday of Lent. Though the observance of these "stations" in Christian Rome has been much studied, it is still not completely understood. As explained above, the practice can most likely be traced to the unity signified by the primitive Roman Church's celebrating the Eucharist together—people, clergy and bishop in the one meeting place. As the community grew and it became impossible for so great a number to gather in one place, the custom developed of having several Masses celebrated at different places within the city on any given day. Only one of these, however—the papal Eucharist—was the official eucharistic worship of the Roman Church. To show that all these priestly Eucharists were one with that of the bishop, acolytes would carry some of the bread consecrated by the pope to these other Masses, where the priests would place it in the chalice at the words "The peace of the Lord be always with you." The pope himself said Mass at each of these ancient meeting places in turn, on the appointed days, according to a list that developed over many years and that acquired all the authority and prestige of an ancient tradition. On these days—they were principally the days of Lent and a small number of other important feasts throughout the year—the pope was said to keep the station at that particular church. A rich and singular ritual grew up around this stational liturgy, involving on certain days a solemn papal procession from a predetermined church to the church of the station. The books that were developed for the Roman liturgy, both in Rome itself and in those other parts of Western Europe to which the Roman liturgy spread, carried a notation at the head of the mass for any day that had a stational celebration announcing the church at which the celebration was held.[52] The practice continued down to the fourteenth century, but was not resumed by the popes on their return from their long residence in Avignon. Missals and other mass books, however, continued to note the place of the Roman station for any given station day right down to the reorganization of the liturgy at the Second Vatican Council.

Scholars have long recognized that there are intricate links between the texts developed for the station days and the churches themselves at which the stations were kept, though they have not yet fully explored these links. Similar links can be found, if to a lesser extent (in itself a curious fact), between the texts for the feast days of early Roman saints and their Roman sanctuaries. Thus the lesson selected for the feast of St. Cecilia on November 22, from Sirach 51:13–17, begins "Lord my God, you have exalted my dwelling-place upon the earth," a clear reference to the story in Cecilia's legend that she gave her house to the Church at her death and that the building became the *titulus Caeciliae*. Such references in the stational liturgy seem far less conventional, however, and among these, the texts that grew up around the *titulus Caeciliae* in Trastevere may be unique in the attention they pay (according to the view I advance in this study) to a pagan cult at the same site. The most remarkable of these texts are the orations and the mass lesson. I shall examine these in some detail, then consider several other texts that take on new significance once the references to the Good Goddess in orations and lesson are understood.

Three orations call for attention: the first from the Gregorian Sacramentary (*Ha* 216), the second and third from the Gelasian (*Ge* 181 and 182).[53]

O God, restorer [*restitutor*] and lover of innocence, direct the hearts of your servants towards yourself, so that the fervor of your spirit having been aroused [within them], they may be found firm in their faith and effective in their works.[54]

May your grace not desert us, we beseech you, O Lord. May it make us dedicated to your holy service, and may it always acquire for us your beneficence [*opem*].[55]

Be present to your servants, O Lord, and bestow your beneficence [*opem*] on those who are asking for it, so that to these who glory in you as their creator and governor you may restore your favors, and when they have been restored, preserve them.[56]

Each of these orations makes an oblique reference to the pagan cult. *Ha* 216, which survived in the Roman Missal as a "prayer over the people," the concluding prayer of the Lenten weekday mass, addresses God as *restitutor*, "restorer." The Christian deity was thus addressed as "restorer" at the very place where the *Bona Dea Restitutrix* had for centuries restored sight to those who venerated her. It can hardly be a coincidence, for this is the only occasion in all the early Roman orations that the title *restitutor* is used. This particular prayer is closely related to two others, both from the Gelasian Sacramentary, one of which uses the first part of the text of *Ha* 216, the other its conclusion. Such seeming dismemberment of orations is a mark of their formulaic character and probably goes back to their origins as improvised prayers—improvised, but according to formula. The first of these related orations, *Ge* 495—the other is *Ge* 646—is of special interest because it asks God for light: "O God, restorer and lover of innocence, direct the hearts of your servants towards yourself, so that those whom you have freed from the darkness of unbelief may never depart from the light of your truth."[57] This prayer is a "collect" prayer for the Saturday after Easter Sunday, the day on which the neophytes, laying aside the white garments they had worn during the week following their baptism, became full-fledged members of the community. Filled with baptismal significance, the prayer applies to the newly baptized a metaphor that parallels exactly the work of the Good Goddess in Trastevere by asking the Christian restorer to preserve his servants, newly freed from spiritual darkness, in the light of truth. It has no immediate connection with Trastevere, but the fact that it and *Ge* 646 are formed from the apparent dismemberment of *Ha* 216 might suggest that this last is the earliest of the three. Thus the association of the phrase "God the restorer of innocence" (*Deus innocentiae restitutor*) with the "restorer of light" in Trastevere might already have been established when the composer of *Ge* 495 spelled out the nature of the divine restoration so clearly.[58]

It is possible, perhaps probable, that the original form of the invocation in *Ha* 216 was not "restorer and lover" (*restitutor et amator*) but "restorer and author" (*restitutor et auctor*), the form the oration takes in certain Milanese sources.[59] A change from *auctor* to *amator* is one that a copyist might easily have made, given the letter shapes involved; and, more to the point, it makes better sense in any of these prayers, the notions of "author" and "restorer" forming a more logical pairing. One notes that the title *auctor* is used of God in another of the three prayers for the Trastevere station day, *Ge* 182, which also asks him to restore and preserve the favors he has already granted.[60] If the title of *Ha* 216 were indeed *restitutor et auctor,* it would correspond even more closely with the attributes of the Good Goddess, who was both a "restorer" and a "giver of increase" (*auctor*). It is in fact this very attribute of hers, of dispensing beneficence, that underlies the two other orations in our group of orations for the Trastevere station day, *Ge* 181 and 182, both of which ask God to bestow *opem*.

Opem signifies power, might, help, support, wealth, substance—in effect, beneficence. It is a defective noun: that is to say, it is not found in the nominative, except as a proper noun, *Ops,* the name of a goddess whose beneficent character the Good Goddess shared and with whom she was often identified. This identification may explain the use of the word *opem* in a Christian prayer on the day when the pope celebrated the Eucharist so close to the shrine of the Good Goddess in Trastevere. If that use was deliberate, and was based on the identification of the two goddesses, then we have in this prayer an oblique reference to a pagan divinity who was worshiped at the very site where the prayer was used and, in all likelihood, composed.[61]

The lesson read at the stational mass at S. Cecilia makes an even more startling reference to Bona Dea than do the orations. It is from an apocryphal section of the Book of Esther, Esther 13:9–11, 15–17, and is a singular choice for a mass lesson on several counts. The Book of Esther received little attention in Christian antiquity and the early Middle Ages, probably because its tale of oriental court intrigue presented such difficulties of interpretation. It was not commented on, nor often quoted, by the Fathers of the Church, and its use on this day in Trastevere was unique in the early Roman mass liturgy.[62] Two other circumstances of this choice of lesson, however, are even more peculiar. First, although the passage selected is spoken by Mordecai in the Scriptures, the liturgical compilers set it on the lips of Esther. The passage, often called "Mordecai's Prayer," is a plea to God to save Israel threatened by the intrigue of Haman. It precedes a corresponding Prayer of Esther (Esther 14:1–19) asking God to give her the courage to approach the king unbidden and plead her people's cause.

The earliest Roman lectionary, the *comes* of Würzburg, is quite clear about this attribution in its summary indication of the passage to be read: "In those days Esther prayed to the Lord, saying, 'Lord God, almighty King . . .'" *down to* "'. . . and do not close the mouths of those who sing your praises.'"[63] The later Roman Missal "corrected" this early "mistake" by putting Mordecai's name back in place of Esther's, just as it was found in the Vulgate. But, one may ask, were the compilers mistaken, or was this attribution of Mordecai's prayer to Esther deliberate? The fact is that medieval lectionaries, and sermons preached upon this passage, almost always keep the attribution to Esther. Preachers would at times point out the "mistake," but did not question that the lectionaries ascribed the text to Esther.[64] The answer, I believe, lies in a mysterious reflection of the Good Goddess's cult in the stational liturgy at S. Cecilia in Trastevere, seen in the significance of Esther's name. Esther in fact had two names, according to Esther 2:7: a Babylonian name, which was Esther (that is, Ishtar), and a Hebrew name, Hadassah. But Hadassah is the Hebrew word for myrtle, the plant sacred to Venus and hence inimical to Bona Dea, whose cult held up the ideals of married chastity to Roman women. Ancient authors are explicit on this point and on the consequent banning of myrtle from the rites and the temple of the goddess, as has been discussed earlier in this chapter.

There are thus two distinct reflections of the pagan cult in the Christian lesson: the significance of Esther's name and the placing on her lips of a text that was spoken by a man in the Scriptures. Esther's name means myrtle, the plant banned from the Good Goddess's cult; and Esther speaks a man's text, as if in some kind of mimicry of the banning of men from those same pagan rites (even pictures of men were covered in the house where the December rites of Bona Dea were held). In addition to the strikingly unique symbolic reference conveyed by the choice of this lesson, we must consider the implications for our argument of the fact that whoever made the selection evidently had some knowledge of Hebrew. It is suggestive that the goddess was served by priestesses, who no doubt functioned about the Trastevere shrine and interacted in some fashion with the nearby Christian community. One should also note that the concluding words of the pericope suggest that even at this early date a link was understood between the liturgy celebrated at the *titulus Caeciliae* and Christian music-making, and that it is from these same words that the title of this study is taken: "turn our mourning into joy, and do not close the mouths of those who sing your praises."

Other liturgical texts—some for this station day, some for the general veneration of St. Cecilia—take on a wider significance when one keeps in mind the references to the nearby pagan cult. The introit, or entrance psalm, for the station day is a case in point: Psalm 37, the third penitential psalm, is full of references to healing, indeed to the healing of sick eyes.

       Caecilia Restituta

In earlier times, of course, the whole psalm was sung, not just the several verses of later use. One can hardly imagine a psalm more suited to a place where healing was sought, nor one that would have carried such meaning for the people of Trastevere: "there is no health in my flesh, because of your angry look . . . my wounds have festered and grown inflamed because of my folly . . . my soul is filled with illusions, there is no health in my body . . . my heart is heavy within me, my strength is fled, the light of my eyes is departed." The concluding verses, 22–23, formed the antiphon or refrain for the singing of the psalm: "Do not leave me, O Lord my God, do not depart from me: bow down to help me, O Lord the God of my health."

Other liturgical texts that formed about the liturgy of the Trastevere basilica and its saint reflect the cult concerns of Bona Dea, but in a way that is completely consistent with the fully formed Christian devotion to Cecilia of the late Middle Ages. The best example is the constant reference on both the station day and the feast of the saint to the prayer that, according to the *Passio,* she "sang in her heart to God" for the preservation of her virginity. The words of this prayer are taken, with slight change, from Psalm 118:80, "Let my heart and my body be kept spotless lest I be cast into confusion." Joined to verse 78 of the same psalm, which begins "let the proud be cast into confusion," these words formed the communion antiphon for Cecilia's feast, on November 22, and were used as antiphons elsewhere in her liturgy.[65] It was the words "lest I be cast into confusion" (*ne confundar*) that attracted the liturgical compilers. They are repeated in the introit antiphon for the feast day, "I shall speak of your testimony in the sight of kings, and I shall not be cast into confusion."[66] The reference is made yet again in the offertory of the station day. The first three psalm-verses that form the antiphon of this chant (Psalm 24:1–3) conclude: "for all who hope in thee shall not be cast into confusion,"[67] while the second of the solo verses in the early *gradualia* (the books that contained the choir chants of the mass), which was a composite of verses 16 and 20 of the psalm, ends: "I shall not be cast into confusion, for I have called upon thee."[68] At this point there would have been a choral repetition of the antiphon, emphasizing even more the allusion to Cecilia's "lest I be cast into confusion."[69]

The liturgical compilers were thus keenly aware of the threat of *confusio* when they selected these texts, fashioning a liturgy and cult at the basilica that prayed repeatedly to be delivered from it. The author of the *Passio,* too, was probably not inventing when he cast Cecilia as one who prays for deliverance from confusion, but was acknowledging existing practice at the shrine. It is interesting to note, in this regard, that he depicts Cecilia as *clarissima,* a noble title but carrying the suggestion of one who is filled with light (*claritas*). Right through the developing cult of Cecilia, to the end of the Middle Ages and beyond, the saint would be associated with *claritas.* The concept permeates Chaucer's treatment of her, for instance, in *The Second Nun's Tale.*[70] But this contrasting of confusion and clarity is precisely what must have fueled the aspirations of the pilgrims who sought relief for their diseased eyes from the Good Goddess in Trastevere. The undercurrent of popular tradition, whose eddies appear faintly on the surface of the liturgy at the basilica and in the *Passio,* was undoubtedly a strong one. It surfaces elsewhere in the unfolding cult of St. Cecilia, nowhere more strangely or more convincingly than at her great shrine at Albi in southwestern France. How and when this magnificent church was dedicated to Cecilia is unknown, yet what legend suggests about those dim origins resonates powerfully with the same associations of blindness, healing, and light-giving that were observed in Trastevere. The founder, according to legend, was a bishop whose very name, *Clarus* (St. Clair), suggests a concern with light, as does Cecilia's. He, too, like the Good Goddess in Trastevere, is hailed as "author of light for the blind" and "restorer" of the sick.[71]

One of the liturgical texts that we have just discussed as pleas for the avoidance of *confusio* would later play a special part in the development of Cecilia's musical iconography. This was the offertory of the station day, from Psalm 24:1–3. Its opening words, the first words of the psalm, are steeped in the sentiments of the converted heart: "To thee, O Lord, I have lifted up my soul." The suitability of the text for this day in Lent is obvious. And for this reason it was chosen also for use on the first Sunday of Advent, the first day of the church year, when the impulse to true conversion, to a new beginning, was uppermost in Christian consciousness. But it was adopted for use on this Sunday not simply as offertory, but as gradual and as entrance psalm as well. As offertory, it was taken over completely and without change, both words and music, from the offertory of the Trastevere station day. As introit or entrance psalm, the first text of the mass, the words "To thee, O Lord, I have lifted up my soul" were the first words in medieval mass books and became the subject of rich miniatures.

One of the most common of these miniatures was the David-in-Penitence, the image of the repentant, truly converted king kneeling before the vision of God in the heavens above, often with a discarded musical instrument on the ground beside him. This detail illustrated the scriptural texts of mourning and joy like Job 30:31 and Lamentations 5:15–16, and formed the basis of the tradition from which developed the musical iconography of Raphael's Cecilia.

One other verse of Psalm 24—a verse that does not appear in the liturgical books, but that would have been sung in ancient usage when the whole psalm was sung at the entrance of the mass—would play a significant role in the development of the imagery of inner, spiritual vision: verse 15, "my eyes are always upon the Lord," which might be a description of Raphael's Cecilia and of the David-in-Prayer, with their gazes turned heavenward. Mystics and writers on spirituality used the verse to describe the pinnacle of mystical achievement, union with the divine, and blended a musical image into the visual one by declaring that in this verse there is contained the "sound of the banqueter."

The evidence we have been considering in these last pages—the inscriptions from the shrine of the Good Goddess in Trastevere, and the texts selected and composed for the early liturgy at the nearby Christian *titulus*—leaves no doubt that the cults of saint and goddess interacted, though exactly how must remain obscure. The fact of the interaction, however, allows us to evaluate the various suppositions that scholars have put forward to account for the origins of St. Cecilia. Father Delehaye's hypothesis is a good starting point.

The weakness of Delehaye's theory, in the light of our new evidence, is its assumption that the cult of Cecilia began when Christians took note of a presumed martyr named Cecilia buried near the crypt of the popes in St. Callistus, and that this cult spread for some unknown reason to the *titulus* in Trastevere. But what was there about the site in Trastevere that suggested that it had been the house of a Cecilia, as the *Passio* has it and as the folk of Trastevere must have come to believe by the time the *Passio* was written? Father Delehaye has little to say about this, except that some now-forgotten circumstance led them to make this identification. Is it at all likely, or even possible, that a totally invented saint, as Delehaye's Cecilia must have been, could so quickly have generated the fervent enthusiasm that seems to have existed in Trastevere? It seems far more probable, given what we know of the interaction of the two cults in Trastevere, that the Christian cult began there, about the site of the *titulus,* and only later was extended to the Cecilia buried in the catacomb, rather than the other way around.

The critical considerations are, in fact, those that revolve about the name of Cecilia in Trastevere. As Delehaye pointed out, the Roman Martyrology seemed confused about Cecilia: it listed three entries for a saint of this name, but the only one to mention Trastevere gives the name in a masculine form. This variation in itself suggests that there was no strong memory of a female figure who had been martyred there, and this suggestion is made more probable by two other considerations. First, the *titulus* was evidently known earlier as the *titulus* of Gordianus, for the author of the *Passio* had to explain the conflict of names to his audience, a fact that indicates the property had neither belonged to, nor been donated by, a Christian woman named Cecilia, but had come to be known as the title of Cecilia for some other reason. Second, the name Cecilia, so suggestive of blindness, of *caecitas,* was applied to the *titulus Gordiani* at a place where a goddess who cured blindness had been venerated for at least four hundred years. It seems highly probable—and this point is fundamental to my hypothesis about the origins of St. Cecilia—that the name Cecilia was applied to the Christian *titulus* precisely because Christian cult there had taken some cognizance of the cure of blindness.

Several other factors will have some bearing on our understanding of this interaction of pagan and Christian cults. One is the general religious condition of Rome following the decrees of the emperor Theodosius banning pagan cults and closing pagan temples in the last years of the fourth century. Another is the power of traditions, like that which enshrined Cecilia's story; no matter how clear the evidence is for a large measure of fabrication, one cannot easily dismiss the likelihood of a core of truth within the legend. Yet a third is the curious fact that those who helped select the Christian liturgical texts had a good knowledge of Hebrew, for they recognized the significance of Esther's Hebrew name. Such knowledge seems highly unlikely in the Greco-Roman Christian community of the time and suggests the involvement of an early Jewish-Christian community.[72]

A cult like that of Bona Dea Oclata would hardly have faded away at a simple word from Theodosius, backed up though it was by harsh legal sanctions. She had been venerated at this place for hundreds of years. The tenacity with which people cling to such ingrained custom, even after conversion (and there must have been many conversions of convenience after Constantine decreed the Peace of the Church), is well attested and can be observed in places where Christianity has been more recently introduced over an indigenous religious culture. Is it likely that the folk of Trastevere (and of more distant places to which the influence of Bona Dea Oclata extended) would have abandoned at once their popular practices, especially those from which they thought they derived benefits of health? Eye disease, at a time when a slight infection could easily result in blindness, was far more common and much more to be feared than is now the case. That a strong devotion to the pagan practices at the Trastevere shrine continued long after Theodosius's decrees is hardly to be doubted—the Christian liturgical texts that were composed and selected there are themselves witness to it.

We need also to note (and this will become clearer when we read the *Passio*) that the legend of Cecilia absorbed certain prominent characteristics of the Good Goddess. The most obvious is the *Passio*'s constant emphasis on vision and true seeing, but there are others. Thus, one of the singular episodes of the *Passio,* the celibate marriage of Cecilia and Valerian, may have a counterpart in the tale of Fauna and Faunus. Fauna was said to have been the wife of Faunus, yet to have lived chastely and to have kept the company of women exclusively; indeed, she was beaten to death by Faunus with rods of myrtle for resisting his sexual advances.

We should note further that certain events and places mentioned in the *Passio* seem to have been based on fact, or at least on popular belief. The bath in which Cecilia was placed seems to have been a part of the original *titulus* and to have been preserved by Pope Paschal I in his ninth-century basilica. So, too, it is possible that the stone on which Cecilia climbed to preach was an actual stone, with some legendary or mythical significance, that was known to the people of Trastevere when the *Passio* was written.[73]

Several ways suggest themselves in which the legend of the Good Goddess could have been transformed into, or absorbed by, the legend of the saint. In one scenario, conflict followed by absorption, the goddess, abhorred by the Christian clergy, might have become the object of contrary

prayers and readings asserting that the Christian deity was the true restorer, the true provider of beneficence. This would not preclude the emer-
gence of a folk heroine, either real or imaginary, who assumed certain characteristics of the goddess and was eventually identified as a saint. Or the
scenario may have been a more peaceful one in which the folk heroine with
the characteristics of the goddess took shape in popular imagination as the
old cult weakened and was forgotten. This figure, eventually considered a
saint, would still retain certain appurtenances of the goddess, though their
origin would by then have been forgotten.

None of this rules out, nor is it meant to rule out, the possibility that
there was an actual person, indeed a saintly person, behind the Cecilia
whose career is so fancifully embroidered in the *Passio*. Vigorous cults of
the kind that revolved around the St. Cecilia of Trastevere do, at times,
flourish in the ground of pure imagination—the cult of St. Philomena, for
example. But it is far more common to find such fanciful legends growing from historically factual roots. It should be remembered that the Good
Goddess was served by *ministrae,* priestesses, who acted as physicians, a
fact that might account for the memory of a healing woman as a folk heroine. The liturgy of the station day probably takes note of this in selecting as
gospel Matthew 20:17–28. This passage tells how the mother of James and
John asked Jesus that her sons might sit at his right and left in his kingdom,
and how Jesus used the incident to instruct his followers in his ideals of
service. He told them that whoever wished to be greater among them must
be a minister to them ("quicumque voluerit inter vos maior fieri sit vester
minister") and that he had come not to be ministered to but to minister to
others ("non venit ministrari sed ministrare"). Most commentators see in
this selection an allusion to Valerian and Tiburtius, who gave themselves
to good works, but the textual reference to "minister" and "ministering"
very likely alludes to the *ministrae* of the goddess as well.

Is it possible that one of the *ministrae* of the Good Goddess became a
Christian and that this woman became the later Cecilia? On balance, at any
rate, it seems more likely that some person came to be venerated by the folk
of Trastevere for her holiness and charity during the fourth and fifth century—some person, say, who "ministered" to sick pilgrims, who preached
to them, who even suffered a death that later passed for martyrdom—
rather than that the legend of the saint hatched fully formed from a refabri-

Caecilia Restituta

cation of the legend of the goddess. In this case, one would have to establish why a person who had not been known as a saint for so long should suddenly appear in a blaze of veneration at the end of the fifth century. Various reasons can be suggested for the long silence about this hypothetical person. If he or she lived after the age of persecutions, there would have been no immediate impetus for a public cult, for only martyrs were generally so honored at that time. Another possible reason for the silence has already been proposed: that the cult began in a Jewish-Christian community, as the compiler's familiarity with Hebrew suggests.[74] Little is known of these groups in the early Church, except that they did exist and that they lived their lives somewhat apart from the more numerous Gentile Church.

If some kind of absorption of the pagan cult by the Christian did indeed take place, one might reasonably expect to find traces of it in the early cult of Cecilia. The *Passio,* for instance, however great the fanciful contribution of its author, must have been based on what was popularly believed about her; and the liturgical texts, both for her feast and for the station day, would probably have been chosen with some reference to the character of her popular cult. The confusion that exists in early references to the *titulus* and in the martyrology entries is perfectly consistent with a process of "transmutation of cult." If there had been a folk hero or folk heroine venerated in Trastevere who was only gradually accepted as a saint, one should hardly be surprised to find conflicts about the date of the feast, the inclusion of the epithet *sancta,* or even the gender of the name. A folk cult of its very nature implies indefiniteness and constant variation. As the cult became officially acceptable, variant and even conflicting elements would have become more stable—by being written down, for instance—and would have led to the kind of disagreement now observed in the sources. The acceptance, and still more the reading, of an "official" version of the legend would have ended the folk cult as such and would have given it a static quality within the Christian liturgy.

If, on the other hand, one accepts with Father Delehaye that the cult of St. Cecilia began with the mistaken attribution of martyr status to a forgotten Cecilia in the catacomb of Callistus, one would expect to find nothing in the *Passio* that is not the sheer invention of the author or his adaptation of certain commonplaces of hagiographical literature to a purely fanciful purpose. The legend would have no roots in popular memory and imagination. But if the cult of Cecilia were derived from a folk cult in Trastevere centering on a figure related to the restoration of sight, and had expanded at some later point to an identification with the Cecilia in the catacomb, one would expect the author's treatment of his topic in the *Passio* to betray this origin. We will see that the most consistent theme of the *Passio* is in fact the bestowal of light by Cecilia while her persecutors remain in blindness. Father Delehaye himself lends unintended support to this assertion when he states that the work is "illumined by mystical glimmerings."[75]

Caecilia Restituta

"illumined by mystical glimmerings"

Three Mourning and Joy in the Passion of St. Cecilia

The *Passio Sanctae Caeciliae,* as its name indicates, is a life of the saint emphasizing her suffering (*passio*), or, in this particular case, her martyrdom. In length it would run to about twenty-five ordinary, modern book pages. It consists of two halves of sixteen chapters each, in the common division followed by Delehaye.[1] The first half begins with a prologue (chapters 1 and 2) and then relates the nuptials of Cecilia and her conversion of her husband, Valerian, and his brother, Tiburtius; all is explained in terms of her leading them to the angelic vision which she already enjoys. The second half tells of the interrogation of the three by the city prefect. In each case, the accused points out that the judge is either blind or deaf. The jailer, Maximus, is converted, and finally all three, along with Maximus, are martyred. The story ends with the burial of Cecilia by Pope Urban and the gift of her house to the Church.

It has been the fashion to dismiss the *Passio* of Cecilia as fanciful, no different in essentials from other fictitious saints' lives, though blessed with a certain poetic gracefulness and "mystical glimmerings," those *lueurs mystiques* discerned by Delehaye. But one must ask whether this work was intended to be what we would call biographical, that is, historical. When one looks carefully at its mystical content, the author's focus seems to change: the narration of events becomes secondary to his (or perhaps her) mystical leanings. After considering the mystical-symbolical interpretations given the *Passio* by later writers, one is inclined to rephrase the question and ask to what degree some mystical purpose may have driven the author as he wrote. The question will receive no answer here, but the asking of it will prepare the reader for the elaboration of mystical considerations as the story of the *Passio* is retold.

Mysticism is a chameleon concept, and dishearteningly difficult to define. It involves always the belief that the world we perceive with our senses is in part a veil for deeper reality—indeed the deepest, and ultimately the only, reality that is significant in and of itself. The mystic seeks to achieve union with that transcendental reality by a motion or process that is often described in terms of perceiving or knowing, but that all who have entered mysticism's ways have identified principally as love. Yet mystics must deny any power of ordinary human perception to apprehend this reality, while using, in their attempts to describe mystical experience, a language that is drawn entirely from sense perceptions and from reflection upon those perceptions.

The prologue, which comprises the first two chapters, urges us to read the lives of the saints, and at once foreshadows the Cecilian theme of mourning turning into joy by pointing out that through such reading "mourning springs forth in the unbelievers . . . and joy in the saints who rejoice with Christ."[2] The saints' victory by martyrdom causes the devil to cry out (*clamat diabolus*), through the mouths of the demented and the possessed (*per lunaticos et energumenos*), that he burns in the flames, and thus to give testimony to that victory. *Clamat,* used four times in the second chapter, is its key word and prepares the reader for the description of Cecilia, at the beginning of the third chapter, as "hearing," *audiens.* The devil cries out so that we may know the rewards of the saints; the sick person, made well, cries out that he is healed (*salvatum*) so that we may know that the saints are with the *salvator.* It is thus, by the cry of the devil and the cry of the healed, that the soul (the soul of one who witnesses this) receives the signs of its restoration (*restauratio*) and is inspired to open the ears of the heart in faith.[3] These ideas—of the devil, the possessed, the demented, the healed—and the language they are expressed in, are fully consistent with the continuity of cult concerns from Bona Dea to Cecilia at the Christian *titulus.* The reference to the cry of the sick man that he is cured is not fortuitous, but is meant for an audience already familiar with the healing that took place in Trastevere, healing that was, in the later Christian context, a proof to the soul of the *restauratio* that had been won for it, and for which one of the orations from the Gelasian mass book made appeal.[4] But there is another cry, the *Passio* continues, that of Christ himself, who cries out constantly: "Come to me all you who labour and are heavily burdened, and I will refresh you." These words, from Matthew 11:28, will later form the beginning of Cecilia's instruction to Tiburtius, her brother-in-law, at his conversion (*Passio,* 196, cap. 3).

It is at this point that Cecilia is introduced, in a sentence that, when fully understood, defines the central characteristics of her cult and shows a striking continuity with the healing aspects of the cult of Bona Dea: "Hearing this voice, the holy and illustrious virgin Cecilia carried the gospel of Christ always hidden in her breast and never ceased by day or night from her divine colloquies and prayer."[5] This sentence, along with the later sentence of this same third chapter that describes her "singing in her heart," contains in embryo the whole of later Cecilian devotion and will bear close scrutiny.

Cecilia is, first of all, *audiens;* she hears the voice of Christ. But she is also (and as a consequence) *clarissima,* not only because of her family— *clarissima* being a conventional title of nobility—but much more (and this becomes clearer with the reading of the *Passio*) because she is filled with light, with divine illumination.[6] Allied with this inner hearing and vision are the keeping of the gospel in her heart, her ceaseless prayer and divine conversation, and of course her virginity: she is a *virgo clarissima.* She is represented, then, as living an inner life, a superior life on a totally different plane, that is appropriate to her as a virgin. This concept of the virgin was articulated in Revelation and richly developed by later writers who equated the life of the virgin with the *vita angelica.*[7] The liturgy took note of these mystic themes in the text chosen as the gradual respond for Cecilia's feast: "Hear, daughter, and see, and incline your ear."[8] One can justly see in this text a line of influence extending from Bona Dea Oclata, the Good Goddess with the Eye, who is elsewhere honored as the Good Goddess with the Ear, and whose altars bear ears as symbols of her healing functions, to a Christian virgin whose essential characteristics include the hearing and seeing of divine things.

Two other elements of the opening sentence of the narrative portion of the *Passio* merit detailed comment: that she kept the gospel hidden in her breast and that she never ceased from "divine colloquies." Both express almost the same idea, and provide fertile ground for the growth of devotion to Cecilia among later mystics, like Jean Gerson and Elena dall'Olio. The phrase "gospel in her breast" or "heart" (*in pectore*) tells us that Cecilia was a contemplative, that she lived ever conscious of God's presence and in prayerful communion with him. It suggests also that her meditation was on the life of Christ, a key recommendation of Franciscan spirituality, particularly to Christians who are embarking on a life of serious prayer. The *colloquia divina,* which surely are a part of what "the gospel in her heart" signified, may perhaps be extended to include those sermons and disputations, those exhortations and discourses, that are her only communications throughout the *Passio.* It hardly seems strange that one thus constantly occupied should become the subject of possibly the most famous example of a genre of painting that goes by the name of *conversazione sacra.*

This Christian virgin is betrothed to a young pagan named Valerian. So deeply is he in love with her, the story continues—with stark avoidance of narrative probabilities—that a day is set for the wedding, and Cecilia, unable to reveal her true love in the face of her parents' wishes and her betrothed's burning eagerness, dons a hair shirt against her skin beneath her outer vesture of gold. "What more was to be done?" the anonymous author asks, and then answers the question with his own most famous sentence. "The day came when the marriage-bed was prepared, and while instruments played Cecilia sang in her heart to the Lord alone, 'May my heart and my body be kept spotless so that I not be cast into confusion.'"[9]

The improbabilities of this episode will be of concern only to one intent on salvaging the historicity of the legend and can be largely ignored here. The important elements are the saint's hair shirt, the music that was played while Cecilia sang her own music in her heart, and the text of her song. Her hair shirt is often mentioned by preachers and spiritual authors. It is a colorful detail; indeed, it was painted by Raphael. It is a reminder and a symbol of the radical remaking of human nature that is implied by grace. The world sees gold without, but there is penitence within; the world's vision is of baubles, while what is interior is of true value and worth in the eye of God. "The animal man does not perceive the things of the spirit," as Tiburtius would later point out to the judge, citing words of St. Paul to the Corinthians (1 Cor. 2:14). The hair shirt and the golden robe, common enough motifs in the lives of the saints, symbolize well this subversion of appearances. But there is perhaps another subversion here, that of the names of the saint and of her penitential garb. It may seem farfetched to remark on the similarity of *Cecilia* and *cilicia* (hair shirt), but the point is worth making in view of the sometime spelling of the saint's name as

Cicilia, making the correspondence of the two words almost exact.[10] That Cecilia wore a hair shirt emphasizes, besides, the Christian belief that all mankind must repent. Only Christ and Mary (and in some views, John the Baptist) were sinless; all Christian perfection, all progress—even the slightest—toward sanctity, begins in, and must always be totally conditioned by, humble repentance.

The *organa* that played at Cecilia's wedding were certainly the instruments of the day, not the organ, at least as we know it. Medieval art, when it depicted Cecilia's nuptials, showed either organ or secular instruments, or even both. The matter is not of great concern, for I propose that the organ Cecilia carries as her emblem in later works did not originate as a simple depiction of the *organa* of her wedding banquet. Of far greater significance for understanding Cecilia's connection with music is the statement that she "sang in her heart," a metaphor which, along with her keeping the gospel "in her heart," was the most influential element of her *Passio.* One must, of course, rid oneself of post-Romantic notions of what "heart" stands for when one reads these and other texts, both ancient and medieval, in which the heart is mentioned symbolically. Yet there is considerable overlap between the two styles of reference; both, for example, embrace the idea of love. The difference in symbolism is, in fact, analogous to the difference between the earlier and later concepts of love. The older notion of "heart" does not exclude the idea of romantic love, but connotes rather the synthesis of the capacities of the whole person. Change of heart for earlier times meant not a change of an unthinking, and in modern terms purely emotional, response, but a change in one's deepest understanding and in the acts of will that flow from such understanding. In that sense, change of heart would mean a new love. Mysticism presents an instructive example, for one of the more unusual, but well-documented, mystical phenomena is the vision of Christ in which he removes the heart of the visionary and substitutes a new heart, sometimes even his own. Such visions are recorded of Blessed Dorothy of Montau; Beata Osanna Andreasi of Mantua, who was a contemporary of Elena dall'Olio; St. Catherine dei Ricci; St. Lutgarde; St. Michel des Saints; and, most notably, St. Catherine of Siena.[11] St. Catherine, whose vision was of Christ substituting his own heart for hers, told her confessor that "I am no longer what I was . . . I am changed into another person."[12]

There is a strong scriptural basis for the use of "heart" to denote renewal of the person. The word appears twice in Psalm 50, the centerpiece of the penitential psalms, in passages that underpin the Christian use of the word. In verse 12 the psalmist prays: "Create a clean heart in me, O God, and give me a new spirit in the depths of my being;" and in verse 19 he declares that "a repentant spirit is the sacrifice God loves; a humble, contrite heart he will never disdain."[13] Two passages of Ezekiel convey similar thought through the same symbol. In Ezekiel 18:31, the prophet records God's command to "cast away all your waywardness . . . make for yourselves a new heart and a new spirit."[14] And in the most colorful of all scriptural uses of the symbol, he relates the divine promise to cleanse and renew Israel: "I shall give you a new heart, and I shall put a new spirit within you; I shall take the stony heart out of your body, and give you a heart of flesh instead. I shall put my own spirit within you; I shall make you walk in the paths of my law, remember and carry out my decrees."[15]

In the New Testament it is Paul and John who express the theme most often and most eloquently. John emphasizes repeatedly, in his Gospel and in the First Epistle, the immanence of the Holy Spirit.[16] And it was Paul's admonition to the Ephesians to sing in their hearts to the Lord that inspired the author of the *Passio* to describe Cecilia's inner prayer as he did: "Do not drug yourselves with wine; that is simply dissipation. Be filled rather with the Holy Spirit; sing to one another, when you are together, in psalms and hymns and spiritual songs; and go on singing and psalming in your hearts to the Lord."[17] This whole passage, and indeed the whole epistle, clearly influenced the construction of Cecilia's legend. Most notable, in the case of Cecilia, with her concerns for vision and clarity, is the important introductory passage where Paul prays for just such enlightenment in the hearts of the Ephesians, asking that God "may enlighten the eyes of your heart so that you may know the hope to which you have been called, and the rich inheritance."[18] One could say that the *Passio* represents Ephesians in action: that the author translated the doctrinal content of the epistle, and the moral admonitions that flow therefrom, into the life of a saint.

In the first three chapters of Ephesians, Paul expounds a mystery that has been revealed to him, the mystery of the nature of the Church as the Mystical Body of Christ; in the fourth through the sixth (and final) chapter, he advises his readers that they must live as the new man, their hearts enlightened, their activities those that flow from charity. His language is filled with images of illumination, of charity centered in the heart; the epistle culminates in the admonition to "sing and psalm in their hearts to the Lord." The *Passio,* by comparison, is a tale of a saint who, bringing light to all around her and "singing in her heart to the Lord," constantly builds up the Church by conversion. She converts Valerian, Tiburtius, Maximus, and the four hundred pagans who hear her preach to the officers sent to arrest her. She is ever preaching, every busy, a "disputatious sheep" from Christ's flock. The similarities between the *Passio* and Ephesians are marked, and the influence becomes immediate at the places where Ephesians is quoted directly: at the passage about singing in the heart and at a later episode when a scroll quoting Ephesians is held out by the old man (he is not named, but is almost certainly St. Paul) who appears in a vision to Valerian.[19]

The content of Cecilia's inner song, "let my heart and my body be stainless, lest I be cast into confusion," has already been touched upon and will be discussed below at greater length. At this point, suffice it to say that the song's abhorrence of "confusion" is all the more clearly delineated because of the contrast it presents with Cecilia's clarity. That clarity marks her as the polar opposite of all that is implied by confusion: the wrong understanding, the wrong love, the wrong deeds associated with the confusion of Babylon.[20]

As Cecilia sings and prays her unceasing song, the *Passio* continues, she fasts for two and three days at a time, entrusting to the Lord her fears about her approaching marriage, and beseeching with tears the angels, the apostles, and the whole Church to help her with their prayers. Inevitably there comes the night on which she is to be bedded with Valerian, and together they seek out "the secret silences" of the bridal chamber. She tells him that there is "a mystery" that she must relate to him, but only if he will promise to keep it secret to himself. When he agrees, she reveals to him that she has "an angel lover, who guards my body with the utmost jealousy." If Valerian so much as touches her out of worldly love (*polluto amore*), the angel will slay him; but if his love is sincere and he preserves her virginity, the angel will love him, too, and will heap blessings upon him. Valerian demands to be convinced, to be shown the angel. Cecilia responds by telling him to go to Pope Urban, hiding in the catacombs, for instruction and baptism; then he, too, will be able to see what she sees.

Here, in the celibate marriage of Valerian and Cecilia, is the most singular element of the *Passio*. Virginity, martyrdom by sword and fire, preachings and conversions—these are commonplaces of hagiography. But an actual marriage in which the partners agree to live virginity within their union is unique to this story, at least among earlier legends. There is a model, of course, in the marriage of Joseph and Mary, as understood in the Catholic tradition; and there are many scriptural and patristic references to marriage in general as a symbol of spiritual union, especially of the soul's union with God.[21] Marriage was commonly interpreted by Christians as an image of the union of Christ and the soul, the locus classicus for this, in the New Testament, being Ephesians 5:22–33.[22] The image was, and continued to be developed as, a primary linguistic vehicle for explaining and fostering the contemplative life. Cecilia's and Valerian's marriage is only a small part of that development, but the theme is prevalent in writings about the saint and recurs often enough in the visual arts.[23] Why did the author choose to weave this episode of the celibate marriage into his account? Did he do so out of some awareness of the figure's mystical implications? Is there a further reason in the Trasteverian background of the legend? Some circumstance of the cult of the Good Goddess? Those circumstances are no doubt too remote, too indistinct to help us propose focused answers to such questions, yet the episode resonates faintly with the woman-centered cult of Bona Dea, which sought to exclude everything male.[24]

In Cecilia's first dialogue with Valerian, the emphasis remains firmly on his need for purification before seeing the angel. While asking to see the angel, Valerian also threatens Cecilia with death should her story prove no more than a subterfuge for concealing a human lover. Cecilia responds that if he will heed her counsel, be purified in the eternal font, and declare his faith in the one God, then he will indeed see the angel. "And who is it who will purify me so that I may see the angel?" he asks.[25] Cecilia replies: "There is an old man who knows how to purify men so that they may be worthy to see the angel."[26] Valerian is to go out along the Appian Way, to the third milestone, and ask the beggars there (these, says the *Passio,* emphasizing Cecilia's charitable works, have always been particular objects of her care) to take him to Urban. "When he has purified you," she concludes, "he will clothe you with new, white garments; as soon as you enter this chamber clad in these, you will see the holy angel, who will have become your lover too, and you will be granted whatever request you make of him."[27]

All happens as Cecilia has foretold. When Valerian conveys Cecilia's message to Urban, the bishop falls to his knees rejoicing, and spreading his hands toward heaven, exclaims with tears: "Lord Jesus Christ, sower of chaste counsel, accept the fruit of the seeds which you sowed in Cecilia. Lord Jesus Christ, good shepherd, Cecilia your servant waits upon you like a disputatious sheep. For her spouse, whom she received as a raging lion, she has now sent to you as a most gentle lamb. He would not have come here if he did not believe. Open, Lord, the gate of his heart to your words, so that acknowledging you as his creator he may renounce the devil and his pomps and his idols."[28]

As Urban continues to pray over Valerian, there appears an old man clad in white garments who holds a scroll emblazoned with golden letters. Valerian falls down in fear, but is raised up by the old man, who bids him read the letters "so that you may be worthy to be purified and to see the angel" Cecilia had spoken of. The words, which Valerian begins to read to himself (*intra se legere*), are the text of Ephesians 4:5–6. A thousand years later the eminent spiritual writer Jean Gerson (1363–1429), whose thought, as we shall see, played no small part in shaping Raphael's picture of St. Cecilia, would characterize them as containing the whole mystical teaching of Pseudo-Dionysius the Areopagite: "One God, one faith, one baptism, one God and Father of all, who is above all things, and is in us all." St. Paul—with whom the old man is usually identified—asks Valerian if he now believes or still doubts. When Valerian cries out his assent with a loud voice (in contrast to his reading *intra se*), the old man disappears. Pope Urban thereupon baptizes and further instructs Valerian, and sends him back to his spouse.

Valerian, clad now in white baptismal robes, finds Cecilia at her prayers, and standing near her a shining angel who holds two crowns made of roses and lilies. The words the angel utters as he gives them the crowns are a direct fulfilment of the prayer that Cecilia had "sung in her heart":

Guard these flowers with an immaculate heart and a pure body, for I have brought them to you from God's Paradise. And this shall be a sign to you: the flowers shall never wither, nor lose their sweet odor, nor shall they be visible to any but those who love chastity as you have shown yourselves to do. And because you, Valerian, have accepted the counsel of chastity, Christ the Son of God has sent me to you so that you may make of Him any request you wish.[29]

Again, one notices the emphasis on vision. The angel can be seen now by Valerian; the flowery crowns are visible only to lovers of chastity. And increasingly one realizes that the *Passio* wishes to inculcate not only the new vision that comes with Christian faith, but the new vision of the Christian ideal of chastity. It should be noted that the chastity motif plays no part in the story of Tiburtius, Valerian's brother, whose conversion Valerian has just asked of the angel and who is introduced following the angel's departure. Tiburtius will accept the faith, abjure idols, succor the poor, bury the dead, and achieve martyrdom, but there is no mention of chastity in his own discourse, nor in the discourse of others with him. Is this because he plays no part in the motif of virginal marriage, and because the author, in consequence, has no wish to exemplify single chastity?

Before departing, the angel heaps praise on Valerian for the petition he has made for his brother's conversion: as Cecilia has gained Valerian for Christ, so Valerian will gain his brother, and both will attain the martyr's palm. Tiburtius, when he enters, finds the couple "banqueting in Christ" and "conversing in holy edification." These phrases, the former in particular, are standard terms of mystical discourse. The spiritual banquet, the scriptural roots of which are in the parable of the wedding banquet, would become one of the most common images of union with Christ; indeed, because this banquet is to be thought of as a wedding banquet, the image is very closely associated with the image of Christ as the soul's spouse. Both, at any rate, have already been encountered in the *Passio*.

Tiburtius greets Cecilia with a kiss on entering the room and remarks at once on the intense and refreshing scent of roses and lilies—a phenomenon that is mentioned rather often in descriptions of higher contemplative states. When his brother tells him of the flowery crowns, which he will be able to see as well as smell if he will believe, Tiburtius wonders aloud if what he hears is only a dream.[30] All their life to this point has been a dream, replies Valerian, adding that he now lives a new life which is all truth, and that the gods they have hitherto worshiped are but demons. An angel of God has instructed him, he adds, an angel whom Tiburtius, too, will be able to see if he will be purified of all taint of idol worship.

Mourning and Joy

As Tiburtius seems to hesitate, Cecilia joins the discourse. Images made of earthenware or plaster, of wood or bronze, or of any metal cannot be gods, she declares; they are covered with spiderwebs and birds' droppings, the storks build their nests upon them, and they owe their existence in the first place to condemned criminals who work in the mines and quarries. How do they differ from a lifeless corpse? Like a corpse, they have limbs and members, but they neither breathe nor speak nor feel; of the corpse one can at least say that it once lived and moved, but the idols began without life and continue without life. When Tiburtius declares that he is convinced, Cecilia kisses him, saying that she now can recognize him as truly kin, "for as the love of God made your brother my spouse, the contempt of idols will make you my kinsman."[31] As he is ready to accept the faith, she adds, he is to go with his brother to seek the purification that will make him worthy of seeing the angel and of finding forgiveness of his sins.

Tiburtius asks to whom Valerian will take him, then recognizes in the name of Urban the Christian pope who has been condemned by the state. If they are found in such company they will themselves be tortured and burned to death, he says. When Cecilia responds that they should not fear to die if in doing so they will gain eternal life, he asks about this other life. Her answer provides further reason for seeing the theme of mourning-into-joy clearly stated in the *Passio*. She delivers a long list of the miseries and uncertainties of the present, which will certainly pass and be succeeded by an eternity of suffering, for the unjust, or of joy, for the just. Tiburtius asks if there is any direct witness to this other life, someone who can give assurances about it.

At this point Cecilia is described as drawing herself up and speaking with great authority and constancy. This is one of several carefully delineated oratorical gestures described in the *Passio* that give her the aura of sage and preacher, a prominent aspect of the medieval view of her. Her words, a preamble to answering Tiburtius's question, are an explanation of the Trinity. When he draws attention again to his request for a witness to the other life, she speaks of the Incarnation and the mission of Christ, and her answer grows into a lengthy allocution, by far the longest in the *Passio*. God's only-begotten Son, born of a virgin, stood upon the holy mountain and called all people to himself, telling them to do penance, for the Kingdom of God had arrived which puts an end to the kingdom of men.[32] The differences between the two kingdoms are explained in the language of mourning and joy. In God's kingdom, rank is measured by holiness. Sinners are punished by eternal fire, the just are rewarded with eternal joy. Christ called on them, then, not to seek the fleeting joys of the present life, but the eternal joys of the life to come. And when his hearers demanded (as Tiburtius now does) some witness of that future life, Christ performed his great miracles for them. Cecilia extends her instruction to an account of Christ's death and resurrection, and ends with an exhortation to Tiburtius to despise this present life so that he may gain the other, immortal life.

Tiburtius can brook no delay, but asks to be taken at once to Urban to be purified. For seven days following the baptism Urban keeps the neophyte at his side, further instructing him and confirming him. So great was the grace God conferred upon him that he saw the angels daily and was granted by God whatever he prayed for. With this, the first half of the *Passio* comes to an end, and the author declares that he will now narrate the glorious martyrdoms of his three saints.

The second half of the *Passio* recounts the interrogations, sentencings, and deaths of the trio in reverse order to their conversion—Tiburtius first, then Valerian, and finally, after their deaths, Cecilia herself. Maximus, the officer appointed to guard the brothers, is converted by Cecilia and is martyred with them. The narrative proceeds by elaborating the mystical themes of attaining true seeing, true understanding, and true joy through knowledge of Christ the light. Cecilia is shown as a mighty preacher, converting hundreds, and also as one who heralds the approaching "day of the Lord." The *Passio* infers that in this she resembles the phoenix, the mythical bird of resurrection that heralds the light of Christ with its singing. Since, in early Christian art, the phoenix became associated with the proclamation of the gospel, the *Passio,* the earliest document to crystallize the meaning of Cecilia for European culture, draws a powerful connection between singing, mystical knowledge, and Cecilia's keeping the gospel in her heart. Thus the *Passio* retains its dual character of mystical document and narrative of high, not to mention gory, drama.

Turcius Almachius, for example, the city prefect who is to be the martyrs' judge, is described as "tearing in pieces the saints of God and commanding that their bodies be left unburied."[33] When Valerian and Tiburtius are denounced for burying the martyrs and for looking to the needs of the poor, they are hauled before Almachius and asked to give an account of themselves. Tiburtius responds first, affirming that the martyrs "have spurned that which seems to be, but is not, and have discovered that which seems not to be, but is."[34] The dialogue that ensues firmly establishes the author's preoccupation with the theme of mourning and joy, and his acute perception of its paradoxical character.[35] When Almachius asks what he means by "that which seems to be but is not," Tiburtius replies that it is "everything in this world which invites souls to perpetual death through temporal joy." What, then, does he mean by "that which seems not to be, but is?" continues the prefect. Tiburtius's answer appeals to two kinds of vision, that of the bodily eyes and that of the "eyes of the heart;" what we see clearly with the latter, we deny with the former. The reward that is the due of the just and the punishment that is the due of the unjust are thus subject to a peculiar and unhappy dissembling. Going against our conscience, we humans manage to see as undesirable that which is really good and to adorn with beautiful descriptions those things that are really evil.

The phrase "eyes of the heart," taken directly from Ephesians 1:18, is a suggestive one, given the almost wearisome emphasis of the *Passio* on the symbolic significance of both organs. Almost a thousand years later, in a work that would affect Raphael's iconography of St. Cecilia, Jean Gerson would refer to this passage in his dialogue between the Solitary Heart and the Worldly Heart, when he cited directly the words of St. Paul that Tiburtius flings at Almachius and that bring his interrogation to a close: "The animal man does not perceive those things which are of the Spirit of God. The spiritual man, however, judges all things, but he himself is judged by nobody."[36]

Laughing at the seeming absurdities, Almachius has Tiburtius removed and Valerian brought forward in his place. "Your brother is not of sound mind," he begins, and suggests that perhaps Valerian can give an intelligible explanation. But Valerian replies in the same vein. It is Almachius's hearing, not Tiburtius's sanity, that is at fault. The prefect bluntly sketches the enormity of their error, initiating a long exchange that contrasts pagan and Christian beliefs ever more firmly in terms of mourning and joy, both worldly and spiritual. No other passage in the *Passio* suggests more strongly that the theme of mourning and joy was not read into the cult texts of St.

Cecilia by later Christians, but was built into those texts from the beginning. And for this reason it is worth citing the passage at length.

Almachius tries to declare the precise nature of the brothers' error. "No one errs as you err—you who have abandoned all that is necessary and useful to pursue what is idle and trifling! You spurn joy, you curse delight, you hold in contempt everything that lends charm to living, you avidly pursue whatever contradicts well-being and happiness!"[37] Valerian answers with a parable similar in message to the parable of the wise and foolish virgins, but even more reminiscent of Aesop's fable of the grasshopper and the ants—a parable that thus serves as an example of the transmutation of pagan themes into Christian ones. Valerian draws a vivid contrast between the idleness, *otium,* of which Almachius has just accused him, and the true idleness of those who are busy with this world's cares but pay no heed to preparation for the life to come. The joy of the dalliers is turned to sorrow, the hardships of the laborers become rejoicing; and the joy and sorrow of each are seen for what they truly are.

I watched in the winter time as people full of laughter and merriment, laden with delight, passed by fields in which peasants were watching over their herds, working with plant cuttings, and carefully setting together the thorny shoots of rose bushes. Some grafted the cuttings, others uprooted weeds, all were wholly occupied in their work. Then the dalliers began to mock the laborers, calling out: 'You unhappy and wretched people, stop this unnecessary work and let yourselves be seen, along with us, as rejoicing in delights and pleasures. Why do you grow faint, like madmen, in this arduous toil, and exhaust your years in labors so desolate?' And as they spoke they broke into laughter over them and clapped their hands, heaping ridicule upon them. And while they all continued thus, the fair weather followed the cold and rainy months. Then the fields, bright with rosy flowers, were adorned with vineclad trees, and the underbrush displayed the curly garlands of clusters at their birth; and they brought forth from various kinds of such trees most luscious fruit on which today we have seen abound charm and fruit as well as beauty. And so while those were rejoicing who had been thought simpletons, those who had seemed sophisticates began to weep. Then those who had prided themselves on their wisdom were ruined in a great pestilence; and giving voice, in too-late repentance, to sorrowing and sighing for their idleness, they began to speak to one another: 'These are they whom we once held in derision; we counted their labor as dishonor, we reviled their life as wretched, we judged their persons unworthy and their meetings without honor. Now they are shown to have been wise, we to have been wretched and foolish and futile, when we neither labored ourselves nor offered help to the laborers. But living in delight, we mocked them and held them to be demented, those whom we now see to be flourishing in glory.[38]

Valerian contrasts the labors and sufferings of the Christians with the present ease and joy of their oppressors. But "a time shall come in which we gather the fruits of this our sadness, and while we rejoice those shall mourn who are now lifted up in their joy. For now is the time of sowing; those who shall have sown joys in this life shall reap mourning and sighing in the next, while those who shall now have sown temporal tears shall reap eternal joys in the life to come."[39] He goes on to apply his emphatic statement to Almachius and the emperors, and to contrast his nameless God with the idols of Rome. The enraged prefect orders him to be beaten, and even as the sentence is carried out Valerian shouts over the voice of the public crier—who is warning that this is the penalty for blasphemy—and calls upon the people not to be frightened from the truth by his suffering, but to grind into powder, to "convert into chalk," the stone gods worshiped by Almachius.

Now the prefect's assessor, Tarquinius Lacca, intervenes, pointing out to Almachius that any delay in executing the brothers will put their goods into the hands of the poor and out of the reach of legal confiscation. And so the order is given that Valerian and Tiburtius be led out to the city's boundaries, where they will be offered one last chance to sacrifice to Jove: if they refuse, they are to be beheaded.

The officer into whose charge they are given, a *cornicularius* named Maximus, is deeply affected by the threat to such noble youths and seeks to persuade them to save their lives. He wonders aloud that they who are going to their deaths should seem rather to be hurrying to a banquet ("quasi ad epulas festinatis"), invoking again the well-known symbol of union with God. Tiburtius speaks to him of the other, eternal life into which they are about to enter and makes mention, for the first time in the *Passio,* of another of the story's conventional symbols, the phoenix: the human body, he says, produced through lust out of earthly seed, is simply returned to its earthly womb so that it may rise like the phoenix at the appearance of the light that is to come. Valerian joins his brother in persuading the officer, promising him that God will open his eyes at their deaths and make him see the glory that is theirs (again the emphasis on vision); and he urges Maximus to take them to his house for this night so that they can bring a purifier who will make him see what they have promised.

Maximus does what they have asked, and at their preaching he and his household—indeed, the executioners themselves—are converted. Cecilia arrives during the night with a group of priests, and all are baptized. Then the *Passio* describes another of Cecilia's symbolically charged gestures, which carries obvious echoes of St. Paul: "And so as dawn put an end to night, and a great silence fell, Cecilia spoke: 'Hearken, soldiers of Christ! Cast aside the works of darkness and put on the armour of light! You have fought the good fight, you have finished the course, you have kept the faith! Go to the crown of life which God, the just judge, shall give you—and not only you, but all who love his coming!'"[40]

Cecilia's heralding of the approaching day in this fashion is almost certainly an elaboration of references in the *Passio* to the phoenix, that legendary and richly symbolic bird whose meaning was deeply embedded in early Christian art and literature. In the traditional reading of Lactantius's fourth-century poem, the mythical creature is said to have welcomed the sun each day at dawn with a wordless song of indescribable beauty. But modern editors transposed the lines that recount this episode to the point in the poem at which the phoenix dies and thus turned a daily song into a unique song at death. They did this not on textual grounds, for the manuscript evidence supports the traditional placement, but because only Lactantius's version of the widespread myth seemed to support a daily singing.[41] The manuscripts of Lactantius, they concluded, must all have followed some early corruption of the text. More recent research, however, has uncovered other versions of the legend that support the traditional reading.[42] There is, then, a strong possibility that the author of the *Passio* intends here to portray Cecilia as doing what the phoenix does, welcoming the Light (who is Christ—I take Lactantius's poem to be a Christian work) that comes into human life. Such an interpretation is not without antecedents and parallels. The double-headed phoenix that was discovered by Margherita Guarducci in the Vatican catacombs called upon Christ for light with the song "Giver of Light, give thy light to the world," just as the deacon did at the Easter Vigil; and the phoenix that sits on the palm tree to the right of the approaching Christ in the apsidal mosaics of Ss. Cosmas and Damian and other Roman churches, including S. Cecilia in Trastevere, is probably a symbolic counterpart of the deacon who sang the daily gospel directly below.[43] Lactantius's phoenix also greets the sun with song at the changing hours of the day, a reference possibly to the chanting of the liturgical hours. Here, at any rate, are ample grounds for seeing an early association of Cecilia with music, with liturgical singing.

Valerian and Tiburtius are led out the next day and given the chance to recant by offering incense to Jove. At their refusal they are beheaded, and it is then that Maximus fulfills Valerian's prophecy by crying out that he has seen their souls leaving their bodies "like virgins from the nuptial chamber." Many are converted by the martyrdoms, and Maximus is ordered by the prefect to be beaten to death. Cecilia has him buried beside the two brothers in a new sarcophagus on which a phoenix is carved, as a sign of his belief in the Resurrection.[44]

Now Almachius, seeking to confiscate the property of Valerian and Tiburtius, commands that Cecilia be arrested. The property having already been distributed to the poor, she, too, is commanded to offer incense to the gods. As she refuses, she begins a dialogue with the arresting officers that leads to her discourse on the worthlessness of this life, to lose which "is not to lose life, but to change it, to give clay and get back gold." After she climbs on a stone to receive the assent of those whom her preaching has converted, she declares that she will bring to her house one who will make them all partakers of everlasting life. Pope Urban comes, and more than four hundred are baptized, "men and women, rich and poor, old and young."[45]

Here occurs the episode of Gordianus, discussed in the previous chapter. One of the newly converted, he thenceforth sheltered Cecilia's house under his own name so that it could function secretly as a church. Undoubtedly this episode betrays the author's need to explain away to his contemporaries the fact that the church he put forward as Cecilia's house was still remembered, by some at least, as the "title of Gordianus."

When Cecilia is at last interrogated by the prefect, her replies are sharper and bolder than those of Valerian and Tiburtius. The conclusion of the exchange is especially remarkable, for she asserts repeatedly and emphatically that the prefect must be not only spiritually but even physically blind to be able to worship idols. The passage seems to reflect strongly the concern with blindness and seeing that marked the area around the shrine of Bona Dea Oclata in Trastevere. When Cecilia tells Almachius that his and the imperial power over life and death is a lie, for such power can give only death and not life, he angrily commands her to cease her audacity and sacrifice to the gods. She replies: "I do not know where you could have lost your eyes, for those whom you call gods both I and all those who have healthy eyes see to be made of stone and bronze and lead. . . . from the moment you opened your mouth, you have said nothing that I could not show was unjust, foolish and empty. But to cap it all you show that you do not even have physical eyesight, for you insist that what we all see to be made of useless stone and rock is really divine! . . . Put out your hand, and let it teach you what your eyes could not, that this is stone."[46] And she goes on to declare, with a final flourish, that it would be better to throw these stone gods into the fire than to let them fall uselessly into ruin, for then their chalky residue would be of some use; left as they are, they can help no one, and certainly cannot help themselves if they should be cast into the flames.

This last insult infuriates Almachius to the point of condemning Cecilia herself to be burned. That he is seeking to fit the punishment to the crime seems obvious, but is never remarked on: because she insists that the idols can be reduced in the fire and that this kind of destruction is the extent of the magistrate's power, Almachius sentences Cecilia herself to the flames. Her power to withstand their destructive force is probably meant as a contrast to the vulnerability to flame that she avers of the idols.

She is to burn not at the stake, but in the bath of her house. There is no real certainty as to what the author understood by this sentence, but it is usually taken to mean death by suffocation in a typical Roman bath as air heated beyond measure was passed through the hypocausts from the furnace beneath. Medieval artists interpreted this punishment more literally, showing Cecilia most often in a great basin over a fire, sometimes with Tiburtius and Valerian alongside her. It should not be assumed that such depiction was due to medieval economies of scale or thought. The image may be an allusion to Sidrach, Misach, and Abdenago in Daniel. They, too, suffered for their hostility to idols, and the song they sang in the fire became one of the most colorful items in early Roman liturgical chant.[47]

Like the three children in the Babylonian furnace, Cecilia, too, is preserved from the flames. "Out came Sidrach, Misach and Abdenago from the fire's heart all of them," says the Book of Daniel, "and with one accord governor and judge and courtiers clustered round them to look. Plain it was, the heat had no power over them" (Dan. 3:94). When Cecilia "was shut up in the heat of the bath, and great quantities of wood were fed to the fires beneath, she remained perfectly protected for a whole day and night as if she were in a place of coolness, so that no part of her showed even the smallest drop of perspiration."[48] The embroidery of Cecilia, Valerian, and Tiburtius on a cope in the treasury of the cathedral of Anagni is reminiscent of the three children in the Babylonian furnace singing God's praises in the flames; like the three Israelites, the three young Romans are accompanied by an angel who seems to be singing from a scroll on which music, too indistinct to be legible, is written.[49]

But Almachius's reaction to the miracle was not that of Nabuchodonosor. On hearing that Cecilia still lived, he sent an executioner to behead her as she lay in the bath. In yet another of the legend's improbabilities, the executioner, even after three blows, was not successful in beheading the saint.[50] She was left for three days to die, during which time the people she had converted came with cloths to soak up her blood, evidently as relics, and she herself "continued to strengthen those she had nourished and instructed in the faith of the Lord."[51] She used the time also to distribute her remaining possessions to the poor, and to confirm to Pope Urban the gift of her house as a church. The last lines of the *Passio* reveal the author's eagerness to explain the presence of the Cecilia in the catacombs, as well as to justify the dedication of the Trastevere basilica to her. They report Pope Urban's burying her "among his fellow bishops," which means in the catacomb of St. Callistus, and his ratification of Cecilia's gift of her house as a church. It was then, as it remained throughout the Middle Ages, a shrine of great note, a place where, as the *Passio* says, "the blessings of God abound even to the present day."[52]

"my harp is turned into mourning"

Four The Discarded Harp in Images of David-in-Penitence

Enough has been said in the previous chapters about the discarded instruments in the miniature of David-in-Penitence to indicate just how important the image and its musical detail are to this study. For, I contend, the compositional similarity of the popular representation of the penitent king to Raphael's painting of St. Cecilia—the gaze turned upward to a heavenly vision, the instruments of music about the feet—is no coincidence, but the result of their sharing in the same iconographic tradition. Something of this has already emerged in the foregoing discussion of the text of Psalm 24:1–3, used as offertory in the liturgy of the Trastevere station day and later adopted as both introit and offertory for the first Sunday of Advent. As introit on this day, the text became one of the common loci of the miniature of David-in-Penitence, reinforcing in picture the lesson of the text, that this attitude—"to Thee, O Lord, I have raised my soul"—is the foundation of the Christian life, with implications close to those of the scriptural phrase "change of heart."

In the present chapter I shall discuss the significance of the David-in-Penitence miniature, addressing the composition itself and its symbolic details, but seeking especially to explain the tradition of thought out of which it developed. Attention will be given to the places where it occurs in illuminated manuscripts, the most important of these being at the head of the seven penitential psalms. The view that life must be grounded in humility, the contrary of pride and thus the foundation of true progress, was universally espoused, at least for public record, in the life of the Catholic centuries, and led to the placing of the David-in-Penitence in its popular loci. The same view, ironically, often brought about the opposite result: the public espousal of humility became the basis for public assertion of right and power. For humility was the source of divine blessing and promise, as asserted most notably in the text of the Magnificat (Luke 1:48, 52): "for he has looked favorably on the humility of his handmaid . . . he has put down the powerful from their throne, and raised up the humble." It became the fashion for the rich and powerful, the patrons of the best art, to associate themselves with the image of the humble and repentant David in the works they commissioned. Whatever the effect of this fashion on the development of the miniature, it undoubtedly led to its wide dissemination. One of the more noticeable of these instances of patronage forms an instructive starting point for a discussion of the miniature itself.

In 1509 Wynkyn de Worde published a set of sermons on the seven penitential psalms by John Fisher, Bishop of Rochester.[1] The sermons were printed, as they had been preached, at the "exortacion and sterynge" of the mother of the reigning King Henry VII, Lady Margaret Beaufort, the bishop's patroness and penitent since his days as master of Michaelhouse and vice-chancellor of Cambridge University. Historians may wonder whether Lady Margaret's wish that the work appear during her son's lifetime (Henry died within months of its publication) reflected simply a mother's desire that her child be perfectly prepared for judgment or a particular fear that some incident in his crafty and ruthless life might yet be an obstacle to divine forgiveness. If of meditative bent and especially sensitive to history's ironies, the same historians may wonder whether Lady Margaret's grandson, another Henry, not yet in his teens, was present at Fisher's preaching. Did Henry VIII sit before the future saint and martyr, whom he himself would deliver to the axe, and hear him tell how "thys weyke and lytell persone Davyd unarmed obteyned the grete and meruayllous vyctory" over Goliath, and how "with the swerde of the same . . . he stroke of his heed"? Did the boy-about-to-be-king, whose rage twenty years later at Fisher's forthright support for the case of Queen Katherine would lead to the bishop's execution, hear that same bishop recount the age-old story of royal lust and willfulness, and of royal repentance, that was the foundation of the seven penitential psalms?

The point of this speculation about Henry VIII and St. John Fisher's sermons on the penitential psalms will be sharpened for the reader by the realization that the king's psalter survives in the British Library and that it includes not only annotations against each psalm in the king's own hand but a number of illuminations in which David is represented in the king's unmistakable likeness.[2] Before Psalm 68, "O God, save me; see how the

Figure 4.1. *King Henry VIII of England as David-in-Penitence*

(By permission of The British Library; Royal MS 2.A.XVI, fol. 79.)

Following a fashion among the nobility, King Henry had himself portrayed in the guise of King David throughout this psalter. Here he kneels in a ruined courtyard, his crown on the ground beside him.

waters close about me, threatening my very life," Henry appears as David-in-Penitence kneeling in the courtyard of a ruined castle. He wears a black cap, while his crown—but no musical instrument, as in so many versions of the composition—lies on the ground beside him (fig. 4.1).[3] More usual before Psalm 68 is a miniature that shows David standing or kneeling in water as suggested by the text. But this scene has clear affinities with the David-in-Penitence, both being fundamentally penitential and suggestive of utter confidence in God. The old Vulgate psalm title, with its suggestion of the radical remaking of corrupt human nature that is available to the repentant, is perhaps even more pertinent: "To the end, for those who will be transformed; for David." The idea of change, of transformation, was in fact a principal meaning of the musical elements that came to be inserted into the images of the repentant David before these psalms.

Henry VIII's self-association with the poet-king who established the dynasty from which Christ was believed to have sprung, and who so manifestly ruled by divine approval, was in no way unique. Many European kings and nobles had cultivated the same association, and had had David painted in their own likeness, or at least had had themselves painted in David's company, just as Henry had done.[4] This habit of the old nobility has aroused considerable interest among art historians and has inspired such fine studies of David-related iconography as Robert Deshman's "The Exalted Servant: The Ruler Theology of the Prayerbook of Charles the Bald." Yet it may be that the emphasis such studies put on the role of the ruler and on theories of governance has given us a lopsided view of

Figure 4.2. *David's Messenger to Bathsheba Removes His Hat*

(By permission of The British Library; *The Psalter of David* [London, 1542], vol. 2, facing p. 1; shelf-number C.25.b.4 [2].)

A discarded crown in the David-in-Penitence miniature symbolizes David's fall when he committed adultery with Bathsheba. The same symbolism may be suggested by this woodcut in a psalter from King Henry VIII's library, which shows the messenger with David's invitation to Bathsheba about to remove his hat.

Figure 4.3. Jan Provoost. *St. Nicholas with Donor* (left panel of a triptych)

(Groeningemuseum, Bruges. Photo: Thomas Connolly)

Just as patrons sometimes had themselves painted in the likeness of David-in-Penitence, at other times they had themselves depicted with a book open to the image of the repentant king. This is the case with the book open before the kneeling donor of this Flemish triptych.

the significance of the iconography of the penitential David by deflecting attention from what is certainly its more basic content: the redemptive work of God in every human soul that stands at the heart of the medieval world view, a work of grace that could begin only in the soul's humble repentance. In this one case of the Tudors, at least, there is nothing in the long court sermons surrounding David's repentance to suggest any special attention to what has been called "ruler theology."

There is, in fact, no study that treats the richly allusive David miniatures

The Discarded Harp

of the old devotional books in a way that matches David's significance in sermons and spiritual writings.[5] But the more deeply one understands the position of David as penitent in Christian thinking and the iconography of the David-in-Penitence miniatures, the more clearly one sees a link between the unplayed instruments in miniatures of David and the discarded instruments in Raphael's painting of St. Cecilia, and the more clearly do these musical images speak of metanoia and subsequent growth in the spiritual life.

No other Old Testament figure achieved so prominent a position in Christian tradition as did David. That position was founded not on Christian theories of kingship, which were of little concern during Christianity's first centuries, but on the place David necessarily occupied in primitive catechesis, as conveyed at the beginning of St. Matthew's Gospel, in the opening words of the New Testament: "The list of the ancestry of Jesus-Messiah, son of David, son of Abraham." Jesus was Messiah, and necessarily a descendant of the royal house of David: his Davidic descent was one of the cornerstones of that early catechesis. A concomitant of this genealogy was the Church's acceptance of the Psalms as the foundation of its public prayer, with the result that consideration of David's life and words became a constant occupation of the Christian mind. No book of the Bible was more profusely commented upon by the early Fathers, the commentaries of Origen, Athanasius, Hilary, Ambrose, Jerome, and Augustine being but the best-known of a much larger number. St. Benedict's stipulation that his monks recite all 150 psalms each week was in no sense an innovation, but merely the confirmation of a deeply rooted tradition. Benedict even recalled to the fainthearted the example of the desert monks who used to recite the whole psalter daily.[6]

It is not surprising, given their content, that seven of the psalms—Psalms 6, 31, 37, 50, 101, 129, and 142 in the Vulgate's numbering—should have been grouped together as the "penitential psalms," nor that their author should have become the principal example of the repentant spirit in the Church, though the processes by which these things came about are obscure. Cassiodorus seems to have been the first to group the seven together under their common name in his commentary on the Book of Psalms. It was the first complete commentary to appear in the West, but is scarcely original, being heavily dependent on the *Enarrationes* of Augustine, commentaries that originated as individual sermons on the Psalms as they were used in the liturgy. As the New Testament itself suggests, however, intense focus on David must go back to the Church's earliest times. David's adultery with Bathsheba, the contrived slaying of her husband, and the king's instant and utter repentance upon Nathan's accusation made up a story of deep human appeal and were principal exempla for preachers and writers.[7] The seven penitential psalms seem always to have been linked with these events in the Psalmist's life, and indeed the fourth of the seven, Psalm 50, which is more than any other *the* psalm of repentance and which is often known simply by its first word as the Miserere, states as much in its title: ". . . of David, when the prophet Nathan came to reproach him for his adultery with Bathsheba." Dante, for instance, would identify David simply as "the singer who in grief for his sin cried 'Miserere mei.'"[8]

The fact that Psalm 37, the third penitential psalm, is the entrance psalm for the mass of the station day at S. Cecilia in Trastevere establishes one link between the figures of David and Cecilia. The presence in that same liturgy of the lesson from Esther 13, with its concluding prayer to "turn our mourning into joy," which is a reversal of the texts that explain the musical content of the David-in-Penitence (Job 30:31 and Lamentations 5:15–16) has already given us some intimation of what that link means. But the meaning of the linkage begins to crystallize only when we read texts such as St. Augustine's Exposition on Psalm 37.[9]

Augustine begins with a discussion of the psalm's title, "A Psalm of David, in remembrance of the Sabbath." One remembers, he says, only that which is absent: thus David composed this psalm while the peace and joy signified by the Sabbath were but a memory, that is, when he was in the anguish and pain of repentance for his sin. How much happier David was, Augustine declares, in this state where peace was a memory than he would have been had his anguish been absent. To the modern ear, Augustine's interpretation may sound peculiar, especially if we hear the words of the Decalogue and recall that there are quite other ways in which to "remember" the Sabbath. And yet his choice merely emphasizes how common was the early and medieval Christian's appreciation of the sine qua non of repentance and the strange changes of joy and sorrow that follow in a life lived with unshaken trust in God. The passage from Augustine is an example of the rhetorical contradictions with which Christian writers have always surrounded the fundamental paradox of Christian teaching, that "he who would save his life must lose it," and that form the basis of the contrast implied in both the visual and literary references to the turning of mourning into joy, joy into mourning. The source of the paradox is scriptural, and scriptural examples abound, the best-known and most frequently cited being perhaps the passage from John's description of the discourse at the Last Supper, in which Christ contrasts the joy of "the world" at his approaching sufferings with the sorrow of his disciples, and promises that their sorrow will be turned into joy.[10]

Cassiodorus continues and adds to Augustine's thought in his comments on the same psalm. Some commentators, he points out, hold that this psalm, with its graphic description of bodily sufferings, refers to the trials of Job, who warred against the flesh, triumphed over immense suffering, and was victorious in the struggle with earthly life. By considering Job's torments, he goes on, penitents find it easier to sustain their own. We should therefore rejoice in bitter afflictions and in the crucifixion of our own flesh, which are able to deliver us from eternal penalties. He emphasizes the happy outcome, the *exsultativa conclusio,* for those who do penance, and the great joy shared in the face of suffering by those who have this source of hope.[11]

Centuries after Augustine and Cassiodorus, one of the most authoritative voices of the Middle Ages, Peter Lombard, pointedly identifies the *exsultativa conclusio* with the most Cecilian part of Psalm 37, those last two verses that make up the introit antiphon for the station day at S. Cecilia in Trastevere. He divides the psalm into four parts and, in discussing the fourth, states that *exsultativa conclusio* is posited "of salvation, so that there may be sure hope for those who are imitating [Christ]. Thus it happens in all penitential acts, *Ne derelinquas me, domine, deus meus.*"[12] We have here a statement that this important Cecilian text, the introit of her station day, is associated with the "joy-filled conclusion" of the inner motion of repentance. The text continued to be used in penitential liturgies. In the modern revisions of the Roman Ritual of Pius V, for instance, it serves as antiphon in the rite of General Absolution for Members of Religious Orders, and in the rite of Apostolic Blessing at the Hour of Death.[13] One of the earliest illuminations of one of the texts of mourning and joy that I have encountered is, in fact, an early-fourteenth-century miniature of a Franciscan priest hearing a nun's confession. The text it accompanies is Isaiah 12:1, "I confess to you, O Lord, for you were angry with me; your wrath has turned; and you have consoled me [Confiteor tibi domine quoniam iratus es michi: conversus est furor tuus: & consolatus es me]."[14]

Earlier Christian texts also bear witness to the theme of mourning and joy in reference to the struggle between virtue and vice (which, in its contemporary Christian context, might better be described as the struggle between grace and sin). A passage in Prudentius's *Psychomachia,* to be discussed in chapter 6, links the theme in a delightfully subtle way with the text of Job 30:31. Passages such as these of Prudentius, Augustine, and Cassiodorus are the remote witnesses of a tradition that would become firmly established in the later Middle Ages, a tradition that would link the idea of converting joy into mourning, and mourning into joy, with the transformation that takes place within human souls in their passage—in both directions—between the states of grace and sin, or (the distinction is an important one) between the suffering of repentance and the joy of grace. Scripture texts that make reference to the idea, like Job 30:31 ("my harp is turned into mourning, my organ into the voice of those who weep"), Lamentations 5:15–16 ("the joy of our heart is fled, our singing is turned into mourning"), and Esther 13:17 ("turn our mourning into joy"), would become commonplaces of the pulpit during the period of penitential fervor and reform that began toward the end of the eleventh century. This period would see the rise of the Canons Regular and the Cistercians, as well as of the mendicant orders, and would culminate in the penitential reforms promulgated by the Fourth Lateran Council in 1215, in particular its prescription of annual confession of sins and of the performance of the penitential acts enjoined by the confessor at the confession.[15] The *quadrigesimale,* a series of penitential sermons preached daily throughout Lent, likewise became one of the great institutions of the Middle Ages. In the many such sermon-series, the most common text for the sermon preached on the Wednesday after the second Sunday of Lent, the station day at S. Cecilia in Trastevere, was the concluding words of the mass lesson of the day, Esther 13:17, "turn our mourning into joy."[16]

It was in this milieu that the image of David-in-Penitence was developed and disseminated in the West. The type of the kneeling, repentant king existed as early as the ninth and tenth centuries in Byzantine and

The Discarded Harp

Figure 4.4. *David-in-Penitence:* Miniature before Psalm 37 in the De Brailes Hours

(By permission of The British Library; MS 49999, fol. 69)

This simple illustration of David-in-Penitence before Psalm 37 in one of the earliest books of hours bears a caption in French stating that it was at this point in his repentance that David began to compose the seven penitential psalms: *la cumenca les vii psaumes.* Psalm 37, so closely associated with the liturgy of St. Cecilia, was seen as a point of transition and radical change in the spiritual journey.

Byzantine-inspired devotional books.[17] In so-called aristocratic Byzantine psalters of that period, it commonly accompanied the fourth penitential psalm, Psalm 50, the title of which states that it was written at Nathan's reproach of David for his adultery with Bathsheba. From this period until the fifteenth century, when the type proliferated and accumulated a wealth of visual detail—the time of Raphael and his commissioners—its development is not easy to trace. The image occurs as early as about 1240 in the De Brailes Hours, which was produced at Oxford and is, according to Nigel Morgan, the "earliest fully-illustrated example in English art of a Book of Hours."[18] Examples certainly exist from the fourteenth century, but are rare in comparison with the fifteenth. In the Douai Psalter, for instance, an East Anglian book dated about 1322, a David-in-Penitence is found at the head of Psalm 119, "Ad dominum cum tribularer clamavi."[19] Several of the common details of the type are already present. David, kneeling, looks up to a vision of God leaning out from a pavilion. He is bareheaded and his harp is on the ground—the first instance known to me of the discarded harp in a version of the David-in-Penitence—but the crown is not to be seen.[20]

An instructive example of the composition—instructive because it includes most of the more usual details and may thus be called typical—is seen in a fifteenth-century book of hours in the Vatican Library (MS Barberini lat. 381, fol. 134; see fig. 4.6). Here the David-in-Penitence is found in its most usual place, before the first penitential psalm. David kneels, his hands joined and his eyes raised, before a bench on which lies an open book. He is bareheaded, and his hat or crown can be seen beneath the bench, while his harp rests on the ground just behind him. From the belt that circles his blue robe and his white, scapular-like outer garment, a small pouch or wallet is seen to hang. An angel hovers overhead, wielding a sword, while in a corner of the sky God leans out from a blue, star-edged

Figure 4.5. *David Seated, with Discarded Harp:* Miniature from a Thirteenth-Century Psalter (Bodleian Library, Oxford; MS Laud lat. 114, fol. 7v)

The visual motif of the discarded harp flourished in images of David repentant in books of the fourteenth and, more especially, the fifteenth centuries. But the first examples of the motif seem somewhat earlier than the David-in-Penitence, as in this example from a psalter dated 1275.

　　　　　　　　The Discarded Harp

Figure 4.6. *David-in-Penitence:* Miniature from a Book of Hours

(Biblioteca Apostolica Vaticana, MS Barb. lat. 381, fol. 134r)

A typical example of the David-in-Penitence occurs before the seven penitential psalms in this fifteenth-century book. The hovering angel, vision of God, discarded harp and crown, book open before David, belt and pouch, city, and stream are all conventional motifs in the popular miniature.

half-circle from which golden rays beam forth. The scene is set on a grassy mound beside a hill from which a spring issues, against a background of a walled city circled in part by a moat or river that seems to flow from, or into, the city wall.

Other common features of the composition are shown in plate 2 and figure 4.7. In the fifteenth-century book of hours from Northern France that we have already encountered in the first chapter (plate 2), once again at the head of the first penitential psalm, David kneels before a high chair or throne, under a canopy whose curtains are drawn back.[21] Two instru-

Figure 4.7. *David-in-Penitence:* Miniature before the Introit for the First Sunday of Advent

(Biblioteca Apostolica Vaticana, MS Vat. lat. 7792, fol. 8r)

In this late fifteenth-century north Italian missal the David-in-Penitence is situated, as it often was (see, for example, plate 5), at the beginning of the church year. Placing it at significant beginnings—it was found also at the beginning of the Psalms, and of the seven penitential psalms—emphasized that Christian living must begin in humility. A harp and viol lie discarded in this example, but there is no vision of God or angel. Two other images that conventionally represent humility appear on the page: the Annunciation at the upper corners and the repentant St. Jerome at the bottom center.

ments—a strangely shaped organ as well as a harp—lie on the ground. Missing from the picture are the hovering angel and the hill; the scene is now set on a checkered stone floor, though it is still outdoors and the city with its stream is in the background. One notes the slightly different posture of the king, the eyes more elevated and the hands raised and apart rather than joined.

The late-fifteenth-century North Italian missal shown in figure 4.7 returns the composition to a grassy place and again shows the hill, or rocky outcrop.[22] As in plate 2, there are two instruments, this time a lute and a viol, and the king's hands are joined. There is no vision of God, no hovering angel, and no bench or book. A notable addition, of a detail that is quite common in the intricate versions of the scene, is the dead tree in the background. Here the miniature heads not the first penitential psalm but the introit, or entrance antiphon and psalm (Psalm 24), of the first Sunday of Advent, the second of its common loci. This is of course the introit that shares its text with the offertory of the station day at S. Cecilia in Trastevere, as discussed in chapter 2.

There are many other variants of the composition, some of them common, others occurring just a few times or even once only, in the great number of examples that I examined during the preparation of this book. The elements from which the David-in-Penitence is composed may usefully be divided into essential, common, and occasional or even unique. Only the kneeling king should be considered essential, there being indeed instances in which he appears against a patterned background with no other detail. All the other details mentioned so far are common, though one could without difficulty find examples of the scene in which one or several of them are lacking. This, it should be noted, applies to the details derived from the texts cited from Job and Lamentations, that is, to the musical instruments and the crown. Though the harp, or some other instrument or instruments, is an exceedingly common element, there are many cases in which it is lacking. There are even occasional miniatures in which the kneeling king plays his harp, though these are rare in the usual loci.

The other more common details should at least be mentioned, along with some of the occasional or unique details. Sometimes, if the angel is not present, it is God who holds the threatening weapons. Sometimes the harp is half-enclosed within its fabric cover; or the book before the king may be half inside its cover, its "chemisette." Quite commonly, a scepter, as well as a crown, is depicted on the ground beside David. There are many examples of the scene's being set indoors, in which case the vision of God, or at least the golden rays, may be seen through or descending from a window.[23] In at least one instance, the scene is set in the courtyard of a ruined castle (Henry VIII's Psalter; see fig. 4.1). The backgrounds of the outdoor scenes are often full of interest. Apart from the already mentioned hill or mountain, the flowing streams, and the dead and living trees, there is sometimes seen a path or road winding across the landscape. David is sometimes shown within or before a cave. Quite often the dead trees are associated with a stony, desert place. Occasionally there are references to episodes from David's youth. Thus he may be seen killing a lion or a bear, as he described it to Saul when he offered himself as Goliath's challenger (1 Samuel 17:34), or even slaying the Philistine giant himself. These last episodes, the slaughter of the lion or bear and of Goliath, are frequently found as border miniatures in later manuscripts. Other subjects in borders are those directly concerned with the story of Bathsheba and Uriah: David observing Bathsheba bathing (which is often a separate miniature at the head of the first penitential psalm); David and Bathsheba together, in bath or bed; Uriah being sent back to Joab with the letter that tells the general to place him where the fighting would be most dangerous; and the death in battle of Uriah.[24]

Though the significance of individual details is not always clear, the texts of the psalms with which the David-in-Penitence is most commonly associated are rich in suggestion; particularly, therefore, Psalm 1, Psalm 24, and the seven penitential psalms. One must be cautious, of course, in connecting visual images with particular passages of Scripture, for these biblical word-images are frequently and notoriously repetitive and commonplace. It is much closer to the mark to suggest that the source of a particular visual detail is the medieval Christian mind imbued with biblical imagery in general rather than any single verse, no matter how plausible the connection of verse and image may seem. The tallying of chapters and verses that follows, then, is meant to show how such a mind was formed rather than to insist on links between specific texts and specific pictorial details.

Psalm 1 is an appropriate introduction to the iconography of humility and obedience; its imagery defines sharply the difference between good and evil and the choice that leads to one or the other. It contrasts the way of the just with the way of the wicked (the winding paths that sometimes appear in the landscapes of the David-in-Penitence come to mind) and declares the just man to be like a fruitful tree planted beside running waters (similes that suggest the living trees and running streams of the miniatures). The just man does not follow the counsel of the wicked; he does not walk in the paths where sinners walk; he does not sit in the chair of corruption. This last image—of the Vulgate's *cathedra pestilentiae*—lends itself to those illustrations of chairs and thrones that are so common in representations of David. The Psalmist enthroned, playing his psaltery or holding his book on his knees, is probably the image most often found at the head of Psalm 1, and hence of the psalter itself. In this case it is the throne of the just man, whereas we should perhaps understand the throne behind the kneeling David in plate 2 as the *cathedra pestilentiae* of Psalm 1:1.[25]

Augustine, whose brief discourse on this psalm runs deep with visual undercurrents, suggests two interpretations of the term. One is that the throne represents earthly power and its pride; this would make the vacated throne, like the abandoned crown, a sign of David's humility. Augustine's other notion is that the term "chair of pestilence" may more truly symbolize harmful doctrine, since its teaching eats away like a cancer. The contrary idea, of a seat of wisdom, was certainly a pregnant one for the Middle Ages, which applied precisely that title to Mary in the Litany; and it has, incidentally, some resonance for those familiar with Cecilia's iconography, for it was as a teacher in the seat of wisdom that the Master of the S. Cecilia painted her, about 1300, in a famous altarpiece now hanging in the Uffizi (fig. 7.5).

In a passage he would later regret as an exaggerated interpretation, Augustine identified the "blessed man" of the First Psalm as Christ, the *homo dominicus,* the Man of the Lord.[26] This enabled Augustine to present the antithesis of the *homo dominicus,* namely, the *homo terrenus,* obviously alluding to the opposed economies of grace and of nature and to those who live under them, and finally identifying the "worldly man" as Adam and Adam's race in his comment on verse 4.

It is not an exaggeration to say that this antithesis between the two economies, and between the "old man" and the "new man" who are their citizens—and it is an antithesis that is crystal clear in Christian readings of the First Psalm—is the foundation of the iconography with which the penitent David came to be surrounded. Many of the elements of that iconography are of the antithetical kind: they either appear as opposed pairs or suggest their matching opposites. Thus we see dead and living trees; the path that crosses the landscape might be the way of the just or the way of the wicked; the stream of water that gives life is contrasted with a dry, stony riverbed; among the white sheep in a field there appears a single black goat. Such visual antithesis is of course biblical in character, and probably in inspiration, matching the antithetical parallelism of Old Testament poetry.

But antithesis does not stop with the unessential details of the David-in-Penitence composition; the figure of the repentant king is itself charged with moral and theological polarities. This is a man transformed, with the radical transformation that only true repentance would effect. He who had let himself be ruled by cupidinous love, by concupiscence, who had looked with hungry eye from his tower on the beauty of Uriah's wife as she bathed, who had brought her to his bed and then contrived her husband's death, has now by his heartfelt cry, "I have sinned against the Lord," given rein to true charity: the love of God now rules within him, and the love of creatures that conflicts with love of God—cupidinous, not charitable love—has been banished from his heart's throne.

Nor is the antithesis confined to the tale of Bathsheba and Uriah; it is heightened when one reads that tale as part of the larger story of David. This was the shepherd boy who went out to battle the dread giant when the boldest of Israel's warriors drew back in fear, felled him with a stone from his sling, and cut off his head. He had been the youngest and least of Jesse's sons, brought before Samuel almost as an afterthought when God had passed over the other seven ("Have no eyes for noble mien or noble stature; I have passed this one by"), yet he was anointed Israel's king. Skilled in the harp and in singing, he was called on to play before King Saul and became his nation's great poet and seer, the "sweet singer of Israel." The fall into sin of such a one, who had been raised from obscurity to the heights by God, was doubly deep, and his repentance and restoration to God's favor were, in consequence, so much more significant a proof of God's love.

Such considerations were a preacher's grist, and might serve as the introduction, the setting-of-the-scene, for any sermon on repentance. They did so, for instance, in St. John Fisher's sermon on Psalm 6 before Lady Margaret Beaufort. This first of his sermons on the penitential psalms begins with his enumerating the blessings of God on David, so that he might the more effectively portray the ingratitude of David's sin, and the love of God who was still, and is always, ready to forgive. David's blessings, David's sin, David's repentance and restoration were, in a word, a commonplace of spiritual counsel and a model that was held up for all Christians. Small wonder, then, that the visual details of the David-in-Penitence should have been so elaborated and that the miniature itself should have been used so often at various parts of liturgical books that constitute beginnings.

The First Psalm with its sharp warning about the way of the just and the way of the wicked is an apt text for the beginning of the Church's songbook, which has perforce been the songbook, and constant companion, of all who have undertaken the way of Christian perfection. The images that decorate its first words, *Beatus vir,* in medieval books are natural visual comments on the journey such souls set out upon, none more so than that of David-in-Penitence with its depiction of radical inner transformation. The First Psalm, with any attendant image, comes not just at the beginning of one section of the Bible, but at the beginning of a number of distinct and important kinds of medieval prayer books—psalters (from which books of hours would later develop), breviaries (with distinct sections for the psalter), and office books of other kinds. It is worth emphasizing yet again that the first picture that would greet a contemplative eye on opening such a psalter in medieval times might well be that of the repentant Psalmist. One of the best-known examples of the miniature at the head of the psalter—an example that may have been known to Raphael, who was a native and citizen of Urbino—is found in the famous two-volume Bible of Duke Federigo of Urbino, now in the Vatican Library.[27]

The second *locus communis* of the David-in-Penitence is in missals and other mass books, where it often decorates the opening words of the entrance antiphon, the introit, for the first Sunday of Advent. Since this is the first day of the Church year, and the introit is the first chant in each day's mass, the miniature of the repentant king is the very first item one finds in such a book after its calendar and other prefatory material. Again, the connection of David with the starting point of a Christian life is clear.

As was pointed out in chapter 2, the text of this introit, from Psalm 24:1–3, serves also as offertory on the same day (in addition, verses 3 and 4 are the gradual) and as offertory on the station day at S. Cecilia in Trastevere, the Wednesday after the second Sunday of Lent. It is a stimulating passage, full of suggestion, full of allusion: "To you I have lifted up my soul; my God, I place my trust in you, let me not be put to shame. Let not my enemies mock me; for those who wait for you will not be cast into confusion."[28] The aptness to this text of the images of the penitent David and the ecstatic Cecilia is obvious. In each case the lifting up of the soul is suggested by the upturned gaze, one of the most distinctive and influential features of Raphael's painting and an ever-present detail of the David-in-Penitence.[29]

One notes, too, the reference to *confusio,* from which all those who wait for the Lord will be saved—*non confundentur.* This "confusion" could hardly have represented mere intellectual disarray to the medieval mind. Rather it implied wider disorder, the disorder of the soul bent on its own ends as opposed to those of God, and so in a state of ruin. Confusion in this sense is another medieval commonplace—a cliché, almost, of the medieval spiritual life. And understanding it thus will support assertions of the antithetical character of the David-in-Penitence. For *confusio* was the common translation of the name Babylon, that mystical city of corruption and home of the economy of corrupt nature. Cecilia, who prays to be kept from confusion, stands in perfect contrast with Babylon and its disorder (and one notes the medieval linking of the city of Babylon to the Tower of Babel and the disarray of language, the confusion of the word, that that implied), for she was the model of clarity, of "the cleernesse hool of sapience," as Chaucer has it.[30]

There is much else within the Twenty-fourth Psalm that shows its aptness to its position in Advent, as the reflective song of beginning. The praise of God's ways and the plea to him to show them to us, thus echoing the thought of the First Psalm, are constant (see verses 4b, 5a, 8b, 9, 10). The plea is repeated in the selections made for liturgical use, not only in the introit but in the gradual and offertory as well, which are also drawn from this psalm. The profession of humble contrition is likewise constant, as in verse 18: "Look upon my humility and my labor, and forgive all my sins."[31] Though this verse has no place in the liturgical texts indicated, it would have been sung in earlier liturgical customs, at those times when the whole psalm was sung, as was certainly the case with the introit, and perhaps also with the gradual and the offertory.[32] The traditions of Christian spirituality are very long, and its roots lie as much in the liturgical use of scripture texts as in any other source.[33]

Although the David-in-Penitence is found commonly enough in the places thus far studied—before Psalm 1 in psalters and before the introit of the first Sunday of Advent in mass books—one cannot say that it is the principal illustration at these points. The case is different, however, with its third *locus communis,* before the seven penitential psalms in books of hours, where it is the scene most often found, with the possible exception of the Last Judgment. Like books of hours themselves, the scene of David-in-Penitence was richly developed in the fifteenth century, particularly in its latter part—just before the time of Raphael—and most of that development took place within the context of the penitential psalms. Of great interest to the art historian (they are often entrancingly beautiful and at times markedly individual), these later examples of the miniature add little to our understanding of its general significance, except in the case of one small class of books that is about to be discussed.[34] The sheer number of images of David-in-Penitence, however, confirms how readily accessible they would have been to Raphael; and their sheer number in the position of visual introduction to the seven penitential psalms confirms beyond all doubt that the fundamental character of the image is humble repentance.

Almost invariably the seven penitential psalms in an illuminated book of hours were decorated with but one miniature, at the head of the section. There exists, however, a small number of *horae* in which each of the seven is decorated with its own miniature, a procedure which prompts one to ask why the artist chose to illustrate a particular psalm with a particular iconographic subject or detail, such as the David-in-Penitence or the abandoned harp, and whether he intended some narrative or thematic connection between that psalm and that subject. Nine such books, the only examples known to me, were examined during the preparation of this study: British Library, MS 49999 (the De Brailes Hours), English, ca. 1240; British Library, Yates Thompson MS 3 (Hours of Jean, Comte de Dunois), French, ca. 1450; Pierpont Morgan Library, MS M.677 (Hours of Anne of France), French, ca. 1473; Pierpont Morgan Library, MS M.1001, French, ca. 1475; Bodleian Library, MS Douce 219–20 (Hours of Engelbert of Nassau), Flemish, ca. 1485–90; Walters Art Gallery Library, MS W.245, French, ca. 1485; British Library, Add. MS 34294 (the Sforza Hours), Italian, late-fifteenth century; Philadelphia, Free Library, Lewis MS 112, French, ca. 1510; and Walters Art Gallery Library, MS W.430, French, ca. 1515. The miniatures these manuscripts provide for the penitential psalms are compared in appendix 2.

A close study of these miniatures will bring into clearer focus both background and foreground of the understanding of the seven psalms that prevailed from about the time of the earliest of these books, the middle of the thirteenth century, down to the time when most of them were made, the era of Raphael. Thus they should help us better to understand the general significance—the background—of the penitential psalms to Raphael, to his commissioners, and to the thinkers and artists of the preceding ages who most influenced them. At the same time the miniatures of these nine books should clarify the foreground, by which is here meant the significance of the visual details that most concern our argument. Most prominent among these will be the discarded harp in the David-in-Penitence, the detail that signifies that "my harp is turned into mourning." We shall be alert, too, to all that these miniatures might reveal about the deeper meaning of the third penitential psalm, Psalm 37, that psalm which we have called Cecilian because of its long and intimate association with St. Cecilia's cult as the entrance psalm in one of the most ancient of liturgical formulations in her honor.

The most obvious background feature of these miniatures is their predominant concern with the story of David's sinfulness and repentance. Though two of the manuscripts illustrate the seven psalms with miniatures of the seven deadly sins, the pictures of the sins riding animals in the first of these, Yates Thompson 3, are explicitly connected with the royal psalmist by the accompanying captions. The captions state that the particular psalm was composed by David when he had committed the pictured deadly sin on some given occasion; as, for example, at Psalm 37 with its figure of Sloth (*Paresse,* Idleness) riding a donkey: "David composed this psalm on account of the great sins he committed idling away his time, as when by his sloth in Jerusalem he sinned with Bathsheba, or when in the desert he became a leader of a robber-band." Thus, except for the seven images in Morgan 1001, every miniature but one decorating these individually illustrated psalms is either of David or is explicitly related to his story. The single exception is the miniature of the commissioner of the De Brailes Hours, identified simply as "Susanna," and even she had herself painted in the attitude of David-in-Penitence.

An equally obvious background feature, and of great importance to our argument, is the association of the miniatures with the spiritual journey of the Christian soul. The miniatures' associations both with David and with the spiritual journey are of course complementary, for the humility David demonstrated in his repentance was the model par excellence held out by preachers and writers as the foundation of all progress in the spiritual life.

When we turn to the foreground features, the details of the miniatures and their significance, we find that most of the details can be readily understood as either events in the life of David or stages of spiritual progress, or frequently both. With regard to the musical details, at the outset it must be said that at first inspection no single or clear pattern emerges from the examination of these nine manuscripts, for the David-in-Penitence, sometimes with its detail of the abandoned harp, is found at the head of the psalms in two books, before the seventh psalm in five, and before various of the intervening psalms. Yet when we look deeper, and especially when we take into account the significance of the notion of spiritual change in the musical symbolism of the abandoned harp, we find that Psalm 37, the penitential psalm we have labeled "Cecilian," can with complete justice, on the evidence of these fully illustrated books, be styled the most musical of the seven penitential psalms. I shall return frequently to this point as I discuss these books in turn.

All the manuscripts, as we have said, connect the seven psalms with the life of David, though they do so with great variety. The Hours of Anne of France devotes five of the psalms to David's sin with Bathsheba and the killing of Uriah; only in the sixth psalm does Nathan rebuke David, and in the seventh David repents. In the Hours of Engelbert of Nassau the first six illuminations show David the shepherd protecting his flocks, his fight with Goliath, and his life as king, harpist, and soldier; again, only at the last psalm does David repent. And so it goes (see appendix 2).

The two cases most suggestive for the present study are the earliest of these examples, the thirteenth-century De Brailes Hours, and the Sforza Hours of the late fifteenth century (with parts dating from the early sixteenth). The historiated initials of the De Brailes Hours, though simple in content, are emphatic in their delineation of David's repentance and in characterizing it as the beginning of the spiritual journey. The first image is of Nathan accusing David, while all of the remainder starkly illustrate his acceptance of the reproof and his repentance. Three of them fit very clearly our stated description of the David-in-Penitence, although none of them includes any visual musical detail such as the discarded harp.

Nevertheless, since William de Brailes added a short description to each of his scenes, this manuscript does identify Psalm 37 as particularly "musical." At Psalm 37, with its simple miniature of David-in-Penitence, the artist advised, in a caption, that it was at this point in the story of his repentance that the king began the composition of the seven penitential psalms (see fig. 4.4). Here De Brailes was relating an old legend suggesting that Psalm 37 was a turning point in David's repentance, a point at which the sorrow he carried in his heart for his sin began to find outward expression: here the singer of psalms begins to sing.[35]

Another of the nine manuscripts, the Sforza Hours, also carries the suggestion that Psalm 37 represented a point of change. There the magnificent miniatures reinforce powerfully, and in a perhaps unique fashion, the character of the penitential psalms as an exhortation to follow the path of the Lord. Each of the seven miniatures except the last falls clearly within our definition of David-in-Penitence, yet each offers visual detail that distinguishes the psalm to which it is attached as having a particular significance within the hortatory scheme. Much of this suggestive visual detail, however, is in the complex background scenes, some of which are difficult to interpret. All but the first miniature are set on a pathway that leads to the summit of a mountain, the "way of the Lord." The first miniature in the series, before Psalm 6, is the most complex, including as it does a background scene of David sitting in judgment in the city square. In the foreground is a splendid example of the David-in-Penitence with harp and crown cast aside, illustrating as always the texts of Job 30:31 and Lamentations 5:15–16, "my harp is turned into mourning . . . the crown is fallen from my head." At the second miniature in the series, before Psalm 31, the crown (but not the harp) is still to be seen beside the kneeling psalmist. And at the third, Psalm 37, David has taken the crown up again, and holds it circling his still-joined hands (see plate 4a). It seems that the process of David's fall is already being reversed by his penitence, that God here gives him back what he had lost. The spiritual crown is about to be restored, and, by implication, the music of the spirit is set to sound again within his heart. The suggestion of change in the heart that is conveyed by the crown encircling David's hands in this miniature is heightened and reinforced by the scene in the background, which shows a donkey, symbol of sloth, carrying grain through a door at one end of a mill while a workman carries a sack of flour out of a door at the other end. The implication of idleness being converted to industry, of fruitfulness and abundance issuing from work, is obvious. Its particular application to this scene and this psalm will become clearer when we discuss the remarks of St. John Fisher on Psalm 37 later in this chapter.

Other illuminated manuscripts in this group of nine reinforce these basic observations: that the seven penitential psalms were linked with, and in part seen as, a narrative of spiritual change; that Psalm 37 sometimes marked a particular point of transition; and that music figured symbolically in the story of change, though not always in connection with Psalm 37. The miniature already referred to before Psalm 37 in Yates Thompson 3 is further evidence that that psalm was a point of transition in a way akin to the corresponding image in the Sforza Hours. Like the Sforza Hours, Yates Thompson 3 illustrated Psalm 37 with a figure representing sloth: it showed sloth personified riding a donkey across a bridge, with a caption declaring that David composed this psalm when he committed the sin of sloth. Again, just as in the case of the Sforza Hours, the significance of sloth in the context of this psalm will become clearer after we consider St. John Fisher's sermon on this psalm.

Two of the nine manuscripts, Walters 245 and Walters 430, show miniatures of David playing his harp at Psalm 37. In both, the illustration fits logically into the particular series, but in one case it seems to represent the spiritual music of David's soul before his fall from grace, in the other the music of grace restored. Walters 430 shows David first in God's favor as he is made king by Samuel's anointing (Psalm 6) and as he overcomes Goliath (Psalm 31), here as so often a symbol of conquered pride. The harp he plays at Psalm 37 would thus seem to represent the grace of innocence, for it is only in the next miniature, at Psalm 50, that David looks lustfully upon Bathsheba and falls into sin. In the following scenes he dispatches the messenger to Joab to seal Uriah's fate (Psalm 101), is reproved by Nathan (Psalm 129), and kneels finally in repentance (Psalm 142). In Walters 245, however, the playing of the harp at Psalm 37 falls within a quite different sequence of depicted events. Here the series begins with David's observing Bathsheba (episodes with Goliath and Uriah are represented in the border), while the second miniature shows Nathan already reproving him (Psalm 31). Thus the music he plays in the next miniature seems obviously the music of grace restored (Psalm 37). All of the remaining miniatures in the series are of David-in-Penitence, emphasizing the restoration that has been granted him.

Here one notes the frequency with which the David-in-Penitence illustrates the seventh penitential psalm in these nine manuscripts. Indeed, it occupies this place in five of the nine, whereas it precedes the first penitential psalm in only two. It would seem that the artists, or whoever planned the iconographic scheme, when confronted with the possibilities of illustrating all seven of the psalms separately, had no hesitation about deferring the picture that depicted repentance itself until the conclusion of the series, that this in fact represented to them a more suitable place than did the traditional Psalm 6. Does the fact that the David-in-Penitence is reserved for the final penitential psalm contradict the observation that penitence and humility were commonly understood to be the starting points of the spiritual life? I think that the choice points rather to the difficulties faced by the visual artist in depicting the spiritual life at all: How *does* one paint the stages of the spiritual life beyond the initial repentance, the stages of ever-closer union with God? There are, basically, two answers to this question. The first is: one doesn't. One chooses rather to paint the much more readily paintable elements of David's life: the boy protecting his sheep, the youth killing Goliath, the soldier, the king, the sinner. The second answer is: one does so only by implication, turning to the rich iconography of music just as Teresa of Avila and John of the Cross would turn to deeply symbolic poetic language when trying to express the ineffable in words. The painter of the Sforza Hours had yet a third solution, showing the David who had already knelt in penitence risen to his feet and beginning to ascend the mountain path. But it was the scriptural musical iconography of mourning-into-joy that served the painter most frequently and most powerfully, whether the miniaturist or Raphael; and that could point so well both to the moment of repentance and to what followed.

To recapitulate: There have been two major foci, background and foreground, in this examination of the nine manuscripts with their diverse but richly symbolic series of miniatures. The background is the close association of the penitential psalms with David's fall and repentance understood as a model for all, as a pointer to the only way of salvation, the "way of the Lord." Whichever parts of David's life the artist might choose to elaborate, and wherever he might choose to start—whether with David's youth, his kingship, or only with his sin—there would, in general, be a certain dramatic naturalness about the sequence: David's blessings, then his sin, then his repentance, perhaps followed by his entering into the way or his restoration to grace. Embracing all detail would be the understanding that repentance permeates the whole texture of these seven psalms as they were reproduced, prayed, and contemplated in the later Middle Ages: not just as a reminder of a historical event, but as a model and figure for all who sought the radical transformation their faith promised.

In our examination of the foreground, the details, we have laid particular emphasis on the occasions when Psalm 37 is seen as a musical psalm or a pivotal psalm or both. The reason in this context is clear: Of the penitential psalms, Psalm 37 is the most Cecilian, being the entrance psalm for Cecilia's station day, the liturgy of which is a powerful early witness to the transformation of mourning and joy, a theme with which music is intricately intertwined. In the story of David's repentance, the musical iconography of the psalms and of the miniatures is symbolic of his spiritual change; and that is the major link between the iconography of the David-in-Penitence and Raphael's musical iconography of Cecilia. But the same analogy is played out at least tentatively in miniature, as it were. When we can examine books of hours in which each psalm is illustrated separately, it is Psalm 37, the most Cecilian psalm, that notably, though not exclusively, serves as a point of spiritual change and of musical symbolism. Given the small number of examples, the analysis must remain suggestive only. In five cases out of nine, the psalm is a point of transformation; in four out of nine it is musical; in only two cases is it both at once. The musical character of Psalm 37 has been seen in the caption accompanying it in the De Brailes Hours, affirming that it is here that the psalmist begins to sing; in the legend from which the caption derives; and in David's playing his harp in the accompanying miniatures of Walters 245 and 430. Psalm 37 also constitutes a pivotal psalm, a point of particular spiritual change, in the Sforza Hours, where the crown rings David's hands; and in the miniature of David facing Goliath (often a symbol of pride) in the Hours of Engelbert of Nassau (fig. 4.8a). This psalm, indeed, is both musical and pivotal in the De Brailes Hours and in Lewis MS 112.

Before leaving this discussion of Psalm 37, we must turn our attention to a related reason for regarding Psalm 37 as the most musical of the seven penitential psalms, a reason that comes from the time of Raphael, though from England and not Italy. When John Fisher preached on Psalm 37 he began by telling his congregation that the Pythagoreans

> were accustomed every morning when they should rise from their beds
> to hear the sound of an harp, whereby their spirits might be more quick
> and ready to receive their studies. . . . For doubtless their sluggish and
> slothful minds by that melody were made quick and merry. Also some-
> time wicked spirits were chased away by the musical and sweet stroke of
> the harp, which thing done is read of King Saul, that when he was vexed
> and troubled by the wicked spirit he had his most and only remedy by
> the harp of David. . . . Let us therefore turn again unto these sweet melo-
> dies of our prophet David which sometime he sang with his godly harp,
> whereby we may chase and put away all sluggishness and sloth put into
> us by wicked spirits, in the which sweet sounds we shall hear so great
> plenty and diversity of tunes as ever was heard before, for sometime he
> speaketh of God, sometime of the devil, sometime of holy angels, some-
> time of damned spirits. Now of hell pains, and sometimes of the pains
> of purgatory, otherwhiles of the rightness of God, sometime of his great
> mercy. Now of dread, anon of hope, sometime of sorrow and weeping,
> and sometime of gladness and comfort, sometime of bodily wretched-
> ness, sometime of the wretchedness of the soul, sometime of the cursing
> of vices and sins, sometime of the praising of virtues. . . . By this diver-
> sity of melody if sinners can not be raised up from the sleep of sin and
> excited unto godly watchings they are thought to be as very dead.[36]

Here Fisher declares the antitheses of the spiritual struggle at greater length and even more eloquently than had Augustine and Cassiodorus, and he finds all those antitheses expressed musically within David's psalms. But he further links them with music on the grounds of music's power to arouse the spirit, following the belief and practice of the Pythagore-ans. Music can change the torpid soul, enabling it to become active; it is a stimulus against slothfulness, against the spirit of idleness. So, too, the music of David's songs of repentance can stir Fisher's hearers to that mo-

Figure 4.8a. *David Confronts Goliath*: Miniature before
Psalm 37 in the Hours of Engelbert of Nassau

(Bodleian Library, Oxford; MS Douce 219–20,
fol. 186v)

David's combat with Goliath is a classic symbol of the
struggle of humility with pride. In this book of hours,
one of a rare group in which each of the penitential
psalms is decorated with an individual miniature, the
young shepherd confronts the Philistine giant before
the third penitential psalm—a situation that reinforces
the suspicion that this "Cecilian" psalm held
connotations of radical inner change.

tion of soul that is necessary for grace to have its effect. If they pray these
psalms, and make these sentiments their own, they will be moved out of
their sluggishness of spirit, which keeps them trapped in sin, and into the
great transformation of repentance and grace. Music's power to excite the
soul is thus seen as a symbol of the most powerful and radical of all trans-
formations. Here our argument moves closer to the reasons for Cecilia's
links with music, for her legend depicts her as a tireless converter, one

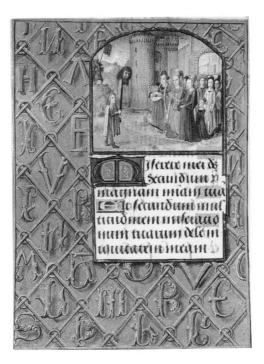

Figure 4.8b. *David Bearing Goliath's Head on His Sword:*
Miniature before Psalm 50 in the Hours of Engelbert
of Nassau
(Bodleian Library, Oxford; MS Douce 219–20,
fol. 190v)
David's combat with Goliath began before Psalm 37
in this book (fig. 4.8a). Its outcome is depicted before
Psalm 50, where David is shown bearing Goliath's
head on his sword to the admiration of music-making
ladies (see 1 Sam. 18:6–7).

who brings light, who transforms; and who calls on those to whom she
preaches at dawn to put off darkness and put on light.[37]

That Fisher should associate this psalm with sloth, praying at the beginning of his sermon that "we may chase and put away all sluggishness and
sloth put into us by wicked spirits," is no coincidence. For in the analysis
and listings of the vices, sloth (*acedia*) was generally equated with sadness
(*tristitia*), which in turn has obvious affinities with *luctus,* that is, with grief,

sorrow, or mourning, but emphasizing its outward expression: an extreme of *tristitia*.[38]

None of the other penitential psalms can support a musical illustration with so clear an explanation as can Psalm 37. The fact that it has such illustration in two of the manuscripts of appendix 2 may not, then, be simple happenstance. And that Psalm 37 is also a Cecilian psalm, with the implications just described, would seem to strengthen the case here advanced for seeing the origins of her musical character as being allied with the musical content of the David-in-Penitence.

That musical content, the common detail of the discarded harp or other instrument, has been explained thus far as a visual reference to two texts, Job 30:31 and Lamentations 5:15–16. These, however, are but two of a large array of similar texts about *luctus* and *gaudium,* any or all of which might have a part to play in the use and development of this pictorial detail in the Middle Ages and Renaissance; the two already cited describe the conversion of *luctus* and *gaudium* in musical terms, and hence are the ones that describe the detail most precisely. This larger group of texts has been gathered in appendix 1. What is most significant about them, for present purposes, is the use to which they were put in the spiritual writing and penitential preaching of the Middle Ages, during the time when the miniature of David-in-Penitence was being formed. But before this is considered, some attention must be paid to the visual detail of the abandoned instruments themselves.

The tradition of using discarded musical instruments to symbolize vice defeated, or the vanities abandoned, was in force long before the painting of the first known David-in-Penitence, and indeed continued well after the time of Raphael.[39] Such imagery was visually so powerful in Prudentius's *Psychomachia* (late fourth century) that it found its way into miniatures in medieval manuscripts of his work.[40] Prudentius describes the conflict of Luxuria (Indulgence) and Sobrietas (Soberness).[41] Cast from her chariot, Luxuria is smashed "with a stone from the rock" by Sobrietas. Her company flee, Jocus and Petulantia first casting away their cymbals; "for it was with such weapons that they played at war, thinking to wound with the noise of a rattle!" The whole company (Amor, Pompa, Venustas, Discordia, Voluptas, and others) rushes about, in agitated flight, dropping various spoils—"a hairpin, ribands, fillets, a brooch, a veil, a breast-band, a coronet, a necklace. These things Soberness and all the soldiers of Soberness refrain from handling; they trample under their chaste feet the cursed causes of offence, nor let their austere gaze turn a blind eye towards the joys of plunder." Thus the vanities are left beneath the feet, along with the cymbals, just as are the instruments in Raphael's *Cecilia*.

In this chapter we have examined a body of scripture texts from which grew the iconographic tradition of instruments representing the turning of joy to mourning, mourning to joy, that is shared in the later Middle Ages by the figures of Cecilia and David. These texts are, principally, Psalm 37, which is the third penitential psalm and the entrance psalm for Cecilia's station day; and Psalm 24, which was the source of the offertory for the station day and of introit, gradual, and offertory for the first Sunday of Advent.

Comments on Psalm 37 by widely separated authors—Augustine in the fifth century, Cassiodorus in the sixth, Peter Lombard in the twelfth, and John Fisher in the sixteenth—have shown how consistent was the habit of explaining the motion of soul involved in repentance in terms of progress from sadness to joy, and of expressing this in musical terms. Though this habit extends to all the penitential psalms, it seems to have been concentrated on Psalm 37.

The whole tenor of Psalm 24, but especially its incipit and verse 15, "my eyes are always upon the Lord," is exquisitely apt to the idea of spiritual perfection and divine union which is the goal of repentance and thus of the attitude engendered in the soul by the seven penitential psalms. It certainly fulfills this function in its position as offertory chant on the Trastevere station day, but does so even more deftly on the first Sunday of Advent at the very beginning of the church year—hence its being pressed into use at three points of the service. Since its most notable text, the opening words ("To thee, O Lord, I have lifted up my soul"), occurs also in the last of the penitential psalms (Psalm 142:8), it is physically, also, in the position of the goal of repentance.

The attachment to this psalm of the image of the repentant David—kneeling, with his eyes fixed upon the Lord to whom he has "lifted up his soul"—is entirely felicitous. Given the habit of seeing the motion of the repentant soul in terms of sadness and joy, and of expressing this by scriptural texts like Job 30:31, Lamentations 5:15–16, and Esther 13:17, it was equally felicitous that there should have appeared in this composition of David-in-Penitence the detail of a harp cast aside, a harp "turned into mourning" as a sign of the sin for which he repents and of the change of heart at work within him. The same aptness attached the same image to its principal locus, at the head of the seven penitential psalms in books of hours, as well as to the head of the psalter itself.

We have yet to pursue the topic of mourning-into-joy into more developed forms of the tradition. This pursuit will lead us into writings and images apart from its scriptural basis, chiefly into the works of certain writers on the spiritual life, but also into those of several more famous authors. We shall see that the tradition has a long literary history that certainly parallels and perhaps antedates its application to the Scriptures. But before proceeding to this particular inquiry, it will make sense to look at the tradition in the form in which it reached Raphael so that we can be more sensitive to the traces of it that appear in the generation that preceded him. This we shall do in the next chapter, in studying the spiritual lineage of the commission he accepted to paint the St. Cecilia altarpiece in Bologna. As we scan the lives and writings of those connected in various ways with the commission, their reception of the tradition of mourning-into-joy and of the scripture texts and spiritual beliefs that support its visual statements, we realize how difficult it is to disentangle the textual and visual threads that are woven into this whole cloth. It may be that even to attempt to do so will be self-defeating in that it will take us further from, not closer to, the medieval minds that read these texts, both literary and pictorial. Those minds, I suggest, saw rather better with the eyes of their heart, heard rather better with the ears of their heart, than do we. As I write this I confess to a strong suspicion that a different sensitivity to the spiritual, a different balance of what we would rather lamely call their psychological makeup, a more robust and willing trust in the spiritual senses, gave them a deeper and richer experience of the music that I shall now address, the music they knew as the "song of the heart."

Five Raphael's Commissioners
and Jean Gerson

If Raphael's painting of St. Cecilia had not presented such problems of interpretation, there would likely have been far less interest in the circumstances of its commissioning than in fact has been the case. But the difficult iconography of the work has for a long time stirred suspicions that the commissioners had an unusually strong influence on its final shape. Already in his *Felsina pittrice* of 1678, Carlo Malvasia reported Francesco Albani's complaint that Raphael's "hands had been tied",[1] and this line of thought has led more recently to serious attempts to lay bare the commissioners' wishes and instructions. Little direct documentary evidence on the commission has come to light, so such attempts have had to be more concerned with materials of an indirect character. There are a few lines by Vasari; a somewhat fanciful anonymous contemporary biography (existing only in manuscript) of the principal commissioner, Beata Elena Duglioli dall'Olio; a few other sparse documents and references dealing with her life and spirituality; and a great deal of information, of varying degrees of pertinence, about her friend and co-commissioner, the noted Florentine ecclesiastic Antonio Pucci.[2] That admirable scholar of things Bolognese, the Oratorian G. B. Melloni, published the best available life of Beata Elena in 1780.[3]

San Giovanni in Monte, the church for which Raphael's altarpiece of St. Cecilia was painted, was an ancient foundation, but it had not enjoyed the patronage of the nobility or the wealthier classes until the Canons Regular began a program of rebuilding in 1474, when the merchants and the legal and medical branches of the professional classes began to attach themselves to the church.[4] Six side chapels had already been added in the ten years from 1440 to 1450, but the later program was far more ambitious. A new façade was completed in 1480; the cupola was rebuilt in 1496; and a new chapel dedicated to St. Michael the Archangel, with a painting by Perugino, was added the following year. This work of Perugino is now exhibited in the Pinacoteca in Bologna, directly facing Raphael's *St. Cecilia*. Some of the more notable works of Lorenzo Costa were executed for S. Giovanni at about this time, in particular *The Madonna Enthroned with St. Augustine, St. Posidonius, St. John, and St. Francis,* still to be seen in the last chapel of the right nave. The work undertaken by Elena dall'Olio, which included the completion of the major chapel as well as the St. Cecilia chapel, represented the culmination of the building phase of this activity, though the program of decoration continued well into the next century and included a magnificent choir in intarsia finished in 1527.

Zarri, analyzing the various opinions that had placed the execution of the commission between 1514 and 1516, is inclined to accept the date of 1515 given by the "Leggenda anonima" as the year of the painting's completion, while she decisively documents the finishing of the chapel itself in 1516.[5] The chapel is the easternmost of the side chapels on the church's north side, and the painting was placed immediately behind the altar in a rich wooden frame carved by Andrea da Formigine.[6] The elegantly carved marble tomb of Beata Elena is set against the east wall of the chapel. Though her cult lessened, it never died out, and is still practiced by a small band of devotees.

In her building project Elena received significant support not only from the Pucci but from another highly placed ecclesiastic as well. Cardinal Alidosi, the first papal legate to Bologna after the return of church rule in 1506, and a man of otherwise dubious fame and character, seems to have been very well disposed toward Elena, giving her a most precious relic of St. Cecilia that he had received, in his capacity as titular cardinal of S. Cecilia in Trastevere, from King Henry VII of England. In addition he made large contributions to her for charitable works, and it may have been through him that she received the privilege of having a private chapel in her house, where he is known to have celebrated Mass.[7]

But it was undoubtedly through Antonio Pucci, with the assistance of his uncle Lorenzo, that the approach to Raphael was made; only they, among her acquaintances, could have commanded the attention of an artist who at that time was free to neglect the commissions of royalty. She was, however, known to Pope Julius II and his successor, Leo X, the Medici pope who was a friend of the Pucci and who met Elena during the brief time in which he served as papal legate for Bologna in 1513.[8] Vasari actually attributes the commission to Lorenzo Pucci, created cardinal by Leo X six months after his election. It seems certain that it was Antonio who paid the expenses of the commission.[9]

Because Elena shaped the painting to some degree, and yet so little is known of her life, scholars have tried indirect ways to discern the nature of her influence; and one such way has been the investigation of her prominent associate, Antonio Pucci. The beginning of Elena's friendship with the Pucci, how and when they made acquaintance, is obscure. But the report of the "Leggenda anonima" that Antonio, who is described as her "spiritual son," lived in the Dall'Olio house in 1513, as well as at various later times, means that there was probably close contact between them just when the project of the chapel at S. Giovanni in Monte, and its decoration, must have been taking shape in Elena's mind. As a member of a wealthy and influential Florentine family with strong ties to the Medici and the papal court, the nephew of the powerful papal official Cardinal Lorenzo Pucci, and already a high official of the Curia, Antonio Pucci was certainly in a position to serve as intermediary between Elena and Raphael. Vasari seems to suggest that it was Lorenzo's elevation to the rank of cardinal that provided the occasion for the approach to the artist. Antonio, like his two ecclesiastical uncles before him (Lorenzo's brother, Roberto, who had held high civic office in Florence as a layman, took orders after his wife's death), was bishop of Pistoia, became a cardinal, and filled the curial office of *sommo penitenziere*. Given the possible connection of the iconography of Raphael's *St. Cecilia* with that of the penitent David, one wonders whether something of the concern of the Catholic Church's chief officer in matters relating to the sacrament of penance—to repentance and the restoration of grace—found its way into the instructions to the artist.[10]

Antonio Pucci considered himself, and was considered by others, to be a spokesman for the strong movement toward reform within Catholicism during the years just before the Protestant Reformation. It was as a reformer that he was chosen to deliver the opening address of the ninth session of the Fifth Lateran Council in May 1514. And it is to his reforming spirit and his connection with reforming circles that some students of *The Ecstasy of St. Cecilia* have attributed the ideas that they think he may have brought to bear on Raphael. His membership in a secret reformist

Raphael's Commissioners

fellowship, the *Oratorio del Divino Amore,* has attracted the attention of several critics, who have seen in its evidently progressive program of reform through personal sanctification and dedication to the ideals of Divine Charity a likely source for Raphael's iconographic scheme.[11] The membership, never large, was a distinguished one, including such prominent names as Jacopo Sadoleto, Gian Matteo Giberti, Gian Pietro Caraffa (afterwards Pope Paul IV), and Gaetano di Tiene (founder of the Theatines, later canonized).

But there is an awkward obstacle to elaborating the idea that the program and ideals of this society exerted any kind of proximate influence on Raphael, and that is its secrecy. Though its membership has been revealed in part, its workings and ideals are known only in a general way.[12] While it is conceivable that Elena may have known something about it from Antonio Pucci, little detailed knowledge of the society has come down to us that would be helpful in understanding Raphael. "Divine Love" and the kind of charitable work that the members practiced are surely too vague to be seen as either principal impulse or principal content of Raphael's thought. Raphael's painting is indeed about divine love, and music can and does symbolize love, both human and divine, but this statement of fact goes no further toward explaining the singularities of the painting's subject matter than it would in any other painting of saints with musical content.[13] Nevertheless, recognizing that even a secret Society of Divine Love would, if orthodox (as this one undoubtedly was), share the symbols, aspirations, and expressions of other schools of Christian spirituality, one can turn directly to Pucci for illumination of some aspects of Raphael's painting, and this has been done admirably by Gabriella Zarri.

Zarri selects, for example, Pucci's elaboration in a homily of words from the Canon of the Mass: "And having raised his eyes to heaven to thee, God, his almighty Father."[14] Pucci's comments deal with the right use of the eyes, with *aversio oculorum* and *conversio oculorum:* the Christian must turn his gaze away from the worldly, from the vanities, toward God. While the thought expressed here in words is undoubtedly related to the thought expressed pictorially in Raphael's painting—Cecilia's gaze turned heavenward, away from the broken secular instruments at her feet—it is also a commonplace of pulpit, of confessional, of spiritual direction. Bernard of Clairvaux (and he was simply echoing St. Benedict's Rule) had made custody of the eyes the polar points of his Steps of Humility and Steps of Pride: Keeping the eyes averted from mundane things (Bernard has them turned down to the ground) is the first step to humility; curiosity, looking about one at worldly things, is the first step of pride. So much is made of this in ascetic and spiritual discourse that one must be scrupulously cautious in asserting lines of dependence between any two occurrences of the idea. The most one can say about the confluence of theme in this passage of Pucci and in Raphael's painting is that they both touch upon a commonplace idea.

One especially notable element in the colorful portrait of Elena that emerges from the "Leggenda anonima" is that she was reported never to have looked a man in the face, but to have walked always with her eyes turned to the ground. Thus, indeed, she is depicted in the several visual representations of her that survive.[15] The attitude, recommended as a defense against concupiscence, draws attention to one of the more unusual features of Elena's story, that she lived virginity within her marriage. This is of course one of the ways she chose to imitate Cecilia, the saint on whom she consciously modeled herself. This imitation is one of the two implications of the title of Zarri's study, "L'altra Cecilia" (The Other Cecilia). The title refers both to Elena, who strove to be another Cecilia, and to Bologna's other famous masterpiece depicting Cecilia, the series of frescoes in the Oratory of St. Cecilia immediately behind S. Giacomo Maggiore.[16] S. Giacomo was the church of the Bentivoglio family, the princely family that was finally overthrown during Elena's lifetime. Zarri considers the rebuilding of S. Giovanni in Monte, the addition to it by Elena dall'Olio of the St. Cecilia Chapel with its great painting by Raphael, and the elaboration of Elena's own legend even while she still lived as being connected to the struggle between the Bentivoglio and the Church, which took over the rule of the city from the Bentivoglio in 1506.[17] For the church of S. Giovanni was very much in the other camp from S. Giacomo, and the aggrandizement of worship and cult there would diminish popular support around the Bentivoglio family and their church.

The web of legend that was woven about Elena makes it difficult to evaluate a person who seems in many ways not unsympathetic. The bald facts of her life, as outlined by Zarri following Melloni and the basic thread of the "Leggenda anonima", are as follows: She was born in 1472, the

Figure 5.1. *Beata Elena Duglioli dall'Olio*

(Pinacoteca Nazionale, Bologna)

Like the several other portraits of Beata Elena, this late sixteenth-century painting by an anonymous artist of the Bolognese-Ferrarese school shows her with her eyes cast down, indicating that she has attained the pinnacle of humility. The man is identified by a later hand as her son-in-law, Andrea Bentivoglio.

daughter of Silvestro Duglioli, a Bolognese lawyer. In 1487, at the age of fifteen, she married Benedetto dall'Olio, also a lawyer, and a man somewhat older than herself. Benedetto was a legal counsel for the Canons Regular who occupied the church of S. Giovanni in Monte, and lived with his young wife in a house close by the church. They had no children, but adopted a niece, and brought up two other children as their own. In 1516 the niece, Pantasilea Monteceneri, married Andrea Bentivoglio, a member of that branch of the Bentivoglio family opposed to the princely rule, and it was their daughter Sibilla who, in 1534, married a nephew of Antonio

Pucci, thus cementing the ties already established between the families by the cardinal's friendship with Elena. The other two adopted children of Elena were a girl who entered the convent and a nephew of the celebrated Dominican, Fra Silvestro da Prierio, who served for a short time as Elena's spiritual counselor.[18] Until about her thirty-fifth year, her life, it seems, was that of a remarkably devout and prayerful woman, but she had not yet been recognized as a living saint by her fellow citizens. Her practice of daily communion, unusual at that period, became a subject of gossip, and it was for this reason that she stopped going to S. Giovanni in Monte for a time and instead went to S. Domenico, where she was counseled by Fra Silvestro. She is known to have been a supporter of charitable work, especially among unmarried mothers.

It was in 1505 or 1506 that talk began to spread in Bologna about the miraculous character of Elena's life. The first element of the story concerned her marriage: it was revealed that she had lived those eighteen years with Ser Benedetto dall'Olio as a virgin, seemingly with his consent, in imitation both of the saint to whom she was so devoted, St. Cecilia, and of the Virgin Mary.[19] This would be the decisive element in her legend, as it was in that of her patron, the element that explains so much else. From that time, the legend of her sanctity, her revelations, and her miracles grew steadily. This contemplative woman was said to have frequent visions, including visions of St. Cecilia, and to hear the heavenly music during these apparitions. The youthfulness of her face, even in her later years (a trait commonly found in reports of married virgins in the Middle Ages), and especially after she had received the Eucharist, was remarked on. It began to be said that she had been born not in Bologna, as was supposed, but in Constantinople, to the Padishah Mahomet II, conqueror of Constantinople in 1453 and its ruler until his death in 1481; that her mother was a Christian princess of the overthrown house of the Paleologi; and that she could trace her ancestry back to the family of the founder of the church of Bologna, St. Petronius.[20] Her presence in Bologna, whither she had been miraculously transported, was due to her descent from St. Petronius (who was said to be a Byzantine): God wished her to live in the city that was so closely associated with her illustrious ancestor. There, by her perfect life in a more Christian atmosphere, she might further the conversion of the Turks.

Raphael's Commissioners

One can safely conclude that the public image of Elena, in Bologna and beyond, developed along these fantastic lines as her life progressed. She was thought of as a living saint, one whose canonization seemed assured even during her lifetime. With well-placed ecclesiastical friends, like the Pucci, who brought her to the attention of the pope, this must have seemed a real possibility. Yet Zarri maintains that there was strong opposition to this view, especially among the Dominicans, with whom Elena had once had close ties, but with whom there had been some kind of falling out when she reattached her loyalties to the Canons Regular at S. Giovanni. The Dominicans of S. Domenico, as Zarri points out, were supporters of the Bentivoglio rule and "faithful guardians of the memory of Savonarola, whom they considered *beato*."[21] Zarri believes that for both these reasons the Dominicans were hostile to the government of the Church, both to its rule by legate in Bologna and to the succession to the papacy of Leo X, the Medici pope elected shortly after the fall of the Florentine republic. Thus they were in political opposition to the Canons Regular and to the aspirations of the congregation of S. Giovanni in Monte.

The opposition of the Dominicans became most evident, according to Zarri, in the dispute that sprang up immediately after Elena's death, on September 23, 1520. Great crowds attended the obsequies and venerated Elena's body as it lay awaiting entombment in the chapel of St. Cecilia, which she had built at S. Giovanni in Monte. But there were also voices of dissent, particularly concerning the public preaching about her career and miracles by her longtime director, Pietro da Lucca.[22] Certainly, Pietro tried to circumvent the drawn-out process of canonization by writing directly to the pope, but the tactic failed because of the death of Leo X the following year and Pietro's own death in 1523. Among the stories and rumors that circulated following Elena's death, it was said that her body remained incorrupt and that her breasts, miraculously full of milk, continued to exude milk after her death.[23] The doubts about this account led to a papal order, delivered via the vice-legate in Bologna, that the tomb should be opened and the body examined by doctors. This was done on November 6, but there seems to have been complete disagreement on the result. The Dominican chronicler, Leandro Alberti, taking evident pains to stress the fact, reported that "the body was corrupt and putrid, and the breast too was full of putrefaction, even though those Canons said it was milk."[24] The

Canons Regular, supported by a group of medical witnesses, claimed the opposite. A second examination of the corpse was made on December 30, resulting in the curious finding that the body revealed "a certain state of incorruption."[25]

Zarri considers that the Dominicans had a more compelling interest in another, far more famous Bolognese mystic, Caterina dei Vigri, who had died in 1463 and was eventually canonized in 1712. St. Catherine's cult, which received official recognition in 1524 and then spread quite rapidly, probably played a part in the slow decline of Elena's status in the customs of Bologna. At the time of Elena's death, Zarri thinks, the Dominicans and other religious orders in Bologna were intent on securing the early recognition of Catherine and would have been displeased by attempts to promote a competing cause.[26] Brought up at the d'Este court in Ferrara, St. Catherine had come to Bologna as superior of a convent of Poor Clares in 1456 at the invitation of the Bentivoglio.[27] Various women of the Bentivoglio family entered St. Catherine's foundation, the Corpus Domini, and this too, in Zarri's estimation, might have prompted the Dominicans, with their ties to the Bentivoglio, to do what they could to stifle the rival cult.

Attractive as it is, Zarri's positing of a strong antipathy between Dominicans and Canons Regular over the matter of Elena seems somewhat overstated. That the two groups leaned in different political directions—the Dominicans were supporters of the Bentivoglio, of Savonarola, and of other causes that conflicted with papal views—is clear. But this is hardly solid enough evidence on which to build a case for Dominican opposition to the cult of a claimed ecstatic with whom they had once had close ties. The allegation of such opposition is largely dependent on one sentence of Leandro Alberti, a gossipy Dominican chronicler, on what was found at the opening of Elena's tomb and on a good deal of conjecture about the Dominicans' preference for the developing devotion to Caterina dei Vigri. However that may be, Zarri is correct in stating that the teaching Elena received from her longtime spiritual director, the Canon Regular of St. Augustine, Pietro da Lucca, helped shape Raphael's painting.

Pietro, it is reported, recounted Elena's miracles and the story of her birth in Constantinople, from the pulpit soon after her death. But one can easily question the assertion (and such assertion is not made directly by Zarri) that it was Elena herself and her director who spread the story of her

Turkish birth and her miraculous voyage to Bologna. Even given the opposition of Dominicans and Canons Regular, and even in an age that could accept without question the miraculous transport of the Holy Family's house from Nazareth to Loreto on the Adriatic coast, it seems hardly credible that the person said to have made the flight and her closest adviser would make such a claim, let alone have it accepted.

Zarri's evidence suggesting that Pietro and Elena themselves propagated the stranger stories about her is quite indirect, and is more plausibly placed in the category of gossip. The authorship, for instance, of the "Leggenda anonima," which abounds in fantasy, is unknown, as is the date of its writing. Like almost all of the biographical evidence in the case, it seems to derive from the mass of idle talk and rumor that circulated about this undoubtedly eccentric figure. There is, moreover, a suggestive, though not probative, alternative explanation for the strange story of Elena's birth in the harem of the Padishah of Istanbul. It is presented here not as an assertion of fact, but rather to show that there are other approaches to this extraordinary episode in Elena's legend.

The lesson for the station day at S. Cecilia in Trastevere, as already mentioned, is from the thirteenth chapter of the Book of Esther, and represents the only occasion during the church year on which this book of the Bible was read at Mass. The story of Esther, a story of intrigue in the harem of an oriental despotic court, was selected originally because of its peculiar suitability to the cult of Cecilia, which began alongside that of Bona Dea in Trastevere. A clear set of parallels can be, and have been, drawn between Esther and Cecilia as we perceive her through a close reading of her *Passio*, and the same sorts of parallels between Cecilia and Esther may account for the Turkish drama of Elena's legend.[28]

Such parallels are not uncommon in medieval preaching, which made so much of this passage from Esther in Lenten sermons. Thus Eudes of Chateauroux, preaching in about 1245 in Paris, began a sermon on the lesson from Esther by announcing that on this day in Rome "pilgrims flock to the church of St. Cecilia, beseeching this glorious virgin just as Mordecai besought Esther to plead for the revocation" of Assuerus's sentence against the Jews.[29] There is, in fact, a great deal of preaching on this text that could easily lead to pulpit elaborations of comparisons between Cecilia and women in the royal harem of Assuerus. Is it not conceivable, even likely, that Pietro da Lucca might have used language linking Elena, Cecilia, Esther, Mordecai, and Assuerus in one long exemplum? Given the literal significance of Esther's story—that she was able to save her people, God's people, from a foreign threat by her prayers to the king—is there not a likelihood that a preacher would try to extract from the story a message for prayers to save Christendom from the Turks, so great a concern in Elena's time? And that this message was misconstrued, and embroidered later in popular retelling? And even if we accept Zarri's picture of a highly partisan community discussing these events in Bologna, is it not likely that both supporters and opponents of Elena's cult and claims would have exaggerated those claims for their own purposes? At the very least, one can counsel caution about accepting the idea that Elena and Pietro da Lucca themselves propounded openly the idea that she was a Christian-Turkish princess miraculously transported to Bologna at birth.[30]

The kind of fanciful embroidery that accumulated so quickly around the people who commissioned the St. Cecilia altarpiece from Raphael, of which the story just discussed is nevertheless an ideal, if extreme, type, should caution us about the difficulty of penetrating their motives and intentions. Nevertheless it is undeniable that the principal motivation for the construction of the chapel was the extraordinary devotion of Elena to St. Cecilia. Elena was said to have had visions of Cecilia and to have remained a virgin in her marriage, as Cecilia is reported to have done. She was an ecstatic, and the painting is fittingly titled *The Ecstasy of St. Cecilia*. If any influence of the commissioners can be discerned in Raphael's achievement, one would expect to find the explanation of that influence in the spiritual life of Elena herself. Gabriella Zarri rightly made this inference and drew attention to Elena's long spiritual apprenticeship to Pietro Ritta, a member of the Lateran Canons of S. Frediano in Lucca. Noted preacher and spiritual director, and author of several modest, but in some cases quite popular, books on the spiritual life, Pietro was the sort of cleric who influences others more by personal qualities than by his intellect or writings.[31] Yet the books are clearly organized and logical, and breathe a patent sincerity and feeling. Zarri suggests that Raphael may have read some of Pietro's texts and points to two in particular that seem to have found a degree of visual translation in the painting.

The first is Pietro's definition of contemplation, "which is called different names by the saints, such as 'hidden wisdom,' 'mystical theology,' 'perfect prayer,' 'charity'—or rather 'charitable love'—by which the rational creature ardently unites itself with its creator and enjoys that union with as much delight as is possible in this life. It so elevates the human mind that in those mental excesses man almost becomes divine, in so far as he leaves the workings of the human senses, experiencing no other thing but his loving creator. He no longer sees, nor hears, nor knows where he is; he no longer fears eternal pains nor demands the glory of paradise, but simply embraces, experiences, and enjoys the supreme good."[32] Secondly, Zarri points to a passage in which Pietro discusses the bodily positions in which it is easiest to meditate. Some meditate with their faces turned toward heaven; others stand upright "supported on their left hand," because in this fashion the heart is at rest; yet others lie prostrate with their faces turned toward the ground.[33]

These passages of Pietro da Lucca do seem to shed some light on elements of Raphael's painting. But, taking Zarri's perceptions as a guide, we can uncover deeper connections between the painting and Pietro's writings if we read these with an eye to the David-in-Penitence and its associations with music and St. Cecilia. First, Pietro insists on humility as the foundation of the spiritual life; he wrote a popular treatise on humility, one edition of which is embellished at its beginning by a tiny woodcut of David-in-Penitence.[34] Second, he resorts to a threefold division of the soul's activity, and to the three ways of the spiritual life that correspond to this division. Third, he constantly refers to Jean Gerson as the principal source of his thought—a reference that Zarri notes but does not pursue.

It is not clear when Pietro Ritta—to give him his family name—was transferred to the house of the Canons Regular at S. Giovanni in Monte, Bologna, but it was early enough for him to claim a long spiritual relationship with Beata Elena as her director. What seems to be his earliest work, the *Regule*, which was first published in Bologna in 1504, identifies him still as a "Canon Regular of S. Frediano da Lucca." Elena's two-year transfer to the ambit of the great Dominican church, S. Domenico, must have occurred fairly early in her career, certainly before the announcement of her status as an ecstatic and visionary in about 1506, by which time her identification with S. Giovanni and with Pietro had already been firmly and clearly established. One can, then, dismiss the influence of the Dominicans, and in particular of Silvestro da Prierio, as of no great consequence in the commissioning. It is to Pietro that one must look if one would understand the lines along which Elena's spirituality developed.

Pietro's ascetical teaching is contained in five little works. These are the *Regule della vita spirituale,* the rules for the spiritual life just referred to; a treatise on humility (the *Fundamento della vita cristiana*); another summary of his rules for achieving spiritual perfection, the *Opusculo di trenta documenti;* a book on preparation for death, the *Doctrina del ben morire,* which was published in the same volume as the *Opusculo;* and a work outlining a method of meditating on Christ's passion, the *Arte nova del ben pensare.*[35]

There is little that is original in Pietro's works, though they are written with clarity and feeling. His authorities are usually quoted by name only, without reference to specific works, and all are within the mainstream of ascetical writing. He often acknowledges the influence of his own congregation, in particular of the Canons Regular Hugh of St. Victor and Richard of St. Victor. Augustine and Bonaventure are mentioned continually, as are also Gregory the Great, Benedict, Jerome, and especially St. Paul. But the name that occurs most often is that of Gerson, who is almost always identified as *Giovanni Gerson Cancelliere Parisiense,* and often with other laudatory descriptions like *il devoto doctore* and *el Christianissimo dottore.* In the third chapter of the *Regule,* in which he lays down the rules necessary for the contemplative life (fol. 15), he mentions explicitly his debt to the many books of the "devotissimo et christ.mo doctore Giovanni Gerson cancielliere parisiense." He says that he does not include the *Imitation of Christ* among Gerson's works (the attribution was very common), but means rather those books in Gerson's great *summa,* especially the *Mistica theologia,* which was for the learned, and the *Mount of Contemplation,* for *li simplici et idioti.*

Gerson's influence, which Pietro himself constantly acknowledges, and which is obvious to anyone who studies his writings, is of critical importance to the proper appreciation of Raphael's painting. For in Gerson there will be found the most effusive and colorful, if at times abstruse, statements of the mutations of mourning and joy; and these statements are made in directly musical terms, defining clearly the song of sadness, the song of joy, and the mixed song that is a blend of both. Within Gerson's works, moreover, there is a definite Cecilian strain, a devotion to the saint and a knowledge of her *Passio*. While these qualities are not found so explicitly in Pietro da Lucca, they are there in germ and will become more apparent as we turn from Pietro to the study of his chief authority.

Highly characteristic of Pietro's teaching is the threefold division of his subject matter: there are three operations of the soul, three generations of men, three states of Christian living, three affections, three steps in the spiritual life. These categories are in fact all commonplaces of ascetical theology, but in Pietro's work, and even more in the writings of Gerson in which it is rooted, they are seen to be related to the three zones of music in Raphael's painting of St. Cecilia. That there are three zones, rather than two, is a fact that is scarcely remarked on by critics, who prefer to see a contrast between two opposed forms of music—secular and sacred, vocal and instrumental, earthly and heavenly. The painting, however, clearly reveals a threefold organization: Broken secular instruments lie discarded at the feet of Cecilia and her companion saints; the *organetto,* the traditional church instrument, bridging heaven and earth, is still in Cecilia's hands, but is falling from them; and the unequivocally heavenly music of the singing angels above her seems to have totally captivated her only moments before.[36]

It is largely in the *Regule* that Pietro stresses these threefold divisions. Setting out to give a method by which one can easily achieve the contemplative state, he begins his first chapter by defining the three operations of the soul: cogitation, meditation, and contemplation.[37] Cogitation is thought about the things of this world, and it is of no worth in his scheme of the spiritual life; it is the kind of thought David spoke of when he sang "the Lord knows the thoughts of men, that they are vain [*novit dominus cogitationes hominis quia vanae sunt*]."[38] In meditation, the soul rids itself of vain thoughts to seize the divine, but at first it can do so only with difficulty. Accustomed to run vainly like a river from one thing to another, the mind must gather itself together, leave aside every idle thought, and struggle to think of one thing only. The difficulty the soul encounters in its striving to meditate is of the utmost importance, for from the difficulty there springs directly the love of God: as the steel against the flint draws fire, so from meditation on divine things the soul draws a burning flame of divine love.[39] The great prophet David bears witness that he has experienced this when he says, in Psalm 38:4, "My heart burned within me and fire blazed in my meditating [*Conculcavit cor meum intra me et in meditatione mea exardescit ignis*]."

Pietro's definition of the third operation of the soul is peculiarly apt to Raphael's Cecilia gazing heavenward, for he calls contemplation an act of seeing: "a penetrating, free, easy and rapid seeing or considering by the mind . . . completely caught up in heavenly things."[40] Contemplation, he says, is the same as meditation except for the degree of difficulty the soul experiences in each: the contemplative soul is practiced, and achieves its mental union with divine things more easily. Here he refers directly to an example Gerson uses "in many of his treatises" to explain the difficulties of the three operations. They are like the difficulties of the apprentice painter: at first he can do nothing, but must learn to draw simple lines; then he begins to learn, but only with difficulty, the true art of painting; finally as a skilled artist he is able to paint easily and with great delight.

In the second chapter of the *Regule*, Pietro undertakes to define the three classes of men: the evil (*captivi*—here one can appreciate the derivation of the Italian word *cattivo*), the good (*boni*), and the perfect (*perfecti*). To each operation of the soul, he says, there corresponds an affection and a manner of living proper to each of these classes. From cogitation, which is "an improvident and vagabond consideration of material things," there flows "an improvident and vagabond and useless affection," which is called cupidity, or libido, or true concupiscence; and those who practice this cogitation are animal, sensual men.[41] They give themselves completely to sensual pleasures, to worldly honors, to avarice for worldly possessions, never raising their understanding to the consideration of the creator. Such men are, of course, the *captivi*, captives of their own sensual desires.

A very different kind of affection flows from the practice of meditation. This is compunction, or devotion, or true prayer, a pious, humble affection that always endeavors to love God's goodness. It is practiced by devout, humble, and kindly men, and it leads them to flee sin and dangerous consorting with the world. And if they should perchance sin, they at once rise from it, and weep with abundant tears for what they have done. These men keep to the middle way, and for that reason are called good and devout.[42]

But from contemplation, the third operation of the soul, there springs an affection that is simply called love, and it contains within itself a sweetness beyond thinking or saying, far surpassing all ordinary human sensation.[43]

It is called different names by different saints—hidden wisdom, mystical theology, perfect prayer, love or charitable love—and by it the rational creature is united with its creator and experiences him with as much delight as is possible in this life. Those who practice contemplation are the perfect: "they are the most excellent, the most wise, the most learned, the most worthy and profound men that are to be found."[44]

In the third chapter of the *Regule,* Pietro lays down a series of rules necessary for the practice of the contemplative life. These, too, fall into the threefold division already proposed. He makes much of the three steps by which the soul advances, the three ways of St. Bonaventure, though he does not call them by the names Bonaventure gave them: purgative, illuminative,and perfective or unitive. But the relationship is obvious, and is acknowledged in his eighth rule, which calls for selecting a skilled and experienced teacher: he appeals to Gerson and Bonaventure on the point, acknowledging his debt to both and stressing the debt Gerson owed to Bonaventure.

In the long ninth rule, Pietro recapitulates many of the triple themes that mark the way toward holy ecstasy. He begins from the insufficiency of purely vocal prayer; to pray with the voice is not enough, one must give oneself to meditating. His description of the state of ecstasy at this point reemphasizes his purpose, which he undoubtedly put before Elena dall'Olio: the soul will reach ecstatic love, which is the same thing as contemplation, and will find itself *come beata,* like those in heaven who already see God in the beatific vision. The ascent to this contemplation occurs in three stages (*tre gradi*), which he describes by a famous analogy (used certainly by Gerson).[45] Damp wood, when it starts to burn, gives off thick smoke but no visible flame, like the soul ridding itself of worldly attachments in the stage of purgation. The smoke represents regret and sorrow for past sin. In the second stage, the flesh is not yet in complete submission to the spirit; worldly attractions are still strong and frequent. The love of God is still small and weak; the love of this world remains powerful. He describes this intermediate stage as a great battle between these two opposing loves, in which there is still much smoke as the flame struggles to take hold. Gradually the soul becomes more secure. It bears more easily the absence of worldly love and begins to feel delight in the love of God, until at last it passes to the contemplative state. The smoke is gone, and the wood burns with the pure flame of contemplative love.

Can one now look at Raphael's *Cecilia* and not see there the imprint of this teaching of Pietro da Lucca? Are not the trampled instruments the vanities, the cogitation of worldly men, those given to worldly pleasures? Does not the *organetto* suggest Pietro's "middle way," and the heavenly choirs the state of union? In addition, however, Pietro explicitly ties what he is saying to St. Cecilia, as well as to St. Paul and St. Augustine. Thus, when he has set forth his rules for contemplation in the *Regule,* Pietro asks on what subjects one should meditate. After suggesting various topics and the practices of several saints, he points out that St. Bernard of Clairvaux, at the beginning of his conversion, gave himself completely to meditation on the life of Christ, "just as one reads was the practice of St. Cecilia and as St. Bonaventure also recommended."[46] One of the most influential and most often cited details of Cecilia's *Passio* is the description of her as one who "kept the gospel in her heart." Pietro's citing of Cecilia in this context accords with other medieval references to her, in which her keeping the gospel "in her heart" is seen to make her a saint of special interest at the beginning of the spiritual life, as we have already seen. Pietro gives a musical twist to his description of contemplation as a pure spiritual flame, clear and without smoke, adding that it is also "without clangor, sound or tumult [*senza ogni strepito: sonito o vero tumulto*]." For Pietro, it seems clangor and tumult belong to the vanities; the sound of contemplation is either "silence, or a great concord." Again, the aptness of this language to Raphael's painting is striking.

Humility, the other great pillar on which Pietro's spiritual instruction rests, likewise has its place in *The Ecstasy of St. Cecilia*. Like his commitment to Bonaventure's three ways, the preeminence of humility is an axiom of Christian spirituality. Just as pride is the root of all sin and permeates all the other vices, so humility is the root of charity, of all love, and permeates all the other virtues. This idea finds constant visual, as well as verbal, expression in medieval works: for instance in the frequent depiction of the Tree of Vices and the Tree of Virtues.

During the period of Pietro's closest association with Elena, the topic of humility was much in his thoughts. In one of his treatises, he sets out to show that humility is the foundation of spiritual progress; thus the book's title, *Fundamento della vita cristiana cioè tractato utilissimo della humilità.* This is the book that went through at least three editions in Bologna from

1504 to 1523, and whose incipit was decorated with images of David-in-Penitence and the Annunciation. The same insistence on the preeminence of humility reappears in the *Opusculo,* published in a single volume in 1518 along with Pietro's treatise on preparation for death, the *Doctrina del ben morire.* In his dedication of the *Fundamento* to Elizabeth Bargellina, the daughter of Giovanni II Bentivoglio, Pietro points out that she has lived in three states of life for which humility is necessary, as virgin, spouse, and widow. This, it will be remembered, was also said of Elena dall'Olio, who maintained virginity within her marriage. In this she resembled Cecilia, who is referred to often enough in sermons as having lived in all three states.

The stories that Pietro uses to illustrate the power of humility are the stock-in-trade of the medieval pulpit and devotional text and will be familiar to anyone who studies the depictions of David's career that accompany the seven penitential psalms. David is Pietro's principal example of humility, based, he says, on a passage of Gregory the Great in the *Moralia in Job.* David had been graced with so many gifts, so many virtues, writes Pietro, yet how vigorously he practiced humility! How far he was from vainglory when he "opened and broke the strong mouth of the lion," when he was chosen king ahead of all his older brothers, when he was anointed and called to the government of the kingdom in Saul's place, when he defeated the giant Goliath with a stone, and when he danced before the ark, to the derision of his wife, Michol. All of these images, found so frequently in the decorative borders of the seven penitential psalms in books of hours, contribute to the sense of humility that is at the heart of the David-in-Penitence. His dancing before the ark was a particularly popular motif in sermons, and is especially germane to my argument because it is literally dancing (*chorus*) that is converted into mourning (*luctus*) in Lamentations 5:15–16: "Defecit gaudium cordis nostri, versus est in luctum chorus noster, cecidit corona capitis nostri; Vae nobis, quia peccavimus."[47]

Elsewhere, in the *Doctrina del ben morire,* for example, Pietro urges the regular praying of the seven penitential psalms. He tells the story of St. Augustine's last hours, when he turned his face to the wall on which the seven psalms had been written and recited them as he lay dying, and stresses their power to inculcate humility and lead the soul to perfect contrition.[48] They thus form an excellent preparation for the individual about to receive communion. Given that Beata Elena received communion frequently, there is reason to suspect that she would have been especially familiar with these psalms.

Pietro pays great attention to the twelve steps of humility, and the corresponding steps of pride, as set out by Bernard. He begins the seventh chapter of the *Fundamento,* which is entirely devoted to this subject, by acknowledging his indebtedness to Benedict and Bernard.[49] The steps are set out in table 5.1, in words taken from Pietro's own brief descriptions, and numbered in the order in which the soul progresses toward either goal.

Let us presume, for clarity's sake, a soul caught in the final stages of prideful sin, the *consuetudine del peccare*—sinning at will, "habitual sin," with no care for any distinction between good and evil. This is the twelfth step of pride, at the bottom of the right-hand column of table 5.1. Such a soul has lost all sense of God's will, and thus all fear of God. It can begin to recover only by beginning to fear God, by climbing onto the first step of the ladder of humility. From this step the converted soul undergoes a radical but gradual change, until it reaches the twelfth and final step, the perfection of humility and of the Christian life. Each step on the way up corresponds to, is the antithesis of, the same step on the way down. The ascending soul, for instance, is ready at the fifth step to confess its guilt and sin; the soul descending to the depths of pride will at this point, its eighth step, begin to deny its sin. The ascending soul will begin to shun the world, speaking less (steps nine and eleven), whereas the soul descending toward absolute pride will at these points (its second and fourth steps) let a degree of levity rule it, then proceed to boastfulness. But it is the final step of humility that impresses one most: the soul attains perfection when it has withdrawn from worldly interests and keeps its gaze on the ground. Yet even at this stage a soul can always slip back, begin the descent of pride; its first step down, which negates the final step of ascent, is admitting curiosity about worldly things, a curiosity that is expressed in vain and purposeless looking-about.

The final stage of humility, which in Pietro's quite orthodox view represents the perfection of the truly contemplative soul, is graphically realized in the portraits of Elena dall'Olio. In all the known portraits of her she looks down, in keeping with her reported attainment of perfect humility, and with the description of her in the "Leggenda anonima."[50] Yet

Table 5.1   The Steps of Humility and the Steps of Pride according to Pietro da Lucca

Steps of Humility	Steps of Pride
12. "In heart and deed always practice humility, with the eyes fixed on the ground."	1. "Curiosity."
11. "Speak few words."	2. "Lightness of mind."
10. "Don't laugh too readily."	3. "Inappropriate joy."
9. "Taciturnity."	4. "Boastfulness, which is to promote oneself and praise oneself with arrogant and proud words."
8. "To hold with the common observance of religion."	5. "Singularity."
7. "To believe, and to state, that one is more vile than all others."	6. "Arrogance."
6. "To esteem oneself as unworthy and useless."	7. "Presumption."
5. "Confession of one's own sins."	8. "Denial of sin."
4. "From love of obedience, to embrace patience in difficulty and hardship."	9. "Simulated confession."
3. "To submit to superiors, in obedience, for love of God."	10. "Rebellion."
2. "Never to delight in doing one's own will."	11. "To sin freely."
1. "To fear God."	12. "Habitual sin."

the pose is in marked contrast to the gaze of Cecilia as Raphael painted her—a gesture that was copied and recopied in other paintings of other saints by other artists, one of the most influential of all painted gestures. Cecilia's upward gaze is a version in paint of the Christian paradox, expressed in one of its many forms in Luke 14:11, "everyone who humbles himself shall be exalted, and he who exalts himself shall be humbled." Cecilia's gaze is of course a spiritual one, not the gesture of the soul curious about earthly things. It is the necessary spiritual concomitant of the freedom from worldly things implied by the downcast eyes of Elena. Cecilia raises her soul, for "the eyes are the windows of the soul," and lives out Psalm 24:15, "my eyes are always upon the Lord." Elena's eyes denote a different aspect of the same spiritual state. She has learned not to look at the things of this world, so that she may look always at God; Cecilia is depicted "seeing" God, having already abandoned all worldly things—they lie broken at her feet, out of her sight. The relationship between the two ladders is a corollary of the relationship between these two kinds of seeing. They are the same, but reversed; to look down in worldly life is to look up in spiritual life; to climb in the world is the spiritual life's descent.

One cannot read the writings of Pietro da Lucca without becoming keenly aware that the saints depicted in Raphael's painting of St. Cecilia held a special place in his spiritual world. Beyond the already noted reference to Cecilia herself, he constantly quotes and refers to both St. Augustine and St. Paul. In the introduction to the *Regule,* he acknowledges his indebtedness to Dionysius the Areopagite (Pseudo-Dionysius), and thus Dionysius's great master, St. Paul. He extols Paul's mystical experience, his being taken up to the third heaven, where God revealed to him "things not given to man to speak," then goes on to claim him as the source for his own mystical teaching, his "secret theology." One should not lose sight of this claim in assessing Paul's presence in Raphael's painting. Pietro's whole thrust is to teach the contemplative life; Elena is his famous disciple, and Cecilia is her model. If we assume Elena's and Pietro's influence on the painting, then Paul's presence must surely be due at least in part to his being the primary source (in Pietro's view) of Pietro's teaching. And Pietro's frequent references to Paul in his teachings on such diverse topics as charity, humility, and ecstasy are but particular manifestations of the general dependence.

Augustine's presence in the painting can similarly be attributed to the reverence in which Pietro holds him, as well as to the fact that the Canons Regular followed the Augustinian Rule. A like reason can be given for the inclusion of St. John the Evangelist, who was in addition the patron saint of the church to which the painting, and the chapel, were given by Elena.

John, like St. Paul, is responsible for basic texts of the mystical and contemplative life, and for the most profound statements on divine love. More will be said about these saints in a later chapter, but it is worth noting here that Pietro links John the Evangelist with Mary Magdalene as the two saints who, with Mary the mother of Jesus, never deserted their master but stayed with him throughout his dying hours.[51] Magdalene, of course, is one of the great penitential figures, and her presence in the painting has posed perhaps more difficulties for the modern scholar than any of the other three companions of Cecilia. Yet it was not her onetime sinfulness that enthralled the Middle Ages, but rather (as Pietro's emphasis on her faithfulness indicates) her reversal of her state of life, her conversion from sinner to supreme contemplative, one especially loved by Christ, who appeared to her before all others following his resurrection. There was a well-established tradition of preaching on Magdalene on the Thursday after Passion Sunday, when the gospel of the Mass told the story of the sinful woman who anointed Jesus' feet.[52] These sermons are a rich source of information on Magdalene's standing in popular opinion during the Middle Ages and Renaissance, about which more will be said at a later point. It should be noted here, however, that Pietro's linking of John and the Magdalene because of their special love for Christ, a love that he was held to reciprocate, has special bearing on Raphael's depiction of them in the painting.[53] It should also be noted that there was a chapel to St. Mary Magdalene at S. Giovanni in Monte, established earlier than the Cecilia chapel built by Elena.

A study of Pietro da Lucca, Elena's spiritual director, has helped us understand some of the currents informing Raphael's painting: the three ways of spiritual progress; humility, repentance, and conversion; the choice of the saints who attend Cecilia. Such understanding can be deepened by shifting our attention to the complex figure who was, in turn, Pietro's acknowledged spiritual mentor. In a poem in praise of music, *Carmen de laude musicae,* Jean Gerson mentions all of these saints except John the Evangelist within the space of seven lines: "O father Augustine, you declare that, moved by the voices of the Church, you watered your cheeks with pious tears. Happy are you, O Mary, whose many sins were covered over, who hear again and again the heavenly voices. We read of Cecilia singing to herself in her heart with a heart filled with God, while instruments played. O Paul, you advised us to sing with our hearts, for such a deed blesses us by a twofold law. Heaven begins here and now, it is here, in exile, in the lives and prayer of the blessed life. Then death comes, it loosens the bonds of flesh, the victor carries on high the soul singing in psalms."[54] In this poem of ninety-eight lines Gerson sings the praises of music, referring to figures in both pagan mythology and the Old Testament, before concluding with the lines cited. Apart from references to St. Agnes, with the fury of divine love in her heart, and to St. Ignatius, whom he credits with attaching antiphons to the psalms, these are the only saints he mentions. That he does so at the climax of the poem, and that he thus groups together four of the five saints in Raphael's painting, must—given his influence on Pietro da Lucca—play an important part in the reasons for their inclusion.

The reasons Gerson has these figures in his verses are clearly stated. Augustine had confessed the affective powers of sacred music; Mary Magdalene constantly heard the angels sing (during the thirty years of solitude of which her legend speaks); Cecilia sang in her heart; Paul had enjoined Christians to "be filled with the Holy Spirit, conversing with one another in psalms and hymns and spiritual canticles, singing and psalming in your hearts to the Lord."[55] That the reasons are related is clear enough, all having to do with the power of music. But it is not "affective power," simply in the sense of emotional response, that Gerson is concerned with; it is much more, extending to the involvement of the whole being with the divine. Indeed, the most prominent characteristic of Gerson's musical imagery is probably the association he constantly makes between music and the heart, "heart" being understood not merely as the seat of the emotions but in the fullest Christian and biblical sense as the synthesis of the powers of the whole person.

Gerson presents a marked contrast to his admirer Pietro da Lucca. Instead of Pietro's five little books, simple and summary, we must now deal with ten hefty tomes of collected writings, much of it as sophisticated and complex as anything written in that age which so delighted in sophisticated complexity.[56] This is not the place for a comprehensive survey of the life or work of this immensely complicated man. Theologian, educator, mystic, poet, littérateur, humanist, politician, preacher, and more—he has not received all the attention he deserves. There is a particular lack of scholarly work on his theories of music and his use of musical allegory and symbolism. In fact, the only recent discussion of this aspect of his writing

Figure 5.2. *Gerson as Pilgrim*

(Photo: University of Pennsylvania Libraries)

Jean Gerson's family name was Charlier. He adopted
the name of his native village because it resembled a
Hebrew word for pilgrim, and the notion that we are
pilgrims was central to his thought. He was
sometimes depicted in pilgrim's garb, as in this
woodcut from the title page of his works published by
Nikolaus Kessler (Basel, 1489).

dismissed the idea that musicologists might have any reason to question
their lack of interest in Gerson.[57]

Gerson was born Jean Charlier in 1363 at Gerson-les-Barby. On entering
the College of Navarre at the University of Paris in 1377, he took the name
of his native place, noting that the name was also a Hebrew word meaning
"pilgrim."[58] That human life was a pilgrimage, that there was a longed-for
place of arrival was a frequent allusion in his writing and preaching, and
he adopted the figure of a pilgrim as his symbol. Indeed, he was sometimes depicted in the guise of a pilgrim, as in the woodcut shown in figure
5.2. The year he came to Paris was the year of Pope Gregory XI's return to

Rome from Avignon, an event that colored Gerson's career, for the problems of papal power evinced from him a conciliarist solution that possibly halted the later movement toward his canonization. Clearly a person of great energy and ability, he became chancellor of the University at a young age, was in demand a a preacher to the royal household, and was a potent representative at several church councils, most particularly the Council of Constance in 1415. He never returned to Paris after the Council, because of the massacre of Burgundians there which so changed the city's atmosphere and which he mourned in his eloquent *Carmen lugubre pro desolatione universitatis parisiensis.* He lived his later years in Lyon, proud to teach small children the rudiments of religion.

Prolific author that he was, he lived at the cusp between the age of manuscript and the age of print, with the result that his works were copied, printed, reprinted, and wrongly attributed, and many works not his were, for obvious reasons, published with his name upon them. The recent publication of his collected works by Glorieux may make it easier for scholars to approach Gerson, though those with an interest in the intensely visual quality of his language and his use of symbolism will regret that so little attention was paid to the rich trove of illumination in the manuscripts and early prints of his works.[59]

Musical allegory and musical symbolism permeate a great deal of what he wrote, though here we are concerned with the connection between Gerson's musical motifs and the thought of Pietro da Lucca, whether expressed in Pietro's writings or suggested visually in Raphael's painting. Several pertinent links are immediately apparent as one turns from the study of Pietro, Raphael, and Cecilia herself to the works of Gerson. Gerson is deeply interested in the symbolism of "singing in the heart," the phrase drawn from Paul's Epistle to the Ephesians that assumed a central place in Cecilia's legend. There is good evidence that he knew the legend of Cecilia well, for he makes oblique references to it. And he expresses the symbolism of the conversions of mourning and joy in a number of important and prominent ways.

Gerson's devotion to St. Cecilia and his understanding of her legend as an allegorical force are already evident from his reference to her in the *Carmen de laude musicae.* He refers to her in similar terms in a number of places. At the beginning of the second part of the second volume of his

De canticis (this volume is entitled De canticordo, a coinage of Gerson's that fuses the words for "heart" and "string," and which he interprets as "the song of the heart"), he sets out to treat the "new song," the canticum novum.[60] Anagogy (the mystical interpretation of Scripture), he begins, tells Christian pilgrims that the new song is something that truly exists and develops (it is "a certain being and becoming") in the heart and in the word of the mind. He recalls that the Church bids them raise their hearts daily, in the dialogue that precedes the preface of the Mass, singing "Lift up your hearts," Sursum corda. This is so that the "new man"—the soul in grace—may seek its new conversation in heaven, where the new song is sung before the throne of Him who says "I shall make all things new" (Revelation 21:5), in fulfillment of Ezekiel 36:26, "I shall give you a new heart and I shall set a new spirit among you." Let these souls sing the new song in their renewed heart, Gerson continues, following the injunction of St. Paul to be filled with the Holy Spirit, to converse in psalms and hymns and spiritual canticles, to sing and psalm in their hearts (Ephesians 5:19). "Thus did St. Cecilia act," he goes on, "who always kept the Gospel of Christ—which is clearly new and clearly the word of God—in her heart, and who sang to God alone, while instruments played: 'Let my heart and my body be immaculate.'"

Here Gerson takes Cecilia as his example of the singer of the new song, and this just at the point at which he is going to discuss the nature of contemplation. For Gerson (and for other mystics, it will be seen) Cecilia is a model of contemplation, a figure who stands in relationship to contemplation as David does to repentance. This corresponds to the position she held for Pietro da Lucca, who held her up as a model for the beginning of meditation on the life of Christ, just as St. Bonaventure had practiced and recommended.

In a work he finished just a few days before his death on July 12, 1429, Gerson took another example from the legend of Cecilia.[61] He was writing on May 25, the feast of St. Urban, the third-century pope who appears in the Passio Caeciliae, and the feast reminded him of what happened when Cecilia sent her pagan husband, Valerian, to be instructed and baptized by St. Urban in the catacombs. During the meeting there appeared miraculously an old man, probably St. Paul, who held out to Valerian a book inscribed in gold with the text of Ephesians 4:5–6, "One Lord, one Faith, one Baptism; one God and Father of all, who is above all, and through all things, and in us all." The old man asked Valerian if he believed this, to which Valerian replied that there could be no greater truth. In these words, says Gerson, is summed up the whole doctrine of Dionysius (Pseudo-Dionysius), one of the pillars of mystical theology and of the contemplative life. Thus, Gerson again sets Cecilia in close association with the foundations of the contemplative life.

One of Gerson's French works, the *Canticordum du pélerin* (The Pilgrim's Song-of-the-Heart) is in the form of a dialogue between the Solitary Heart (*cuer seulet*) and the Worldly Heart (*cuer mondain*), which should be thought of as a struggle within a single soul—probably Gerson's own—rather than between two distinct souls. At one point Solitary Heart challenges Worldly Heart, citing 1 Corinthians 2:14, "you cannot see or perceive what it is that delights me within, for 'the animal man does not perceive the things of the spirit.'" Worldly Heart replies, "Tell me why I cannot see them. Do you think that I am blind, without eyes, or a foolish head without sense? Why do you judge me thus? I am considered a worldly-wise person, while you are held to be foolish, sad, melancholy, in line with the saying of Scripture: 'I go mourning all day long.'"[62] This passage of Gerson is connected with the *Passio Caeciliae,* though Gerson does not say so. When Valerian and Tiburtius are questioned by the prefect Almachius, Tiburtius tells him that they, like those martyred before them, have contempt "for that which seems to be and is not, because they have found that which seems not to be, but is."[63] Almachius doubts that he speaks with his right mind, to which Tiburtius responds with the same words of 1 Corinthians 2:14, "the animal man does not perceive the things that are the spirit of God." Tiburtius is removed, and Valerian is questioned. Almachius begins with "since your brother is not of sound mind . . . ," the likely source of Gerson's "foolish head without sense."[64] Later, when Cecilia is commanded angrily by the prefect to sacrifice to the gods, she replies: "I do not know where you have lost your eyes. I, and all who have sound eyes, can see that these things you call gods are but stone and bronze and lead."[65] But this would seem to be the source of Gerson's "Do you think that I am blind, without eyes?" Furthermore, the psalm verse that Worldly Heart quotes, "I go mourning all day long," is Psalm 37:7, from the psalm already noted as intensely Cecilian, the entrance psalm for the Trastevere station day, as well as the third penitential psalm. Once again, Gerson draws upon the legend of Cecilia to make an important point about the foundations of the contemplative spirit, which lie in the God-centered heart.

It is possible that Gerson is reacting to an echo from the liturgy of Cecilia at the beginning of the first volume of the *Tractatus de canticis,* when he calls Christ "the lover of innocence."[66] This epithet occurs in the "prayer over the people" for the station day at S. Cecilia in Trastevere, and has been shown to be unique in early Roman orations, though it is admittedly a sufficiently neutral expression that its use may have become widespread in later medieval literature.[67] But one may reasonably suspect that Gerson drew it, consciously or unconsciously, from his familiarity with the Cecilian liturgical texts.

It is, however, in the *Tractatus de canticis* that Gerson's closeness to the themes enunciated above—Cecilia's "singing in her heart" and the conversions of mourning and joy—is most evident. The work itself is full of musical symbolism, even in its organization. He divides his material among three volumes, each of which is further divided into three tomes; but these, he declares, he will call "tones" (*toni*), and the points within them will be "notes" or "little notes" (*notae seu notulae*), symbolic titles that he deems appropriate in view of the subject matter.[68] The first volume, *De canticorum originali ratione,* treats music from the historical perspective in its first "tone," from the philosophical in the second, and from the theological in the third. In the second volume, which is about the "song of the heart" (*De canticordo*), he deals in the successive "tones" with the distinctions between the "song of the mouth" (*canticum oris,* music of the senses) and the "song of the heart" (*canticordum* or *canticum cordis*), with the more fundamental characteristics of the "song of the heart," and with "the new moral and mystical gamma." His third volume is again divided into three "tones," more, he says, out of respect for traditional ways of viewing its material than from any inherent distinctions within the material itself. The first "tone" is a collection of six of his poems about music; the second and the third are each a collection of fifty "notes," consisting of aphorisms, rules, and theorems about music—about songs (*de canticis*) in the second "tone," and about the expression of consolation (*verbum solatii*) in the third. These last two "tones," he adds, constitute a single entity, a collection of one hundred aphorisms entitled *centilogium de canticis.*[69]

Gerson's use of musical imagery and musical metaphor is far subtler and more complex than is generally realized, and still awaits its great explicator. One of his chief images, pivotal in itself an in its function within his musical thought, is that of mutation. It is a concept foreign to twentieth-century musicians, and it must be explained if the reader is to follow Gerson's thinking.

Although the notion of the octave interval in music was understood perfectly in the Middle Ages, it was not used as a basis for determining melodic movement. This was done rather by means of the hexachord, a grouping of six consecutive notes with the same intervallic pattern as the six notes ascending from C to A, that is to say, intervals of whole step (C-D), whole step (D-E), half-step (E-F), whole step (F-G), and whole step (G-A). This basic hexachord was called the "natural" hexachord, becuase its intervals occurred without having to sharpen or flatten any of its notes. There were two other identical hexachords available, but they involved the use of the one note within the octave that medieval theorists regarded as ambiguous in its relationship to its neighbours, the note B (which, of course, did not occur in the "natural" hexachord). B could be either *durum* ("hard" = modern B natural) or *molle* ("soft" = modern B flat). Using B natural, there was a hexachord available from G to E; using B flat, there was a hexachord from F to D The B-natural hexachord, from G to E, was thus known as a *durum* hexachord, while the B-flat hexachord, from F to D, was a *molle* hexachord. The notes of any of the hexachords, however, were primarily known not by their letter names but by the solmization syllables ut, re, mi fa, sol, and la.

If one is to understand the significance of Gerson's figure, it is essential to keep in mind that the hexachordal system developed before a system of fixed pitch was in force. But because the hexachordal system, in the age of expanding polyphonic awareness, became inextricably intertwined with fixed-pitch symbols, and because it is practically impossible to explain the system to those brought up on modern music theory without referring to pitch symbols, the modern letter-names simply have to be used in explanation. The situation would be comparable to trying to teach classical Latin to an English-speaking person without using English. But the reader should be aware that musicians of Gerson's time were well able to think of the hexachordal functioning of notes without reference to any letter-names.

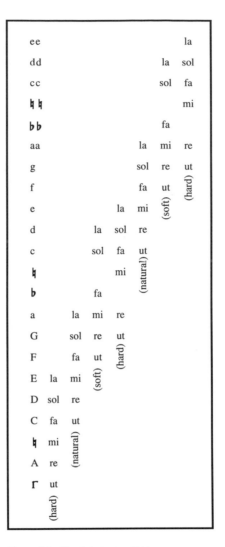

Figure 5.3a. The Solmization Table

(Design: Bob Rex)

Until about 1600 musicians defined melodic
movement by the position of pitches within a system
of interlocking hexachords (six-note groupings) rather
than within successive octaves. The solmization table
shows this hexachordal structure (fig. 5.3a), which
was taught to students by means of a didactic device,
the Guidonian Hand (fig. 5.3b). The series begins with
the syllable *ut,* for which the Greek letter gamma
might stand in a fixed-pitch system—hence the name
gamma or *gamut* for the entire system.

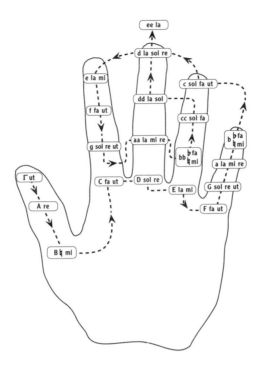

Figure 5.3b. The Guidonian hand

(Design: Bob Rex)

Musicians learned the steps in the hexachordal system (the *gamut*) by associating them with positions on the hand. The system begins at the top of the thumb with *ut,* and the succeeding steps are indicated by the arrow. By tracing a melody on the hand, a singer could know at once which changes of hexachord, or mutations, were available. Hexachords were hard if they included B-natural, soft if they included B-flat, and natural if they did not include the ambivalent note B.

The customary range of notes employed, from low G to E in the third octave above, was thus made up of seven overlapping hexachords, as shown in figure 5.3a. As letter-names began to be used, notes were given names that reflected both their letter-name and their hexachordal function. The letter-name would distinguish a note within the octave, but would not characterize its function within the melody; for that, one of its hexachordal names would have to be applied. Thus, to pick a random example, the note A *la mi re* would remain always an A by pitch, but according to the character of the melody in which it was employed, it would be classified in a particular situation as la (within the natural hexachord from C to A), mi (within the soft hexachord from F to D), or re (within the hard hexachord from G to E). Now, the process by which a single pitch changed its hexachordal function was called "mutation." Through this process, a single pitch, the same pitch, suddenly changed character because of the nature of the melody in which it occurred. There is no exact counterpart for this in modern musical terminology, but the concept of harmonic modulation comes close enough. Modulation does, in fact, have something of a history as a literary metaphor, the best example perhaps being Robert Browning's "Abt Vogler," in which the great extemporizer, his tormented spiritual-musical journey at an end, "seeks for the common chord" (a chord that functions in two keys, the key he is leaving and the key he is entering) and then, after modulating, finds his resting place, "the C-major of this life."

Gerson's writings abound in similar musical references to change. Pietro da Lucca, too, comes to mind, when he speaks of penitence as a "great mutation." The term *mutation* can, and more often does, refer to change in general, but given Gerson's references to "the mystical gamma" and his many discussions of spiritual change in musical terms, one always suspects a musical underpinning to his (and Pietro's) use of the word.

Gerson's is the medieval world of mutability, a world subject to the turns of Fortune's wheel, set between the eternally fixed realms of God and of Satan. For Gerson, the musics corresponding to these realms are the mixed song, the song of pure joy, and the song of pure sadness:

The song of pure joy is found in God in a way that is proper to him alone, and in the faithful angel and in the man who has reached heaven. . . . The song of pure (or almost pure) sadness is found in the devils in hell, in damned men, and in those living without hope. . . . The mixed song is the song of pilgrims [the living, whose salvation is not yet decided], which mixes hope and fear according to their three states. There are the beginners, who are being purged [of worldly attachments], the proficient, who are being illumined, and those nearing the goal, who are being perfected. In these we sometimes observe joyful laments, sometimes mournful rejoicing, according to differences of purpose, as when a mother rejoices to hear her child seek her in tears, or a master to hear a pet dog's barking after an absence.[70]

Here, in the tripartite division of the "mixed song," is a very close correspondence to the three zones of music in Raphael's painting of Cecilia. The division follows exactly the progression of Bonaventure's three ways, from the purging of worldly vanities, through the illumination that comes to those in "the middle state," to the more perfect union with God that is reached by those advanced in sanctity. The pilgrims or wayfarers (one must keep in mind that Gerson took the name of his native town as his surname because it meant "wayfarer" in Hebrew; there is always a degree of self-identification in his talk of *viatores*) in whose hearts the mixed song is sung do not experience it as an unchanging melody, but rather as one that fluctuates according to their spiritual condition. And what constitutes these changes or fluctuations is the varying degree of mourning and joy, *luctus* and *gaudium*.

While Gerson repeatedly identifies these qualities of mourning and joy as "affects," it is a mistake to think of them as the equivalent of the modern "emotional states." His psychology is vastly different, and his exposition is sufficiently hedged with elaborations and distinctions to make a simple analysis more confusing than helpful. Fortunately, he wrote his own simplified discussion in the French dialogue already cited, the *Canticordum du pélerin,* and it is this interpretation that will be advanced here. His explanation of "mystical mutation," in particular, is found a number of times throughout his works, in varying degrees of completeness. It should be noted, however, that his much longer *Tractatus de canticis*—which may be called an explanation by musical analogy of all divine dealing with human souls, and which contains all that is in the *Canticordum du pélerin,* but more diffusely expressed (his "mystical gamma," for instance, is explained twice)—is completely set in terms of the fluctuations of *luctus* and *gaudium*. He begins and ends with, and constantly returns to, the parable of the children in the marketplace of Matthew 11:16–17. The conclusion, in particular, makes it clear that the change in the mixed song varies with one's loving conformity to Christ, a conformity also expressed in the Pauline phrase "putting on Christ" that Gerson appropriates: "The consolation of Christ follows him who puts on Christ, that is him who is conformed in living to Christ as his exemplar. Nor will a consoling angel be lacking to such a one when he is in his last agony. Whoever, therefore, is downcast, let him look to this exemplar and make psalmody with good spirit, exulting at the rejoicing Christ, mourning with the lamenting Christ, as he taught in the parable of the children sitting in the marketplace and calling out to their friends, 'We piped to you and you would not dance, we sang dirges to you and you would not mourn.'"[71]

In seeking to understand Gerson's mystical gamma, one must remember that in the fourteenth and fifteenth centuries the gamma, or gamut, would have been conceptualized in the circular fashion of the "musical hand" (fig. 5.3b), rather than in the modern, linear style of figure 5.3a. The hand (often called the Guidonian hand, after Guido of Arezzo, who used an incomplete solmization system but not the hand itself) was an aid for memorizing the structure and relationship of the hexachords and for understanding mutations. The device was used in other disciplines besides music, but the "musical hand" was the best-known, and was accorded great prestige and authority in the time of Gerson.

Gerson derived his mystical gamma by extracting the vowels from the solmization syllables and letting each vowel stand for one of his mystical affects. Since la and fa have the same vowel, he was left with five symbols rather than six—with all five vowels, to be precise—to which he attached the following meanings: A is joyful love, E is hope, I is compassion, O is fear, U is mournful hate.[72] Gerson identifies these with the four passions to which the eleven Aristotelian passions were traditionally reduced: love, hope, fear, hate. He adds a fifth, compassion, from what he calls "mystical considerations," meaning that there was a compelling theological reason for doing so. Like earlier writers, Gerson finds support for the reduction in several authoritative sources. The principal one seems to have been the final verse spoken by Philosophy in book 1 of Boethius's *Consolation of Philosophy,* but Gerson also cites Virgil (*Aeneid* 6:733–34) and a liturgical text.[73] In Gerson's diagram of his mystical gamma, A, E, O, and U are arranged about X (which he explains as crossed I's), thus giving a cross, a square, or four points on the circumference of a circle, grouped around I (represented by X) at the center, as in figure 5.4.

Gerson begins his long discussion of his gamma by calling it the *Gamma canticordi,* the gamma of the heart's song, to hear or know which one must

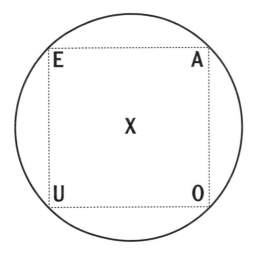

A : *Amor gaudiens (sometimes amor, gaudium, joye).*

E : *Spes.*

I : *Compassio.* [**X:** I *crossed*]

O : *Timor.*

U : *Odium dolens (sometimes tristitia, luctus).*

Figure 5.4. Gerson's mystical gamma

(Design: Bob Rex)

Gerson frequently refers to this device. As the musical
gamma (see fig. 5.3a) showed the changes of
hexachord in melodic movement, so the mystical
gamma displayed the changes in the music of
the heart.

"put off the old man, put on the new, and become like a child—even a
fool—in Christ." [74] As examples he cites Mary, the mother of Jesus, and
John the Evangelist, who as an old man uttered nothing but the sound
of the new love with his constant repetition of "Little children, love one
another." It is also the *gamma novum,* the gamma of "the new song," which
is the song of "the new man." Such a new man, even though he is "pretty
well grown up" (*grandiusculum*) in Christ, will not spurn this gamma, for
in accepting it he accepts humility, which is to be great in Christ, to be
advanced in Christian perfection. The mystical gamma, he goes on, is fashioned after the exemplar of Christ crucified. For this is the seal that Mary
had "on her heart in meditating, on her arm in her works." [75] And it was

this sign, Gerson continues, that renewed Paul, forming his new self from the old Saul and leading him to declare that he gloried only "in the cross of Christ, through which the world is crucified to me and I to the world."[76]

Gerson explains the several ways of viewing his diagram. It represents "the length and the breadth, the height and the depth," of creation.[77] The A of joyful love is thus at the top, near the heaven where there is no activity but that of joy; and this vowel is the beginning of the mystical gamma. The U, which designates pain and hatred (*dolorem et odium*), properly stands at the bottom, for what else but pain and hatred is heard in the depths of hell, *ubi dolor et fletus et stridor dentium?* On the tone at the right arm of the cross stands the E, which signifies hope or desire (*spei significandae seu desiderio*), for the good thief, who hoped in Christ and heard him say, "this day you shall be with me in Paradise" (Luke 23:43), was crucified at Christ's right hand. The O of fear is then placed on the left of the cross; and what more fearful sound could there be than that which will sound at the left hand on the Day of Judgment, "Depart from me you cursed, into everlasting fire"?

Gerson states that the letters also signify the four corners of the world, with A to the east, U to the west, E to the north, and O to the south. Further, he continues, they thus stand at the places of the common expressions designating changing fortune on medieval representations of the turning wheel of Fortune. A thus can mean "I reign" (*regno*), E "I shall reign" (*regnabo*), O "I have reigned" (*regnavi*), and U "I am bereft of a kingdom" (*sum sine regno*).[78] He points to other interpretations, but does no more than name them: the gamma can represent the four elements and their chief qualities; the arrangement of the planets; or the composition of the human complexions from the humors. In the last pages of his longer discussion in the *De canticis,* he does compare the mystical gamma to the manual gamma, that is, to the well-known "hand" of musical theory depicted in figure 5.3b, and shows that the mystical gamma has its own consonances, its own temporal and rhythmic divisions.[79]

It is fair to say that Gerson's deepest concern in expounding the mystical gamma is conversion, the leading of the soul from worldliness to the closest possible union with God. While this is evident even amid the profusion of figures and comparisons in the *De canticis,* it is even clearer in the simpler *Canticordum du pélerin.* Close to the beginning of the former,

Figure 5.5. *The Decline of Venus*

(By permission of The British Library; Sloane MS 3983, fol. 43)

This miniature from a fourteenth-century treatise on astronomy is one of four depicting the phases of Venus: *exaltatio, domus* (house), *declinatio,* and *casus* (fall). They correspond to the positions of Fortuna on her wheel. Here, in Venus's decline, the crown and instruments fall, as they did in the David-in-Penitence.

when he is still dealing with the music of the senses (*canticum sensuale*), he repeats the common medieval belief in healing through music, but does so in terms of the wonderful mutations it effects: "mirabiles fieri mutationes per musicam sensualem."[80] In the same section of work he compares two instruments, the cithara and the psaltery, as symbols, noting that they have the same shape but turned upside-down and that they proceed in different directions passing from low notes to high.[81] The psaltery, he finds, thus more suitably represents the motion of the contemplative soul while the cithara represents the penitent soul that ascends from the valley of tears.

Here again, he is concerned with the changes, fluctuations, mutations in states and affects between those things that cause *luctus* and those that cause *gaudium*.

The *Canticordum du pélerin* is the story of a conversion, which takes place in a series of seven colloquies between the Worldly Heart and the Solitary (or Contemplative) Heart. Probably Gerson never finished the tract as planned, for he broke off after three colloquies and compressed the remaining four into a series of brief notes. What distinguishes this tract from the *Tractatus de canticis* is the great narrowing of treatment and purpose. Where the *De canticis* took a cosmic view of God's dealings with creation, the *Canticordum du pélerin* is concerned only with his dealings with an individual soul. The principal result of this narrower focus, for present purposes, is that the universal sweep of Gerson's listing of the passions and affects is reduced to their significance for the individual. Thus, the *Odium,* or Hatred, of the larger treatise, which had been the opposite of his *Amor gaudiosum,* and which had been broken down into a great number of specific passions, of which *Tristitia* was but one, is now defined almost completely in terms of *Tristitia,* for that is how it reveals itself in the human soul.[82] Another result of the refining of Gerson's discussion in the *Canticordum du pélérin* is that the reader gains a much clearer view of the *nuances* and *mutaciones* that are central to his view of the process of conversion and spiritual advancement.

Within the mystical gamma itself, the letter *I* (or *X*, which has the same meaning, since he intends it as *I* crossed) plays the principal role, for it represents the compassion of the humble and loving Christ who alone can render concordant the other passions. Thus, *amor* (A) and *tristitia* (U), *spes* (E) and *timor* (O), are discordant if they are not tempered by the *pitié*, the compassion, of Christ. All of these passions have a bad and a good sense. Thus, in response to Worldly Heart's question as to how *doleur* can be sweet and pleasant, Solitary Heart answers that St. Paul distinguishes two kinds of *tristesse,* one worldly and one "according to God."[83] The reference is to 2 Corinthians 7:9–10, in which Paul rejoices at the repentance of the Corinthians: "I rejoice, not because you were made sorry, but that your sorrow led you to repentance. For you became sorrowful as God intended. . . . Godly sorrow works repentance that leads to salvation, but wordly sorrow brings death."[84] Sorrow of the worldly kind brings no hope of pardon and salvation, whereas godly sorrow brings both hope and joy to the point that the soul no longer pays heed to the painful character of its repentance but rather rejoices in it. Of repentant souls, according to Solitary Heart, "the Gospel says, 'Blessed are those who mourn for they shall be comforted.' Is there not here a beautiful and profitable music, of weeping turning to song, of sorrow turning to joy? 'Your sorrow shall be turned into joy . . . and your joy no one shall take from you.'"[85]

This passage of Gerson, and what follows, is set squarely within the scriptural tradition of the music of mourning and joy, which has already been observed in connection with Cecilia and with the abandoned instruments of the David-in-Penitence. Worldly Heart comments immediately, agreeing with what Solitary Heart has said, that it is indeed a beautiful nuance, a heavenly mutation.[86] Solitary Heart adds that this same nuance occurs often in the music of the *Canticordum,* that any of these mystic notes or pitches can be transformed into another. Thus "from good sorrow the heart leaps to good joy, as from ut to la, or from good fear to good hope, as from re to sol. And compassion, *pitié,* joins itself sometimes to one, then to another, and sometimes to all at once, in many guises and modulations."[87]

The interplay of the spiritual passions that Gerson sets forth in such variety in these treatises is in certain respects a commonplace of devotional literature and sermons. Fear and hope, for example, are always seen as complementary, fear of divine punishment impelling the soul to amendment, hope in the divine promises drawing it by a kind of attraction. Gerson and Pietro da Lucca both use the common figure of the soul as a bird that flies with the two wings of hope and fear, deriving greater power now from one, now from the other, but needing both if it is to reach its goal. But nowhere else is the world of God and soul portrayed in more vivid and elaborate musical images than in these treatises of Gerson. In them, through the mediation first of his devoted reader, Pietro da Lucca, and then of Pietro's disciple Elena dall'Olio, lies the surest explanation of the imagery of instruments and music that Raphael employed in painting *The Ecstasy of St. Cecilia.* Gerson's last sentences in the *Canticordum du pélerin* provide as succinct a reading of the musical iconography of the work as can be given: "If we have spoken of the song which belongs to the reasonable creature during this mortal pilgrimage, it is so that his song may more closely approach that of Paradise for unending eternity. This song of the heart we call the Canticordum of the high gamma, which is the song of the heart since it has been sensual, then spiritual, and has then become celestial. It is to progress in knowledge from devotion to speculation to contemplation. 'O God, I will sing to you the new song, with all my heart I will praise you.' " [88]

Six Mourning, Joy, and Music

in Medieval Spirituality

Before returning explicitly to visual representations of Cecilia in the Middle Ages, and in the last chapter to Raphael's painting of her, we should survey what medieval textual sources tell about her—not so much about the events of her legend, but about the inner significance of those events. We should ask in particular whether these sources support the view that has been suggested thus far in this study: that her links with music were based on early views of change, and most especially of spiritual change, change in the heart, change that was sometimes represented by the figure of mourning-into-joy. The survey begins with a writer who was a principal conduit for the thought of antiquity to the Middle Ages, the fourth-century Christian poet Prudentius. It looks at the use of the figure of mourning-into-joy by two of the greatest medieval poets, Dante and Chaucer. Dante makes no mention of Cecilia, but Chaucer does so quite explicitly in a way that sees her as working a kind of change that is the spiritual equivalent of alchemy.

The spiritual roots of these poetic views are sought, and found, in the words and writings of medieval preachers, philosophers, and mystics. Sermons were a fundamental method for the communication of ideas in the Middle Ages (a fact still not properly appreciated), and this survey can only skim the surface of that vast trove of belief about Cecilia. The few examples presented are, nonetheless, persuasive. The view of the saint and of her links with beliefs about spiritual change and music that these sermons suggest echo ideas of change as far apart in time as those of Augustine and Aquinas. Yet it is in the mystics and spiritual writers that the most clearly stated and most deeply felt views of Cecilia and the idea of mourning and joy are found. Richard Rolle, Julian of Norwich, Margery Kempe, Camilla Battista da Varano, and Catherine of Siena are the principal names. In all of them, the theme of mourning-into-joy is clearly present and important, and in several the reference to Cecilia as a model of the kind of change the theme represents is explicitly stated.

The survey begins with Prudentius's *Psychomachia,* an allegorical poem about the struggle of the virtues and vices that is itself the source of much medieval allegorizing in both the literary and the visual arts. In it there is a spirited description of the combat between Patience and Wrath. Patience stands her ground before a hail of blows until her adversary, utterly enraged, seizes one of her own discarded weapons and impales herself upon its upturned point. Proclaiming victory, Patience makes her way through the ranks of the applauding Virtues. She is accompanied, the poet tells us, "by a noble man; for Job had clung close to the side of his invincible mistress throughout the hard battle, hitherto grave of look and panting from the slaughter of many a foe, but now with a smile on his stern face as he thought of his healed sores."[1] The present-day reader is likely to pass over this description of Job's grave look dissolving to a smile as a natural enough dramatic device to illustrate the mental state of one who has endured bitter torments and now sees his long-suffering rewarded, but there is probably more to it than that. This literary figure describes the metamorphosis of the human soul from vicious to virtuous, from the state of wounded nature to the state of grace, in terms of the fluctuations of the passions of the soul between sadness and joy. It is closely related to—if it does not indeed derive from—the medieval application by preachers, spiritual counselors, and spiritual writers, of those scriptural texts of mourning and joy that have already been discussed at length and that are listed in appendix 1.

The most famous smile in medieval letters, that of Beatrice throughout the *Paradiso,* is an even more instructive example for our purposes, since Dante plainly allies it with music, thus enabling one to see the influence of the popular musical texts of mourning and joy like Esther 13:17, which forms the conclusion of the mass lesson of Cecilia's station day: "Turn our mourning into joy . . . and do not close the mouths of those who sing your praises." This is a text that reverses the thought of Lamentations 5:15–16, "The joy of our heart is fled, our singing is turned to mourning," or of Job 30:31, "My harp is turned into mourning, my organ into the voice of those who weep." For Dante, the Woeful Kingdom far behind him and the way of purgation traversed, sadness has given way to swelling joy, lamentation to songs of heightening bliss.[2] At each of the lower spheres Beatrice's smile shines on Dante with increasing brightness, her beauty and her joy increase, and the songs of the spirits they encounter change and intensify.[3] But when they reach the sphere of Saturn, the last of the planets, all is silent, the singing is gone, and Beatrice smiles no more. The reason is explained to the poet by both Beatrice and St. Peter Damian, who point out that Saturn is the sphere of the contemplatives, those elect souls who have come closest in this life to true union with God. Smile and song have indeed vanished, but this is not because they have no place here, not because the sphere of contemplation is a cheerless place. Rather the opposite is true: the joy here is so great that Dante's mortal powers could not withstand it, but must first be strengthened. "Your hearing is mortal, like your sight," says Peter Damian, "and it is for this reason that there is no singing here, for the same reason that Beatrice does not smile."[4]

Joy (along with love, with which it is often equated, as by Gerson) is of course the passion that is theologically appropriate to the souls of the blessed, for whom desire (and indeed all of the passions, except love and joy) has ceased and who are impelled only by the charity that envelops them in the clear vision they enjoy of the divine essence. Equally, unremitting sadness is the passion of Satan and the damned, who by their own election have turned away from that charity and are now fixed in their choice for eternity. Joy is similarly the passion appropriate to those still living who progress successfully in the ways of spirituality and mysticism. Saint Augustine, for example, states the final goal of mysticism in the words of Matthew 25:21, "Enter into the joy of the Lord."[5] Such observation is commonplace, though Dante (unlike many of his modern critics) would surely have counseled against light dismissal of the thought for that reason. Less common, however, is an awareness of the extent to which Dante has based his whole cosmography on the contrasting concupiscible passions of sorrow and joy, and has used figures drawn from music to emphasize the contrast. The fierce laments of the Inferno express the everlasting mourning of the subjects of the Emperor of the Woeful Kingdom, who had himself once been part of the song of unchanging praise and joy in the first circle of the Empyrean; between these there are songs of lesser joy, and songs that fall closer to sadness. Dante's musical-cosmological scheme is close to the plan of mystical music spelled out by Gerson in the *De canticis,* with its song of pure joy, song of pure sorrow, and mixed song.

That Dante intended his cosmography to reflect the scripture texts of mourning and joy is made evident by the speech of the beautiful lady he meets at the stream bordering the Earthly Paradise. She is later called Matilda by Beatrice, and is perhaps to be identified with the German mystic Mechtilde of Hackeborn, who died in 1298 and whose writings treat sensitively of the Earthly Paradise.[6] When the poet first sees her, she is singing and gathering flowers, and he asks her to come nearer so that he may hear the words of her song. She is in fact singing the fifth verse of Psalm 91, which expresses her joy in the Lord's works: "You have delighted me, Lord, in your doings, and in the works of your hands I shall exult." The smile with which she greets him is the first of many that he will see in the journey ahead, always in some way betokening the joy of the blessed. Matilda's first words to the poet, in explanation of the beautiful garden in which she stands, are of human subversion of God's first plan, a subversion that she expresses entirely in terms of the turning of joy into mourning: "The Supreme Good . . . made man good and for good, and gave him this place as a pledge of everlasting peace. But through his fault, he lived here only a short time; through his fault, he turned honest laughter and sweet pleasure into tears and toil."[7] As we have already seen, and shall further discuss shortly, the scripture texts of mourning and joy were so used so commonly in the Middle Ages, both in preaching and in spiritual writing and discourse, that we must suppose some echo from the pulpit in references such as this.

Matilda's joyous song and smile are in any case the starting point in a progressive sequence of these same symbols that reaches a singular level in the sphere of Saturn, with its sudden silence imposed to shield the poet's mere human faculties from the overpowering joy that prevails there. No passage in Dante shows forth more potently his mystical sense, his strong belief in the radical remaking of human nature through Christian redemption and in the potential of restored human nature to be wedded to the divine.

It is helpful to our deeper understanding of music and mourning-into-joy to consider for a moment why Dante chose Saturn as the sphere of the contemplatives. The god Saturn had of course reigned over the golden age of the Romans. The sphere of the planet named for him, held to be the furthest and the coldest of all, was in medieval belief the sphere of temperance, positioned both to influence and to represent abstraction from the sensible world in favor of the spiritual. Perhaps more to the point was its situation as the last of the planets. To Dante it represented the final stopping place before he was led by Beatrice into the Empyrean and the direct knowledge of the divine essence. Its closeness to the divine realm, its position as the last outpost of the visible universe before the strange convolution, conversion, from the geocentric scheme of revolving spheres (where the true center was actually occupied by the Emperor of the Woeful Kingdom) to the God-centered circle of the Empyrean, made it an apt location for those who in life had in some mysterious way loosened the constraints of flesh and known God directly.

Dante does, indeed, hear the great cry of the contemplatives before he and Beatrice ascend the ladder that joins Saturn directly to the divine realm, but it is a cry of indignation at the grievous condition of Christ's church rather than any song of joy. The ladder is a further indication of Dante's belief that the true contemplative enjoyed a species of direct access to God, unmediated by the faculties of sense. Before they make their swift ascent Beatrice tells the poet that he should realize from the intense emotion the contemplatives' cry has aroused in him just how unready he is for the sudden burst of joy that her smile and the song of the spirits in this place would have enkindled: he would have been wholly changed, "transmutated."[8] Dante seeks to emphasize, in this episode, that the sphere of the contemplatives represented a cardinal point in his journey, and that contemplation itself effected a radical change in the souls and the powers of its practitioners. This change he typified by a dramatic increase in the force of the two symbols of joy, the smile and the song.

Radical change expressed in terms of the flux of the contrary passions of the human soul is surely not surprising from a poet whose thought is so clearly based in the experience of his own conversion. Such change is even less surprising given the reforming spirit of the mendicants and other evangelical groups of that era. If we wish to understand the popularity of the scriptural texts of mourning and joy, we must first appreciate the climate in which they developed.

Siegfried Wenzel, one of the leading authorities on medieval preaching, comments on this phenomenon: "As Rosemary Woolf has shown, certain favorite meditative passages in Latin were translated again and again into

English verse and expanded into longer lyrics. The same is true of the humbler tags used in preaching. A good case is Lamentations 5:15–16: *Defecit gaudium cordis nostri: versus est in luctum chorus noster. Cecidit corona capitis nostri: Vae nobis, quia peccavimus.*"[9] Wenzel then gives several instances of such use of the passage. The frequent use of this text (and of others like it) indeed justifies his labeling it a "humbler tag." But what, one may wonder, was the reason for its popularity in the Middle Ages?[10]

That popularity may perhaps be traced in some measure to the citation of Job 21:12–13 and 30:31 and to the development of the theme of mourning and joy in the treatise *On the Wretchedness of the Human Condition* by Lotario dei Segni. This work, written by the future Pope Innocent III in the winter of 1195, just three years before his election, quickly assumed great influence, becoming the most popular work on *contemptus mundi* down to the seventeenth century, when the theme fell from favor. Lotario intended to balance the dismal view of the human condition that he set forth with another work on human *dignitas,* but was evidently hindered by the press of affairs following his election. His prologue declares that he sought in the *De miseria* to humble the proud, intending in the subsequent work to exalt those who had been so humbled. The spiritual dynamic thus envisioned, along with the contents—its three sections discuss, with a wealth of lurid and at times repulsive biblical citation, man's "wretched entry" into the world, his "culpable progress" through it, and his "damnable departure" therefrom—lends itself readily to the application of the texts of mourning and joy. The texts from Job are cited in chapters 20 and 21 of book 1, titled respectively "Of Brief Joy" and "Of Unexpected Sorrow."[11] In strict accord with his theme, Lotario applies the texts solely to worldly pleasures and sorrows, and to the penalties for sin, with no trace of the spiritualized applications that would interpret this "joy" as the joy of the blessed, such as are found in Dante, or that would see in "sorrow" the kind of sorrow that, if suffered for Christ's sake, would be turned to joy, as envisioned in John 16:20: "You shall lament and weep, but the world shall rejoice; you shall be saddened, but your sorrow shall be turned to joy."

Who, Lotario asks, knows even a day of joy that is not alloyed with distress? And the last of the scripture citations he applies to his thought is Job 21:12–13, "They take the timbrel and the harp and rejoice at the sound of the organ. They spend their days in wealth, and in a moment they go down to hell." As an example of sorrow's inevitable intrusion into worldly joy, he points to the sudden calamity that befell Job's children, and adds that the father thereupon said justly, "My harp is turned to mourning, my organ into the voice of those who weep" (Job 30:31). This strict application of the texts to worldly pleasure and sorrow was probably the most common if for no other reason than it seems the easiest and most obvious. It is the kind of application that probably underlies most of the use of the texts as "humble tags" of which Wenzel writes. Innocent III, the most forceful of the reforming popes, was the presiding genius of the Fourth Lateran Council, with its vast influence on preaching, as well as the advocate, and in a sense the co-founder, of the new mendicant and preaching orders. In the prodigious growth of preaching to the common folk that grew out of this work, including the initiatives of Francis and Dominic and those who followed them, the theme of worldly sorrow was used and reused, and varied and refined in the process.

An overview of J. B. Schneyer's huge catalogue of sermons from the years 1150–1350 reveals many occurrences of several of the scripture texts of mourning and joy among the themata listed, but none is more prominent than that from Esther 13:17, "turn our mourning into rejoicing, so that living we may praise thy name, O Lord, and do not close the mouths of those who sing thy praises, O Lord our God." The concluding words of the lesson for the Wednesday after the second Sunday of Lent, the verse occurs rather frequently as the principal text for this day in those collections of sermons for every day of Lent that went by the name of *quadrigesimale*. This Wednesday is, as already noted, the station day at S. Cecilia in Trastevere, a liturgical assignment that was listed as a matter of course in the Roman Missal, and that was drawn to the congregation's attention in some of these sermons. Thus the Dominican Eudes de Chateauroux, a chancellor of the University of Paris in the mid-thirteenth century, who preached on this verse of Esther to the Choir of Paris (*coro parisiensi*), began by telling his hearers of the great throngs that visited the Trastevere basilica on this day to honor the saint.[12] He does not explicitly refer to her as the patron saint of music, but given his audience and the content of the sermon, it is more than plausible to understand a link between Cecilia and the interests of the *corus parisiensis* to whom he was preaching.

A survey of the whole corpus of sermons listed by Schneyer is indeed revealing for our purposes, and shows the popularity of the theme among medieval preachers. It would be well to preface such a survey with a consideration of the way penitential preaching developed in the time of reform that began about the end of the eleventh century and that embraced so much social change and unrest in both church and state. These expressions about mourning and joy, their musical implication often made explicit, are seen to become endemic, commonplace. This was the age when the focus of life shifted more and more from country to town, when even those monastic reforms that resulted in such new orders as the Cistercians, the Carthusians, the Premonstratensians, and the Augustinians in their several varieties were inadequate to the new religious spirit that had so much to do with the developing urban classes. Alongside the more successful of the mendicant orders, Franciscans and Dominicans, there sprang up a variety of similar groups and organizations, some clerical and some lay, some clearly heretical and all of them involved with, and accused of, heresy to greater or lesser degree. There were the Humiliati in their three orders, the Sackites, the Brethren of the Common Life, the Brethren of the Free Spirit, the Béguines and Beghards, the Gesuati, the Waldensians, the Valdesi, the Wickliffites, and others. The thirteenth century saw the sudden bursting forth of the extraordinary penitential movement of the Flagellants, in whose songs mourning and joy took on a special significance. All were involved in preaching, reform, calls to repentance. Lay preaching and preaching by women were common, at least in certain areas, and drew down the ire of the more conservative and orthodox. The basis of this ferment was the will to see and effect reform; and the call to reform was in every case the call to repentance.

In this milieu it is not surprising to find the theological language and the rhetorical expression that have been such central concerns of this study become pervasive in sermons. In the Lenten Series, as already noted, the text of Esther 13:17, "converte luctum nostrum in gaudium," became a stock text for the sermon of the station day at S. Cecilia in Trastevere. Esther was a savior of her people in one of the great crises of their exile, a fact that surely had a part to play in the development of Cecilian spirituality. Often enough the figure of Esther forms the starting point of medieval sermons on this day, the Wednesday after the second Sunday of Lent, as in an anonymous sermon preserved in a collection in the Bodleian Library, which directly equates that Jewish captivity with man's expulsion from Paradise.[13] There survive sermons by many famous preachers that were preached on the text of Esther 13:17 on this same day, among them those of Aldobrandinus de Cavalcantibus, St. Thomas Aquinas, Nicholas of Ascoli, John of S. Gimignano, and Eudes of Chateauroux.[14]

Apart from these sermons on the lesson from Esther, there are many other medieval sermons on the theme of the conversion of mourning and joy. Isaiah 61:2–3 ("Dabo coronam pro cinere, oleum gaudii pro luctu") was a popular source of texts for Ash Wednesday and for the Octave of Easter.[15] Jesus' promise to the apostles in the Holy Thursday discourse, "Tristitia vestra vertetur in gaudium" (John 16:20), provided a text for the Easter season.[16] Matthew 5:4 ("Beati qui lugent") and Jeremiah 31:13 ("Convertam luctum eorum in gaudium") were texts in a series of sermons devoted to the Beatitudes and were filled with the language of humility and change of heart.[17] "Convertisti planctum meum in gaudium" (Psalm 29:12) served both for St. Mary Magdalene, the great penitent, and for Easter Sunday.[18] For Palm Sunday we find "Risus dolore miscebatur" (Proverbs 14:13).[19] The profusion of such sermons underscores how common the whole theme of mourning and joy had become.

A good example of what may be called the spiritualizing of the figure is found about 1400, in the most influential of all Christian spiritual texts after the Bible, *The Imitation of Christ*—the "fifth gospel," as Bossuet called it. Here Psalm 29:12, "You have turned my mourning into joy . . . and with gladness surrounded me," is applied (along with several other verses of the same psalm) to the sense of spiritual consolation that is experienced, in alternation with periods of desolation and dryness, by serious travelers on the way of perfection, and that is to be regarded as a free gift of God, not as something to be sought after for its own sake.[20] The figure undergoes further refinement at the hands of Gerson, especialy in the mystical gamma: here, sorrow and distress become joy through the acceptance of the cross of Christ and its values, which are diametricaly opposed to those of this world.

Nothing better symbolizes the embedding of the theme of mourning and joy in the spirituality that grew among the mendicants and the reforming currents of which they were part than its appearance in the legend of St. Clare of Assisi, where one encounters it in the description of the act that shows as much as anything else in Francis's life the importance he attached to contemplation, namely, the establishment of that branch of his order dedicated to contemplation in utter poverty. When, over the fierce objections of her family, he finally installed Clare in S. Damiano as the nucleus of the first community of Franciscan women, he arranged things so that "on the day of the feast [it was Palm Sunday], elegantly clad, she would receive the palm in the midst of the crowd, and on the following night leave her lodgings to turn the joy of this world into the mourning of the Lord's passion."[21]

Here, however, there is no linking of the theme of mourning and joy with music. The strongest evidence suggesting that the two were commonly joined in Franciscan spirituality betrays further links both with Cecilia and with the milieu of Raphael. This evidence is found in the spiritual memoir of a late-fifteenth-century mystic who had undoubted ties to the Urbino court circle in which Raphael was brought up, as well as ties of a less direct kind to Elena dall'Olio and perhaps even to the Pucci family. Camilla Battista da Varano was born in 1458 into the ruling family of the cultivated humanist court of Camerino in the *Marche,* some fifty miles southeast of Urbino. She had both taste and talent for letters, her writings being among the more expressive of mystical works. Drawn early to Franciscan spirituality, she entered the convent of the Poor Clares at Urbino when she was twenty-three, then returned to Camerino just two years later (the year of Raphael's birth) to establish a new foundation for her order in a monastery abandoned by the Olivetans. Here she lived until her death in 1524, except for two years (from 1505 to 1507) at Fermo, where she established another convent at the request of Pope Julius II.[22]

In the account she wrote of her spiritual formation, the time from about her tenth to her thirty-fourth year, Camilla Battista spoke of Cecilia, and mentioned Cecilian themes and texts, in ways that strongly suggest a particular influence of the Cecilian legend on the schooling of contemplatives. Thus God told her, as she began her spiritual journey, to "keep her body and her heart immaculate as Cecilia had done."[23] Like virtually all the mystics, she underwent a time of tremendous spiritual trial, which she describes in the fifteenth chapter of her autobiography by citing the words of Job 30:31, "and therefore the harp of my trusting was turned into mourning."[24] Her liberation from this torment is related in the following chapter.

For three months, she says, she experienced a feeling of interior flame, a burning desire to be freed and to be with Christ. It was not a feeling of dying, but rather "a going to nuptials while instruments played [*uno andare a noze 'pulsantibus organis'*]."[25] But this last phrase, *pulsantibus organis,* is a direct reference to the famous *cantantibus organis* passage of the *Passio Caeciliae* in which the saint's wedding is described. It comes from the same pasage Camilla Battista had already cited in the sixth chapter of her autobiography, when she told of God's express command that she imitate Cecilia by keeping her heart and body immaculate.[26]

The suggestion that Cecilia was in some ways held up as a model for contemplatives finds support in other mystical and spiritual writings of the late Middle Ages and early Renaissance. One such case is St. Catherine of Siena. Another is Julian of Norwich, who is increasingly seen today as a key figure in the history of mysticism.

Blessed Raymond of Capua, the confessor and biographer of St. Catherine of Siena, describes in these words the saint's habit of constant prayer: "It was a continuous prayer to the Lord, that He would guard her virginity. And she sang with Saint Cecilia the verse of David: 'O Lord, may my heart and body be immaculate.'"[27]

Julian of Norwich, who was born about 1343 and died some time after 1416, left two versions of her revelations, the first, or Short Text, being written almost immediately after they took place, in 1373.[28] In the first chapter of the Short Text, and thus almost immediately after she received her revelations, she tells how at the beginning of her spiritual journey, of her conversion, she desired three things of God. The first was to have a recollection of Christ's Passion; the second to experience a bodily illness so severe that it would seem certain even to herself that she would die, but from which in fact God would preserve her; and the third to suffer "three wounds."[29] She explains that the third desire was aroused when she heard "a man of Holy Church" tell the story of the three wounds that St. Cecilia received in the neck. "Moved by this," she goes on, "I conceived a great desire, and prayed our Lord God that he would grant me in the course of my life three wounds, that is, the wound of contrition, the wound of compassion, and the wound of longing with my will for God."

This image of Cecilia's wounds became not only an underpinning of Julian's spirituality, but also the framework of her revelations. In her thirty-first year, she writes, God granted her the bodily illness she had sought, thus fulfilling her second desire. A seeming paralysis came over the lower part of her body, she received the last rites, and as she gazed up at the crucifix held before her, it seemed to her that the upper part of her body, too, began to die, so that she could scarcely feel anything.[30] At this moment, as she looked on the crucifix, all her pain suddenly vanished, and it came into her mind to ask for the second of the three wounds—"that my body might be filled full of recollection and feeling of his blessed Passion."[31] It was with this prayer, and at this point in her spiritual development, that the series of sixteen revelations began. She makes it clear "that the sickness . . . and the miraculous cure . . . were God's immediate preparation for her to receive the revelations which ensued." She also makes it plain that the first revelation, the one that flowed immediately from the granting of the "second wound," was the source of all that God revealed to her, the revelation in which all the others are summed up—that "it stands to the other fifteen as the Prologue stands to the rest of St. John's Gospel."

The revelation began as a bodily vision of Christ's head bleeding under the crown of thorns. The translators and editors of *Showings* point out how short and austere her description of this vision is, particularly in contrast to the second and eighth revelations. "In the long text the reason for this becomes clear," they go on, "when she writes that 'suddenly the Trinity filled my heart full of the greatest joy, and I understood that it will be so in heaven without end to all who will come there.'" There is no reference throughout this revelation to the dolors of the Passion. The stress is on the consolation that the vision brought; and she tells us of her first reaction to the sight of Christ, "glorified and exalted, yet on his Cross."

What has happened is, in essence, as follows: Julian has been granted the second petition she had made when young, an illness that seems deathly but from which she believes she has been miraculously saved. At this moment, recognizing what God has given her, and acting, she is convinced, under divine guidance, she asks again for the second wound that she had desired so long ago and that had been inspired originally by the story of Cecilia, the "wound of loving compassion." The wound is given her in the vision of the bleeding Christ, and she amplifies her description of it as "loving compassion" by pointing out that she asked "that my body might be filled full of recollection and feeling of his blessed Passion . . . for I wished that his pains might be my pains, with compassion which would lead to longing for God" ("longing with my will for God" was the third wound).[32] Finally the principal meaning of the vision—that this tremendous suffering is the greatest joy, the greatest consolation, the greatest love—is revealed to her. Thus the revelation occurs within the framework of the "three wounds" of Cecilia that Julian had asked for; and it consists of Christ's utter pain and sorrow being revealed to her, through the gift of compassion, as the glory, the joy, the consolation of the vision of God. Julian has here stated the Christian paradox, that the suffering of Christ becomes eternal and infinite joy, and that the change has been effected only through compassion. Mourning, *luctus,* has become joy, *gaudium,* through the medium of compassion, in exact correspondence with Gerson's mystical gamma, as was discussed in chapter 5.

Julian's first revelation shows how intimately the consideration of Cecilia, and of Cecilian themes, could be associated with the contemplative life. Indeed, the realization, through compassion, that "mourning" is "joy" seems, in Julian's mind, to be the principal matter, and the foundation, of all contemplation. The importance of Cecilia for Julian is further reinforced by the fact that the sources of her developing spirituality were Franciscan. Meditation on the Passion, the summoning to the imagination of its physical details, is a well-known tenet of the Franciscan approach that finds a natural point of convergence with Cecilian devotion in the often repeated phrase of the *Passio* that Cecilia "kept the Gospel within her heart."[33] It is this convergence that gave rise to Cecilia's appearance in a celebrated copy of one of the most popular manuals of Franciscan piety, Pseudo-Bonaventure's *Meditations on the Life of Christ.* In this work, Cecilia, who is introduced at the very beginning, is depicted in an illustration as a Poor Clare and described in the text as a model for the sisters precisely because she "kept the gospel in her heart."

A further point to remember as we examine the place of Cecilia in the lore of spirituality concerns the "man of Holy Church" from whom Julian heard the story of Cecilia. One's first inclination is to think that she was recalling a sermon, but she does not say so, and it is at least equally possible that she heard the story in the course of spiritual direction. Such direction, the spiritual communion and consultation between the disciple and the master in the search for the ways of contemplation and perfection, remains one of the oldest and least explored of all oral traditions, yet it is unquestionably the principal channel for the transmission of the learning and practice of spirituality. A Pietro da Lucca writes in his books the merest fraction of what he discusses and teaches in his conferences with an Elena dall'Olio; and for every Pietro, who manages to pen at least a distillation of his discourse with Elena, there must have been hundreds of directors whose discourse with their disciples was just as constant but who wrote never a word of their conferences. The sudden surfacing of Cecilia at the beginning of Dame Julian's revelations is like the mention of Cecilia, and the surfacing of Cecilian themes, in the writings and the spiritual histories of other medieval mystics and contemplatives: it smacks not of the study, not of the lecture hall, not of the pulpit, but of the spiritual director's cell.

Julian casts further light upon that most pervasive of Cecilian themes, the turning of mourning into joy. The seventh of the sixteen revelations, which she summarizes at the beginning of the long text of *Showings,* is "the frequent experiences of well-being and woe," evidently synonymous with *gaudium* and *tristitia-luctus.* And her explanation of the revelation, in her fifteenth chapter, indicates that she meant by the expression the fluctuations of a sense of consolation and a sense of desolation that are much discussed by writers on the spiritual life, and that often precede the attainment of the state of union. It was to this experience that both *The Imitation of Christ* and Camilla Battista da Varano applied texts of mourning and joy. In Julian's case, as in Camilla Battista's, the fluctuation from one state to the other occurred many times and with unusual rapidity, and was perceived by her as a deep and special mystical experience.

"And after this," she writes, "he revealed a supreme spiritual delight in my soul. In this delight I was filled full of everlasting surety, powerfully secured without any painful fear. . . . This lasted only for a time, and then I was changed, and abandoned to myself, oppressed and weary of my life and ruing myself, so that I hardly had the patience to go on living. . . . And then presently God gave me again comfort and rest for my soul, delight and security so blessedly and so powerfully, that there was no fear, no sorrow, no pain, physical or spiritual. . . . And then again I felt the pain, and then afterwards the delight and the joy, now the one and now the other, again and again, I suppose about twenty times."[34] Given medieval understanding of the passions, it is very easy to see how the sudden departure of fear and the arrival of a sense of "securety" that seemed to transcend hope would be token and pledge of the divine presence, for passions such as fear are inconsistent with the direct knowledge of God, and will—according to constant Scholastic teaching—disappear in the next life when God is possessed eternally.

Julian's whole spirituality is in fact shot through with the consideration of "well-being" and "woe," understood not just in the sense of changing emotional states but rather of fundamental spiritual and even ontological conditions. Joy and sadness are, for her, the stuff of the long, cosmic struggle in ways that parallel the thinking of Jean Gerson. Though she does not discuss the problem of evil head on, she plainly enough meditated about it long and hard. She offers no hint of a solution, but she believes, from a private revelation, that by a mysterious action on the Last Day, God "will make everything well which is not well."[35] Declaring her firm adherence to Catholic teaching, she professes belief in hell, and that the rebellious angels and those men who die outside the divine love will be eternally condemned to suffer there. The conflict in logic between this belief and the revelation that "all would be made well" puzzled her, and she assigned it to the realm of divine mysteries: "And all this being so, it seemed to me that it was impossible that every kind of thing should be well, as our Lord revealed at this time. And to this I had no other answer as a revelation from our Lord except this: What is impossible to you is not impossible to me. I shall preserve my word in everything, and I shall make everything well. And in this I was taught by the grace of God that I ought to keep myself steadfastly in the faith, as I had understood before, and that at the same time I should stand firm and believe firmly that every kind of thing will be well."

That "well-being" and "woe" had broad significance for Julian is evident from her whole text, for there is scarcely a chapter in which she does not discuss this, or a seemingly equivalent, polarity. Her text seeks, of course, to translate a deep experience, of the kind that is most unyielding to words, into ordinary language; yet it is not an irrational text, but rather a text that reaches the outer confines of human utterance, a text that seeks to portray an experience shared by very few. She can be read most clearly only if we take into account the theological basis of her terms and discussion, and the similar experiences of other mystics. "Well-being" and "woe" seem to have

Mourning, Joy, and Music

both an internal, personal meaning, and a wider, even universal and "cosmic," import. She uses these terms (or equivalents) to speak of the final state of creation, after the Last Judgment (as in the paragraph cited above); of the singular personal experience during which she received her revelations, her "showings"; of the states of grace and of sin; of the fear and hope, sorrow and gladness, that the thought of these things arouses (something closer to our concept of emotions); of the activity of the "spiritualized" senses; and more.

Thus far we have examined explicit modeling on Cecilia in the case of two important medieval women mystics, Julian of Norwich and Camilla Battista da Varano; both responded strongly to the scriptual and mystical connections between Cecilia and the transmutation of sorrow and joy. In one case, Camilla Battista's, these Cecilian themes were explicitly connected with music, in the other case not. Another, and singular, feature of Cecilia's story that left a powerful imprint on women mystics of the Middle Ages was Cecilia's virginity within marriage. Adopted by Elena dall'Olio, this arrangement also appealed to mystics like Marie d'Oignies, Frances of Rome, Angela of Foligno, Bridget of Sweden, Aldobrandesca of Siena, Umiltà of Florence, Umiliana dei Cerchi, Gherardesca of Pisa, and Catherine of Genoa, all of whom adopted the celibate state within, or after, marriage, and who seem also to have perceived their marriages as presenting some hindrance to their progress in sanctity.[36]

In her astute and sympathetic study of a group of medieval Italian women mystics, a study that sheds light far beyond the women with whom it is principally concerned, Elizabeth Petroff points to the stresses endured by such women as a result of the social and sexual customs of their times—"their families' determination to marry them off once they reached puberty," and the like.[37] The aptness of Cecilia's solution to the problems that sexual pleasure might present to such women is obvious. It seems likely that Petroff's judgment about the way their lives were transmitted is part of the explanation: "The oral tradition of which these women were a part can now only be traced in . . . official writings. . . . the biographer's intention was not to reveal how unusual or unconventional a woman was, but to demonstrate how conventionally good she was. The tradition of female sanctity and power which medieval women followed is always covert, either ignored . . . or interpreted from a male point of view." It is not, I think, mere coincidence that among the women we have mentioned thus far the two who so firmly assert Cecilia's place in their spiritual growth are the two who are known to have been well educated and to have written their own memoirs, Camilla Battista and Julian of Norwich.

If Cecilia is not mentioned directly in more of these women's lives and writings, it is nonetheless astonishing how closely the careers of some of them seem to have followed the Cecilian pattern. Consider, by way of argument, a Christian woman who aspires to the contemplative life yet finds herself married to a man far removed from her in religious sympathies. Though it seems to those about her that she has wed him willingly enough, her heart is troubled by their obvious differences, and she confides to him her strong sense that God wishes her to live the life of a Christian virgin within their union. She warns that God will slay him if he does not respect her wish and disturbs him with her seemingly wild talk of a heavenly lover. To obtain the grace of perfect chastity within her marriage, a grace she says she desires more than anything else in the world, she undertakes a program of severe fasting and prayer, constantly beseeching the Lord to preserve her and keep her chaste, and even donning a hair shirt beneath her ordinary attire. So close does her communion with the Lord become that celestial music seems constantly to flood her soul, and she tells her friends that not a day goes by that she does not hear the angels singing.

How unmistakably Cecilian this story sounds! Yet it was not, in fact, written about Cecilia at all, but about the late-medieval mystic, and author of the first autobiography in English, Margery Kempe. Simple, unlettered Margery, forever weeping and wailing, a profound irritant to her acquaintances, long married and the mother of fourteen children, seems a far cry from the eloquent Roman virgin who so mockingly defied her judge. Yet their spiritual careers are so similar that one can easily suspect the weeping pilgrim of Lynn of having modeled herself upon Cecilia, even though Cecilia is nowhere mentioned in her book.[38] While it may be objected that the resemblances between them are common enough in medieval mysticism (other mystics sought celibate marriage, wore hair shirts, claimed to hear the angelic music, and so forth), and hardly grounds for a theory of conscious imitation, one important fact about the case of Margery Kempe keeps this supposition alive.

When Margery felt an inner stirring toward a martyr's death, she said she would prefer beheading, which is the kind of death Cecilia was sentenced to.[39] The peculiarity is not that she would prefer this kind of death, but that the statement so closely parallels the experience of the one other female mystic Margery knew personally, the one female authority on the spiritual life whom she is known to have consulted, the anchoress Julian of Norwich. For Julian, as we have seen, a figure of far greater stature and intellect than Margery, founded her spiritual life on the wish to receive "three wounds," like Cecilia. Certainly the flux of mourning and joy is one of Margery's chief underlying narrative strategies and she does at times cite related scripture texts to defend her constant weeping.[40]

It has already been pointed out that the sources of Julian's spirituality, like those of Camilla Battista, were heavily Franciscan. While the Franciscan spirit was clearly imbued with what we have identified as Cecilian themes, those same themes were popular with other reformist groups that flourished from the eleventh century on, particularly the Dominicans and the Umiliati. Joy in poverty, in what this world regards as misery and wretchedness but which is transformed in and through the love of Christ, is at the heart of Francis's spirituality. The little man in the brown robe who ran barefoot through the snow, singing and exulting, was the inspiration for a style of preaching that assailed worldly, material living, yet ended in a jubilant singing of the infinite, all-embracing, all-forgiving love of God. Two hundred years after Francis's death, one of his followers would end an Easter sermon with a song which he introduced by admonishing his hearers to "sing devoutly in your heart"—the kind of singing for which Cecilia was famous.[41] No wonder that the style of song that came out of (or at least accompanied) the Flagellant movement should have been based on the same principle, beginning with the flagellation of the pride of world and flesh, and ending with rejoicing in God's love, a true *exsultativa conclusio*. Such, at least, is the pattern of a great number of early *laude*, most noticeably those of the most famous of the early Franciscan singers, Jacopone da Todi.[42]

The suggestion that Cecilia herself had some special appeal for the medieval reformist groups is intriguing. Is it coincidence, for instance, that among the handful of contemplatives who formed the first communities of Dominican and Franciscan women there should have been two who took or kept the name of Cecilia in religion? In any case, the importance of Cecilia to Dominic is clear, and it was recorded by one of these Cecilias.

The Dominican Sister Cecilia was one of a group of women Dominic gathered in Rome, just a year before his death, at the little church of S. Sisto Vecchio. A few years later she went to Bologna, where she became prioress of the convent of St. Agnes in 1237. She lived to the age of about ninety, dying in 1290. In a book she wrote about Dominic's miracles, she described an apparition he had of the Virgin Mary in the company of St. Cecilia and St. Catherine of Alexandria, in which Mary told him that she had taken his order under her special protection.[43] In view of the Dominican ideal of contemplation and preaching—of preaching to others only what they have themselves mastered through study and contemplation, expressed in the motto *contemplata aliis tradere*—the appearance of these two saints on this occasion is suggestive. For if Catherine, who put to intellectual rout the fifty philosophers sent by the Emperor Maxentius to debate her, was so obviously apt a model for Dominic's preaching friars, a symbol of the ideal of "handing on" (*tradere*) to others the fruits of contemplation, then Cecilia, who kept the gospel, the Word, in her heart, who gave herself to unceasing prayer and divine colloquies, and who "sang in her heart," is an equally apt model for the life of contemplation from which the ideal Dominican preaching had to derive. Cecilia also appears in a significant way in the legend of one of the most famous Dominican preachers, St. Peter the Martyr. He was accused of entertaining women in his cell, but after inquiry it was revealed that he had been conversing with St. Cecilia and St. Catherine of Alexandria.[44] Both Cecilia and Peter were praised in sermons because they had won the threefold aureole of preacher, virgin, and martyr.[45]

The Franciscan Cecilia, who joined St. Clare as one of the first group of Poor Clares at S. Damiano in Assisi, was the daughter of Gualtieri Cacciaguerra of Spello. She, too, lived to a great age, was Clare's close companion for forty-three years, and gave testimony, still extant, at the process of her canonization.[46]

Cecilia's appeal for the reformist movement that grew from the late eleventh century onward is also discernible in the dealings of one of the earliest groups to be motivated by that spirit, a group that predated the Franciscans and Dominicans and provided a model for Francis in the planning of his new order. Several scholars, noting that churches in the possession of the medieval order of the Umiliati were frequently dedicated to Cecilia, have suggested that the order had a special devotion to the saint.[47] Though the history and character of the now defunct order have been obscured, enough is known of them for us to see the logic behind such a devotion. The Umiliati began as a lay group, given to evangelizing and preaching; and Cecilia is as apt a model as could be found for the lay preacher, especially, of course, the woman preacher. Women seem to have been equal and prominent members of the movement at the time of its lay beginnings, and special arrangements were made for them to be members of the order that was eventually established (though on different lines from the Franciscans and Dominicans). The Umiliati were not mendicants, but preached a doctrine of labor and self-support (their foundations were established among the urban laboring and artisan classes); Cecilia, noted for her industriousness in the Lord's behalf (Chaucer, following Pope Urban's comparison of her to a bee, celebrated her "bisyness" and called her "ful swift and bisy ever in good werkinge"), was surely an apt model in this as well. The Umiliati labored and prospered mightily in the wool and textile trades; would not Cecilia, with both her rough penitential robe and her noble, golden vesture, have been a perfect symbol for this activity as well?

The history of the Umiliati is still too obscure for us to accept these assumptions as anything more than that. That the order did possess a number of churches dedicated to the saint is beyond question, however. It has been noted that various of their churches stood beside streams near city boundaries, preferred sites for those engaged in dyeing and washing wool. Curiously, a number of other Italian churches dedicated to Cecilia, but not known to have been associated with the Umiliati, were situated in similar locations, suggesting a possible link between Cecilia and the trades mentioned, not just between Cecilia and the Umiliati.[48] Whatever the truth of the matter, it is certain that one famous church dedicated to Cecilia came under the care of the Umiliati, and this the most famous of them all, S. Cecilia in Trastevere. The Umiliati occupied the basilica and the attached monastery from 1344 to 1419, and again from 1438 to 1527.[49]

Thus far in this chapter our focus has been on Cecilia's place in the spiritual thought of particular individual figures (chiefly mystics) and particular religious groups in the Middle Ages. At this point, it will be helpful if we view the saint in the broader context of the language used in medieval thought to describe inward changes. Our ultimate aim will be to grasp how St. Cecilia was understood in the Middle Ages to be related to music, and this will require a discussion of medieval concepts of change. Central to the cult of Cecilia was the activity of the heart. Those texts of her legend that described her as keeping the gospel in her heart and as singing in her heart were read as powerful descriptions of the changes that took place within the souls of Christians who followed faithfully the path of divine love. When the medieval thinker came to describe such inner changes, he chose his words from a vocabulary common to what today would be called a variety of disciplines. For the Middle Ages was not the age of the specialist; there was still a profound belief in a unity of purpose, of final cause, at work in the universe; and the wise and learned sought to explain it all.

The theologian, for instance, in explaining how at baptism the soul was imprinted with a character or seal that marked it indelibly for all eternity and that endowed it with new and real powers, would argue to his conclusions from the pertinent texts of Scripture, while at the same time drawing upon his metaphysical training to describe that character as an accident (as opposed to a substance), a quality, and an instrumental power that resided in the intellectual part of the soul. When the same theologian sought to elaborate the activity of this baptized soul, he relied on his understanding of Aristotle's *De anima* and its Scholastic expositions. Aristotle's eleven passions, in their categories of irascible and concupiscent, formed the matrix of his formulation, but now they were spiritualized and extended beyond the domain of the merely sensitive appetite. To the Christian mind, God was the supreme object of love, of joy, of desire, and so forth; loss of him, the object of hatred, of sorrow, of aversion. And just as the concupiscent passions were used to explain spiritual activity, so, too, were the irascible passions—hope and fear, despair and boldness, and wrath (the one passion that had no contrary)—all elevated to the spiritual plane.

Our theologian would discern within the baptized soul five spiritualized senses, corresponding to the physical senses of sight, touch, hearing, taste, and smell; for the natural passions could operate only through the senses, and there was a logic in positing the same kinds of instrumentalities for the functioning of the spiritual passions as for the natural. The passions themselves he would explain as habits of the soul under one aspect, as activities springing from these habits-of-soul under another. When he sought to explain further the activities and changes of the soul he might even borrow the terminology of another branch of his natural philosophy, which we of the modern era would be inclined to call mechanics, discussing these changes as examples of motion. And if he sought illustrations and examples from the world about him to help him explain, he might even introduce the terminology of alchemy or of magic.

The most common of the concepts applied to supernatural activity may well be that of motion, a term whose scope was wider then than it is today. Its fundamental sense was that given it by Aristotle in the third book of the *Physics*. He defines it as the entelechy, the act (in the hylemorphic sense), of that which exists in potency insofar as it is in potency (Aquinas, *Commentary on Aristotle's "Physics,"* par. 285), or the act of the possible insofar as it is possible (par. 290). Aristotle and his Scholastic commentators, such as Aquinas, spent great intellectual energy in considering, expounding, refining, and distinguishing this concept. Though their work defies summary, several observations about it will help show how closely it pertains to the topic of Cecilia.

Motion for Aristotle meant much more than movement in place, though this was one of its principal species. Its sense was closer to that of change in general, embracing all activity within the realms of divine creation. Indeed, Aquinas, following Aristotle, declared mobile being to be the subject of natural philosophy, saw nature itself as a principle of motion and rest in that in which it is, and defined natural science as dealing with those things which have within themselves a principle of motion.[50] The character of such change—of motion, if you will—was not restricted to the tangible world, but was considered valid for the whole created universe. It was held to apply just as truly to the workings of the human mind, and to the angelic order, as to the material world. Thus spiritual activity, the changes effected by grace and by living under grace, came within its terms.

One of the best-known and most influential transfers of the terminology of motion to spirituality is found in Pseudo-Dionysius's threefold categorization of spiritual motion as straight, oblique and circular.[51] This formed the basis for later threefold divisions of the spiritual life, such as Bonaventure's three ways. In circular motion, the soul perceives God before all else, after putting away created things. In straight motion, the soul perceives God only through created, visible things. Oblique—or, more properly, spiral—motion was explained as a combination of the other two forms, wherein the soul turns to God in response to the enlightenment received from him, but does so after its own fashion. Circular motion thus designated the highest type of contemplative activity, and might be loosely equated with perfect union with God. Circular motion was seen as the only local motion that could be continuous and eternal: the point that constituted its center was itself motionless and fixed, while the circumference was considered to be derived from the center and at the same time to represent endless motion about it. Dante made profound use of this thought in the *Commedia*, in depicting the souls of the blessed as revolving spheres, and in the circular cosmography of both the visible universe and of the Empyrean.[52] Gerson, too, as we saw in chapter 5, made reference to it by asserting that his mystical gamma could be interpreted as a circle, with all that that implied.

An even more eloquent application of the language of motion to the spiritual was the use of terms related to mutation. *Mutatio* is of course the normal Latin word for change of any sort, as are also its various forms in the Romance tongues. But it has a number of technical applications as well, those in music and in Aristotelian-Scholastic natural philosophy being especially germane to the way it was used in spiritual and theological writing. This consideration in fact does much to explain the relationship of St. Cecilia to music. It will further help explain how Cecilia and music are both linked in medieval thought to the inner life of the contemplative. And it will cast a revealing light upon some of the mysterious ways of medieval literature, particularly the musical-mystical background of Dante's thought and the curious treatment of St. Cecilia by Chaucer.

We have already discussed mutation as a musical concept that signified change of hexachord and so of melodic character, and that provided the symbolism whereby Gerson portrayed the spiritual activity of the human heart and soul. When Gerson did this he was making reference to the medieval understanding of motion as "mutation according to contrariety [*mutatio secundum contrarietatem*]," and of the passions of the soul as "motions of the soul [*motus animae*]." Mutation and motion in the strict sense were not synonymous, the former being the broader term. That is, there were mutations that were not species of motion, but all motion was mutation, and its distinguishing feature was the qualifier *secundum contrarietatem*.[53]

The Aristotelian-Scholastic view confined motion per se to the categories of quantity, quality, and place; and regarded action and passion, in their metaphysical sense, as synonymous with motion itself—they simply added an intelligibility, *ratio,* to the idea of motion. The concept of mutation according to contrariety (it is important to note the distinction between contrariety and contradiction) may be expressed more clearly as "progression from one positive term to another positive term which excludes the first in the same subject." The usual examples are of black and white, and of qualities that change gradually like hot and cold.[54]

The flux of the passions of the soul fitted integrally into this system. In a precise sense, they were not simply the terms of motion but were synonymous with motion: "to say that there is motion in action and passion is the same as to say that there is motion in motion," says Aquinas commenting on Aristotle. The contrariety of the passions (that is, their occurrence as pairs of contraries) is well established in all Aristotelian-Scholastic explanations.[55] Both St. Thomas and Gerson, as discussed in chapter 5, appealed to a tradition founded on a passage from Boethius's *Consolation* and another from Virgil, which reduced the eleven passions to four, while St. Thomas appealed to Aristotle as well.[56] The idea that these four passions summed up all motion within the universe, the macrocosm, and within the microcosm of the human soul, inspired Gerson's device of the mystical gamma. The gamma could represent both the motion of the natural universe and of the natural man, corrupted by the Fall, and the motion of the universe and of the human soul as transformed by sanctifying grace. The point at which this transformation takes place, where the "old song" is mutated to the "new song," is compassion, understood as a new supernatural element added to the cosmic gamut to bring about the mutation of the natural to the supernatural hexachord. Compassion is at one level the divine pity, in no way owed to humanity by God, but freely and lovingly given; it is manifested through the Passion of Christ, which indeed turned the sadness of sin to the joy of the Lord. The baptized human soul that enters into this compassion within the Church is entering into the divine pity by the Passion that the Mystical Body shares with Christ its head.[57]

In making compassion the "note" that would mutate the old song to the new, Gerson was a perfectly orthodox theologian. His thinking also reflected contemporary currents in both speculative and mystical theology, for compassion was the core of the theology that developed in the early Franciscan centuries with their great emphasis on affective piety, on contemplation of the events and the meaning of Christ's Passion.[58] Nor could it have been lost on him (for his writings abound in musical wordplay and punning) that this compassion, which held the secret of the response to God's offered salvation, was the Latin equivalent of the Greek *sympathia,* sympathy, with all that it implied for musical response by sympathetic vibrations. A sympathetic vibration is one that is transmitted from one vibrating body to another. It can happen only when the two bodies are capable of vibrating at the same frequency. Thus if one sings the note C loudly into, say, an open grand piano, the piano string of that pitch will begin to sound. The effect was certainly known in antiquity and the Middle Ages, and Gerson seems to use the idea in a sermon that sums up his teaching about the "mutation" of souls. Fittingly, this sermon was preached on the feast of All Saints, and its text, the third of the Beatitudes, was a central statement of the Christian paradox as well as of the theme of mourning and joy: "Blessed are they who mourn for they shall be comforted."[59]

Gerson's thought, unique in some respects, is a logical enough development of the view of music that goes back at least to the Pythagoreans, received its most influential development from Plato in the *Republic* and the *Timaeus,*[60] and was adopted without question by the Middle Ages. Its significance is well stated by Cassiodorus in the sixth century: that all things are governed by musical laws, and that the divinely established proportions of the music of the spheres are mirrored throughout the universe in the healthy body and mind, and in the virtuous soul.[61]

Though its application to the Christian economy of grace can be observed in countless medieval writings, it has still not received a satisfactory and comprehensive scholarly treatment. This is particularly true for the writers and writings that are closest to the subject of this study, mystics and writers on mysticism like Hugh and Richard of St. Victor, St. Bernard of Clairvaux, St. Bonaventure, Richard Rolle, and so many others who use musical imagery to describe the inner activity of the contemplative and mystical life, of whom Gerson is one of the most prominent.

That musical law applied to motion, or change, was a given of this world view. How it did so when the changes were in the inner life of man, and particularly when that inner life was transformed by the grace of Baptism, was a question that beguiled many thinkers, with Augustine foremost among them. The astonishing, and difficult, sixth book of the *De musica* states fairly explicitly the philosophical and theological basis for later speculation about the inner musicality of the contemplative soul. While Augustine's teaching falls outside the scope of this study, it must be observed that there is considerable compatibility between his speculations about musical rhythm and motion and the theme of mourning-into-joy. For Augustine's starting point was a famous definition of music that tied it intimately to motion, understood in the broad sense of change.

Music, he states in the first book, is the *ars bene modulandi* (the art of modulating well), while *modulatio* (modulating) is the *scientia bene movendi* (the knowledge of moving well, of the perfection of motion). The best rhythms, in his view, achieve some kind of correspondence with the equality found within the unity of the godhead. (Here we might note the parallel with the idea that the divine love moves all things, setting in motion the outermost sphere and, through its agency, transmitting motion to the whole of the mutable universe.) Thus, for Augustine, motion, which begins from divine action, finds its perfection in the attempt to return to, or at least in some way to mirror, that from which it originates. The consequent balancing of unity (and the oneness of creatures is only a reflection of the oneness of the divinity) and multiplicity, the attempt of created number to match the perfection of the divine unity, became a persistent strain in mystical thinking, often associated with music, which was intimately tied to number in ancient thought.

Having grasped this much of medieval thinking about change and music, we are now prepared to understand what medieval commentators had in mind when they linked Cecilia with these topics. Saint Aldhelm, for example, a West Saxon monk and bishop of the late-seventh century, praised Cecilia in his *De virginitate*. He left two versions of the work, the first (which we will examine here) in his high-flown, abstruse prose, the second a simpler treatment in verse.[62] In discussing Cecilia, he dwells heavily on the episode described by the *cantantibus organis* passage; for the rest, he simply says that she converted her husband and his brother, that they were granted the vision of the angel, and that the angel gave them crowns of flowers from paradise, exhorting them to guard these with pure hearts. That there is not a word about their trials, about their judge, about

Plate 1. Raphael. *The Ecstasy of St. Cecilia with Sts. Paul, John the Evangelist, Augustine, and Mary Magdalene*

(Pinacoteca Nazionale, Bologna)

Three zones of music mark the saint's spiritual journey. Worldly enticements have been cast aside; the mixed music—the earthly and the heavenly intertwined—no longer serves and slips from her grasp; the music of divine union fills her heart. Like her companion saints, Paul, John the Evangelist, Augustine, and Mary Magdalene, she knows the radical change wrought in the heart by a deeply contemplative life.

Plate 2. *David-in-Penitence:* Miniature from a book of hours

(Bibliothèque Municipale, Laon; MS 243⁴, fol. 87. Photo: Thomas Connolly)

Before the seven penitential psalms in a fifteenth-century book from northern France, David kneels in repentance for his adultery with Bathsheba and his murder of Uriah. The abandoned musical instruments tell us that his "harp is turned into mourning" and his "organ into the voice of those who weep" (Job 30:31).

Plate 3. *David-in-Penitence:* Miniature from a North Italian Bible

(Biblioteca Apostolica Vaticana; MS Urb. lat. 2, fol. 5r)

The miniature of David-in-Penitence was often found at the beginning of the Book of Psalms, as it is here in the Bible of Duke Federigo of Urbino. Raphael, a native of Urbino and the son of an artist who filled commissions for the ducal family, may have seen this miniature.

Plate 4a. Giovanni Birago. *David-in-Penitence*: Miniature from the Sforza Hours

(By permission of The British Library; Add. MS 34294, fol. 218)

Before the third penitential psalm, David's hands are encircled by the crown "fallen from our head" (Lamentations 5:16), which he has taken up again. Closely linked with the cult of St. Cecilia, this psalm represents a point of radical change in the spiritual journey mapped out by the penitential psalms. In the background a slothful donkey bears grain to a mill, and a man carries out the flour that has been transformed by the working within.

Plate 4b. Giovanni Birago. *David Ascends the Mountain:* Miniature from the Sforza Hours (By permission of The British Library; Add. MS 34294, fol. 233v)

Before the seventh penitential psalm, David has risen to his feet and sets out up the mountain path toward the goal of the spiritual journey.

Plate 5. *David-in-Penitence, with Patron*: Miniature from a North Italian Missal

(By permission of The British Library; Add. MS 15814, fol. 7)

This subject often illustrates the entrance psalm for the Mass of the first Sunday of Advent, the beginning of the church year, as in the late fifteenth-century missal of Laurentia de Castilione Aretino Sforza. Its position buttresses its message: true Christian living can begin only in humility. The tiny figure above David's hands reflects the first words of the accompanying psalm, Psalm 24: "To thee, O Lord, I have lifted up my soul."

Plate 6. Master of the St. Bartholemew Altarpiece. *St. Agnes, the Donor, St. Bartholemew, and St. Cecilia: The St. Bartholemew Altarpiece*

(Alte Pinakothek, Munich)

The portative organ Cecilia holds has by this date, the late fifteenth century, become one of her prominent attributes. She has taken up the organ cast aside by the repentant David, his joy turned to mourning; her prayer to "turn our mourning into joy" has been heard.

Plate 7. Anton Woensam. *The Mystical Betrothal of Sts. Cecilia and Valerian*

(Wallraf-Richartz Museum, Cologne. Photo: Rheinisches Bildarchiv, Cologne)

Woensam painted Cecilia's organ, as did Raphael, with the longer pipes to the right and the shorter to the left, contrary to the order of an actual instrument. But the Flemish artist reinforced this symbolism, with its implication of the contrasting musics of mourning and joy, by placing the mouths or sound-holes of the pipes at the top rather than the bottom.

Maximus, nor, except for the simple fact, about their martyrdoms, is not really surprising, for Aldhelm's theme is virginity, and he selects only those parts of the legend that refer to it: the beginning, therefore, with its story of the crisis of Cecilia's wedding.

Aldhelm reserves his most extravagant language for describing the music of the wedding instruments, the *organa cantantia,* and Cecilia's resistance to it. It is a music of multitudinous sounds—one hundred and fifteen, to be precise ("bis quinquagenis et ter quinis sonorum vocibus")— and, like the music of the sirens, it entices the unwary to their destruction. This "numerousness" of the sounds, compared to the simplicity implied for Cecilia, seems the key to Aldhelm's meaning. To understand why, one must note the context in which he has brought her into his book. In the passage immediately preceding he has described the preeminent virgin, Mary, and has given her, among many titles, one drawn from the Song of Songs 6:7, "a dove amongst the sixty queens and eighty concubines."[63] He declares that his contemplation of Mary, who was a virgin before she conceived and remained so afterwards—that is, after the Annunciation by Gabriel and her answering *Fiat*—put him in mind of Cecilia, who like Mary was a virgin both before and after her marriage and whose continued virginity followed the intervention of an angel.

Following Aldhelm's statement that Mary has put him in mind of Cecilia, and that he intends to compare the two, the reader coming upon the numbers of the instruments at Cecilia's wedding immediately recalls the numbers in Mary's title. The sense of this image from the Song of Songs is clear enough, and its application to Mary is obvious: the king may have his great retinue of official queens and even more concubines, but they are worthless in comparison with the dove, that is, with the single love of the shepherd-lover who is the book's hero. Thus Aldhelm, in describing the great number of the sounds of the wedding music, is saying that just as Mary is among the host of queens and concubines, the single dove, so is Cecilia among the multitude of instrumental sounds at the wedding; she sings the single song, the song of union between soul and God. And this is a song, we observe, that fulfills Augustine's preference for the rhythm based on the equality of one to one. Such a preference for the simplicity of unity over multiplicity, applied thus to the contemplative versus the worldly state of mind, seems a medieval constant.

In the tenth century, Flodoard of Rheims penned a description of Cecilia's heart-music that confirms how suited the imagery was to contemplative expression, though he says nothing of motion, nor of contraries, except for setting contrary musics in opposition. Flodoard clearly understood *cantantibus organis* to refer to the music of the wedding feast, yet he did not hesitate to use the image of an instrument for Cecilia's inward singing: "while the instrumental music of the wedding sounded, she sang her own feasts to God with the cithara of her mind, asking him to grant her a pure heart in a chaste body."[64] From about the same time there survives a Mozarabic hymn that expresses much the same thought, calling Cecilia's unceasing prayer, the keeping of the gospel in her heart, "the music of her mind."[65]

The best-known of all medieval texts about St. Cecilia is Chaucer's *Second Nun's Tale,* though few admirers of the great poet would rank his terse and rather bland retelling of the saint's legend among his finest achievements.[66] Written originally as a separate work, and only later pressed into service for *The Canterbury Tales,* this text bears the marks of its solitary birth. There is, for instance, no description of the Second Nun's actually telling the story, nor any mention of her at all except in the poem's title and in the list of the company in the General Prologue. Nonetheless, and of late, interest in the tale has quickened with the realization that Chaucer had intended it to appear side by side with the *The Canon's Yeoman's Tale,* which follows it in Fragment G, and that the juxtaposition blends an unexpected piquancy into the blandness.[67] Yet if there is agreement that the two tales are related, there is no consensus on the nature of that relationship. Here our study of Cecilia and the contrary passions of mourning and joy may be of use to the Chaucerians. For if we are correct in giving primacy, in our understanding of Cecilia, to the idea of motion—in her case, of radical spiritual change—we can see at once the aptness of coupling a poem that recounts her legend with another about the kind of motion that is held to take place in alchemy. I shall maintain that Chaucer sees Cecilia as one through whom God works a kind of spiritual alchemy. This is more than implicit in Chaucer's opposing her to Idleness, and in his celebrating her "busynesse," her constant "working." But before we pursue this train of thought, it would be well to look at recent scholarly inquiries into the alchemical connection between the two tales.

In his fine investigation of the iconography of Cecilia's fiery bath, Professor V. A. Kolve pays tribute to the solidity of Joseph E. Grennen's and Bruce A. Rosenberg's work establishing the kinship of the two tales, but chides them because they "deny *The Second Nun's Tale* any substantial literary merit of its own, valuing it only as a prefatory occasion for something better, *The Canon's Yeoman's Tale* of alchemists and their craft."[68] Later, and after he has succeeded in showing us something of the "beauty and complexity in *The Second Nun's Tale* that the visual arts of the time can help us to recover," he concludes that "if Grennen and Rosenberg have too readily dismissed the Cecilia legend as negligible on its own, they may also, in their enthusiasm for it as a preface to *The Canon's Yeoman's Tale,* have overstated that relation in one respect closely associated with the present theme: the alchemical gloss they provide for the wedding of Valerian and Saint Cecilia."[69] Kolve then goes on to demonstrate—from miniatures in alchemical treatises showing the coupling of the Red King (sulfur) and the White Queen (mercury) in the work of achieving material union—that the eroticism of Cecilia's "fiery bath" is also suggested by the baths the alchemists used in pursuing their "great work" of transmutation. But this leads him to doubt Grennen's suggestion that Chaucer intended us to think of this kind of alchemical union as we read about the marriage of St. Cecilia. "Her marriage *does not* take place in the flames (read by Grennen as analogous to the fire under the alchemists' crucible)—indeed, her husband has been killed *before* she is subjected to the fire—and the higher thing that is born of their union—the increase of a Christian community—neither waits upon her martyrdom in the bath nor is completed therein. In the words of the Prologue, the 'busynesse' of the saint continues in heaven."

To be sure, Kolve has no quarrel with Grennen and Rosenberg for proposing that *The Second Nun's Tale* illuminates *The Canon's Yeoman's Tale,* but he does not think that illumination "significantly reciprocal and retrospective." He considers *The Second Nun's Tale* the "most absolute of the Canterbury narratives—uncompromised by irony, unmediated by larger context, and uncolored by the idiosyncrasies of a personal narrative voice." And he believes that

> Chaucer chose to begin the concluding movement of *The Canterbury Tales* with it precisely because it is *about* clarity, light, brightness, fire.

It exemplifies the *claritas* of truth . . . the light this tale casts upon the darker corners of what is to come . . . is like a searchlight moving outward from its source, not a candle whose flame is made brighter by reflection within a hall of mirrors. The legend of St. Cecilia might more accurately be said to imply a Christian answer to the alchemist's failure—the possibility of spiritual conversion and moral change—than a Christian parallel to their vision of success. I think it is a mistake, however, to read the tale in terms of that relationship only. The legend itself is powerful and complex, in ways that can be lost to us if we focus our attention too exclusively on what lies ahead.

Professor Kolve's esteem for *The Second Nun's Tale* is as refreshing and as well founded as it is unusual. I suggest, however, that his difficulties about this "forward reading" of the tale would be greatly lessened by taking a larger view of the "contrariness" of the tales than he has done, or indeed than Rosenberg and Grennen have proposed. He has been most perceptive, it seems to me, in suggesting that Cecilia's work of conversion is an answer to (a contrary of) the alchemist's failure to "convert," to transmutate. But, as should by now be apparent, I would read such "conversion" as the radical remaking of the Christian soul through grace rather than as the change of belief; as faith fulfilled by grace rather than as faith taken alone. Kolve bends slightly to our modern tendency to separate the intellectual side of true religiosity from the moral in allowing himself the redundancy of distinguishing "spiritual conversion" and "moral change."

What I am going to suggest—and this will strengthen Professor Kolve's arguments for the individuality of *The Second Nun's Tale*—is that Chaucer aimed first to establish the true kind of conversion, of transmutation, in the story of Cecilia; and that *The Canon's Yeoman's Tale* is a reflection, by a sort of parody, on this kind of conversion. The first of the two tales thus holds the center of gravity in the author's intent, while the meaning of the second stems from its sly backward glance. The Cecilia legend is not an anticipated answer to the alchemist's failure, but asserts the eternal and absolute success—God's "great work"—which is enhanced, in human eyes, by the parodic contrast that is appended in *The Canon's Yeoman's Tale*.

Before turning to the evidence for this view in Chaucer's tale of Cecilia, I wish to draw attention to certain details of *The Canon's Yeoman's Tale* that clarify the kind of contrast between true conversion and false transmutation that I believe Chaucer intended. When the Yeoman has finished telling how the Canon fleeced the wealthy priest by duping him into believing in his power to turn base metal to gold, he proceeds to draw the moral from his tale. "See," he says, "here is the reward in that gay game: it will turn a man's mirth to grief."[70] But this, surely, is an ironic echo of the theme of mourning and joy, and of pulpit lessons like those for Cecilia's station day, which asked God to "turn our mourning into joy." That echo would trigger other thoughts and sentiments, some now lost to us, about the "working" of Cecilia by which she achieved true transmutation.[71] Our study of medieval ideas of change in connection with music also sheds light on Chaucer's two lines immediately preceding: "If a man has money, he can easily learn how to multiply it into nothing!"[72] This contrasts St. Augustine's ideal rhythm, which would reduce the multiplicity of worldly desires to the unity of union with God, of which Cecilia is an exponent, with the Canon's rhythm, which would reduce multiplicity to nothing, to zero.

A glance at some of the sermons preached about Cecilia in the fourteenth century will reveal that the idea of describing her work of converting (again, with the sense of total, interior conversion) in terms consistent with an alchemical enterprise did not originate with Chaucer. Indeed, the idea was close to the surface of the *Passio* itself. It would have been hard, for instance, not to think alchemical thoughts while reading Cecilia's answer to the officers sent by Almachius to induce her to sacrifice to Jove. And this was a text Christians had been reading for nine hundred years before Chaucer. When these *apparitores* wept that one so young and beautiful chose thus to die, and pleaded with her "not to turn such beauty into death," Cecilia's reply was full of the imagery of transmutated metals: "This does not mean to lose one's life, but to change it;" she told them, "to give clay and to get back gold; to give a lowly dwelling and receive a spacious palace built of precious stones and gold; to give a dark little corner and receive a bright court shining with pearls; to give something that will perish and to receive something that knows neither end nor death; to give a common stone that is trodden underfoot and get back a gem which gleams and shines in a royal crown."[73] And she went on to ask them if they would not run to the shop of a merchant who offered gold coins in exchange for bronze, rejoicing at such a *commutatio*. When she had finished speaking she climbed upon a stone that lay at her feet, as if to mark the starting point of the great change she offered, and received the declaration of faith from all around her: "'Do you believe what I have said?' But they all answered together: 'We believe that Christ, the Son of God, is truly God. . . .' 'Go and tell the unhappy Almachius,'" she cried, "'that I ask for a delay to my martyrdom, so that I may bring to my house those who will make you all sharers in eternal life.'"[74] And when Pope Urban came, he baptized more than four hundred souls.

Hardly any of these details appear in Chaucer's telling of the story, but that is not to say that they were not otherwise known, discussed, and preached about.[75] Two Dominican preachers who were active in the early-fourteenth century, Jacobus de Losanna and Johannes de Biblia, discussed this alchemical passage of the legend in sermons for Cecilia's feast day.[76] Both, furthermore, made use in the same sermons of Proverbs 31:10–31, the famous verses in praise of the "valiant woman" which formed a popular preacher's quarry for biblical texts and images to apply to women saints. Used by long tradition as the lesson for the Common Mass of Holy Women (the Mass, that is to say, for female saints who were married, or otherwise not virgins), the passage was perhaps less usually applied to virgins. (It is not the lesson for Cecilia's feast day, which is rather from Sirach 51:13–17.) But since Cecilia was often held up as the one saint who, like Mary, practiced perfection in the three conditions of virgin, spouse, and widow, the application of the text to her is not surprising. The passage from Proverbs is the encomium of the virtuous wife, the valiant woman, the *mulier fortis*. Her husband has entrusted to her the management of his house; her price is above pearls; she seeks wool for the weaving of garments; she knows that her trading, her *negotiatio,* is profitable; she trades to advantage with the Canaanites, a great mercantile people. The passage crafts a portrait of the wise and capable woman who manages the affairs entrusted to her with unsurpassed skill, who turns everything into profit.

There is reason to suspect that this pericope, along with Christ's parable of the children playing in the marketplace (which contains one of the more evocative texts of mourning and joy, used by Gerson at the beginning and end of his *Tractatus de canticis* to describe the great transmutation that Christ's redeeming work made possible), underlies one of alchemy's murkier references to transmutation, namely the tag *opus mulierum et ludus puerorum.*[77] This is not to suggest (nor, indeed, to rule out) that our preachers thought about alchemy when they cited these passages. It is meant to suggest that there was a solid basis for such thinking which might easily have come to Chaucer's attention and led him to link the two tales of Fragment G.

The Dominican Johannes de Biblia, who was attached to the great convent of St. Dominic in Bologna for roughly the first four decades of the fourteenth century, cites the "alchemical" passage of the *Passio* in one of his several sermons on St. Cecilia.[78] Beginning from a discussion of Cecilia's "evident beauty," her *pulcritudo spectabilis,* he protests that she is to be praised for her spiritual beauty, not that of the flesh, and describes her as knowing only too well, in the words of Proverbs 31:30, that "winning ways are vain, and beauty a snare."[79] Like the woman of this famous passage, he goes on, she was a "wise dealer who turned these gifts into something better [*tamquam sapiens negotiatrix ipsas in melius commutavit*]." God gave her a corruptible beauty so that she might acquire one that was incorruptible, and it was for this reason that she responded as she did to the officers come to summon her before the judge. When they wept that she was doomed to die, she told them that she was not losing life but changing it, giving dross to receive gold, giving something perishable to receive something that would endure forever.

In the very next sermon in the same collection, also on St. Cecilia, Johannes delves deeper into Proverbs 31:10–31. Some of it is in similar vein, explaining what is implied by Cecilia's beauty. Some of it offers us quite specific explanations of details in Chaucer's poem and in Raphael's painting—why Chaucer calls Cecilia "round and hool in good perseveringe," for instance, and why Raphael painted her with an ornament on her arm, and with sandals on her feet when the other saints in the painting are barefoot. Most arresting is the Bolognese Dominican's description of Cecilia's spiritual functions in explicitly musical terms. But of these passages more will be said in the proper place.[80]

Jacobus de Losanna, another Dominican of the same generation (d. 1322), referred to this passage of the *Passio* in a more oblique, yet even more suggestive way, again in a sermon for the feast of Cecilia. From the words Christ spoke before raising Jairus's daughter to life—"The girl is not dead, but asleep"[81]—Jacobus leads his congregation to a consideration of the life of sanctifying grace. By God's gift, he says, citing Augustine, the soul lives through grace just as the body lives through nature; and as the body lives while it has a conjoined soul, so, too, with the soul, which cannot die by sin while it is joined through fervent charity with Christ. Almachius, he continues, tried to induce Cecilia to sin by sacrificing to idols, but failed because she was so perfectly joined to Christ in love. Here Jacobus introduces a singular "example from nature" (*exemplum ex natura*), suggested to him by the episode of Cecilia's dialogue with the judge's *apparitores,* in particular by her climbing upon a stone to receive the declaration of faith that led to the conversion of the four hundred souls. He says nothing of her "alchemical" statement that she does not lose life but changes it, that she gives dross and gets back gold. Rather his attention is completely upon the image of the stone and the power it symbolizes for him.[82]

Jacobus's exemplum is less exotic than it at first seems, being taken pretty much exactly from Pliny's and Isidore's descriptions of asbestos and its fire-resistant properties.[83] Both authors mention that it afforded protection against the spells (*veneficia,* which Jacobus has described as *incantationes*) of magicians, but only Isidore refers to its use in fire-resistant clothing. As an example it serves the preacher well, giving solidity to the image of a Christ who lends life and power to the soul that rests upon him. Cecilia's power over the fires of lust is matched by her power over the fires of the bath in which she was plunged, powers that come from Christ with whom she is conjoined in love. None of this is explicitly alchemical in character (though the example seems to suggest magic). But, as the preacher makes amply clear, there is another power Cecilia displays, transmitted to her from the rock on which she stands, and that is the power to convert, which is after all the power to change and transform. As with the sermon of Johannes de Biblia, this is fertile ground for direct alchemical reference.[84]

Of great interest in the present context is the preacher's reference to Cecilia as able to resist the powers of the singers of hell. Jacobus draws a parallel with a popular belief that this substance, or stone, conferred power to resist the incantations, the sung spells, of magicians. Quite evidently, Cecilia was perceived at that time, the beginning of the fourteenth century, as a musical figure.

Even if there is no overt reference in the sermon to alchemy or its powers, its imagery fits alchemical processes, and the stone itself may recall one of the powerful stones of alchemy, in particular the fourth and most precious of all, the so-called angelical stone. Elias Ashmole's description of the power of this stone in his summary of St. Dunstan's *De philosophia occulta* recalls the spiritual powers exercised by Cecilia: "A stone that will lodge in the fire to Eternity without being prejudiced. It hath a Divine Power, Celestial, and Invisible, above the rest; and endows the possessor with Divine Gifts. It affords the Apparition of Angels and gives the power of conversing with them, by Dreames and Revelations: nor dare any Evill Spirit approach the Place where it lodgeth. Because it is a Quintessence wherein there is no corruptible Thing: and where the Elements are not corrupt, no devil can stay or abide."[85]

Whether these or any other preachers of Chaucer's time intended to compare alchemical transmutation to Cecilia's power to convert is a question that must await a more exhaustive study of a much greater number of sermons. But one can at least feel sure that there was a solid basis for such a comparison, and that even if the idea of making it originated with Chaucer himself there was already a world of reference that it would evoke to the delight and instruction of his readers. I wish to proceed now to such a reading of those passages of Chaucer's tale where the results of this study of the saint's cult can be brought to bear most advantageously. Though Chaucer's tale of Cecilia is shorter than the *Passio,* in other respects they differ hardly at all. The Prologue, however, with its three distinct sections (the first four stanzas, elaborating the contrast of Idleness and Busyness, which I shall call the preface; the invocation to Mary; and the interpretation of Cecilia's name), represents a considerable addition to the legend itself and will receive most of my attention.

Chaucer does not mention Cecilia before the last line of the preface. Until then, his concern is the vice of Idleness, for which he declares the "busyness" he has spent upon his translation to be an antidote. Near the end of the Prologue, spelling out the qualities he finds in Cecilia's name, he proclaims that she is the model of Christian works and working; that as people look to the heavens and see there sun, moon, and sundry stars, so in Cecilia they see the magnanimity of faith (the sun), the clarity of wisdom (the moon), and "sundry works, bright of excellence" (the stars). She was in this like the heavens themselves: as they are—so the philosophers tell us—swiftly moving, round, and ever-burning, so, too, was Cecilia. For she was "swift" and "busy" in "good working," "round and whole in persevering," and, finally and most importantly, "burning ever in charity full bright." Her "working" led, as it was bound to do, to perfect love of God.

It was not entirely by free poetic choice that Chaucer began his Prologue with Idleness, and ended it with the image of perfect charity. It was plain Christian teaching that Idleness (sloth, *acedia*) becalmed the soul, and that the only escape was the working of charity, which would result in joy. The contrast of Idleness with Working (or "busyness") has been closely discussed by Chaucerians, but not, I think, exhausted. That the terms are contraries is obvious (the poet himself points it out in the first stanza), as is also the association of "working" with alchemy, whose transmutations and operations were very commonly labeled the "work" or the "great work." Chaucer makes precisely this reference throughout *The Canon's Yeoman's Tale*.

Cecilia's "busyness," many would say, is based on the passage of the *Passio* in which St. Urban commended her as "a busy bee" following the conversion of Valerian.[86] This view would generally restrict "busyness" to the performance of good deeds and charitable works, to the active life traditionally characterized by Martha's being "busy about many things." *Operatio,* however, has a much wider sense in spiritual discourse. Indeed, Gregory the Great used it as the second of the three stages of the spiritual life: purgation, "working" (*operatio*), and contemplation.[87] What seems to have escaped the eagle vision of the Chaucerians, however, when they consider Chaucer's contrasting of Idleness with the busy Cecilia, is the traditional association of Idleness with Sadness, that is, of *acedia* (or Sloth) with *tristitia*. John Cassian had listed *tristitia* and *acedia* as distinct vices, but Gregory the Great combined them into one, under the name of *tristitia,* and they generally remained thus compounded thereafter.[88] This identification of "sadness" and "sloth" means that Chaucer's view of Cecilia's "working" may encompass a motion broader in scope than mere movement from inaction to action; it may in fact be seen as the motion from sadness to joy, the kind of "increase" that is the opposite of that which the Canon wrought in his crucible and which caused the Yeoman to complain so bitterly that it changed mirth to grief: "A mannes mirthe it wol torne un-to grame."

John Cassian's definition of *acedia* as "anxiety or weariness of the heart [*anxietas sive taedium cordis*]" again draws attention to the activity of the heart as the principle of Cecilian devotion. The "working" that Cecilia practices is in fact the working of the heart, spiritual working, nothing less than motion within the heart, just as spiritual sloth (*acedia*) is in essence a weariness, an inertness (*taedium*), within the heart. These notions of weariness and sadness remained essential parts of the concept of spiritual sloth through the Scholastic age. Aquinas, for instance, defined it as "weariness in working well [*taedium bene operandi*]" and "sadness about spiritual good [*tristitia de bono spirituali*]."[89] Since joy is one of the essential, and principal, effects and characteristics of charity, which Chaucer has set as the term of Cecilia's "working" (see the very end of the Prologue), the equation of that "working" with motion from sadness to joy within the heart is seen to have a firm theological basis.[90]

Aquinas's lucid presentation of the nature of *acedia,* in the thirty-fifth question of the *Secunda secundae partis* of the *Summa theologiae,* explains precisely how and why this vice keeps the soul becalmed in spiritual sadness and torpor, unwilling to move to the joy that charity brings; and in doing so explains many of the symbols within Cecilia's legend and in Chaucer's retelling of it. St. Thomas begins his discussion by citing St. John Damascene on *acedia* as a kind of sadness, explaining that "it so depresses the soul that no action is pleasing to it; just as those things which are acidic are also cold."[91] The discovery of the mineral acids is regarded as one of the chief scientific advances of the thirteenth century, and observers were undoubtedly astonished that a substance not hot in itself could yet generate heat.[92] St. Thomas quotes John Cassian's warning that *acedia* is a particular peril to monks, in part because of the routine of their lives, and that its danger is greatest about the middle of the day: "*Acedia* will unsettle a monk about the sixth hour, like a fever bringing burning heat to a sick person as it runs its preordained course."[93] The terms of the analogies and the metaphors change, but the point remains clear: the vices are accompanied by disordered temperatures, while Cecilia in her graced virtue, and working against the diseased coolness of spiritual torpor, retains a supernatural coolness against both the heat of lust and the bath of martyrdom. And the remedy proposed for this *acedia* is another Cecilian characteristic: perpetual contemplation of divine things, "keeping the gospel in her heart" and "praying night and day." "The more we think about spiritual things," says Aquinas, "the more pleasing they become to us, and this causes *acedia* to vanish."[94]

In discussing whether *acedia* is a particular vice, or whether it pertains to all the vices, St. Thomas states that it is a form of sorrow, and that its contrary is joy. He does so in presenting an objection to the view that it is a particular vice, the ground being that joy, its opposite, is not a particular virtue. But he answers that objection by offering an enlightening distinction. *Acedia* is sadness concerning spiritual good (*tristitia de spirituali bono*). If spiritual good is understood in the general and broad sense, there is no basis for regarding *acedia* as an individual vice. But in the sense that all the spiritual goods encompassed in the acts of the individual virtues are ordered to the one supreme spiritual good (namely, the divine good) and that there is a particular (and supreme) virtue relating to this good (namely, the virtue of charity), it can be said that *acedia* is indeed a particular, individual vice. "To be sad concerning the divine good, about which charity rejoices," concludes Thomas, "pertains to a particular vice, which is called *acedia*."[95]

Explaining how *acedia* can be a mortal sin, Thomas asserts that it breaks the commandment to keep holy the Sabbath, which enjoins the mind to rest in the Lord: sadness of mind concerning the divine good is of course contrary to such rest, and therefore breaks this commandment. Here one can usefully recall Augustine's comment on Psalm 37, the psalm "in remembrance of the Sabbath," which formed the introit for the station day at S. Cecilia in Trastevere.[96] The soul remembers only a peace that is absent. This, then, was a song of David when he felt the need for and the absence of that peace and rest.

Two final observations of St. Thomas about the workings of *acedia* are pertinent. Among the "daughters" of *acedia*, *otiositas* holds a prominent place. But this is idleness explicitly, the source of that personified Idleness, or *Oiseuse*, who is the portress at the door of the Garden of Déduit in the Romance of the Rose, and who is presented in the first line of the Prologue to *The Second Nun's Tale* as the clear contrary of what Cecilia stands for. Of this more will be said shortly. The second observation is innocent and unremarkable in itself, but singular in the context of St. Cecilia. In explaining how and why *acedia* is a sin, and in response to John Cassian's remarks about monks at midday, St. Thomas lays down the standard Aristotelian-Scholastic doctrine of the workings of the sensitive appetite. The passions of the sensitive appetite, he says, can in themselves be only venial sin;

but they can incline the soul (through its full knowledge and consent) to mortal sin. Because the sensitive appetite has a bodily organ, it follows that through change in the body (*per transmutationem corporalem*), a man can be rendered more susceptible to sin. Therefore it can come about that by certain corporeal transmutations that occur at particular times, certain sins can assail us more vigorously. But every bodily lack disposes one to sadness; thus it is that those who are fasting are more vigorously attacked by *acedia* about midday, when the sun is hot and they are feeling the lack of food.[97]

When Thomas speaks here of bodily organs, of human physiological instruments and processes, he is speaking of the instruments through which the soul effects and expresses transmutations, or, to use another term, of the instrumental causes of those changes. Though he does not say so explicitly here, the medieval view was that such changes within the body, within the microcosm, were effected according to musical laws. Since Cecilia was so closely associated with the soul's changes from sadness to joy —with what I have called the fluxes of sadness and joy—one is led to wonder if the *cantantibus organis* passage might not have been understood to refer to such musical instrumentality within the soul and its organs. Musical organs were in origin, after all, precisely that: instruments of music, the instrumental causes of music and its motions. Bodily organs were instruments of bodily transmutations, the instrumental causes through which the soul's appetites expressed their motions. It may seem incongruous to us in the twentieth century, when the distinction between "organs" as musical instruments and "organs" as bodily instruments is such a wide one, to propose that, because both suggested motions of the soul to the Middle Ages, the musical organ might have been an eloquent symbol of the instrumentality through which changes were wrought in the human soul. There are good reasons, however, for thinking that such was the case.

In a collection of anonymous sermons by Benedictines, from the late thirteenth or early fourteenth century, there is a sermon for St. Cecilia that moves directly from its chosen text, the *cantantibus organis* passage, to a discussion of the different kinds of impetus that the soul is subject to. " '*Cantantibus organis* Cecilia the virgin sang to the Lord in her heart, saying: Lord, let my heart and my body be spotless lest I be cast into confusion.' As Blessed Gregory says, in the elect and the reprobates there are

different impetuses. For the elect follow the impetus of the spirit, the reprobates are ruled by the impetus of the flesh. But the impetus of the spirit is
to spiritual things, that of the flesh to fleshly. The former is to interior gifts,
the latter to exterior."[98]

This is a sermon, then, about the war of the members, about the salu-
tary impetus or impulse of the spirit (the effect of grace within the soul)
and the destructive impulse of the flesh, of unhindered carnal urgings. It
is only by following the former, by admitting the rhythms of peace and
concord, that the soul can achieve harmony. Something similar has already
been encountered in the remark of Camilla Battista da Varano, when her
time of trial ended and she felt the joy of spiritual nuptials, that it was like
"a going to nuptials while instruments pulsed [*uno andare a noze pulsantibus organis*]." Highly cultivated as she was, Camilla knew the implications
of impetus and impulse for the *cantantibus organis* passage, and substituted
pulsare for *cantare* to delineate the "musical" effect of grace upon her body
and spirit. Something of this is reflected also in Dante's statement that
the divine influence is transmitted through the hierarchy of the spheres,
"these organs of the world." As organs, they are instruments in effecting
motion, but they nonetheless operate within musical law and actually emit
a cosmic music.[99] Whether or not one accepts such an interpretation of the
cantantibus organis passage, there seems little doubt that the "working" and
"busyness" of Chaucer's Cecilia implied much more than a mere unspecific
activity intended as a counterbalance to inactivity and laziness. His styling
Idleness "the minister and nurse unto vices" confirms Aquinas's teaching
that *acedia* permeates all the sins.[100]

How original was Chaucer when he compared and opposed Cecilia to
Idleness, the portress at the entrance to the garden of Déduit? There is,
over the door of the choir in the Cathedral of St. Cecilia in Albi, a statue
(fig. 6.1) that provides a strong visual confirmation of Chaucer's idea, suggesting that he may simply have been repeating a traditional view of the
saint. The statue, in polychromed stone, dates from the end of the fifteenth century, hence somewhat later than Chaucer's time. It shows Cecilia
dressed as a noblewoman, crowned with flowers, holding a palm in her
right hand and a portative organ—its pipes reversed—in her left. What
is most distinctive about the statue, however, is its location, its relation to
what is around it. It stands just within, and over the entrance to, the choir,

Figure 6.1. *St. Cecilia as Portress*

(Coecilia Albigeoise)

A polychromed stone statue of St. Cecilia, carved c. 1485, stands above the inner side of the entrance to the choir of Albi Cathedral. Her position as portress recalls Chaucer's contrast of Cecilia with the figure of Idleness, who was portress of the Garden of Déduit in *The Romance of the Rose*.

Mourning, Joy, and Music

on the inner side of the *jubé,* or rood-screen, very much in the position of a doorkeeper, and presides over a throng of seventy small angels standing in their niches about the choir walls. Above the door on the outside of the *jubé* is a large crucifix, with figures of John and Mary, and Adam and Eve, beside it.[101] The overall intent is obvious. Outside the choir we are still in the world of salvation. The first sinners are here, outside the gates to paradise, and above them is the Crucified One through whom sinners find their way to redemption. As one passes through the portal, immediately above and within is Cecilia, holding in her hands the music that has changed the hearts of all who enter here. Her position is not unlike that of the contemplatives in the sphere of Saturn, at the point where the music suddenly becomes too joyful for Dante's human ears. It is the point, also, at which the full clarity of true vision envelops the entrants, the clarity that is the hallmark of the *virgo clarissima,* and the antithesis of the "confusion" that is caused by Idleness.[102]

Chaucer's transition from the preface to the invocation to Mary, if abrupt in execution, is not at all awkward or contrived in concept, but a carefully considered element in his view of Cecilia, and a natural outcome of the way she was regarded in the Middle Ages. The invocation is based on the hymn to the Virgin in the final canto of the Paradiso, in which St. Bernard asks Mary to remove the last clouds that hinder Dante from the divine vision and so disclose to him the supreme joy. Chaucer's version of the hymn includes the same petition, a plea for vision purified of mortal contagion and of the effects of earthly lust and false affection. The point of the invocation is not so much that the poet invokes Mary, but that he invokes her for vision, to dispel the fog of concupiscence ("fals affeccioun") and let him see with the clearness of charity. But this is a principal cult concern of St. Cecilia herself, the clarity that comes with the mutation from sadness to joy.

The third section of Chaucer's Prologue, the interpretation of Cecilia's name, is based squarely on the introduction to the saint's story in the *Golden Legend.* Here, too, the abruptness of the transition from the Marian invocation to the interpretation of Cecilia's name does not result from the poet's lack of focus, but more likely from the unfinished state of his work. The unity of concept is evident in the emphasis Chaucer gives to familiar Cecilian themes: her "light of sapience" and, more particularly, the perfection of charity that prompts the extended planetary comparison with which the Prologue ends. The final etymology the poet offers of Cecilia's name is "heaven of people." As men look up and see sun, moon, and stars, so in Cecilia the spiritually sensitive see the magnanimity of faith (the sun), the "cleerenesse of sapience" (the moon), and a multitude of good works (the stars). But he goes beyond this comparison to liken her to the great sphere of the visible cosmos itself. Philosophers tell us that the heavens are swift and round and ever burning. So too is Cecilia: utterly swift and always busy in her "working," round and whole in her persevering, and always brightly burning in her great charity, her pure love of God.

This kind of comparison, involving spherical shape and the activity of the cosmos, is common enough in medieval writing and preaching about women saints. The circle is a depiction of perfection, since (among other things) circular motion knows no contrary and thus represents the immutable.[103] For similar reasons, Pseudo-Dionysius held that circular motion represented the pinnacle of contemplation, the prayer of divine union. This elaboration of the idea seems to have been the one that most influenced Dante in his reliance on the circle as a cosmographical symbol.

Preachers certainly applied the figure to Cecilia in sermons. Johannes de Biblia, the fourteenth-century Bolognese Dominican already mentioned, did so in expounding the text of Proverbs 31:10, "Mulierem fortem quis inveniet? Procul et de ultimis finibus pretium eius." "No rare and precious thing, to be sure no valuation of any earthly goods, bears any equivalence to the worth of this kind of strength. This is why it is said, 'Far distant from the furthest boundaries is her value.' In a spherical body, the circumference is greater the further it is from the center. The universe has a spherical shape; and the Empyrean heaven, which is of the greatest size, is at the furthest distance from the center of the earth in which we live. It is there that this woman has her value."[104]

Chaucer may also have had in mind a more strictly alchemical meaning of the symbol of the circle when he compared St. Cecilia to the circling of the heavens. The circle with the point at its center was the zodiacal sign of the sun as well as the hieroglyph of gold, and as such was used in alchemical writings to symbolize transmutation.[105] Indeed, it stood for the "Infinite, Eternal One," which represented perfectly the great cycle of the universe and the "Great Work" that reflects it: perfect stillness (the point at the center) and perfect motion (the circumference). The legendary father of alchemy, Hermes Trimegistus, called alchemy the "operation of the sun" in his Emerald Table.[106]

Chaucer's application of the symbolism of the circle to Cecilia, then, should not surprise us, for it was a well-understood signifier of salient features of her cult. It could represent the highest degree of contemplation, a goal Cecilia had achieved, and for the attainment of which she was held up as a model. The circle of the visible universe encompassed all that was mutable, all that knew change, for beyond it, beyond the sphere of the Empyrean, was the realm of the immutable God. The circle was thus an apt symbol of motion, of *operatio*, of "working" (including, evidently, the "working" of alchemical transmutation), an idea which, more than anything else, seemed to receive Chaucer's attention in his characterization of St. Cecilia.

Enough has been said above about the Scholastic understanding of *acedia* and its relationship to *tristitia* to suggest that the kind of working Cecilia engaged in was more than physical activity, more than her carrying out of the corporal works of mercy. It was a deeper and broader working, a working within the heart, which moved the soul from the sadness of merely human loves to the joy that wells up from true charity. It was, in a word, the working of charity itself. This seems even truer when we take into account the way Cecilia was viewed elsewhere, by mystics like Camilla Battista and Julian and preachers like Johannes de Biblia.

Oddly enough, but perhaps not coincidentally, such an understanding of the saint's "working" has roots in a classic patristic exposition of one of the principal scriptural texts that link the motion from mourning to joy with music. Gregory the Great, discussing Job 30:31 ("my harp is turned into mourning, my organ into the voice of those who weep") in the *Moralia in Job,* explained the harp as "good working [*bona operatio*]" and the organ as "good preaching [*bona praedicatio*]." [107] The demands made on the human person by the precepts of the gospel must be properly balanced, neither too slack nor too tense, and thus resemble the tuning of the *cithara* if it is to sound well. And the organ, whose sounds are produced by air through pipes, is a worthy symbol of the proper pronouncement of the word of God, which comes through the action of the spirit of God within. Gregory's exposition of this text would seem to offer a ready explanation of the organ's appearance as Cecilia's symbol—she nourished the word within, and preached it to others, a model of the Dominican injunction *contemplata aliis tradere*. Even more attractive is the suggestion of *operatio* as the middle step of spiritual progress, following Gregory's listing of the three steps as purgation, *operatio,* and contemplation, for this is the meaning to be found in the organ that hangs upside down in Cecilia's hands in Raphael's painting.

Yet Gregory is too remote for us to allege any direct influence of this passage on the appearance of the organ among Cecilia's emblems, and eventually as her principal emblem. Indeed, though repeated by later writers, the passage seems to have been taken over in rather mechanical fashion and not to have been the subject of further elaboration. But its indirect influence is another matter. *Operatio,* "working," is in a very deep sense divine working within the heart, which is itself a species of motion within the microcosm of the soul, a motion that in earlier belief could take place only in accordance with musical laws and that was defined as the flux of the contrary passions of joy and sadness. While the biblical expression of this "working" was found in several often repeated scripture text, its perfection was declared by the text from Esther that had its place in the liturgy of Cecilia and that defined her as the saint in whom the working of divine love turned mourning back to joy.

images of st. cecilia before raphael

Seven

The gaze that Raphael's Cecilia turns heavenward, to sights and sounds that seem meant for her alone, is the painting's most influential detail, copied upon the faces of countless saints throughout the sixteenth and seventeenth centuries. Yet although the gesture inspired Domenichino, Guido Reni, Bernini, and many lesser artists, its use by Raphael was hardly original.[1] The thought that gave rise to it—the thought that the holy and the virginal seek the light from which they sprang—is in fact among the most ancient themes of Christian art, and is expressed in unmistakable ways in the earliest representations of virgin saints. Cecilia's origins in the cult milieu of the Good Goddess with the Eye who restored light to the blind at the little shrine in Trastevere made her doubly suited for such symbolism, and early images of her do indeed betray her beginnings as light-seeker and light-giver.[2] These images, depictions of her in absolutely stylized fashion with little to distinguish her from other virgin-martyrs, constitute the first of three stages or phases in her iconography. The second, beginning in about the eleventh century, consists of historiated scenes (often arranged in narrative cycles) and of images that attribute to her traditional emblems. These are principally the book (she "kept the gospel always in her heart"); the palm (of martyrdom); the crown of flowers (received from the angel who watched over her); the sword (of the martyr's death); the ring (for her marriage to St. Valerian, and her mystical nuptials with Christ); the throne or chair on which she sometimes sits (suggesting her authority as a teacher or preacher); and, fairly late, a bird, usually a falcon (said to depict nobility, but perhaps suggestive of her seeking the light). Third, there are those scenes that connect her with music. They begin much earlier than has been thought, perhaps as early as the late thirteenth century, but almost certainly no later than the first half of the fourteenth. In some of these she is listening to music; in some she holds an instrument, almost always a portative organ; and in others—these are generally the latest, the end of the whole pictorial development—she actually plays.

The earliest images of Cecilia are mosaics at Ravenna and at Poreč in Istria. Just before A.D. 500—about when the *Passio* was written—she appears for the first time in the mosaics of the chapel of the Archbishop's Palace in Ravenna, a small, stylized bust, one of a number of almost identical virgins inside the arch on the gospel side.[3] There is nothing in the image itself to suggest that this is Cecilia, only her name above the roundel. The appearance of these virgins and other saints in the architectural setting of the vaults and apses of early Christian churches, however, is a fact of great importance for understanding the liturgical and artistic minds that created them. The dominant position of Christ in the apse at the east end, as if coming from the orient, is evidence of the Christian adoption of the poetic language of light that is common to all the religions of late antiquity and that springs from a mythic reverence for (and worship of) the sun. But the virgins and saints who gleam alongside him and about him in mosaic are part of the process, too. Virgins especially, because their spiritual gaze was directed away from the earthly, from the material (in particular, the sexual), were understood to share already, here on earth, the life of the angels and, like them, to be in a state of special communication with God. The virginal condition, moreover, necessarily encompassed the true musical proportions transmitted through the music of the spheres. For Christians, there was a special basis for this belief in the text of Revelation 14:1–5, which tells of John's vision of the virgins singing before the Lamb.[4] For the whole of the ancient world the thought was essentially Neoplatonic, founded on the *Timaeus* of Plato, and given later expression by, for instance, Martianus Capella and Macrobius. Virgins, they held, maintained their links to the realms of light beyond the spheres, links that play a part in their association with music, too, for the Neoplatonists believed that the purest souls had the clearest memory of the music of the spheres from the time before their descent into the material world, and that these souls were most perfectly attuned to that music.[5]

This same thought is part of the background to the splendid mosaic depicting the procession of virgins and saints above the nave of S. Apollinare Nuovo in Ravenna, from about A.D. 560. Cecilia appears among twenty-two virgins who are proceeding toward Mary and the Christ-Child enthroned amid four angels (fig. 7.2). Except for St. Agnes's lamb, nothing distinguishes one virgin from another. Each is richly dressed, each holds her crown in her hands, each stands beside a palm tree, the sign of paradise, of the abode of light and of victory. Cecilia's association with the source of light accounts in part for her presence, along with other saints, in the vault of the triumphal arch at the east end of the Cathedral of Poreč, about A.D. 540 (fig. 7.3); and perhaps for the medieval wall-painting, of

Figure 7.1. The earliest known image of St. Cecilia

(Photo: Thomas Connolly)

Inside the arch on the gospel side of the Archbishop's Chapel, Ravenna, Cecilia and a group of other virgins are depicted each in her own mosaic roundel. These mosaics date from just before 500, about the time the *Passio Caeciliae* was composed.

Figure 7.2. *St. Cecilia in a Procession of Virgins*
In about 560, Cecilia appears as one of twenty-two almost identical virgins in this famous mosaic above the north side of the nave in S. Apollinare Nuovo, Ravenna.

uncertain date, that adorned the light shaft in her crypt in the catacomb of St. Callistus (see fig. 2.3). Here a large image of her, in the posture of the orant, appeared in the source of light that fell upon the worshipers below. Yet another image of her as orant was painted onto the wall of the same crypt, beside the burial niche, which now holds a replica of Maderno's famous statue. The image in the light shaft has almost completely faded, but the wall-painting has been recently restored.

One of the best-known images of Cecilia from the early Middle Ages is in the apsidal mosaic of the basilica in Trastevere built by Pope Paschal I, in about A.D. 820, following his rediscovery of her remains in the cemetery of Praetextatus (see fig. 2.5). This mosaic, an example of the so-called *Adventus in gloria* scene, depicts Christ coming from the east in the clouds of

Figure 7.3. *St. Cecilia*

(Photo: Thomas Connolly)

A mosaic roundel of the saint in the triumphal arch of
the Basilica Eufrasiana in Poreč, Istria, dates from
about 540. It provides one of several instances of
unusual spellings of the saint's name, here as Cicilia.

heaven.[6] He is the Light of the World, who will come at the end of time on
the "Day of the Lord"; who judges and rewards all men at their death, just
as he here receives Cecilia into paradise; and who sheds his light daily on
those who worship him. The saints in the scene are standing on the banks
of the heavenly Jordan, in paradise.[7] Peter is to the right of Christ, with
St. Agatha and St. Valerian; Paul is to the left, and beside him is Cecilia,
dressed as a noble Byzantine lady and wearing a crown. She rests her hand
on the arm of Pope Paschal I, who holds a model of the new basilica. Flank-
ing the whole scene are two palm trees; the tree on the left has a phoenix in
its branches. Tree and bird confirm that this is a paradisal scene; and the
phoenix is, as always, a symbol of resurrection and immortality. But it is
also the phoenix that, in Lactantius's poem, welcomes the rising sun each
day at dawn with a song of indescribable beauty.

Among the more important early medieval images of Cecilia are two Roman frescoes—one in S. Maria Antica; the other, a further example of the *Adventus in gloria,* in the apse of the little church of S. Sebastiano al Palatino. Here again, in S. Sebastiano, we find the stylized Byzantine manner of the Trastevere apse; Cecilia again is crowned, but with no distinctive emblem to identify her, nothing really to mark who she is except the inscription of her name.

In the twelfth century there was executed at S. Cecilia in Trastevere a series of frescoes depicting the life and martyrdom of the saint, and the events surrounding Pope Paschal's rebuilding of the basilica. Destroyed in a remodeling in the seventeenth century, they are known from a carefully painted copy made at the order of Cardinal Francesco Barberini and now in the Vatican Library.[8] This cycle was not, however, the first one of the saint to have been painted. An early eleventh-century series, now much faded, may be seen in the Church of S. Urbano alla Cafarella near the catacomb of St. Callistus. Such series of paintings, the beginning of what I have called the second phase of paintings of Cecilia, point to growing artistic interest in the historical details of saints' lives, and in the emblems that came to distinguish them and to figure so prominently in their cults.

Another, and more detailed, cycle of wall paintings on Cecilia's life was painted in the ancient church dedicated to her in Cologne, a church badly damaged in the Second World War but since restored and now serving as the Schnütgen Museum of Medieval Art. Though the cycle of paintings was destroyed, photographs of them remain for study. A window in Bourges Cathedral presented a series of twenty-two episodes in the saint's life, but several of the panels were destroyed and have been replaced by abstract patterns. Other cycles followed, two of them in Bologna. Francesco Francia, Lorenzo Costa, and others illustrated her life and martyrdom in ten frescoes in the Oratory of St. Cecilia immediately behind S. Giacomo Maggiore, just a few years before Raphael completed his altarpiece. And Ludovico Carracci, Amico Aspertini, Guido Reni, and others executed a famous series, which included a painting of Cecilia modeled on Raphael's, in S. Michele in Bosco, the Olivetan church and monastery that still overlooks the city from the south, and which was home to the organist and theorist Adriano Banchieri, the same Banchieri whose description of Cecilia's abandoned instruments recalls their relationship to the scriptural texts of

Figure 7.4. *Three Episodes from the Life of St. Cecilia*

(Fratelli Alinari, Florence)

Cycles of scenes from the saint's legend were common before Raphael's time. Three fresco scenes from such a cycle in the sacristy of S. Maria del Carmine, Florence, painted in the style of Bicci di Lorenzo in the fifteenth century, show her distributing her goods to the poor, preaching to the pagans as she stands upon a stone, and attending the consequent baptisms.

mourning and joy. Yet another painting that tells the story of the saint is the fifteenth-century fresco, in the style of Bicci di Lorenzo, in the Church of S. Maria del Carmine in Florence. Several episodes are shown in figure 7.4, including her standing upon a stone to preach.

Of all the cycles of the life of St. Cecilia, none can match the painted altar frontal in the Uffizi, executed by an anonymous artist known as the Master of the St. Cecilia in about 1300 (fig. 7.5).[9] The saint is shown at the center of the panel, a dominant figure in what is by far the largest picture of the series, and around her are eight paintings of episodes from the *Passio*.[10] Veiled, crowned, and with a pearled nimbus, she is seated on a throne or chair ornamented with supporting angels. Her dress is the same as that worn by the figures in a well-known manuscript of Pseudo-Bonaventure's *Meditations on the Life of Christ,* considered to be Franciscan.[11] In her right hand she holds a palm branch, in her left a book. Her position on the chair or throne need not signify only the rewards of heaven: taken in conjunction with the book she holds so prominently, it might very well indicate that she is a teacher. This function of teaching, of preaching, of converting, is in fact the predominant theme of the series. After the wedding banquet Cecilia instructs Valerian and they both receive the crowns of flowers; then she instructs Tiburtius, and with the two brothers attends the baptism of another of their converts; she stands upon the stone and receives the profession of faith of the court officers and bystanders she has just preached to; she engages Almachius in debate; and finally she is shown being beheaded in the "fiery bath." Almost every episode depicted, and certainly the story as a whole, revolves about the idea of Cecilia as the converter, the changer of hearts, as one who, in Chaucer's words, was ever busy and "working," being "fruitful" for Christ and building up his Mystical Body.

There is a wonderfully organic unity in the series thus understood, for the first image, of the wedding banquet, can be understood as referring not simply to the troubles that surrounded Cecilia's vow of virginity and the crisis that her wedding presented to her, but also to that most common and potent image of the Church as the Bride of Christ. Paul uses the image in the fifth chapter of Ephesians, immediately following his injunction to his readers to converse "in psalms and hymns and spiritual songs, singing and psalming in your hearts to the Lord." This spiritual singing is the sign of the divine unity they have in Christ; and it is a consequence of that unity that husbands must love their wives "as Christ loved the Church, giving him-

Figure 7.5. The Master of the St. Cecilia. *St. Cecilia with Episodes from Her Legend*
(Uffizi Gallery, Florence; Photo: Fratelli Alinari, Florence)
This anonymous artist, a contemporary of Giotto, painted the saint on a throne, or perhaps the chair of a teacher, in the center panel. About her are grouped eight scenes from her legend.

St. Cecilia before Raphael

self up for her so that he might make her holy, washing her with the laver of water in the word of life."[12] In Ephesians, which is so fundamental to the story of Cecilia, the laver of water is undoubtedly the laver of baptism. But baptism itself meant immersion, and immersion in the death of Christ, so that the laver in which Christ washes his bride has overtones of the waters of death that confer life, and thus of the bath in which Cecilia herself is placed and is finally and completely united with her true bridegroom.

While this worldly wedding is in progress, Cecilia is already wedded to Christ and hears the music of those spiritual nuptials. She builds up that union, she helps make it fruitful, as she goes about Christ's "great work" of change, conversion, mutation. The final scene evokes an image of Cecilia in the bath that spells both death and life, that changes one to the other; and another of her being tested by fire, and issuing from that test fully proven as true and tested metal.

The eye's progression from this panel to the central panel of Cecilia enthroned recalls Revelation 3:15–22, the letter to the seventh of the churches, that of Laodicea. The imagery of this passage may be in some measure the source of the imagery of the *Passio* and of Cecilia's medieval cult: the warning against tepidity (and hence against *acedia*), an invitation to purchase true gold (gold tested in the fire), white vesture, the "confusion" of nakedness (and of eroticism, as Kolve discusses), blindness healed (and resultant clarity), the injunction to penance, the command to listen to the voice and the knocking at the door (surely of the bridegroom without), and, perhaps above all, enthronement as the reward for those thus tested:

> Because you are lukewarm, and neither hot nor cold, I shall begin to vomit you out of my mouth. You say: "I am rich; I have acquired wealth and lack for nothing." But you do not realize that you are wretched, pitiful, poor, blind and naked. I counsel you to buy from me gold tested in the fire so that you may become rich, and may wear white garments lest the confusion of your nakedness be apparent; and anoint your eyes with salve so that you may see. Those whom I love, I rebuke and chastise. Be earnest, then, and do penance. See, I stand at the door and knock. If anyone hears my voice and opens the door to me, I will come in and eat with him, and he with me. To him who overcomes, I will give the right

to sit with me on my throne, just as I overcame and sat with my Father on his throne. He who has an ear, let him hear what the Spirit says to the churches.[13]

Apart from presenting this unified theme, the Uffizi series also contains many of Cecilia's popular emblems: the crowns of flowers, the book, the bath, the palm and sword of martyrdom, the chair or throne. Research into any of these emblems or objects (as well as a number of others that do not appear in the Uffizi Cecilia, such as the phoenix) would certainly advance our knowledge of her medieval cult. Considered together, these emblems would demonstrate that medieval society's understanding of the lives and symbols of the saints was as intricate and complex as its understanding of the Bible, and would help put to rest the facile observations often ventured in explanation of such symbols. A brief consideration of just two of these objects, the phoenix and the fiery bath (other choices would have done as well), will strengthen the view that music was not a fortuitous medieval addition to Cecilia's repertory of emblems, but was inherent in the way she was regarded in earlier times (in keeping with Neoplatonic thought and with early Christian ideas of virginity), and that the overt musical symbolism that developed around her in the high Middle Ages was a logical outcome of this earlier stage in her cult.

Though it is mentioned in the *Passio* and is depicted in several important early representations of St. Cecilia, the phoenix has not generally been regarded as one of her emblems, though it should be.[14] Other birds have received such recognition, particularly the falcon, which may symbolize her noble origins because falconry was a sport of the nobility.[15] This is surely so, but I doubt it is the whole story. Some medieval miniatures depict Chastity as a female figure holding a bird.[16] The falcon, like its cousin the eagle and its mythical relatives the phoenix and the griffin, was a bird of the sun, a classification that carried a heavy freight of symbolism in the ancient and early Christian worlds.[17] It may well be that something of this earlier symbolism carried over into medieval times, and into the falcon's association both with noble origin and with Cecilia. Is it coincidence that Chaucer, following Jacques de Voragine, derived Cecilia's name from its association with blindness, which was undoubtedly present in the origins of her cult (though neither Chaucer nor Jacques could have known this), while Chaucer's century emblematized her with a bird that was kept hooded and in darkness until it was sent aloft to seek its prey in the realm of light and of the sun? The phoenix, at any rate, in addition to symbolizing resurrection and virginity had a strong connection to light and sun, and through them to music. In many versions of the myth it was the herald of the sun, who each day at dawn welcomed the light-giver, asking him to give his light to the world. In Lactantius's influential poem, written about the beginning of the fourth century, the welcome is not in words but in musical tones of indescribable beauty. Lactantius's phoenix dwells in the grove of the sun, to the farthest east, a place that is probably to be identified with paradise. As the dawn is about to break, the mythical bird washes itself in the sacred spring of the grove, drinks a little of its water, then flies to the top of the highest tree. As soon as the first glow appears in the east it sings its exquisitely beautiful song. Then, when the sun has fully risen, the phoenix worships it by a threefold beating of its wings and falls silent.[18]

The *Passio* describes Cecilia in a way that quite possibly implies a comparison of her to the phoenix as the singing herald of the sun. After the sentencing of Tiburtius and Valerian, the former instructs Maximus in the Christian belief in future resurrection: "The body, which earthly seed gave through lust, is given back to its earthly womb, so that reduced to dust it may, like the phoenix, rise again at the appearance of the light that will come."[19] Just after this, while Maximus keeps the brothers at his house overnight to prepare for their execution the next day, Cecilia comes with priests, and the officer and his household are baptized. As dawn breaks she greets the light, calling on them all to "cast off the works of darkness and put on the arms of light" (a reference to Romans 13:12) and to go accept the crown of life that the Lord will give "to all who love his coming."[20] The scene is described with special reverence, the author emphasizing the great silence that falls upon the assembly before the light and Cecilia's solemn announcement. Shortly after, when Maximus has been put to death following the martyrdoms of Valerian and Tiburtius, Cecilia has him buried near them in a new sarcophagus on which she has a phoenix carved in memory of his faith in the Resurrection.

The simple proximity in the *Passio* of these three episodes, Tiburtius's description of the phoenix, Cecilia's welcoming of the light, and the sculpting of the phoenix on Maximus's tomb, may not seem sufficient grounds for asserting that the saint was meant to play a phoenix-like role in this episode. But the evidence grows stronger when we consider how the phoenix legend seems to have been received in Christian Rome around the time of the *Passio*'s composition. Let us consider three instances of this reception: the double phoenix and accompanying inscriptions found in the necropolis beneath St. Peter's Basilica, the phoenix in the apsidal mosaic at Sts. Cosmas and Damian, and the phoenix on the robe of St. Agnes in the apse of Sant'Agnese *fuori le Mura*. These images carried far more detailed meanings to their viewers than did, say, the simple palm that signified victory at so many Christian burial sites in Rome. Thus, while the phoenix always and primarily signified resurrection, many other elements of the legend were evoked by the architectural setting of these examples.

Close by the remarkable double phoenix she discovered in the Vatican necropolis, and evidently associated with it, Margherita Guarducci found early Christian inscriptions that bear witness, if her reading of them is correct, to the mythical creature's role as herald of the sun.[21] She dated her discovery at about A.D. 300. The curious drawing shows a head of Christ from the upper part of which arise two phoenix heads inscribed to indicate that one is the dying, the other the living, bird. Van den Broek adumbrates, but does not develop, the idea that this particular drawing signifies not just Christ as an individual, but also those who live a new life because of him.[22] That this must be so is due in the first place to the pervasiveness in the early Church of the doctrine of the Mystical Body, the belief that the Christian's new life in Christ had already begun at baptism, and that the baptized formed with him one organism.[23] The artist who left this rough outline on the wall of the tomb of the *Valerii* was declaring his belief not simply that Christ himself had risen, nor that those buried here would rise again bodily at some future time, but that they already lived with Christ a new life that would be completed and perfected when he came again. In the second place, the attestation of the inscriptions that this bird sings to welcome the light means that the bird is not exclusively the individual Christ, for Christ is the light that is welcomed. The members of Christ—the dead Christians who have cast off their old life to live with him—are in some way included in the meaning of this Vatican phoenix. As the bird sings to welcome the light, so they, too, herald and welcome the light that is Christ, now shining upon them as never before.[24]

St. Cecilia before Raphael

Thus understood, Guarducci's findings lend new meaning to some of the better-known examples of the Christianized phoenix, such as the phoenix carved on early Christian sarcophagi in the scene known as the *Traditio legis*,[25] and even more the phoenix in the apsidal mosaic of Sts. Cosmas and Damian. This is the earliest and most beautiful example of the so-called *Adventus in gloria* scene (which derives from the *Traditio legis*) and was the model for the apsidal mosaic in S. Cecilia in Trastevere (fig. 2.5). Mosaic has an advantage over carved marble of allowing the artist to depict a sky of deepest blue against which the majestic Christ stands, emphasizing that this is his coming—a true *adventus domini*—as the light of a new day. It is of course the "day of the Lord" of biblical reference, but not just his coming at the end of time: it is equally his coming into the Christian soul through faith and at baptism, and his daily sacramental coming through the liturgy to those who worship here. If one accepts Van den Broek's conclusions that the phoenix indeed greets the sun in Lactantius's version of the myth, corroborated for Rome by Guarducci's discovery in the Vatican necropolis, then the phoenix that sits atop the palm tree on the left-hand side (the liturgical north, or gospel, side) of the mosaic in Sts. Cosmas and Damian can be understood as signifying not simply "resurrection," as practically all commentators have it, but as having a far richer sense that includes its welcoming of the sun—that is, of Christ—at its coming, its advent. This understanding in turn leads to provocative questions about the placement of these figures in the apse of the basilica.

By transferring the scene from sarcophagus to apse, the artist sought, on the one hand, to emphasize the deeper theological implications of the notion of Christ's advent: that it is not just a single and future event but a continuing and ever-developing one within the Christian community and in the individual soul; and, on the other, to underline the correspondence between the scene and this particular liturgical setting. Gregory the Great, who must have seen the liturgy celebrated many times in Sts. Cosmas and Damian, and who stood so often at the center of its apse as he celebrated that liturgy himself, immediately below the great figure of Christ and flanked by attendant clergy, may well have had this correspondence in mind when he penned his famous description of the Mass:

> For this victim preserves the soul, in a singular way, from eternal ruin by renewing for us, through a mystery, the death of the Only-begotten.

Though "rising from the dead he now dies no more, and death has no more dominion over him," nevertheless, possessing within himself immortal and incorruptible life, he is immolated for us again in this mystery of sacred oblation. . . . For who amongst the faithful can doubt that at the very hour of the offering, at the words of the priest, the heavens are opened, the choir of angels are present in that mystery of Jesus Christ, the lowest are joined with the highest, the earthly with the heavenly, and the visible and the invisible are made one?[26]

To the Romans in the nave who saw their bishop and clergy standing just below the great figure of Christ with his attendant apostles and saints, coinciding with them but in a different plane, Christian belief in the handing-on of priesthood and jurisdiction from Christ to those in orders must have added weight to the visual correspondence. Indeed, it is hard to avoid the conclusion that the artists intended exactly this effect when one recalls that Sts. Cosmas and Damian was not built as a Christian church, but was a particularly significant adaptation of a Roman imperial and religious building. It had been the library of the Temple of Peace, and its rededication represented "the first encroachment of the Church into the area of the Imperial Fora."[27] If this correspondence of Christ with celebrating bishop, and of apostles and saints with attendant clergy, can be accepted, it is not at all farfetched to understand a like correlation between the phoenix in the palm tree, heralding the light in song, and the deacon, one of whose primary functions was to sing the gospel at Mass. To people who knew the phoenix as a bird that welcomed the dawn with song, its representation in mosaic above and in line with the deacon singing in the ambo must have had a more extensive and richer symbolism than is conveyed simply by "resurrection." This kind of correlation between deacon and phoenix seems even more cogent if we consider the role of the deacon at the Easter Vigil. When the lights had all been extinguished and a new fire kindled and blessed, the great Easter candle was lit to symbolize the newly risen Christ. As the deacon carried the candle into the darkened church, he hailed the candle three times, singing "Light of Christ!" The tall candle was then set upon the ornate candelabrum and the deacon sang the praises of the new light in the most joyful of all chants, the Exsultet.

The third image of the phoenix that I wish to consider says nothing directly about the bird's light-heralding function, but much about its relation to the virginal and the angelic. In the apse of Sant'Agnese *fuori le mura* in Rome is a mosaic of Agnes with a small phoenix decorating the lower part of her robe, dating between A.D. 625 and 640. Van den Broek is no doubt correct in seeing this phoenix as primarily representing virginity itself, as a sign of the virgin's equivalent angelic state, marked by the same symbol that adorns the robes of the archangels in S. Apollinare in Classe, in Ravenna.[28] Yet even here one cannot rule out all reference to the phoenix's role as singing herald of the light. Agnes, not Christ, is the dominant figure in this apse, but the apse is at the east end, the end from which the light comes. And as a virgin—indeed, in many ways, the model and prototype of Roman virgin-martyrs—Agnes is the constant companion of Christ, who "follows the lamb wherever he goes" and sings "a song none else might learn to sing."[29] This passage of Revelation played an important role in shaping the Christian view of virginity and became a principal source for medieval theologizing about the virginal state. One of its consequences was the common appropriation of song to the choirs of virgins, who alone among the choirs of confessors, martyrs, bishops, and others were deemed to sing.[30] Thus the Middle English treatise *Hali Meidenhad* interpreted the passage from Revelation exactly in this sense: "no saints but virgins alone may sing in heaven; and who follows God almighty, the fulness of good, whithersoever he wends, as others cannot, though they be all his sons and daughters."[31]

One other detail of this apsidal mosaic adds to the complex of ideas that clarify the role played by the phoenix in the legend of Cecilia, while at the same time posing new and intriguing questions. It will also introduce the second of those Cecilian emblems (or "objects") whose implications for the saint's cult we undertook to outline. At Agnes's feet the artist portrayed her instruments of martyrdom: the fire from which she was, like Cecilia, miraculously preserved; and the sword or dagger that pierced her throat. The significance of a phoenix on the garments of a saint who stands, glorious and unharmed, upon raging flames, is hardly likely to have escaped the attention of its first viewers, familiar with the legend of the bird that regenerated in fire. A more difficult question, however (but certainly one that merits further study), is whether the bird's function as singer and herald can be associated with these flames. True, the phoenix in some versions of the myth sings before it dies, but the two activities of singing and dying

Figure 7.6. *Sts. Cecilia, Valerian, and Tiburtius with Singing Angel*

(Reproduced by permission of Oxford University Press from Christie, *English Medieval Embroidery*, plate LIX)

On this panel from a cope of English manufacture given to Pope Boniface VIII in about 1300, and now in the Cathedral Treasury at Anagni, Sts. Cecilia, Valerian, and Tiburtius are shown together in a boiling cauldron. Next to them is an angel, who seems to sing from a leaf of music.

seem not to have any mutual influence. The flames in which the phoenix expires, on the other hand, have themselves a regenerative power in some forms of the story. That such a power is attributed to fire should stimulate the curiosity and the suspicions of those who have been considering the influence of music and song in change and mutation.[32]

Is it possible that a tradition of this kind lies behind scenes that show Cecilia and her fellow martyrs being burned together, even though such a detail is contrary to the narrative of the *Passio?* One such scene may indicate her musical character as early as the late thirteenth century: it is on a cope, a singer's vestment, manufactured in England and presented to Pope Boniface VIII, and now in the treasury of the Cathedral at Anagni (fig. 7.6). On one of its panels Cecilia, Valerian, and Tiburtius are shown in a cauldron together, while, next to them, an angel seems to be singing from a scroll. This scene does not necessarily reflect a medieval misunderstanding of the Cecilia legend, nor a wish to economize or summarize in depicting the martyrdoms. It could, for instance, be a reference to a biblical story that gave a powerfully symbolic color to "singing in the fire," the story in Daniel 3:1–97 of the three young Israelites condemned by King Nabuchodonosor to be cast into the fiery furnace for refusing to adore his golden statue. Miraculously preserved, they were seen walking about in the fire and singing a hymn in praise of their God, while the flames devoured their executioners.

A general similarity between this event and the preservation of Cecilia is obvious, for she was condemned to the "fiery bath," as were Valerian and Tiburtius to the sword, for refusing to sacrifice to idols. A visually more specific correspondence to that story is established when Cecilia is shown standing amid flames, without any "fiery bath" or cauldron (fig. 7.7).[33] More suggestive, though, is the fact that this episode from the Vulgate Daniel formed a rather singular chant and ceremony in S. Cecilia in Trastevere during the Easter Vigil as early as the eleventh century. The later Roman liturgy almost universally took the third chapter of Daniel as the twelfth reading of the Easter Vigil, and followed it with the chanting of the Hymn of the Three Young Men in the furnace. But in parts of southern Italy at least, this reading and chant seem to have been accorded a place of special veneration in this most venerated of all liturgical celebrations, as can be judged from the character of the music and ritual. The matter has not yet been adequately studied, though various service books that contain the elaborate music and strange rubrics are known, and some have been published in facsimile. One of the more important and more interesting of these (it is in private hands and remains unpublished) is a lectionary from S. Cecilia in Trastevere, which shows that the southern Italian custom was practiced there, seemingly with its own local elaborations and peculiarities.[34]

There was, then, at Cecilia's ancient shrine in Trastevere, a tradition that gave an exceptional emphasis to the story of the three young men in the fiery furnace, not for its own sake, but—the point is an important one—as a liturgical symbol of the transformation of souls brought about by Christ's death and resurrection. As with the double phoenix in the tomb of the

Figure 7.7. *St. Cecilia Standing amid Flames*

(By permission of The British Library; Add. MS. 29704–05, fol. 160v)

This late fourteenth-century miniature from a Carmelite missal shows the saint standing in flames, without bath or cauldron. The flames of the bath, the overcoming of the flames of lust, and the flame of divine love may all be suggested.

Valerii, the question here is not of Christ purely as an individual, but of the Mystical Christ, head and members in the symbolic language of the doctrine of the Mystical Body. The story from Daniel spelled out for the worshipers of Trastevere the same lesson they knew from Cecilia's legend: that they had been radically transformed in Christ. And like Cecilia's legend, and the legend of the phoenix that was alluded to in the apse of their church, the images in which it was conveyed—whether by words or by pictures—were of a richness and density of allusion that the twentieth century is hard put to recover. And by their very nature, the implications are fluid rather than fixed. Nevertheless, this long, digressive inquiry into the images of fire and phoenix in Cecilia's legend should help to show why the spare musical allusions within that legend provided fertile ground for the elaborate musical symbolism that grew up in her cult in the later Middle Ages.

Musical images of Cecilia mark the third phase that I have distinguished in her iconography. When such images were first made is a question of obvious importance to this study, and about which there has been a good deal of confusion. Again and again it is repeated, in encyclopedias of art and of music and in dictionaries of the saints, that images of Cecilia holding or playing instruments were unknown until the fifteenth century, just a short while before Raphael painted his altarpiece. Statements of this kind are self-perpetuating; an opinion that has been repeated often enough in so many authoritative sources takes on a life of its own and finally achieves a canonized status. The case was compounded by the too-ready identification of some familiar medieval images as St. Cecilia, such as the angel playing the organ in the Van Eyck altarpiece at St. Bavo, in Gand, or Andrea Pisano's angel with rebec in the Bargello Museum in Florence. When such identifications are discredited, and shown to have been rather foolish, it is all too easy to conclude that any identification of a medieval musical figure as Cecilia is wrong. This kind of thinking seems to have led the curators of one collection of medieval art to remove the organ held by a thirteenth-century wooden statue of St. Cecilia simply on the grounds that the organ was not one of her emblems at that early date.

At least one well-authenticated image of a musical Cecilia dates from the early fourteenth century, and several others, some from as early as the late thirteenth century, have evidence strongly in their favour. I shall describe four of these early images in some detail to support my position that musical images of the saint were known much earlier than scholars have hitherto maintained, and to illustrate some of the peculiar problems that can arise in trying to make identifications of this kind. The works are a large, stone statue in the Castelvecchio Museum, in Verona (fig. 7.8); a fresco in the Church of the Annunziata, Minturno (fig. 7.9); a panel (already referred to) on a late thirteenth-century cope in the treasury of the Cathedral at Anagni (fig. 7.6); and a small, wooden statue from Wille-badessen, now on display in the Diocesan Museum at Paderborn.

Figure 7.8. The Master of St. Anastasia. *St. Cecilia*

(Museo di Castelvecchio, Verona. Photo: Thomas Connolly)

Sculpted toward the middle of the fourteenth century, this statue in tufa is the earliest image that can be said with assurance to represent St. Cecilia with a musical emblem.

Of these four images the Verona statue can be proposed with the greatest security as a true musical Cecilia. It came to the museum in the late nineteenth century along with a number of other statues of saints from abandoned churches; it belongs stylistically to a group of statues by a clearly identifiable, though anonymous, artist of the early fourteenth century known as the St. Anastasia Master; one of the churches, presumed to be the place of origin of the statue in question (though I have found no written record of this), was an ancient church of St. Cecilia that was prominent in the city's life; the statue itself is in the exact tradition of the other early Cecilias holding the organ as her emblem; and there is little possibility that the organ was added later, as is alleged of the statue at Paderborn.[35]

About the massive Verona statue, carved in tufa like other works of the St. Anastasia Master, there hangs an air of impressive dignity. It has at-

St. Cecilia before Raphael

Figure 7.9. *St. Cecilia with Angel Musicians*

(Photo: Thomas Connolly)

This fresco, executed ca. 1325–50 in the style of the Florentine Maso di Banco, once adorned the vaulted ceiling of the sacristy in the Church of the Annunziata, Minturno. It is now displayed in the sanctuary. The central figure with the portative organ should probably be identified as St. Cecilia, at least if the sacristy was originally a chapel to her, as some believe.

tracted some notice because the garment and headband of the figure are thought to portray popular Veronese dress of the time, but it has been over-looked in lists of possible early musical Cecilias. The portative organ the saint carries has several unusual features. It is pumped by a bellows on its underside rather than at the back, and it has a singular keyboard, its "black" keys being grouped only in pairs (rather than the alternating twos and threes of modern keyboards) about a single "white" key, and with three "white" keys separating each pair. The pipes are arranged in two rows, one row behind the other. The front row of thirteen pipes extends across the instrument the "wrong" way, that is, with the shorter pipes to the left as one faces the keyboard. The second row of pipes increase gradually in height, in proportion with the front row, but in reverse direction, becoming higher from right to left. This row, however, of seven pipes, extends only halfway back across the organ. The arrangement of pipes is of some importance, as it seems to signify a "reversed" organ, like the one Raphael's Cecilia carries.

If this is so (and it cannot, I think, be insisted upon, as we know so little about organs of the period: it may have been modeled on a true, working instrument of the time), this early musical Cecilia already possesses a particular symbolism that was employed by Raphael some one hundred and seventy years later.

The identification of the Minturno fresco (fig. 7.9) as a musical Cecilia, or as Cecilia at all, is a little more open to challenge than the Verona statue. It does not, for example, come from a church of St. Cecilia, but belongs to a group of frescoes from the sacristy of the Church of the Annunziata, though that sacristy is reputed to have once been a chapel of the saint. The identification of this chapel, and of the particular figure as St. Cecilia, is made in earlier scholarly writing, but evidently with no more justification than that this was the locally accepted opinion.[36] Minturno is a medieval hill town, a little inland from the ruins of the Roman Minturnae, on the coast about forty miles north of Naples and some twelve miles below Gaeta. Built in the fourteenth century (the fresco seems to have been part of the original decoration), the Annunziata was severely damaged in an attack by the French in 1799 and was devastated by fire in 1888. Restored in 1930, it was reopened the following year; since then, further restorations have been carried out on the frescoes and other works of art. The fresco in which Cecilia appears is one of a group of frescoes that decorated the vault of the reputed chapel of the saint now used as the sacristy. The artist is unknown, but the style is considered close to that of Maso di Banco, active in Florence from about 1335 to 1350.[37] During the restorations, two frescoes of this group were removed from the wall, and are now exhibited alongside the high altar. Neither is well preserved. The surfaces are cracked and gapped, and the colors have disappeared in some areas and deteriorated in others; but the outlines remain, and the content is clear.

One (let us call it Fresco A) contains twenty-two figures, the other (Fresco B) twenty-four, arranged in two rows in each case. Several figures in each fresco are playing instruments. When they were exhibited at Gaeta in 1976, the catalog described the figures simply as *Angeli musicanti*, "Angels Making Music." The accompanying text, however, at one point placed "angels" in quotation marks: "These 'angels' belong to a clearly Florentine sphere of influence, as Toesca had already asserted," indicating, it seems, some doubt as to whether all the figures are angels.[38] The doubt

St. Cecilia before Raphael

stems from the absence of wings on several figures—all of whom are, none-theless, nimbed—which suggests that these musicians are mingled angels and saints. In particular, the central figure in the front row of Fresco A, who plays a portative organ (as does the winged central figure in Fresco B) is without wings, and it is this figure that may represent St. Cecilia. If it does, it means that Cecilia is first represented as an actual performer at about the same time she is first shown holding the unplayed instrument as her emblem.

The little wooden statue of St. Cecilia in the Diocesan Museum at Paderborn, which is reliably dated about 1300, or perhaps a little earlier, presents a different kind of problem.[39] It came to the museum, along with much other important material, from the monastery of Willebadessen, when the religious houses were secularized in the eighteenth century. As the museum received it, and as its catalogers described it, the statue carried a small portative organ in the left hand. But this has since been removed, and a note added to the case in which the statue is displayed stating that this was done because the organ did not become Cecilia's emblem until the fifteenth century. I have not been able to determine whether there were other reasons for believing that this organ was a late addition to the original statue. If it was, one can question whether the statue was of St. Cecilia at all, for there is nothing else to identify her. If it was not, then we can place the first musical Cecilia even earlier than the Verona statue, perhaps into the second half of the thirteenth century.

The Anagni cope, already mentioned in the discussion of images showing Cecilia, Tiburtius and Valerian in the "fiery bath" together, presents yet another kind of problem. Here there is no question that this is Cecilia, only whether the artist intended any relationship between the three martyrs and the angel who seems to be singing from a leaf of music in the next panel (see fig. 7.6); that is, whether he meant to show Cecilia listening to music, with obvious implications for "singing in the heart" and for the contrasting of the old song and the new. Images of the saint listening to music, rather than holding an instrument or playing one herself, are an important subcategory of musical Cecilias that will be discussed shortly.

There are angels elsewhere on the vestment, but not in any pattern that would explain the presence of this one. The case is complicated by two facts. First, it is quite possible that the angel should be interpreted as reading rather than singing. Second, the angel does not sing toward the three saints in the cauldron, but away from them. This situation, however, could be explained by the overall design and the need to have the angel face forward, like the other figures on the cope. It should be noted that the cope, or *piviale,* was generally, though not exclusively, a vestment of cantors, which may explain the presence here of Cecilia and a singing angel and at the same time strengthen the view that the three saints in the "fiery bath" are a reference to the three israelites in the fiery furnace, since they, too, are noted for singing in the fire into which they were cast.

The following statements summarize the conclusions that can be drawn from our review of the early musical Cecilias, and on which our consideration of the more numerous music-related images of her from the fifteenth and sixteenth century will build. First, the Verona statue establishes fairly conclusively that musical Cecilias are known at least from the middle of the fourteenth century. Second, in view of the Paderborn statue, it is likely, though not certain, that this *terminus a quo* should be set back into the late thirteenth century. Third, it is possible that all three distinct types of musical images of the saint—one in which she carries the organ as an emblem (as in the Verona statue), another in which she listens to angelic music (as in the Anagni cope), a third in which she actually plays an instrument (as in the Minturno frescoes)—are all of equally early origin. But even if this last possibility should prove correct, it is nonetheless quite evident that images of Cecilia as a performing musician did not become common until much later.

Since I have been arguing that the scriptural texts of mourning and joy played a fundamental part in the development of Cecilia's musical imagery, I wish to note here Cecilia seems to have acquired musical emblems in stages that parallel the appearance of the musical instruments in the David-in-Penitence. Instances of abandoned instruments first occur in the David-in-Penitence in the fourteenth century, but they are few and scattered, like those of musical Cecilias. But in the fifteenth century the David-in-Penitence, very often with its musical motif, becomes exceedingly common. The case is similar with the musical Cecilias in the fifteenth century. Though not as common as representations of David-in-Penitence, they are found much more frequently than they had been in the hundred years preceding. Allowing for some delay between the introduction of the idea behind such pictorial representation and the actual artistic rendering of that idea, we are able to declare a highly probable time-frame for the spread of musical imagery in the David-in-Penitence and in depictions of Cecilia. It was the popularity of the texts of mourning and joy in the penitential attitudes of the twelfth and thirteenth centuries, most especially in the spiritual fervor that grew along with those attitudes and in the preaching of the mendicants, that led artists to depict instruments abandoned on the ground beside the repentant David: he has cast his music aside, for his joy has turned into mourning and his organ into a weeping voice. It was the application of one of those texts to Cecilia, the lesson of whose station day asked God to turn mourning again to joy and not to close the mouths of those who sing his praises, that led artists to depict an organ in her hands. It is almost as though she picked up the organ that David had cast down. And in both cases, with David as with Cecilia, this musical element enters their iconography at the same time, during the fourteenth century or perhaps a little earlier, and proliferates in the subsequent century—though much more so in the case of David, who was a more central figure in the spiritual scheme of things.

The chief questions we face as we study the musical images of Cecilia that preceded Raphael, and that constitute the iconographic tradition within which he worked and against which his painting must be seen, are questions of meaning. These questions can be clearly framed only if we carefully account for the kinds of image that Raphael knew, the kinds of image that we distinguished above: images in which an unplayed instrument forms an emblem (it may be held, or rest beside her, or even take the form of an ornament she wears); images in which she actually plays an instrument; and images in which she listens to music (whether this be the music of her wedding feast, music played by an angel, or even music she plays herself). Is there a general significance shared by the musical symbols in all these images? Or does each type represent something quite different? Or is the answer somewhere between, the different types simply adding degrees of nuance to some basic sense? Chronology might help us here. If, for instance, the image with the organ were well established before the other types appeared, we could look for some development out of that particular symbolism. But with the evidence suggesting that two types, and perhaps all three, appeared at about the same time, no such help is forthcoming.

The difficulties are in fact much reduced if we concentrate our attention on the most basic of Cecilian texts, and apply it to all three categories: "While instruments (*organa*) played, Cecilia sang in her heart to God." The derivation of this passage from Ephesians 5:18–20, "sing and make music to the Lord in your hearts," is certain. And since it is the only explicit musical reference in her legend, and was the most popular Cecilian text in liturgical use, it surely permeates all her musical imagery. The contrast the text posits between the sounding organs and her "heart's voice" is also fundamental, and it is the same kind of contrast that we encounter in the story of the repentant David. A medieval Christian familiar with the tale of Cecilia and with the liturgical texts that shaped it would have been reminded of this contrast by any of the saint's musical images, whether she was singing or playing, listening to music (whether of an angel or of the wedding banquet), or simply displaying an organ about her person as an emblem. The act of listening to music was in fact an act of inner musicalizing, an activity of the heart, just as surely as was the making of one's own audible music. All the music-making that Cecilia engages in is a reflection of her "singing in her heart": the inner music of contemplation that is at the same time the kind of music St. Paul enjoined upon the Ephesians, the virgins' music announced in Revelation, and the music of pure, virginal souls in Neoplatonic theory. The point will become apparent if we consider some examples.

An excellent one occurs in an early fifteenth-century manuscript in the Fitzwilliam Museum at Cambridge, in a historiated initial for the antiphon *Cantantibus organis* (fig. 7.10).[40] When this artist painted his picture of Cecilia turning away from the portative organ played at the wedding feast, and gazing with joined hands toward the divine light that streams down upon her, he worked consciously within the rich tradition that understood her to be singing a better music, the music of the heart. This contrast is, indeed, what the antiphon, the most famous of Cecilian texts, is all about, even on the surface. While the "organs" play for the wedding feast in preparation for the carnal marriage bed, Cecilia sings in her heart to God alone the music of the heavenly nuptials, of union with her heavenly spouse. It is the music of divine joy, that comes from seeing with divine vision. Its practitioner sees that the music of merely worldly joy is in reality a song of sorrow and mourning, and that her own spiritual music is the music of

Figure 7.10. *St. Cecilia Spurning the Music of the Wedding Feast*

(Fitzwilliam Museum, Cambridge; MS McClean 201, fol. 26)

In an exquisite fusion of text and image—the image decorates the C of *Cantantibus organis* in an early fifteenth-century breviary—Cecilia turns from the music of sadness to sing in her heart the music of joy. If one were to set an upturned *organetto* in her hands, the concept would be close to that of Raphael.

supreme gladness. If we were to unjoin the hands of this Cecilia, and set a little organ upside down within them, the conception would be close to Raphael's. This secular organ, to be sure, is being played; it does not lie broken on the ground. But Cecilia spurns it nonetheless, and the spurning is as evident in her upturned gaze, fixed on a vision none other may see and on a music none other may hear, as it is in the gaze of Raphael's Cecilia.

The same contrast is implied in any of the paintings that show secular musicians at Cecilia's wedding feast, for instance, in a panel of the early-fifteenth-century cycle of frescoes, already referred to, in S. Maria del Carmine in Florence.[41] It is easier, however, to see the reference to Cecilia's inner music, her song of the heart, in those pictures that show her obviously withdrawn into herself and listening to the music of a nearby angel. We may indeed regard the presence of the angel as a kind of visual gloss on the notion of "singing in the heart," an attempt to render outwardly what is of itself so spiritual, so inward. As a visual tradition, this motif of the angel-musician singing or playing to Cecilia goes back at least to the embroidering of the Anagni cope in the late thirteenth century, if we accept that this is a singing angel related to the three martyrs over the flames. There is no doubt that the motif is found at least in the fourteenth century, however, for there is a splendid example of it in the Breviary of Jeanne d'Evreux, dated about 1325.[42] Here, a historiated initial *C* at the beginning of the first reading of matins shows Cecilia and Valerian sitting together while an angel crowns them with flowers. Another angel sits nearby and plays a lute in the presence of a serpent, which perhaps represents the enticements of the world and the flesh.[43]

A more puzzling example is found in a miniature cut from an Italian service book of the later fourteenth or early fifteenth century and now preserved in the British Library as one of a group of twenty-six similarly mutilated fragments (fig. 7.11).[44] Within a large initial *C,* probably beginning either *Cantantibus organis* or *Cecilia, virgo clarissima,* Cecilia kneels while God looks down upon her from the heavens, blessing her. Her garb is bluish grey, her eyes are raised heavenward, her hands are joined, and with the celestial figure above, the whole is reminiscent of the David-in-Penitence composition. In front of her are three musicians: one, seated, plays a positive organ, behind which two blow on long trumpets, while another figure pumps the bellows. But these seem human, not angelic, figures, and one is left in doubt as to whether this is a secular music the saint spurns or a spiritual music that floods her heart.

The best-known and most beautiful image of Cecilia enthralled by angelic music before Raphael's altarpiece is in a work painted in about 1490 by Riccardo Quartararo for Palermo Cathedral (fig. 7.12). There is no new feature about the music, or Cecilia's listening to it. She stands calmly entranced, holding her closed book and the palm of martyrdom, her gaze turned downward toward a kneeling angel lutenist whose playing transmits to her the impulses of heaven. Yet this painting has novelties of other kinds, principally in the landscape and in the strange architectural setting. The saint stands in front of a peculiar construction that seems made up of incongruous components—an incomplete and illogical building— one of whose doors opens upon a scene not of an interior but of a garden. A landscape stretches into the far distance behind the structure. De

Figure 7.11. *St. Cecilia Listens to Music*

(By permission of The British Library; Add. MS 29902, fol. 6)

Cecilia kneeling before the divine presence resembles David kneeling in repentance. The musicians seem men, not angels, suggesting that their music is a worldly music which the saint spurns rather than a spiritual music that floods her heart. This miniature, within a large C (most likely *Cantantibus organis* or *Cecilia virgo*), is a cutting from a mutilated Italian service book of ca. 1400.

Figure 7.12. *St. Cecilia Listens to an Angel Lutenist*
(Fratelli Alinari, Firenze)

In Riccardo Quartararo's painting, executed c. 1490
for Palermo Cathedral, St. Cecilia holds book and
palm, two of her common symbols, and listens to an
angel lutenist. The door of the strange building before
which she stands seems to lead to a garden. This may
symbolize the cultivated soul, and Cecilia's position
by the door may suggest that she is its portress.

Mirimonde is probably right in understanding the building to refer to her
house, which she left to the Church at her martyrdom, but this does not
solve the problem of its inconsistency or of the inward garden.[45]

It is only after Raphael, if we leave aside the doubtful case of the Minturno fresco, that Cecilia is seen to concertize with the angels in true musical ensemble. But there are depictions of the saint being helped in her
music-making by angels, and these must rank among the earliest representations of her actually playing (again, ignoring the Minturno fresco).

On the St. Bartholemew Altarpiece, in the Alte Pinakothek at Munich, St. Cecilia plays a portative organ that is supported by a little angel (see plate 6). The anonymous artist, who is identified by this work simply as the Master of the St. Bartholemew Altar, was active from 1470 to 1510, and so of a generation earlier than Raphael's but overlapping with it. He painted a similar *Cecilia* on a wing from another altar that is now in the Wallraf-Richartz Museum in Cologne, in which the angel not only supports the organ on a strap around his shoulders but reaches out a hand toward the bellows as well. To list instances of this motif after Raphael would take us well beyond our purpose, but we should nonetheless note that its later popularity indicates that the connection of Cecilia's music with the angels had particular appeal to artists and their viewers around the beginning of the sixteenth century.[46]

If this heart-centeredness of Cecilia's music is evident in the more elaborate depictions I have presented, it is at least equally so in the standard, simple representation of her holding an organ, the kind of picture that confirms our acceptance of the organ as her emblem. These pictures are plentiful before Raphael, contrary to what has been often alleged, and the fact should be noted, since our interpretation of the Bologna altarpiece will be much influenced by our knowledge of the visual tradition of Cecilia within which its creator worked. Cecilia's organ, whether she holds it, plays it, wears it as an ornament, or stands or sits beside it, is meant always to recall the contrasting musics that began her story: the worldly music of the wedding banquet and the heart-centered music of her union with God. But because that heart-centered music is divine love and complete joy, this organ recalls also the music lost by disrupting that union, defecting from that love, and having that joy turn into mourning: the music that was lost by David when he sinned, when his organ was turned to the voice of those who weep and the crown fell from his head; the same music that the virginal Cecilia, the companion of the angels, carried in her heart, and for the restoration of which in the hearts of the worshipers her Lenten liturgy prayed.

It is important to stress that the musical iconography that had developed around Cecilia was not only well known by Raphael's time, but was also well known about Europe. This can be brought home by considering two examples that were being painted within a few years of the Bologna

Figure 7.13. *St. Cecilia Plays a Positive Organ*

(Copyright Bibliothèque Albert 1er, Brussels; MS 5648, fol. 262r)

A miniature in a gradual from the Abbey of Gembloux, painted in 1514 and thus almost contemporary with Raphael's painting of St. Cecilia, shows her seated at a positive organ. This is one of the earliest images of the saint playing an instrument other than the *portativo*.

altarpiece. One of these was small, the other the most complex of all artistic renderings of the idea of Cecilia. In 1514 Jean Massy, an artist from the Low Countries, painted a miniature in a gradual for the Benedictine Abbey of Gembloux, near Brussels, in which Cecilia is shown playing a positive organ (fig. 7.13). It is perhaps the first example of Cecilia seated at a keyboard, the first time in fact that she plays anything except her little portative organ.[47] The proximity of its date to that of Raphael's painting shows that by no means all of the development of Cecilia's musical iconography can be laid at the Italian master's door.

Just two years earlier, at Albi in the southwest of France, a group of artists finished one of the most prodigious labors in the whole history of painting when they completed the frescoes on the twelve vaults of the Cathedral of St. Cecilia. Its technical demands at least equalled those made upon Michelangelo in the Sistine Chapel, and if it fell short of that master-

St. Cecilia before Raphael

piece in inspiration it was nonetheless executed at a high level of technical mastery and exhibits a refreshing charm and sincerity. In several important respects it remains unique, not least in the intricacy and cohesiveness of its iconographic plan. It is perhaps unique, too, in that it has never been restored—its position so far above the ground preserved it from that, as well as from more malicious assault during the French Revolution. Called to Albi by the archbishop, Cardinal Louis II d'Amboise, these obscure artists painted the thirty side chapels, as well as the vaults, in an astonishingly short period of time. The painting of the vaults, an area measuring some one hundred metres by thirty metres and reaching thirty metres above the pavement, took just three years, from 1509 to 1512, as we know from the dates they added to their work.[48] Interestingly, they were from the region of Bologna, so there can be some presumption that the ideas they incorporated into their considerable treatment of St. Cecilia were in a tradition shared with Raphael.

That there is a strongly unified, though intricate, iconographic plan to the painting of the vaults has been argued by Marcel Bécamel, who took issue with a common view of art historians, as expressed by Emile Mâle, that the ensemble was put together rather haphazardly, that it represented *un programme un peu flottant.*[49] Bécamel's detailed mapping and analysis of the ceiling also help us to see that an important part of this iconography, a major subprogram, revolves around Cecilia. There are in fact two parts of the cathedral's decoration that claim the attention of students of Cecilia. One is the statue that presides over the choir, sculpted in about 1480; the other is the ensemble of musically allusive subjects in the fifth and sixth bays of the vaults.

I have discussed the polychrome stone statue of the saint (fig. 6.1) in the previous chapter, pointing out that its position over the door of the choir marks Cecilia as a portress, the antithesis of Idleness in the Romance of the Rose and so identified by Chaucer in *The Second Nun's Tale.* But the siting of the statue is meaningful in other ways. First, Cecilia here presides over a throng of seventy small angels standing in their niches at regular intervals around the choir. They are not explicitly musicians, for they carry escutcheons, pennants, instruments of the Passion, and other symbols, but they are nonetheless clearly meant as a choir, and Cecilia's position over them as a kind of leader or precentor confirms our view that her musical imagery derives from her long association with inner, paradisal, angelic music, not from a mistaken belief that she actually made audible music here on earth. Second, the statue is situated immediately below the fifth and sixth bays of the ceiling, those in which Cecilia is represented. This relating of the statue to the iconography of the ceiling, it seems to me, is likewise intentional, particularly in its linking of Cecilia to the Annunciation and Incarnation, the events in Mary's life that led the medieval Church to style Mary the Gate of Heaven, *Ianua Coeli*. But this will be understood only on closer viewing.

There is reason to think that Francesco Donnella, the principal painter of the ceiling, was a student of Pinturicchio; if so, he may well have known Raphael.[50] At least, as Bécamel points out, while the technique of Donnella's painting was new (it represents the initial penetration of the First Italian Renaissance into France), its spirit was traditional and utterly Christian, its iconographic theme was thoroughly medieval, and its creators appear as late disciples of the Italian primitives.[51] The whole vast composition comprises a summary of Jewish-Christian religious history, with a predominant and symmetrical intermingling of the Old and New Testaments. In general the Old Testament figures are found in the central parts of the vaults, while the New Testament figures and saints occupy the outer parts. But some of the vaults depart from this scheme, including the sixth, where Cecilia and Valerian share the central ground with the Annunciation (figs. 7.14, 7.15). The plan of the fifth and sixth vaults, the two that include the Cecilian iconography, is shown in figure 7.16.

In the fifth, Cecilia and Valerian stand facing each other from opposite sides. They are richly clad and crowned with flowers, and both carry books. Cecilia holds also the palm of martyrdom. Matching them to the west are the figures of Tiburtius and St. Agatha. But it is the sixth vault that compels our attention. It is the focal point of the whole design (there are twelve vaults in all), and by its position immediately above the entrance to the choir, it reinforces the symbolism of the statue of Cecilia with the organ that stands directly below at the entrance to the choir. Valerian and Cecilia kneel, each set within a great nimbus, each receiving a crown of flowers from an angel. Below them are the texts: "The angel gave a crown to Cecilia," and "The angel gave another to Valerian."[52] To the east are Mary, opposite Cecilia, and the Archangel Gabriel, opposite Valerian, over the

Figure 7.14. The southern half of the sixth vault, Cathedral of St. Cecilia, Albi

(Photo: Zodiaque, La Pierre Qui Vire, F-89630 St. Léger Vauban)

In the two halves of this vault (see also figs. 7.17 and 7.18) the crowning of Cecilia and Valerian is compared to the Annunciation. As Mary is the mother of her creator, Cecilia is the spiritual mother of her spouse; Mary receives the Word, Cecilia has the word of the Gospel always in her heart.

first words of the Ave Maria, which are the words Gabriel spoke at the Annunciation, with the addition of Elizabeth's greeting to Mary, and Mary's reply to Gabriel: "Hail, thou who art full of grace, the Lord is with thee, blessed art thou," and "Behold the handmaid of the Lord, may it be done unto me according to thy word."

Here the thought is as symmetrical as the composition. The archangel makes his announcement to Mary and she becomes the mother of Christ, though remaining a virgin; at the angel's appearance to Cecilia and Valerian, she who is Christ's bride becomes, while remaining a virgin, the

Figure 7.15. The northern half of the sixth vault, Cathedral of St. Cecilia, Albi

(Photo: Zodiaque, La Pierre Qui Vire, F-89630 St. Léger Vauban)

On the northern border of the vault is Musica, seated at a positive organ. Opposite, on the southern border (see fig. 7.16), is Theology, a woman crowned and throned, bearing a book in her right hand, a scepter in her left. The linking of the two attests a medieval conviction that the principles of music are the foundation of all that transpires in the cosmos, even of theology.

mother in a spiritual sense of her earthly husband. It is a thought that is expressed in a number of medieval texts about Cecilia. Thus the tenth-century Flodoard of Rheims, speaking of Cecilia in his poem "On the Triumphs of Christ": "opening the way completely, she conceives her pupil; with her breasts, with the milk of wisdom, she nourishes the brothers. When did it happen that, on what was believed to be the wedding-night, the one who was thought to be the bride gave birth to her husband?"[53] A related thought is expressed by Dante at the climax of the *Paradiso*, in the

St. Cecilia before Raphael

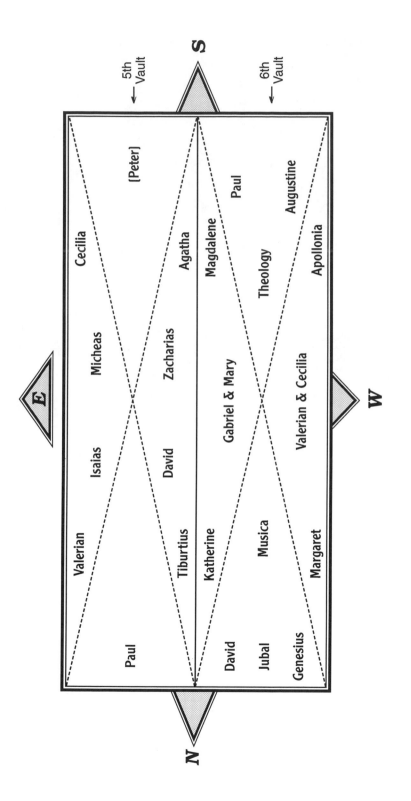

S

5th Vault

6th Vault

E

W

N

[Peter]

Cecilia

Magdalene

Paul

Agatha

Augustine

Micheas

Theology

Zacharias

Apollonia

Valerian

Isaias

Gabriel & Mary

David

Valerian & Cecilia

Tiburtius

Katherine

Musica

Paul

Margaret

David

Jubal

Genesius

first words of St. Bernard's profound prayer that God grant to Dante the power of supreme vision he needs at the final goal of his journey, "Maiden yet a mother, daughter of thy Son . . . ,"[54] which Chaucer borrowed in his invocation to Mary at the beginning of *The Second Nun's Tale*. Chaucer's borrowing indicates that he would have understood well the reason for the juxtaposition of Cecilia and Valerian with Mary and Gabriel in the Albi vaults. Dante's thought is not only that Mary became the mother of her creator, and thus gave physical being to him who had given physical being to her. It concerns also Mary's role in the bringing-into-being of the Mystical Christ, the Mystical Body. Mary's position, her singular preeminence in grace before all other creatures, was due to her share in that Mystical Body, owed (before the fact) to the redemptive work of her son. Yet that Body, along with the human body of her son, took form only on the utterance of her *fiat* to the announcing archangel. She is thus in a second and different sense the begetter of Christ's Body, of which she was at the same time a member, brought into spiritual life through the birth that came by Christ's death and resurrection. Thus she begets and is begotten by the Mystical Christ.

There is an important quality to this mothering prerogative of Mary's that finds frequent visual expression in medieval art and at times migrated into the iconography of Cecilia. It was expressed by Dante immediately after his proclamation that Mary was her son's daughter: "lowly and exalted more than any other creature."[55] Generation, the act of love and of giving, was an act of humility that at the same time conferred the highest dignity upon the giver. Mary sang this in her Magnificat: "My soul glorifies the Lord, and my spirit has rejoiced in God my saviour. Because the Lord has looked on the humility of his handmaiden; for behold! from this time forward all generations will call me blessed."[56] Grace in the form of generation for those who have humbled themselves is a constant visual allu-

Figure 7.16. Plan of the fifth and sixth vaults, Cathedral of St. Cecilia, Albi

(Design: Bob Rex)

The central position of Cecilia and Valerian in the plan of the twelve vaults, the artists' wish to compare Cecilia's spiritual generation of her husband to the facts of the Annunciation, and belief in the relation of music and theology are evident in the arrangement of the iconographic topics in the fifth and sixth vaults. The plan is here set out in the manner of a ground-plan, as if viewed from above.

St. Cecilia before Raphael

sion in medieval representations of David, and the same details are found in depictions of the Annunciation. Both Mary and David kneel humbly, while the golden rays of the divine power beam down upon them. David was of course a key step in Christ's genealogy, and there is constant visual allusion—as witness the beds in the background of scenes of David's repentance and of Mary's Annunciation—that because David has humbled himself, the divine promise will ultimately be fulfilled out of his loins.

A miniature of Cecilia and Valerian in a French breviary of the early fifteenth century shares these same visual implications (fig. 7.17).[57] The couple kneel as the angel presents the crowns of flowers. Cecilia is in the pose taken by Mary in so many scenes of the Annunciation: kneeling humbly at the prie-dieu, on which rests the book (the Word was in Mary's heart, as it was in Cecilia's), and half turning as her attention is caught by the angel. Behind her, a canopied bed with drawn curtains (again, as in so many scenes of the Annunciation) speaks of the kind of generation that her humility, her humble and unquestioning acceptance of God's will, has brought about and will continue to bring about, the birth in Christ of Valerian, of Tiburtius, of Maximus, of those she preached to, of those who came to her house-turned-church. This same implication of generation proceeding from humility is present in the overall plan of the Albi vaults, which along with its representations of David himself, and of the Annunciation linked to Valerian and Cecilia in the very center, shows ten of the twelve figures listed by Matthew in the third part of his genealogy of Christ, that part which extends from the Babylonian exile to Joseph. These are the figures found on the five last branches of the Tree of Jesse, which represent essentially the conclusion of God's plan of generation from David's repentance to its fruition in the Incarnation (Matt. 1:12–16).

What has been said in chapter 6 about music in the heart, and about music as a concomitant of impulse and impetus in medieval thinking, should leave us not unprepared for the exuberant visual statement of Cecilia's musical involvement in the same sixth bay of the Albi vaults that contains, side by side, the Annunciation to Mary and the crowning of Cecilia and Valerian. Cecilia's involvement here is not with music alone, but equally with theology. Theology appears at the southern border of the composition, as a woman crowned and throned, bearing a book in her right hand and a scepter in her left (see fig. 7.14). She is identified by the

Figure 7.17. *Sts. Cecilia and Valerian Being Crowned by an Angel:* Miniature from a fifteenth-century French breviary

(By permission of The British Library; MS Harley 2897, fol. 440v)

Cecilia's pose, kneeling at a priedieu with an open book, and with a canopied bed in the background, invites comparison with scenes of the Annunciation and recalls the way these scenes were set side by side in the sixth vault of Albi Cathedral.

words *Theologia est,* though one suspects that this tag is meant to link her to the complementary figure of Music on the opposite border of the bay, and thus to be completed as *Theologia est Musica.* She resembles closely Raphael's figure of Theology on the ceiling of the Stanza della Segnatura at the Vatican Palace, or the figure of Cecilia in the altar panel at the Uffizi painted by the Master of the St. Cecilia (see fig. 7.5). Pinturicchio, the reported teacher of Francesco Donnella, painted similar female figures to represent the liberal arts in the Borgia Apartments at the Vatican. These may have been models for Raphael's Theology.[58] The resemblance of the seated Cecilia of the Uffizi altar panel to these other female embodiments of learning is of course no coincidence, and it demonstrates the degree to which the saint was regarded as a teacher and a figure of wisdom in serious piety, the *doctrix* of medieval hymns.

Grouped around Theology at Albi are four saints, three of whom are among the companions of Cecilia in Raphael's painting of her and are also singled out in Jean Gerson's poem in praise of music. These are St. Paul and St. Augustine, two of the greatest Christian teachers, and St. Mary Magdalene. The fourth is the virgin St. Apollonia.

Paul and Augustine are represented here in incidents that involve heavenly intervention and heavenly enlightenment, just as was the case with Cecilia and Valerian at the time of their marriage. All three saints were the subject of sudden, dramatic conversion, the recipients of the Word in lightning-bolt experiences: Paul on the road to Damascus; Augustine in the voice heard across the garden wall, "take and read . . ."; Magdalene by the casting out of seven devils. All went on to become models of, even founders of, Christian contemplation and mysticism. Magdalene, customarily understood to be the Mary who sat at Christ's feet and listened to his words rather than busy herself with housework, became a symbol of the contemplative, one deeply imbued with the understanding of divine truths. This view was stressed in the rich legend that later grew up around her, in which she enjoyed the constant companionship of the angels, and seven times a day—at the time of the liturgical hours—was raised to heaven, where she heard the angels sing. The painters of the Albi vaults showed Paul in the event that so utterly transformed him, the apparition on the road to Damascus. About St. Augustine they depicted a legend that was known only from the thirteenth century on, and that tells of his pondering the mystery of the Trinity as he walked by the seashore. He observed a child pouring water from the sea into a hole in the sand, and asked what he was doing. When Augustine smiled at the child's reply, that he was trying to empty the ocean into the hole, the child told him that it was just as foolish to hope to understand the mystery of the Trinity, then disappeared.

The mystic musicality of Cecilia is the principal meaning of every musical symbol applied to her at Albi. It is also the principal meaning of the figure of Musica on the northern side of the bay, directly opposite the figure of Theology enthroned. Musica is here a woman playing a positive organ while an angel stands behind it and pumps a bellows. She is of course seated, but not crowned, and resembles closely enough those later depictions of Cecilia herself at the organ, like that in the Gembloux Gradual of 1514 (see fig. 7.13). But there can be no confusion, for she is identified, like Theology, by her name written in a large roundel. Other instruments appear in the surrounding decoration, and there are two musicians of the Old Testament, David with his harp, and Jubal, the legendary biblical founder of music, as well as another saint closely associated with music, the martyred Roman actor St. Genesius.

The Cecilia of the Albi vaults, then, like the Cecilia known elsewhere in the medieval visual arts, is a Cecilia deeply involved with music and with the knowledge of God—not with music simply in its limited modern sense of artistically organized pitches and sounds, but with music as it was understood in the ancient and medieval worlds, a science whose principles formed part of the underpinnings of both the observable and the spiritual universe. Music was in the interstices of things, it shaped the liberal arts, and it was necessary to theology both in its scientific, speculative aspect and in its practical aspect; thus music (as Gerson was the first to distinguish and insist upon) was in no way distinct from contemplation itself, nor indeed from the love of God in its purest form. She is a Cecilia whose cult holds no extraordinary mysteries, but simply demands a little understanding. Music is here not because anyone misunderstood an antiphon from her office or a sentence from her legend, but because Cecilia had come to be understood, in a way that developed naturally and logically from consideration of what her office and her *Passio* said about her, as one who had particular vision, particular access to divine impulse, particular sensitivity to all the instrumentalities of God working within the world by the proportions that He had himself established. She was, then, a true and perfect musician, who heard and sang and played the inner, divine melody.

"my eyes are always upon the lord"

Eight   Raphael and St. Cecilia

So unalike in scope and dimensions, the Albi vaults and the Gembloux miniature are at one in showing that a firm tradition associated Cecilia with music in Raphael's time, and that his Bologna altarpiece, while not without its novelties, was not quite as revolutionary in its concepts as has been supposed. Indeed, its roots go back to the foundations of Cecilia's cult, as our look back at images of Cecilia before Raphael has shown. When we come to consider the Bologna altarpiece itself, then, we need to distinguish what, of its musical content, is new, and what is old. We shall also take stock of a famous engraving, by Marcantonio Raimondi, which is generally believed to have been made from one of the early sketches Raphael prepared for the painting (fig. 8.1). In comparing the two—engraving and painting—we may be able to identify some elements in the finished work that were introduced at the suggestion of the commissioners.[1]

But before beginning this consideration, it will be well to remember that our concern is not with the painting's value as a work of art, but with its "aboutness," with its objective content and especially with its musical content. The new perspectives our study gives us for doing this will naturally affect the interpretation of other aspects of the painting—the presence and arrangement of Cecilia's companion saints, for example. But our principal focus is on the musical iconography, and on how the understanding, developed in the previous chapters, of music insofar as it signifies aspects of Christian spirituality, affects the picture as a whole. It would be crass to attempt to summarize the "meaning" of the painting, to try to encapsulate what Raphael was about in a few words (or, for that matter, in any number of words at all). Yet ideas and meanings there are in the work, and in abundance, even if their sum does not make up the whole of the painting. If I seem to give greater weight to certain of these ideas and meanings over others, this is not because I believe that I have discovered some key that lays bare the artist's soul, but only because what insights I have developed

Figure 8.1. Marcantonio Raimondi. Engraving from an early sketch of Raphael's *St. Cecilia* (Pinacoteca Nazionale, Bologna)

Elements that changed between this early conception and the finished altarpiece include the gazes of the saints and the music of the angels.

Raphael and St. Cecilia

do have important consequences for our appreciation of what it is that we are seeing.

Most striking, to me, considering Cecilia's long association with light, with clarity, with vision, is the disposition of the gazes that she and her four companions cast about them. None looks in the same direction as another; rather their gazes seem to span the universe. Only Cecilia looks up, to a point somewhere before the angels singing from the rift in the clouds, while Paul's deeply thoughtful gaze seems to penetrate the ground they stand on, a visual comment on the idea of "profundity." John and Augustine look to either side, and Magdalene looks directly out of the picture as if to engage the viewer with a look that might be termed frank, candid, questioning, or inviting. This was not how Raphael first planned his composition, however, for in Raimondi's engraving both Augustine and Paul, and John to a degree, look downward, while Mary Magdalene joins Cecilia in gazing at the heavens. In the engraving, in fact, Magdalene's upward glance is far more direct than Cecilia's distracted look.

Why did Raphael change the disposition of the five figures in this way? Like so much else about the painting, the reason must be looked for in the thought of the spiritual mentor of Pietro da Lucca, Jean Gerson. It is not unlikely that the change was made following the artist's consultations with his commissioners, perhaps even his own reading of some of the writings of the French mystic. One of Gerson's principal interpretations of his mystical gamma (the symbolism of this device permeates the painting to an extraordinary degree) is that it represents the dimensions of the universe, "the length and the breadth, the height and the depth." He was thinking not just of physical dimensions, however, but of the divine love that suffuses that universe, hidden from mortal gaze, but visible to those who see with the eyes of the spirit. For this was the point of Paul's phrase: that the Ephesians might know the *supereminentem scientiae charitatem Christi,* the love that underpins the cosmos.

This whole third chapter of Paul's letter to the Ephesians can be read, in fact, as a model, a cartoon, for Raphael's painting. Paul declares himself to be the appointed minister of the mystery of Christ that had been hidden heretofore but is now revealed: to him, the least of God's people, has been committed the grace to spread word among the Gentiles of the inexhaustible riches of Christ, to enlighten all about the economy and the working out of this mystery. He prays to God on bended knee that the Ephesians may be enriched and strengthened through the Holy Spirit "unto the inner man" (an expression of radical inner change); and (this is the central point) that Christ may dwell through faith in their hearts, which will be rooted in, founded upon, charity, so that they may comprehend "the length and breadth, the height and depth," and know "the supereminent love that comes in the knowledge of Christ." (Whether or not the mystery Paul speaks of is to be identified with this love of Christ, as the Greek Fathers maintained, that love is at least closely related to the mystery; and it is either the mystery together with Christ's love, or else simply Christ's love, that they will, if Paul's petition is fulfilled, comprehend in all its infinite dimensions.) Thus the four dimensions are the dimensions of Christ's love that floods the universe, visible only to the eyes of the spirit, of faith. It is this love—and, it is fair to presume, this mystery—that the saints of the painting take in with their all-encompassing vision.

Paul's subsequent thought leads logically to the idea that those who are thus rooted in charity, and in whose hearts Christ dwells, should "sing and psalm in their hearts to the Lord." For he goes on to admonish the Ephesians to unity (Ephesians 4:1–16), and then to discuss the nature of Christian sanctity that flows from this faith, this love, and this unity (Ephesians 4:17–5:20). Singing in their hearts is, indeed, the end point of the process, faith leading to love, to unity, to the perfection that the heart's music expresses. All of this is contained in Raphael's vision, and it is Cecilia, her eyes fixed on the heavens, on the mystery of Christ's love, who here embodies Christian perfection—faith, unity, love, and "singing and psalming in her heart to the Lord." She is thus the answer to Paul's prayer for the Ephesians, one who has experienced the transformation, the great mutation, that the mystery of Christ's love entails.

Yet before we turn our attention to Cecilia herself as she was envisioned by Raphael, we must look longer at her companion saints and their divergent gazes. That their looking indicates the dimensions of the love of Christ is a fair enough assumption, it seems, given what Gerson has said about the interpretation of his gamma. It is nonetheless remarkable that the five figures are so disassociated from one another and seemingly so uninvolved with one another. Indeed, this was a frequent objection to the composition of the painting in earlier criticism. Only Augustine seems to look directly at one of his companions, at St. John. Augustine, who left us the first explicit statement of mystical experience in the Western Church, and who is rightly regarded as a foundation of Christian mysticism (as he is of so much else), drew heavily upon John, so the look can be explained naturally enough.[2] Of the gazes of Mary Magdalene, of Paul, and of Cecilia herself, there is likewise no doubt. All three seem absorbed in attitudes that are not at all concerned with the other saints in the painting. Paul is introspective and Cecilia is caught up in the heavenly vision and music, while Magdalene engages the viewer with a look that may be frankly curious, or questioning, but is most likely an invitation. John, however, is a different case, for it is not absolutely clear that he is looking at Augustine, as most critics assert. Indeed, Shelley, it will be remembered, thought—mistakenly—that he was looking at Cecilia. It is possible that he is looking at Magdalene, which if really so would lend support to a curious but interesting speculation that the *St. Cecilia* makes reference to the legend that associated John and Magdalene as the bridal couple at Cana.[3]

We do not need, however, to probe the strange legend of John's and Magdalene's betrothal to understand the solid reasons for the presence of these four saints as Cecilia's companions, and thus to counter the old objection that the artist had brought together a group of saints who had no particular association with Cecilia and little special association with one another. Excellent reasons there are, which were no doubt suggested to Raphael by the principal commissioner, whose devotion to these saints is known. Their presence in the painting is not simply a matter of purely personal devotion, however, but is part of a coherent understanding of the four as powerful representatives of the links between music and the heights of contemplation, or of music as both expression and cause of the highest union with the divinity that can be attained by the human soul. It is for this reason that Cecilia, Paul, Magdalene, and Augustine have so prominent a place in Gerson's *Carmen de laude musicae*—a poem which, we must remember, forms part of his *Tractatus de canticis*. John's addition to the group is readily explained, for it was he who sang of divine love in his gospel and of the power of the virgins' song in Revelation. And he was singled out by Gerson as a singer of the new song, the new gamma, at the beginning of the third tome of the *De canticordo,* the second volume of his *De canticis.*[4]

This basis for associating these saints with music, the basis expressed by

Gerson in allying them with the heights of the contemplative life, is likely to have played a greater part in determining their presence in Raphael's composition than those superficial, but more commonly advanced, reasons: that the church of the commission was dedicated to St. John the Evangelist; that it was served by the Lateran Canons, who followed the rule of St. Augustine; and that it contained a chapel dedicated to Mary Magdalene, to whom Elena had a particular devotion through her work for repentant women. But it will be best to consider these saints, as they appear in the altarpiece, individually and in some detail.

St. Paul is the founder of the Christian contemplative tradition, his writings the principal source from which that tradition springs. His mystical experience began, by his own description, with the apparition on the road to Damascus.[5] It was an experience so startling that the name of its site has become synonymous not just with conversion, but with conversion in its more radical aspects, with change that is sudden, total, uncompromising, and quite unforeseen. It must have been shortly after his conversion that the experience he described in 2 Corinthians 12:2–12 took place, when he was caught up to the third heaven and "heard mysterious words which it is not given to man to utter." The passage became a constant point of reference among mystics and those who have written about the contemplative experience, including Gerson and his disciple Pietro da Lucca. But it was Paul's admonition to "sing and psalm to the Lord in our hearts" that most often caught Gerson's attention in his allusions to Paul's contemplative character. And he understood the words, as did Paul himself, as indicating in some way the expression and effects of divine love in the human soul. He mapped the dimensions, the infinite dimensions, of that love in his gamma, whose corner points mark the height and depth, the breadth and length, of that love.

Paul's downward gaze, in Raphael's painting, thus signifies the depth of divine love, but of course should not be read apart from the gazes of the companion saints, which in conjunction express its limitless bounds. It may be, however, that Raphael had something else in mind when he prepared his early sketches for the altarpiece. For between Raimondi's engraving and the finished painting, only Paul's and Cecilia's gazes kept the same general direction, and of these two Paul's was modified less.[6] Paul's head remains fixed downward on exactly the same line in both versions of the scene, directed seemingly at the broken instruments at his feet, though his eyes seem raised to a higher plane. Other aspects of Paul's figure did change more noticeably from version to version, however. Most notably, the sword moved from the apostle's right to his left hand, while the book he held in his left in the engraving became leaves of paper held in the same hand, along with the very top of the sword, in the painting. Very likely Raphael wanted to achieve a deeply pensive, contemplative look by having Paul rest his chin on his right hand.[7]

But if the look is bent toward the instruments, the symbols of the vanities and of the power over the soul of earthly, fleshly enticements, this is enhanced in the altarpiece by having Paul's sword-point thrust through the triangle. The sword here is the word of God received from the Spirit, as set forth in Ephesians 6:10–20. It is also the symbol of martyrdom, of the ultimate severing of flesh from spirit for love of God. Such martyrdom is the logical conclusion or culmination of the process indicated by the cutting off from the spirit of the flesh these symbolic instruments represent. The sword is laid to the vanities, and there ensues the process of purgation, which is the beginning of all conversion and of all spiritual progress, the first step on the way that leads on through contemplation to union. That Paul should point out this beginning with his sword is exquisitely appropriate, for it was he who gave the vanities their musical shape: "If I should speak with the tongues of men and of angels, but not have charity, I have become no more than sounding brass or tinkling cymbal."[8] Paul's words literally refer to the hollowness of witness that is not informed by love, but the worldly instruments were frequently equated with "the flesh"—not least by Gerson himself. The depth of divine love, then, that the apostle's gaze measures is one of spiritual more than physical distance: a depth plumbed not be a gaze down to the furthest boundaries of the universe, but by a gaze to the depths of degradation that the vanities imply, to which divine love willingly descended so that it might raise and transform us.

John the Evangelist, too, is here because, as Gerson described, he "heard and knew the gamma of the heart's song," putting off the old man and putting on the new, becoming like a child even, and a fool, in Christ. This was evident in his old age, when he was renewed like the eagle, speaking only of love: "Little children, love one another." In both the altarpiece and the engraving we see a youthful John; and in both, the evangelist's symbol of the eagle is apparent. It may be that Gerson's text on John was brought to the artist's attention early, and that he wanted to paint a man renewed by love. Though the inclination of the head is so different in the two versions, other details are unchanged. One notices, for instance, the pose of the left hand on the heart. Neither in engraving nor in painting does one see John's thumb. It is folded out of sight, while the fingers are arranged in the same pose in each case, the first being slightly elevated and the remaining three grouped together. One thinks first of the unity and trinity of God, but other explanations are possible. Paul, not John, said that there remain now faith, hope, and charity, and that the greatest of these is charity, yet the thought is appropriate to John.

Gerson included St. Augustine, along with Paul, Cecilia, and Magdalene, in his poem "On the Praise of Music," citing Augustine's declaration that he was so moved by the songs of the Church that his cheeks were furrowed by his tears.[9] But this metaphor is not just the expression of an emotional response to music. It is rather an expression of change, of conversion. For the whole poem is about change, particularly of the kind that is effected through divine love. Augustine's weeping is the weeping of repentance that transformed him and brought rest to his restless heart. There is no doubt of the importance of music to Augustine and to his writings. His realization that he could be beguiled by the beauty of the sound away from the contemplation of the words bespeaks a deeper response to music, not a suspicion of it. His description of his own mystical experience, in a sermon on the Forty-first Psalm, is stated in clearly musical terms, the first of many such in the annals of the Western contemplatives.[10] The music he has heard in "the house of God," by which he quite evidently means a deeply personal encounter with God, is not the music of transient earthly joys but of endless holiday in God's vision, the "sound of the banqueter" (or "the sound of endless holiday"), the *sonus epulantis* of verse 5.

This *sonus epulantis* became an important expression for later mystics, and was explained (by Denis the Carthusian, for instance) as carrying the meaning of Psalm 24:15, "My eyes are always upon the Lord." It was in seeing God eternally, without cease, that the contemplative reached his goal in the unceasing joy of the divine presence. Thus the overriding purpose of the contemplative life and endeavour, the vision of God, is described by Augustine—the "prince of mystics," in Cuthbert Butler's phrase—as a

Raphael and St. Cecilia

thrilling music, a "sweet and melodious strain" that "strikes on the ears of the heart," originating in the everlasting, perpetual festivity of "God's house," of his intimate and unmediated presence.

In all this discussion of saintly gazes, and of the equivalence for the contemplative of the "sound of the banqueter" and the "eyes . . . always upon the Lord," we must recall again that Psalm 24 expressed the same thought in its opening verse ("To thee, O Lord, I have lifted up my soul") as it did in verse 15 ("My eyes are always upon the Lord"), and that this opening verse was used in Cecilia's stational liturgy as the offertory chant, and on the first Sunday of Advent as offertory, gradual, and introit. As introit on this day, and thus as the first chant of the year in medieval mass books, it became a common site for the image of the kneeling, repentant David, sometimes with his instruments and his crown beside him, but almost always with his eyes raised to the vision of God in the sky above.

In this David we have the image of hope that is intrinsic to repentance. The music of the divine presence that he lost by his sin is promised to him again, it is there in the divine face that is again turned upon him. In his painting of Cecilia, Raphael has carried to its logical conclusion the inherent comparison of this David, his "joy turned to mourning," to the musical Cecilia in whom the flux of these two passions has been reversed. Her eyes are upon the Lord, and there strike upon the ears of her heart the "sound of the banqueter" in the everlasting holiday of the divine presence.

Between the scheme of Raimondi's engraving and that of the finished painting, Augustine's was the figure that changed the most. He wears his bishop's mitre in the early sketch, but his head is bowed forward and his eyes are hidden. Clasping a large, closed book to his breast, he is obviously deep in prayer. One notes, besides, that his sandaled foot is visible beneath his robes. In the painting, the mitre is gone, the bald, strongly profiled head is raised and is turned directly to his right. Gone, too, is the book. Instead, he holds a bishop's crozier in his right hand, while his left is raised in a rhetorical gesture. The crozier itself is richly ornate, and the vestment he wears—a cope (over a black, monkish robe) in place of the former chasuble—is lavishly embroidered with human figures. The saint's foot is no longer visible, being hidden behind the shadows and the robes.

There seems to be no one compelling reason for any of these changes. Perhaps Raphael found the bishop's mitre jarring among those otherwise bare heads, and then added the crozier because he needed to replace the lost sign of episcopal rank. Two of the new details—the hidden feet and the bald head—may have some deeper significance. If the commissioners were aware of Augustine's famous description of the music of contemplation, in his Exposition of the Forty-first Psalm, as they most likely were, they were also aware of his interpretation of its Hebrew title, "For the sons of Korah." These represented one of the family groups from among the Levites who were set apart by David for special musical duties in the Temple.[11] Augustine knew that the Hebrew root of the name signified baldness, and in this psalm, as well as in several others of the same title, he elaborates on this, relating the name sometimes to the traditional meaning of the word *Calvary,* the "place of the skull" and the site of Christ's death, at other times to the incident of 2 Kings 2:23, in which children mocked Elisha's baldness and were attacked by two bears for their disrespect. Baldness, in Augustine's interpretation, was thus associated allegorically with those marked out by God to sing his praises, as well as with Jesus' redemptive death. As for Raphael's concealing of Augustine's foot in the final version of the altarpiece, we shall have more to say about this when we come to discuss Cecilia's dress and the artist's decision to put sandals upon her previously bare feet.

None of the other saints who stand with Cecilia is as arresting as Mary Magdalene. Her gaze in Raimondi's engraving was raised to the music-making angels in even greater rapture than was Cecilia's, yet in the altarpiece this look has shifted completely. It is now directed straight at the viewer, and indeed seizes the viewer's attention as soon as one looks at the painting. Her formerly flowing, uncovered hair is now gathered up beneath a lace veil, but other notable elements of her posture, such as her firm grasp of the vessel of perfume and her bent left knee, remain the same. The gleaming, silvery whiteness of her dress (one cannot, of course, tell from the engraving whether Raphael intended this from the beginning) is another detail that serves to attract the viewer's attention to her immediately. It may also have an important symbolic significance.

Magdalene's links to music in medieval thinking are much stronger than students of Raphael's painting have realized. Unraveling those links, however, is no easy task, for her legend is a convoluted one. It tells of her thirty years of seclusion near Aix, in which she is said to have lived in ceaseless contemplation, without food or drink of any kind, and to have been borne aloft every day by angels at the time of the canonical hours to hear with her bodily ears the glorious chanting of heaven. Beyond this tale, one notes some parallels with Cecilia. Her name, like Cecilia's, is interpreted as light-giver by Jacques de Voragine. The threefold interpretation he gives of her name matches the symbolism of the three zones of music in Raphael's painting: it can mean "bitter sea," "light-giver," and "enlightened," says the *Golden Legend,* and thus symbolizes penance (the purgative stage), inward contemplation (the illuminative way), and heavenly glory (divine union). Her kissing of Jesus' feet in her great act of repentance was held to have endowed her mouth with the gift of eloquence, so that, again like Cecilia, she became a great preacher.

Other elements of her story are more individual. Christ's declaration that many sins were forgiven her because she had loved much took deep root in the Christian imagination, and led to her being regarded not only as the person who, of all mankind, loved Jesus the most, but also as the person who was most loved by him. In discussing Jesus' great love for her, writers and preachers would make due exception for his mother, but one senses that in this instance Magdalene had the greater appeal, and this precisely because she had shared the universal experience of being a sinner. John the Evangelist was the other figure whom Jesus was said to have loved before all others, and this parallel between him and Magdalene is probably why they are sometimes linked as the couple of Cana. Luke's story that she sat listening at Jesus' feet while Martha was busy at housework, and that Jesus defended her seeming indolence as "the better part," was further reason for attributing great contemplative gifts to her. Her transition from great sinner to great lover and greatly loved was surely the fundamental element in her story. This transformation made her a perfect example of the mutation effected by repentance (and thus by divine compassion); and therefore, in Gerson's estimation, she was a saint to be listed in his poem in praise of music.[12]

One critical factor in medieval linking of Magdalene to music was the belief, attested by both Mark and Luke, that Christ had cast seven devils out of her.[13] On the one hand, this helped shape the general image of Mary as quintessential sinner; on the other, it led to more precise associations through the symbolism of the number seven. One of these was an association with the liberal arts, in the belief that the arts in Christian hands were healers of the wounded spirit, that they could correct the aberrant ratios and proportions of the soul mired in sin. It is no accident, I think, that there should be so clear a statement of this in the milieu from which Raphael sprang. Antonio di Bitonto, a Franciscan who lived in Urbino at the time of Count Guidantonio (1404–43), the grandfather of Duke Federigo, makes this kind of connection in a sermon for Good Friday, one of a set of Lenten sermons in dialogue form dedicated to the count.[14] He has Magdalene mourn Christ's death with the seven liberal arts, with music last of all: "In the seventh and last place Mary Magdalene mourns her master with music, saying: 'O musicians, change your mode and weep, for the true cantor and musician today died on the cross.'"[15] The change of mode is called for out of reasons of compassion—the exact mutation called for in Gerson's mystical gamma.

The first viewers of Raphael's *Cecilia* may well have brought some such understanding of Magdalene—though even more complex and detailed— to their viewing of the painting. They would have been struck, as we still are today, by the tasteful boldness of her figure. The white garment, which draws our attention merely by its brilliance, no doubt attracted their eyes, too. But it had other connotations as well, among them the dedication of female life and virginity to Christ. Margery Kempe, even though she had had fourteen children, decided to wear white at the beginning of her spiritual (and worldly) journeying.[16] It was indeed by Christ's own instruction, she asserted in the face of ecclesiastical disapproval, that she took this step. In so doing (and in her later mystical marriage to Christ, in Rome), she highlights the doubts and ambivalence that were sometimes expressed about the exaltation of the virginal state at the expense of the married, even of the married who decided to live in chastity as Margery and her husband did.

Magdalene's white probably held for its first viewers some connotation of virginal consecration, and of sanctity regained. They would surely have noted that it covers a garment of reddish hue. White was the color of certain penitential groups, in particular the flagellant *Bianchi*, who flourished in Italy and across Europe in the previous century. It seems that they assumed white robes precisely to indicate that repentance had restored what had been lost, that the soul colored scarlet by sin could yet become whiter than snow. The common interpretation of Magdalene's name as "light-giver" strengthens the case for seeing her white robe in this way.

It should not surprise us to find that Raphael dwelt at length on Magdalene's penitence in the iconographic treatment of her figure, for she has always been the supreme example of repentance in Christian thought. Indeed, Raphael's whole intent in his depiction of her is to show that her penitence means a total absorption of her being into the world of divine love that is shared in by all of these saintly figures, that her new being in Christ is not a wounded being, scarred still by the lesions of her former sin, but a being totally renewed with even her sins turned to good. The two details of her figure that most clearly distinguish her from the other saints of the group may be references to this transfiguration: her bent left knee and the gaze she fixes so directly upon the viewer.

Magdalene's knee is bent in the engraving of Marcantonio, showing that this detail was part of Raphael's early thinking about the composition and was perhaps requested by the commissioner. It has been suggested that she has just arrived on the scene, that the knee is bent because she has not quite come to rest.[17] But there seems no reason why Raphael should have intended this. More likely the gesture is simply a regular *contrapposto* seen from the side, meant perhaps as a kind of visual counterpoint to the otherwise statuesque poses of the group as a whole. The gesture was by no means unknown in Renaissance art. A frontal drawing of a female Greek statue with left knee bent in just this way is attributed by some to Raphael himself.[18]

But there is another possibility, which is not inconsistent with the use of a conventional pose; and although it cannot be insisted upon, it merits consideration given the painting's emphasis on the notion that divine union springs from repentance and the casting away of the vanities. Could it be that Magdalene has, in fact, been kneeling, and has just risen to her feet? Her posture is certainly consistent with such an action. In rising from one's knees, one rises first to one foot, then draws the other into line with the first, just as Magdalene seems here to be doing. And the action is equally consistent with the character of Christian understanding of her spirituality. She knelt and kissed Christ's feet to ask forgiveness, washed them with her tears and anointed them with perfume from the vase that became her emblem.[19] Christ explained to Simon the Pharisee, in whose house this occurred, that her actions were the sign of great love, for which many sins were forgiven her. In the thirty years of repentant prayer that her legend describes, she knelt constantly, being raised up only to be regaled with the music of the angels, which took the place of her earthly food and was all the sustenance she knew or needed. This may well be what is happening in Raphael's painting: she is rising to her feet, the perfume in her hands, at the sound of the music that fills the spiritual heart.

But there is deeper significance to this kneeling and rising than simple correspondence with the legendary narrative. That narrative itself formed part of the great body of contemplative lore that was buit up by the masters of the Christian spiritual life. For them, there was a special significance attached to kneeling at Christ's feet. Bernard of Clairvaux described spiritual progress in a figure that paralleled Bonaventure's three ways, and that was applied particularly to Magdalene. In a most influential teaching, he distinguished the three stages of spiritual progress by the figure of a threefold kiss: the kiss of the feet, the kiss of the hand, and the kiss of the mouth.[20] The first corresponds to purgation, the second to contemplation, the third to union. And one of the common examples used to describe the first kiss (and developed to include the others) was that of the kneeling Magdalene who kissed the feet of Christ. We find it, for example, built into Margery Kempe's description of a vision she had of Christ's passion and death.[21] When the body was taken from the cross, Jesus' mother received it in her arms and kissed it upon the mouth. "And then this creature thought she heard Mary Magdalene say to our Lady, 'I pray you, lady, give me leave to handle and kiss his feet, for at these I get grace.'" When leave was given, "Mary Magdalene soon took our Lord's feet, and our Lady's sisters took his hands, the one sister one hand and the other sister the other hand, and wept very bitterly in kissing those hands and those precious feet."

More than any of the other saints in Raphael's scheme, Mary Magdalene represents the initial step of purgation that sets the soul in the way of divine love, and it is for this reason that she looks directly out at the viewer. If Cecilia's gaze is the most influential detail in the painting, Magdalene's is the most arresting. Hardly have the viewer's eyes alighted on the work's surface than they are seized, gently yet surely, by the steady gaze of the great penitent. The quiet power of the look is not inwrought, but is due rather to the whole visual context, to the simple fact that Magdalene alone, among these five contemplatives, seeks the viewer. It is not, as in other paintings by Raphael, the look of the young Bindo Altoviti, who gazes at us just as directly, confident of his good looks and golden locks, nor anything like that of *La Fornarina,* with its utterly private invitation, for both of these are essentially singular, individual. It is because Magdalene looks at us directly while her companions are absorbed in their own affairs, unaware of the viewer, that her gaze has such attractive power. The look has been called—and not inaccurately—bold, frank, candid; yet more than any of these it is, I think (how like, yet how unlike, *La Fornarina!*), inviting.

The invitation is to be a part of the little group, to join them in their sacred conversation, which is nothing less than direct and unmediated commerce with God. Where the gazes of those other saints figure for us the infinite dimensions of the all-encompassing divine love, Magdalene, herself drawn wholly into that love, looks out invitingly, asking the world to take the first step in the way of love as she has done, to forsake sin and kneel at Christ's feet. If you will do that, her look tells us, you, too, will be raised up and taken up into his love even as I have been. When Raphael decided, between the sketch used for Raimondi's engraving and the finished altarpiece, that he would seek to represent in the looks of the other four saints the dimensions of divine love, just as Gerson had done in the four points of his gamma, he intensified the spiritual message of his work by showing visibly the infinite possibilities of love that are open, through divine compassion, to all humanity, if they will but allow love's power to transform them, if they will make the great mutation. Those possibilities are laid before our eyes in the seeing of these saints and most especially in the heavenward seeing of Cecilia herself. And the way to achieve this seeing is the way that Cecilia has followed, the discarding of the music of sadness to possess only the music of joy. What better way to invite the viewer than the appealing look of the Magdalene, which so draws our gaze into the company and eventually to the God-seeing gaze of Cecilia herself? In representing Magdalene thus, Raphael simply gave visual expression to one of the essential characteristics of her cult, for more than any other saint, Mary Magdalene was held up as the model of what is achieved through repentance and the humility from which it grows.[22] It was for this reason that the gospel of the Thursday after the fifth Sunday of Lent told the story of her forgiveness, with its emphasis on Christ's declaration that many sins were forgiven her because she loved much. This day, more than any other in Lent, became the occasion in the Middle Ages, and remained so still in Raphael's day, for the most powerful appeals of preachers for humility and repentance, all built upon Magdalene's example.

Magdalene's invitation is to be a part of what the picture so firmly yet delicately portrays, in the figure of the saint who stands at the group's center. For whatever else this work is about, it is most assuredly about what Cecilia herself is doing. One concludes impulsively on first viewing the painting (and it is an impulse that can easily linger) that Cecilia looks and listens. That rapt heavenward gaze sees sights that it is not given to others, least of all the viewer, to see; and it seems a fair assumption that she hears, too, what others do not: the music of heaven. Why else are those earthly instruments abandoned at her feet, the organ held so distractedly in her hands, while the little group of angels sings in the clouds above her? Yet her gaze is not toward the angels, who are actually behind her, but to something in the heavens before them and out of the viewer's sight. One could make a strong case for saying that her rapture is not engendered by the sounds from the angels bent over their part-books, but by whatever vision it is that has so completely captured her eyes. That this is the vision of God, and that her gaze represents the goal of all contemplation, that of union, seems obvious, and is hardly controversial. Yet what does this say about the singing of the angels? Does her distractedness, her ecstasy, signify a turning-away even from their music as she is caught up into seeing God? Or is one simply straining a metaphor too much by seeing some logical conflict in the idea that Cecilia is here enraptured by the divine vision and the angelic music at the same time? The angels themselves, after all, are understood to enjoy the beatific vision while they sing.

The issue is not a trivial one, for the concept of the spiritual senses and their capacity to deal with divine things was well developed in mystical theology. The topic was of special concern to Jean Gerson.[23] One might turn to medieval theologians to understand the background on which Raphael's portrayal of the heavenly seeing and hearing of Cecilia ultimately depended, to learn that spiritual vision and spiritual hearing were the pre-eminent senses, with vision occupying the first place alone. For the vision of God is the goal of all spiritual journeying, and when it is finally achieved there is no longer need for faith, which is dependent on hearing. Faith in

God, which is received through his word, is fulfilled in the fully perceived presence of God, by vision of his very being. At that point love is perfected, desire ceases, hope is fulfilled. But a sharper insight will come, I think, if we consider how Dante dealt with vision and hearing as the soul attained to full vision in the final cantos of the *Paradiso*. This is not to assert (or deny) that Raphael realized his conception with Dante in mind, but rather to rely on the shared background of belief that both painter and poet brought to their work.

We have already noted the way in which Beatrice's smile and the music of the heavenly citizens increase in joy as Dante rises through the spheres and passes into the Empyrean. There the music of the angels circling around the great rose forms an unending symphony of praise, of love, of joy, that is described in almost every canto. Yet at the very last, when the poet himself passes to the direct vision of God, all of this ceases. There is no music, no speech, no smile, only light and vision. Saint Bernard is the last to speak in the *Divine Comedy,* and his speech is a prayer to the Virgin Mary that the poet be given the final powers of vision, that he may see God: "This man, who has seen the lives of the spirits one by one from the deepest pit of the universe to here, now begs for strength great enough, by your grace, that with his eyes he may rise higher still, towards the last salvation."[24] When Bernard has finished, Mary turns her eyes on him, then raises them to the Eternal Light. Bernard signals the poet with a smile (and he is the last to smile as he has been the last to speak) that he too should look upwards. But Dante, invested with new power, is already doing so; and from that moment his vision surpasses speech, and renders it useless. Nor can memory contain or recall the vision. He can only appeal to God for some spark of recollection, so that he may dimly illumine the minds of those who will come after and thus implant in them a clearer conception of the divine victory. Decrying thus his ability to relate what he had seen, the poet goes on to tell that vision in language as powerful as any he ever used, but direct and forthright, and less dependent on the symbolic artifices that he has thus far employed.

This rhetorical device of Dante at the very end of the *Divine Comedy,* his abandonment of music, of speech, of the whole world of sound that has till now formed so eloquent a part of his language, is mirrored in the gesture Raphael attributes to Cecilia. Language has ceased among these saints, all of whom are silent, who exchange no glance, though they are obviously bound close by the tie of divine love. But it is Cecilia, more than the others, who seems to have left the world of sound behind; whose soul, indeed, seems to have soared to its meeting with the infinite love. Not only are the instruments of this world left broken at her feet, not only does the silent organ lie forgotten in her hands, but even the singing of these angels seems to go unheard, or only faintly heard, as her gaze is flooded with a vision that is beyond all merely human seeing or knowing. That dictum of Augustine which so impressed Gerson seems, for her, to have been made real: *visio est tota merces.* We might almost say that she does not hear the music because she sees it.

Yet what exactly are these musics that Raphael has painted into his vision of Cecilia? That they are founded upon Gerson's threefold musical-spiritual scheme seems certain given not only the powerful influence he exerted on Pietro da Lucca, but even more the perfect fit of the painter's image to the theologian's thought. We must, however, inquire further, for Gerson describes two threefold schemes of music—closely related schemes, to be sure, but nonetheless distinct. At the more basic level, he posits the song of pure joy, the song of pure sadness, and the mixed song, as the musics of heaven, of hell, and of the world. But the mixed song (which is the song of the pilgrims, the wayfarers, the living who are still on their spiritual journey) is itself threefold, according to the state of the individual's soul. If one has made little progress in the spiritual life, and is still in the state of purgation, when the vanities and the call of sin are yet dominant, then the strain of sadness is preponderant in the mixed song. For those who have achieved some proficiency in the spiritual life, those who are being illumined (according to the common scheme propounded by Bonaventure), the strain of joy reaches a balance with that of sadness. Finally, in the higher reaches of perfection, in the souls of those who are in the unitive way, the music of spiritual joy becomes ascendant.

It seems clear enough that Raphael's musical scheme follows the pattern not of Gerson's basic division of the cosmic music into the strains of pure sadness, of pure joy, and of joy and sadness mingled, but of his threefold distinction of the mixed song itself. For the discarded instruments are an image not of the fierce laments of the damned, but of the things of this life that can entice the human heart to damnation with their siren call. The angels over Cecilia's head are not a sign that she is in paradise—they sing, after all, through a rent in the dark clouds—but that she has achieved such union with God that paradisal joy fills her soul even in this world. And the scene is, without a doubt, set in this world, with its church upon the hill in the background between Cecilia and Augustine. Though held by some to be the church of San Luca that overlooks Bologna from the hills, the case has also been made that it represents the church of S. Giovanni in Monte, for which Elena had commissioned the Raphael, and which she had assisted so materially in its program of rebuilding.[25]

Yet we ought not insist too firmly that one rather than the other of Gerson's threefold musics was the source of Raphael's thought, for the two schemes do not wholly exclude each other. The strains of sadness and joy that make up the mixed song are, after all, echoes in this life of the eternal musics that lie beyond the mutable world, echoes that ebb and flow in all human souls as they feel the calls of divine and worldly love, of charity and concupiscence, and variously respond to them or deny them. But Cecilia is the model of those who have traveled the spiritual journey to their true home. It was this that made her so appealing a figure to the mystics—to Elena, to Umiltà, to Julian of Norwich, to Camilla Battista da Varano, and others, who seem largely to have perceived her in the context of bringing joy out of sadness. The vanities that din so insistently in the ears of those not yet purged from their allure are shattered on the ground about her. She has successfully passed through the state of those who are progressing, who are being illumined, as the upturned *organetto,* with its mingled associations of church and world, of spirit and flesh, bears witness, and her heart sings with the single music of the love of God.

The upturned *organetto* that Raphael placed in Cecilia's hands is an apt symbol of the point in the process of spiritual mutation where the strains of sadness are dimmed by the growing music of joy—the point, that is, at which mourning is turned into joy. As the middle point in the process, it can fittingly represent the great work, to borrow the alchemist's term, of spiritual transmutation. Here it is worth recalling that Gregory the Great described the three steps to perfection (and his description is one of the many precursors of Gerson's three musics and of Bonaventure's three ways) as purgation, working, and contemplation. Working, *operatio,* was thus his name for the middle phase of Gerson's mixed song, for the illuminative way of Bernard, for the step in which the subjugation of the vanities is achieved and which prepares the soul for true union with its eternal lover.[26]

This is the kind of "working" that Chaucer's Cecilia ("ful swift and bisy ever in good werking") is engaged in. It is the only "working" that can change the soul's enmeshment in the material to its liberation in God, a mutation that can take place only in the mutable world, between the fixed states of utter concupiscence and utter charity. For when the end comes, the night "in which no man can work" (John 9:4), concupiscence and charity will be revealed for what they truly are, and either fierce lament or joyous heart-song will become the eternal melodies of the souls in which they have been sounding. This kind of "working," the operation within the soul by which the love that proceeds from wounded nature is transmuted into charity, into supernatural love, is the essence of the symbol of the organ that Raphael had painted, reversed and upside down, in Cecilia's hands. The characterization of this precise operation as music is more than a plausible inference from the spate of allegorical references I have advanced. Indeed, it is consonant with the role of music in all instrumentality within the cosmos, a role amply delineated in chapter 6, and is stated quite explicitly by various mystics and spiritual writers of the late Middle Ages. Thus Mechtild of Magdeburg describes the passing from tears to joy as music, music which she goes on to define as the cessation of carnal concupiscence (when concupiscence turns to charity): this melody, she adds, banishes "trouble," or sorrow.[27] And Richard Rolle describes the soul's progress to contemplation by deliberately reversing the text of Job 30:31, by making in words the reversal that we have discovered in the images of abandoned instruments in the David-in-Penitence and in musical representations of Cecilia: "The man condemned to sorrows, uttering his laments to the whole world like a learned teacher, will say: 'My harp is turned into mourning, and my organ into the voice of those who weep.' But I, taken up into love, praising Him who raises me up after washing me from my impurities, turn round about the song of the captive, mutating the melody of sorrow. I dare to sing out this tenor: 'My mourning is turned into a harp, and my weeping voice into an organ.'"[28]

Gerson, a proximate source of Raphael's thought, seems not to have addressed directly the symbolism of the reversed organ, even though his writing is shot through with the scriptural texts of mourning and joy, which are so full of the implications of reversal. He does, however, discuss a parallel case that makes it easy to believe that he would have understood the reversed organ in this way. The passage, from his "Centiloquium," concerns the reversed shapes of the psaltery and the cithara. Because one is the mirror image, the exact reverse, of the other, he says, they can symbolize the contrary musics of sorrow and joy.[29] But this is the meaning I would give to the images of organs that are held by Cecilia, discarded by David. It is the meaning I have posited in Cecilia's assumption of the organ at about the time it appears discarded beside the penitent David, following the reversal in a Cecilian text (Esther 13:17, "turn our mourning into joy") of the symbols in a Davidic text (Job 30:31, "my harp is turned into mourning").

Thus the organ in Cecilia's hands, upside-down and back-to-front, is a sign of the saint's powerful working, of the transmutation within the soul that she effected and of which she was a patron. The idea is confirmed in other depictions of the saint, most particularly in the complex rendering by Anton Woensam (see plate 7) in his *Mystical Betrothal of Sts. Cecilia and Valerian*. This highly allusive work, painted not long after Raphael's *Cecilia,* shows her organ not merely reversed, but with the mouths of the pipes at the top instead of the bottom—a detail that cannot possibly be attributed to the artist's misconception of the instrument or to his reliance on a reversed print, but must be seen as a deliberate use of symbolism.[30]

Raphael reinforced this idea of Cecilia with other symbolic details, particularly those of her dress. This rich vesture is most likely modeled on the imagery of the figure of Judith, whose heroic figure formed a common enough point of comparison with Cecilia for preachers. Thus Johannes de Biblia, the Bolognese Dominican who elaborated the alchemical undertones of the Cecilian legend and who applied to her the opulent imagery of the "valiant woman" of Proverbs 30:10–31, vividly described Judith's rich vesture in a sermon for St. Cecilia: "She decked her head with a turban, clad herself in her richest robes, and put sandals upon her feet. She wore an armlet on her right arm, she took lilies, rings for her ears and fingers, and adorned herself with every kind of ornament."[31]

Some of this finery is copied into Raphael's image of Cecilia, who is shown wearing turban, armlet, and sandals, as well as the gold robe over her penitential sackcloth. André Chastel, noting the turban, thought it made the saint some kind of magician, "une sorte de magicienne."[32] But the Dominican preacher's interpretations are surely closer to what the painter had in mind. The turban, he says, denotes hope, for it is upon the head, and hope comes from above. The rich garment is the nuptial robe, the symbol of fraternal charity. Sandals, being open at the top, are signs of the raising of the affection. Finally, and most significantly, for it confirms a characteristic of Cecilia that is central to Chaucer's understanding of her, Johannes interprets the armlet (one can be seen on Cecilia's left arm, her right being partly hidden beneath the folds of her garment) as a token of her "strength in working [operationis fortitudo]."[33]

Thus the Bolognese preacher and the English poet, composing their different testimonies to the saint a generation and several countries apart, both saw her "working," operatio, as a fundamental trait of her spirituality and cult. Chaucer's espousal of the idea has puzzled the Chaucerians, largely because the associations that "working" and "busyness" arouse in the English mind are so different from those aroused by operatio in the Latin. The remarks of Johannes de Biblia, on the other hand, would go unnoticed if they were read casually, for they seem to be a commonplace of preaching, an application of a text that was used frequently in sermons and writings about saintly women: Cecilia was a valiant woman, who did mighty deeds in God's service. But the implications are much deeper. They go to the core of the mysterious cult of St. Cecilia and her association with music. For operatio was one of the broad descriptions of the medieval idea of motus, motion, and was thus the process by which change was effected. Motus, mutatio, operatio were indeed used synonymously, if somewhat equivocally.[34]

Yet Johannes de Biblia, unlike Chaucer, leaves his readers in no doubt that the saint's spiritual working was a musical working, for in the next section of his sermon he employs an explicitly musical figure to express just this idea. If he does not say, in so many words, that Cecilia was the patroness of music, or that she was considered in some sense a musician, it is because he did not need to, and because saying so was pointless for him and his contemporaries.

From his discussion of the ornaments of Judith, the Bolognese Dominican proceeds (fols. 224v–225) to describe how Cecilia adorned the house of the Church, taking as his text Sirach 32:7, "A carbuncle set in an orna-

Raphael and St. Cecilia

ment of gold, the matching of musical instruments in a banquet of wine [*Gemmula carbunculi in ornamento auri, et comparatio musicorum in convivio vini*]." The banquet, he says, is celebrated in the life of the Church, and in it the truly spiritual are inebriated with the wine of devotion and exaltation. He explains the phrase *comparatio musicorum* as the correct proportion of sounds of musical instruments, both high and low; when a high and a low string are sounded together in correct proportion, a sweet sound is produced. Cecilia gave forth just such sounds in this banquet. The low string was her resistance to evil, the high was her swiftness to do good; from such a double string in the banquet of the Church there sounded forth this sweet melody.[35] For Johannes, then, all that Cecilia was and all that she achieved resulted from the instrumentality of true musical proportion, applied in the spiritual realm. Though he lived and taught a century before Gerson, his imagery is remarkably close to that of the French theologian, who taught that all inner change unfolded in accordance with the mystical gamma.

Change—deep change, in the spiritual order—is the constant in the veneration of Cecilia, the single theme on which most of the cult terms encountered in this study are but variations. Light from darkness, clarity out of confusion, mutation, *motus,* working, *impetus,* busyness, *operatio—* all are manifestations of the love that moves the sun and stars, and whose influence, transmitted in the works of grace, turns mourning into joy. No bizarre details (like the elevation of Magdalene seven times a day into heaven) were added to her existing legend, no quaint folk customs (like the carrying of Agatha's remains around Catania to stay Etna's eruptions) crept into her cult. Only the appearance, some time late in the Middle Ages, of music festivals and celebrations held in her honor breaks the otherwise even tenor of the cult's history. And even this circumstance, which has puzzled those who consider Cecilia's association with music to have come about suddenly and inexplicably, is a perfectly natural development in devotion to a saint who was always musical in the ancient sense.

The kind of veneration accorded Cecilia at the time of Raphael, and Elena, and Pietro da Lucca, is no superstitious outgrowth. It stems rather from the centuries-long pondering, by subtle and deeply contemplative souls, of the texts in which the Christian Church had expressed the saint's cult: the *Passio,* certainly, but even more, it seems, those scriptural texts that defined the significance of Cecilia in the context of Christian worship. It may seem strange, or coincidental (but it is neither), that the saint whose origins lay in the turning of darkness into light at the shrine of Bona Dea in Trastevere should have been venerated by a psalm text that carried the image, in illuminated books, of the kneeling, penitent, Godward-gazing David: "To thee, O Lord, I have lifted up my soul." It is neither strange nor coincidental that the fifteenth verse of that same psalm, "my eyes are always upon the Lord," should have been characterized as the heart of contemplative activity, the "voice of the heart" and "the song of the banqueter"; nor that the central gesture of Raphael's painting of Cecilia should have mirrored the traditional gesture of the David-in-Penitence. That gaze, like the gaze of Beatrice inviting Dante to look upward to infinite light, carries the soul to the source of true love and joy, and away from concupiscence, from false love. Here *acedia,* sloth, and sadness have been left behind and trampled underfoot; here is the great work, the great mutation, the turning of mourning into joy. Cecilia, like Dante beyond the sphere of Saturn, hears music, or sees music, that surpasses human powers. And if the *organetto* that hangs silent and forgotten in her hands tells us that she has ceased to sing, here in her new world of divine vision, can we suppose that she has also—and again, like Beatrice in a higher joy—just ceased to smile?

Appendix 1

Selected Scripture Texts of Mourning and Joy

Old Testament

Tobit 2:5–6. "When he had hidden the body he ate bread with fear and trembling, remembering the words the Lord had spoken through the prophet Amos: 'Your days of feasting shall be turned into lamentation and mourning' [*Cumque occultasset corpus, manducavit panem cum luctu et tremore, memorans illum sermonem quem dixit dominus per Amos prophetam: dies festi vestri convertentur in lamentationem et luctum*]."

Esther 9:22. "For on those days the Jews took revenge on their enemies, and their mourning and sadness were turned into mirth and joy. And these would become days of banqueting and joy, when they would send one another portions of food and give gifts to the poor [*Quia in ipsis diebus se ulti sunt Iudaei de inimicis suis, et luctus atque tristitia in hilaritatem gaudiumque conversa sunt: essentque dies isti epularum atque laetitiae, et mitterent sibi invicem ciborum partes, et pauperibus munuscula largirentur*]."

Esther 13:17. "Hear my prayer, and be merciful to thy lot and thy inheritance, and turn our mourning into joy so that we may live and praise thy name; and do not close the mouths of those who sing thy praises [*Exaudi deprecationem meam, et propitius esto sorti tuo et funiculo tuo, et converte luctum nostrum in gaudium, ut viventes laudemus nomen tuum domine, et ne claudas ora te canentium*]."

1 Maccabees 1:41–42. "Her sanctuary is desolate, like a wilderness; her festival days have been turned into mourning, her sabbaths into a reproach, her honors have been brought to nothing. Her dishonor has become as great as had been her glory, her honor has been turned into mourning [*Sanctificatio eius desolata est sicut solitudo, dies festi eius conversi sunt in luctum, sabbata eius in opprobrium, honores eius in nihilum. Secundum gloriam eius multiplicata est ignominia eius, et sublimitas eius conversa est in luctum*]."

1 Maccabees 9:41. "And the wedding was turned into mourning, and the voice of the musicians into a lament [*Et conversae sunt nuptiae in luctum, et vox musicorum ipsorum in lamentum*]."

Job 19:9. "He stripped me of my glory and took the crown from my head [*Spoliavit me gloria mea et abstulit coronam de capite meo*]."

Job 21:12–13. "They take the timbrel and the harp, and rejoice at the sound of the organ. They spend their days in wealth, and in a moment they go down to hell [*Tenent tympanum et citharam, et gaudent ad sonitum organi. Ducunt in bonis dies suos et in puncto ad inferna descendunt*]."

Job 30:31. "My harp is turned into mourning, and my organ into the voice of those who weep [*Versa est in luctum cythara mea, et organum meum in vocem flentium*]."

Psalm 29:6. "Weeping shall last through the night, but in the morning there shall be joy [*Ad vesperum demorabitur fletus, et ad matutinum laetitia*]."

Psalm 29:12–13. "You have turned my wailing into joy; you have cut off my sackcloth and clothed me in gladness; so that my glory may sing to you and that I may not regret [*Convertisti planctum meum in gaudium mihi; conscidisti saccum meum, et circumdedisti me laetitia; ut cantet tibi gloria mea, et non compungar*]."

Psalm 76:4. "My soul would not be consoled; then I remembered God and was filled with delight [*Renuit consolari anima mea: memor fui Dei et delectatus sum*]."

Psalm 125:4–6. "Turn back our captivity, O Lord, like streams in the southern desert. Those who sow in tears shall reap in joy. They shall go out weeping, scattering their seed; they shall come back rejoicing, carrying their sheaves [*Converte, domine, captivitatem nostram, sicut torrens in austro. Qui seminant in lacrymis, in exsultatione metent. Euntes ibant et flebant, mittentes semina sua; venientes autem venient cum exsultatione, portantes manipulos suos*]."

Proverbs 14:13. "Laughter shall be mingled with sorrow, and mourning will be the end of joy [*Risus dolore miscebitur et extrema gaudii luctus occupat*]."

Sirach 22:6. "A tale told at the wrong time is like music in a time of mourning [*Musica in luctu importuna narratio*]."

Isaiah 12:1. "I shall confess to you, O Lord, for you were angry with me. Your anger has faded, and you have consoled me [*Confitebor tibi, domine, quoniam iratus es mihi; conversus est furor tuus et consolatus es me*]."

Isaiah 35:10. "Those who have been redeemed shall be brought back by the Lord, and shall enter Sion in praise. And there shall be everlasting rejoicing upon their heads, they shall have joy and gladness, and sorrowing and sighing shall flee away [*Et redempti a domino convertentur, et venient in Sion cum laude; et laetitia sempiterna super caput eorum; gaudium et laetitiam obtinebunt, et fugiunt dolor et gemitus*]."

Isaiah 61:2–3. ". . . so that I might comfort all who mourn, all those who mourn in Sion; so that I might give them a crown in place of ashes, the oil of joy for mourning, a cloak of praise for the spirit of grief [. . . *ut consolarer omnes lugentes, ut ponerem lugentibus Sion, et darem eis coronam pro cinere, oleum gaudii pro luctu, pallium laudis pro spiritu moeroris*]."

Isaiah 66:10–11. "Rejoice, Jerusalem, and gather together all you that love her. Rejoice joyfully you who were in sorrow, that you may exult, and be filled from the breasts of consolation [*Laetare, Jerusalem, et conventum facite omnes qui diligitis eam: gaudete cum laetitia qui in tristitia fuistis, ut exsultetis, et satiemini ab uberibus consolationis vestrae*]."

Jeremiah 31:13. "Then shall the maiden rejoice in the dance, the old men and the young men with her; and I shall turn their mourning into joy, and shall console them and make them joyful after their sorrow [*Tunc laetabitur virgo in choro, senes et iuvenes simul; et convertam luctum eorum in gaudium, et consolabor eos, et laetificabor a dolore suo*]."

Lamentations 5:15–16. "The joy of our heart is fled, our singing is turned into mourning, the crown has fallen from our head; woe unto us, for we have sinned [*Defecit gaudium cordis nostri, versus est in luctum chorus noster, cecidit corona capitis nostri; Vae nobis, quia peccavimus*]!"

Baruch 4:34. "And the rejoicing of her throngs shall be cut off, and her joy shall be turned into mourning [*Et amputabitur exsultatio multitudinis eius, et gaudimonium eius erit in luctum*]."

Ezekiel 2:9. "And I looked, and lo! a hand was stretched out to me, holding a book rolled up; and he spread it out before me; and it was written on within and without. And written in it were lamentations, and song, and woe [*Et vidi: et ecce manus missa ad me in qua erat involutus liber, et expandit illam coram me, qui erat scriptus intus et foris, et scriptae erant in eo lamentationes, et carmen et vae*]."

Amos 8:10. "And I will turn your feasts into mourning, and all your songs into lamentation. And I will put sackcloth on every back, and baldness on every head. And I will make it like the mourning of an only son, and your last end like a bitter day [*Et convertam festivitates vestras in luctum, et omnia cantica vestra in planctum; et inducam super omne dorsum vestrum saccum, et super omne caput calvitium; et ponam eam quasi luctum unigeniti, et novissima eius quasi diem amarum*]."

New Testament

Matthew 5:5. "Blessed are those who mourn, for they shall be comforted [*Beati qui lugent, quoniam ipsi consolabuntur*]."

Matthew 11:17. "We piped to you, and you did not dance; we sang you dirges, and you did not mourn [*Cecinimus vobis, et non saltastis; lamentavimus, et non planxistis*]."

Luke 6:21. "Blessed are you who now weep, for you shall laugh [*Beati qui nunc fletis, quia ridebitis*]."

Luke 6:22–23. "Blessed shall you be when men hate you. . . . Rejoice and exult on that day [*Beati eritis cum vos oderint homines. . . . Gaudete in illa die et exsultate*]."

Luke 6:25. "Woe to you who now laugh, for you shall mourn and weep [*Vae vobis qui ridetis nunc, quia lugebitis et flebitis*]."

Luke 14:11. "Everyone who exalts himself will be humbled, he who humbles himself will be exalted [*Omnis qui se exaltat humiliabitur et qui se humiliat exaltabitur*]."

John 16:20. "You shall wail and weep, but the world will rejoice; you shall be sorrowful, but your sorrow shall be turned into joy [*Plorabitis et flebitis vos, mundus autem gaudebit; vos autem contristabimini, sed tristitia vestra vertetur in gaudium*]."

2 Corinthians 8:9. "For you know the grace of our Lord Jesus Christ, that though he was rich, yet for your sake he became poor, so that through his poverty you might become rich [*Scitis enim gratiam domini nostri Jesu Christi, quoniam propter vos egenus factus est, cum esset dives, ut illius inopia vos divites essetis*]."

2 Timothy 2:11–13. "Here is a trustworthy saying: If we have died with him, we will also live with him; if we endure, we will also reign with him [*Fidelis sermo: Nam si commortui sumus, et convivemus: si sustinebimus, et conregnabimus*]."

James 4:9–10. "Be wretched, mourn and weep; let your laughter be turned into mourning, your joy into lamenting. Humble yourself in the sight of the Lord, and he will exalt you [*Miseri estote, et lugete, et plorate; risus vester in luctum convertatur et gaudium in moerorem. Humiliamini in conspectu domini, et exaltabit vos*]."

Revelation 7:17. "For the Lamb at the center of the throne will shepherd them, and lead them to the springs of living water, and God will wipe away every tear from their eyes [*Quoniam Agnus, qui in medio throni est, reget illos et deducet eos ad vitae fontes aquarum, et absterget deus omnem lacrymam ab oculis eorum*]."

Appendix 2

Books of Hours with Miniatures before Each of the Seven Penitential Psalms

Books other than those cited here no doubt exist but must be comparatively rare. They would most likely be found among the more lavishly produced books of hours.

1. London, BL, MS 49999. The De Brailes Hours. Copied at Oxford, ca. 1240, by William de Brailes for a certain Susanna. One of the earliest books of hours. Each of the penitential psalms begins with a historiated initial. A caption describes each miniature. David is crowned throughout; there is no harp or musical reference in any of the images.

66 Ps. 6	David is accused by Nathan.	
67v Ps. 31	David buried in the ground.	
69 Ps. 37	David-in-Penitence. The caption states that at this point in his penance, David begins to compose the penitential psalms.	
72 Ps. 50	David is scourged as penance.	
75 Ps. 101	The donor, in penitence.	

78 Ps. 129   David-in-Penitence.

79 Ps. 142   David-in-Penitence.

2. London, BL, Yates Thompson MS 3. Hours of Jean, Comte de Dunois, Bastard of Orleans. Probably produced in Paris ca. 1450. Each psalm is associated with one of the deadly sins by a miniature of that sin personified and riding an animal that also symbolizes the sin in question. The David-in-Penitence appears before Psalm 6, quite evidently as an introduction to the whole series of seven psalms. Between Psalms 6 and 31 there is a miniature with two sins, Pride and Envy. Clearly Pride is meant to be associated with the previous psalm, Psalm 6.

157 Ps. 6   David-in-Penitence. Harp discarded, musical angels with God above.

159 Ps. 31   Pride on lion, Envy on camel.

162 Ps. 37   Idleness on donkey, crossing bridge.

165v Ps. 50   Wrath on leopard, kills self with sword.

168v Ps. 101 Gluttony on wolf, holds cup.

172v Ps. 129 Luxury on goat, holds two arrows and a mirror. David and Bathsheba in background.

174 Ps. 142   Avarice on monkey, with chest of money.

3. New York, Pierpont Morgan Library, MS M. 677. Hours of Anne de France, by Jean Colombe, ca. 1473.

211 Ps. 6   David observes Bathsheba bathing.

213v Ps. 31   David holds Bathsheba's hand.

216v Ps. 37   David gives letter to Uriah.

221 Ps. 50   Uriah leads the assault on Rabat.

225 Ps. 101   Uriah's body is carried into camp.

230v Ps. 129 Nathan reproves David.

232v Ps. 142 David-in-Penitence.

4. New York, Pierpont Morgan Library, MS M. 1001. Hours. Miniatures painted in Poitiers, ca. 1475, by Robinet Testard. Over each penitential psalm is a miniature of a deadly sin personified and riding a beast. Associated with each is a presiding demon, and a scene in the border depicting the particular sin.

84 Ps. 6	Pride, holding a mirror, on a lion. Border: Lucifer and the proud.
86 Ps. 31	Envy, holding a magpie, on a camel. Border: Beelzebub and the envious.
88 Ps. 37	Wrath, on a leopard, stabs himself. Border: Men and women fighting.
91 Ps. 50	Avarice on a wolf holds one moneybag, empties another. Border: The avaricious hoard money.
94 Ps. 101	Gluttony on a pig, holds a ham in one hand, spills wine from a jug in the other as he tries to drink. Border: Berich and a gluttonous feast.
97 Ps. 129	Sloth, about to fall from a collapsed donkey. Border: Astarot and sleeping cobblers.
98 Ps. 142	Luxury on a goat, holds a bird in his right hand, the goat's horn with his left. Border: Asmodeus with men and women revelling.

5. Oxford, Bodleian Library, MS Douce 219–20. Hours of Engelbert of Nassau. From the hand of the Master of Mary of Burgundy, ca. 1485–90. Probably originally presented to Philip the Fair. The section with the penitential psalms is introduced by a miniature of the Last Judgment.

181v	Last Judgment.
182 Ps. 6	David and dog defend flock from a bear.
184 Ps. 31	David defends flock from a lion. Lion's paws are on an upturned beehive. David holds the lion's jaws.
186v Ps. 37	David attacks Goliath with sling and staff. Army tents in background, also towers.
190v Ps. 50	David holds head of Goliath on a spear. Ladies at the castle gate hold musical instruments, lute and harp.
194 Ps. 101	David, crowned, plays harp before two ladies. All seated within castle courtyard.
198v Ps. 129	David asleep in tent. Soldier raises flap of tent. Another soldier holds banner. David bareheaded, hand rests on crown on the ground.
200 Ps. 142	David-in-Penitence. David kneels, harp and crown on the ground, hands raised. Angel, winged, with spears

above. David kneels on a pathway, which leads to a
gateway with gates opened.

6. Baltimore, Walters Art Gallery Library, MS W. 245. French Hours, ca. 1490.

31 Ps. 6	David observes Bathsheba. Border: Death of Goliath; David and Uriah.
31v Ps. 31	David, on throne, weeps before Nathan.
32v Ps. 37	David, crowned, plays harp.
33v Ps. 50	David kneels, crowned, hands joined, harp on the ground, angel above with sword.
34 Ps. 101	David kneels, crowned, God above, dragon before.
35 Ps. 129	David kneels, harp on the ground, rays descend from above.
35v Ps. 142	David kneels, crown on the ground, patroness behind, God above.

7. London, British Library, Add. MS 34294. The Sforza Hours. Executed by Giovanni Birago in the late fifteenth century for Bona Sforza. Parts were stolen soon after its completion, and these were replaced by Gerard Hornebout in the early sixteenth century for the book's new owner, Margaret of Austria. The penitential psalms were illustrated by Birago, and thus are from the fifteenth century.

212v Ps. 6	David kneels in penitence, looks up to vision of God and an angel brandishing arrows or spears. Harp, crown and sceptre are discarded beside him. In the background, David sits as judge for a line of supplicants.
215 Ps. 31	David kneels in penitence. Crown on the ground before him.
218 Ps. 37	David kneels in penitence. He has taken up the crown, which now circles his joined hands.
223 Ps. 50	David kneels in penitence. Nathan reproves him and points out the way of repentance.
227 Ps. 101	David kneels in penitence.
232 Ps. 129	David kneels in penitence.

233v Ps. 142   David has risen to his feet and makes his way up the
                mountain path.

8. Philadelphia, Free Library, Lewis MS 112. French Hours from Lyon,
ca. 1510. Has a full-page miniature before the penitential psalms, another
before Psalm 6, then a historiated initial before each remaining psalm.

47   Job on dunghill, attended by wife and friends.
48 Ps. 6   David and Bathsheba with the body of Uriah.
49 Ps. 31   Nathan upbraids David; harp on the ground.
50 Ps. 37   Angel appears to David; harp on the ground.
52 Ps. 50   David with his dead son by Bathsheba; harp on the
                ground.
53 Ps. 101   David inclined in repentance, but not kneeling; harp on
                ground.
55 Ps. 129   David and the young Absalom.
55v Ps. 142   David and the dead Absalom.

9. Baltimore, Walters Art Gallery Library, MS W. 430. French Hours,
ca. 1515. Miniatures by the workshop of Jean Poyet.

84 Ps. 6   David anointed by Samuel.
86 Ps. 31   David faces Goliath.
88 Ps. 37   David plays harp.
91v Ps. 50   David observes Bathsheba.
94v Ps. 101   David gives letter to Uriah.
98 Ps. 129   David kneels before Nathan; scepter and crown on the
                ground.
99v Ps. 142   David-in-Penitence; harp on the ground.

Abbreviations

In citing works in the notes, short titles have generally been used. Works frequently cited have been identified by the following abbreviations.

AaSs   *Acta sanctorum collecta . . . a sociis Bollandianis.* Antwerp, 1643–; 3d ed., Paris and Brussels, 1863–.

AFP   *Archivum Fratrum Praedicatorum.* 1931–.

AH   *Analecta hymnica medii aevi.* Edited by G. M. Dreves, C. Blume, and H. M. Bannister. 55 vols. Leipzig, 1886–1922.

BibSanc   *Bibliotheca Sanctorum.* 13 vols. Rome: Istituto Giovanni XXIII della Pontificia Università Lateranense, 1961–70.

CIL   *Corpus Inscriptionum Latinarum,* 1863–.

DACL   *Dictionnaire d'archéologie chrétienne et de liturgie.* Edited by F. Cabrol, H. Leclercq, et al. 15 vols. in 30. Paris: Letouzey et Ané, 1907–53.

DAGR   *Dictionnaire des antiquités grecques et romanes.* Edited by C. Daremberg, E. Saglio, et al. 5 vols. in 10. Paris: Hachette, 1887–1919.

DSAM   *Dictionnaire de spiritualité ascétique et mystique, doctrine et histoire.* Edited by M. Viller, F. Cavallera, J. de Guibert, et al. Paris: G. Beauchesne, 1937–.

DocTemp   *L'estasi di Santa Cecilia di Raffaello da Urbino nella Pinacoteca Nazionale di Bologna.* Documenti del tempo. Exhibition catalogue. Bologna: ALFA, 1983.

DTC   *Dictionnaire de théologie catholique.*

FontFran   *Fonti Francescani.* 2 vols. Assisi: Movimento francescano, 1977.

Ge   *Liber sacramentorum Romanae aeclesiae ordinis anni circuli. . . .* ["Gelasian" Sacramentary.] Edited by L. C. Mohlberg with L. Eizenhöfer and P. Siffrin. 3d ed. revised by L. Eizenhöfer. Rerum ecclesiasticarum documenta, Series maior, Fontes, 4. Rome: Herder, 1981.

Ha   Sacramentary text according to the *Hadrianum* version. In *Le sacramentaire grégorien: Ses principales formes d'après les plus anciens manuscrits.* 3d rev. ed. Edited by J. Deshusses. Spicilegium friburgense, 16. Fribourg: Editions universitaires, 1992.

Indagini   Emiliani, Andrea, ed. *Indagini per un dipinto: La Santa Cecilia di Raffaello.* Bologna: ALFA, 1983.

Pa   Sacramentary text according to the *Paduensis* version. In *Le sacramentaire grégorien: Ses principales formes d'après les plus anciens manuscrits.* 3d rev. ed. Edited by J. Deshusses. Spicilegium friburgense, 16. Fribourg: Editions universitaires, 1992.

PalMus	Paléographie musicale: Les principaux manuscrits de chant grégorien, ambrosien, mozarabe. Solesmes, 1889–.
PL	Patrologiae cursus completus, series latina. Edited by J. P. Migne. 221 vols. Paris, 1844–64.
Pauly-Wissowa	Pauly, August F. von, ed. *Paulys Realencyclopädie der classischen Altertumswissenschaft.* 24 vols. in 39. Hrsg. von G. Wissowa. Stuttgart, 1894–1963.
RCMI	*Inventory of Musical Iconography 3.* International Repertory of Musical Iconography. Edited by T. Ford and A. Green. Pierpont Morgan Library Medieval and Renaissance Manuscripts. New York: Research Center for Musical Iconography, 1988.
RepSerm	J. B. Schneyer. *Repertorium der lateinischen Sermones des Mittelalters für die Zeit von 1150–1350.* 11 vols. Münster i. W.: Aschendorff, 1969–90.
SacVer	*Sacramentarium Veronense.* Edited by L. C. Mohlberg with L. Eizenhöfer and P. Siffrin. 3d ed. revised by L. Eisenhöfer. Rerum ecclesiasticarum documenta, Series maior, Fontes, 1. Rome: Herder, 1978.

Notes

One   Raphael's St. Cecilia

1. See Shelley, *Letters* 2:49–53.
2. The gallery was that of the Accademia delle Belle Arti, the present Pinacoteca Nazionale. "Guido" is, of course, Guido Reni.
3. "Today (Nov. 10) we first went to see those divine pictures of Raphael & Guido again." Shelley, *Letters* 2:53.
4. The theft and subsequent adventures of the painting are admirably recounted by Gilberte Emile Mâle in "Le transport, le séjour et la restauration à Paris de la Sainte Cécile de Raphael 1796–1815." See also *DocTemp,* 94– 98. The French seem to have considered the *St. Cecilia* the supreme masterwork of Raphael.
5. Some explain this as an artist's choice in the interest of a more harmonious composition; others as a result of his having worked from a woodcut, in which the correct arrangement had been reversed by the process of printing. See e.g., Mirimonde, *Sainte-Cécile: Métamorphoses d'un thème musical,* 41.
6. They are a viola da gamba with broken strings, its bow lying across its broken belly, three recorders, two tambourines, two small kettledrums (one with its skin pierced) with their drumsticks, a triangle, and a pair of cymbals. The instruments were painted by Giovanni da Udine, as Vasari tells us in *Le vite* 6:551.
7. No one, to my knowledge, has tried to identify these figures, or to explain the cope any further.
8. Thus Mossakowski, "Raphael's 'St. Cecilia,'" 14: "she is shown at the moment of joining the group of other saints."
9. The story is reported by Vasari, *Le vite* 3:545–46. Among early critics who praised the work so highly were L. Dolce in 1567; R. Borghini in 1584; G. P. Lomazzo in 1584; A. Banchieri in 1609; and F. Scanelli in 1657. Their encomia, with the passage of Vasari, are collected in *DocTemp,* 253–55.
10. Pope-Hennessy, *Raphael: The Wrightsman Lectures,* 230, says that belief in the tight control of the commission-

ers stems from a statement of Francesco Albani, cited by Malvasia: "When Francesco Albani migrated from Bologna, to join the studio of Annibale Carracci in Rome, he complained, in the light of his experience there, that the *St. Cecilia* was unrepresentative. Raphael's hands, he said, had been tied by the patron who commissioned the painting." See Malvasia, *Felsina pittrice,* 2:245.

11. Bosio, *Historia passionis,* 59, attributed the connection with music to the *cantantibus organis* passage of the legend. Gurlitt, "Die Musik," 63, declares that "only during the second half of the fifteenth century, in Italy, was the Christian martyr alleged to be associated with music." On p. 85, Gurlitt cites the statement of Herder in an essay of 1773 that "no patron saint of any art came to be so with so little reason as Cecilia . . . who had nothing to do with music, indeed she turned her thoughts away from it to busy herself with higher concerns." Hammerstein, *Die Musik der Engel,* 257, says that since about 1480 Cecilia is almost always shown with a portative organ in her hands. See also Winternitz, *Musical Instruments,* 137 n. 1. Recent popular reference works in music continue the trend. Thus *The New Penguin Dictionary of Music,* s.v. "Cecilia": "her connection with music is purely legendary and dates only from the 16th century, apparently through the misreading of a Latin text." Similarly, *The Norton/Grove Concise Encyclopedia of Music,* s.v. "Cecilia": "Her status as patroness of music probably resulted from a misinterpretation of a phrase relating to musical instruments in the Acts of St. Cecilia."

12. There are some early representations of her in which she listens to other music. Thus the painting by Riccardo Quartararo, where she listens to an angel lutenist (fig. 7.12), and perhaps the Anagni cope, on which she may be listening to a singing angel (fig. 7.6).

13. The best discussion of this document remains that of Delehaye, *Etude sur le légendier romain.* Erbes, "Die heilige Cäcilia," had shown that the largely fictitious story was based on a tale in the History of the Vandal Persecutions by Victor Vitensis. This, coupled with the citation of the *Passio* itself in a portion of the *Liber pontificalis* (edited by Louis Duchesne) known to have been written before 535, gave a secure dating of the *Passio* between 485 and 535. The *Passio Caeciliae* is one of the more stable saints' legends, with comparatively few variants in its tale, none of them of any substance.

14. *Passio,* cap. 3, p. 196. I have chosen to translate the *ne confundar* of the *Passio* as "lest I be confounded" simply so as to keep close to the sound of the Latin. The implications of the word in early Christian and medieval writings are manifold, and too much would be lost in opting for any single English equivalent. *Confundar* of course implies *confusio,* which was commonly equated with Babel and Babylon in patristic and medieval writings. Cecilia, *clarissima,* was a model of the opposing quality, clarity, and was celebrated as such by, for instance, Geoffrey Chaucer. (See below, chapters 3 and 6.) Chaucer's linking of Cecilia with alchemy may suggest the sense of "pouring together" as well.

15. This was the second such invention of Cecilia. The first was under Pope Paschal I (817–24) following a vision in which Cecilia told the pope that her relics had not been carried off by the Lombards, as was commonly supposed, but were hidden in the catacomb of Praetextatus. Paschal found them there and brought them to the new basilica he had built in Trastevere over the old one, which had fallen into decay. On the prob-

lems surrounding these inventions, and especially on the report that Cecilia's body was found incorrupt in 1599 and that Stefano Maderno's magnificent statue of her was modeled on what was then observed, see Delehaye, *Etude*, 88–96. Bosio was an Oratorian and a disciple of the great Oratorian scholar Baronio, who was also present at the opening of the tomb in Trastevere.

16. Antiphons, short sentences sung before and after psalms, were of their nature more likely to stay fast in the memory. In addition, vespers was quite commonly a service for the laity, whereas matins, with its longer reading of the passage, was commonly sung only by clerics and religious.

17. Quentin, "Cécile," cols. 2721–22. Luckett, "St. Cecilia and Music," 23 n. 37, found the opinion as early as 1838 in A. Botte de Toulmon, "Des puys de palinods en général, et de puys de musique en particulier," in *Revue française* 7 (1838): 107.

18. Banchieri, *Conclusioni nel suono dell'organo*, 2–6. The frontispiece of Banchieri's work— one notes that it appeared just ten years after the opening of Cecilia's tomb, and nine after the publication of Bosio's edition of the *Passio* with his opinion on how the organ came to be the saint's emblem—is decorated with a small woodcut of Cecilia standing before an organ with reversed pipes and holding an open book, another of her common symbols, in her left hand.

19. "Gitene, gitene, suoni, canti, & voi tutti mondani piaceri alla gran madre antica, che io altro non bramo solo essere assignata nella santissima Capella Musicale trà quei Musici, & Organisti elletti vittoriosi gli quali concertano continuamente avanti il mio dolcissimo sposo IESU santo, santo, santo."

20. Ps. 136:2, "In salicibus in medio eius: suspendimus organa nostra." Job 30:31, ". . . organum meum in vocem flentium." Throughout this work the psalms will be numbered as they are in the Latin Vulgate, the Bible used in the Middle Ages.

21. The passages are reprinted in *DocTemp*, 258–75. For Addison, see *DocTemp*, 92, where A. Sorbelli, *Bologna negli scrittori stranieri* (a. c. di G. Roversi [Bologna, 1973]), 314, is cited.

22. Ruskin's lack of interest in, even disdain for, the instruments in the painting is typical. See Ruskin, *Modern Painters*, 3:36. "Yet Raphael painted fiddles very carefully in the foreground of his St. Cecilia—so carefully that they look as if they might be taken up. So carefully, that I never yet looked at the picture without wishing that someone *would* take them up, and out of the way."

23. See *DocTemp*, 270–78.

24. Justi, "Raphaels heilige Cäcilia"; Gurlitt, "Die Musik"; Chastel, *Art et humanisme*; Mossakowski, "Raphael's 'St. Cecilia'"; Arasse, "Exstases et visions"; Zarri, "L'altra Cecilia"; Osthoff, "Raffael und die Musik."

The present study will in general pay little attention to the Neoplatonic content of Raphael's iconography. This is not meant to deny such content but rather to address the imbalance by which this content has been studied to the near exclusion of a less arcane perspective.

The demonstration by Mossakowski of the work's Neoplatonic symbolism, which he attributes to the Neoplatonism that was so popular in humanist circles of the time, particularly in the entourage of the early Renaissance popes, is persuasive. Antonio Pucci, curial official and adviser of the principal commissioner, Elena dall'Olio, is known to have been friendly with Orlandini and other followers of the intensely Neoplatonist Marsilio Ficino. Mossakowski argues, e.g., that Raphael's six singing angels are grouped as they are in order to suggest the ratios of the perfect consonances (the octave, the fifth, and the fourth) and thus to declare symbolically that perfect harmony is the basis of the right ordering of the universe. He points out, p. 7, that "in the centre of the group are placed three angels singing from a common choir-book. At the side they are joined by a fourth angel, represented heraldically on the right, who sings from a separate sheet of music, holding it in his left hand while with his right he supports the choir-book of his companions as if he wanted to stress that he is not independent but also belongs to their group. The six person group of the choir is completed by two angels singing from a book placed heraldically on the left." This yields natural groupings of two, three, and four, from which one derives immediately the ratios of the octave (4:2 = 2:1), fifth (3:2), and fourth (4:3). Mossakowski goes on to show how this accords with Neoplatonic ideas of love, especially as expressed by Ficino. These ideas of Mossakowski might be profitably developed by studying further the order of the pipes that are falling from the *organetto* held by St. Cecilia. Counting from right to left if the organ is viewed right way up—that is, in order of ascending pitch—these pipes are the fourth, the sixth, the eighth, the twelfth, the sixteenth, the eighteenth, and the nineteenth. Curiously, if one counts the other way, from left to right—and the thought of doing so should not be dismissed as nonsensical in dealing with this strangely "reversed" instrument—the falling pipes are the first, second, fourth, eighth, twelfth, fourteenth, and sixteenth.

One important expression in Ficino's difficult lexicon has an insistent resonance for those who know the language of the seven penitential psalms, which this study will hold to be central to the iconographic tradition from which Raphael's painting sprang. Ficino was much concerned with the raising of the soul to God. He labeled it *furor divinus* and distinguished its several varieties, which, he held, lead in ascending order to the state of ecstasy. (Thus Mossakowski, "Raphael's 'St. Cecilia,' " 9 nn. 103, 104, which document these references to Ficino.) But *furor divinus* is found in the first sentence of the first penitential psalm (Psalm 6), which shares its opening text, "Domine ne in furore tuo arguas me," with the third (Psalm 37). Psalm 6 is the most common site of the David-in-Penitence, the source of Raphael's iconography in the view here advanced, while Psalm 37 is the entrance psalm for the Trastevere station day and has undoubted Cecilian implications. Both, then, have a firm verbal link—the word *furor*—with a central idea of Ficinian thought about divine love and ecstasy. It should be noted further that the Greek for the Vulgate's *furor* is *orge*, which may suggest a further linguistic link with *organ*.

25. Several examples of early musical Cecilias will be discussed in chapter 7.

26. Randall, "In Honor of Janet Wurtzburger," describes a sixth-to-eighth-century Coptic textile on which David appears as harpist, and refers to a manuscript of A.D. 547 that shows that the subject was already known.

27. Lam. 5:15–16, "Defecit gaudium cordis nostri, versus est in luctum chorus noster. Cecidit corona capitis nostri; vae nobis, quia peccavimus." Job 30:31, "Versa est in luctum cithara mea, et organum meum in vocem flentium."

I have in general understood *chorus* as "singing," though it might more properly be translated as "dancing." But my concern is with the musical implication, which is present in either case. (The David-in-Penitence miniature is discussed in chapter 4.)

28. Laon, Bibl. munic., MS 243⁴, fol. 87.

29. The stational liturgy of the medieval popes, the masses and associated liturgies they celebrated at the twenty-five or so principal churches of the city on the more significant liturgical days, visiting them in traditionally established order, has long been recognized as a factor of great importance in medieval culture. A station day at one of these churches is often of more significance to the early cult of the church's patron saint than is the saint's feast day. The liturgies of the two days of St. Cecilia—the station day at her Trastevere church on the Wednesday after the second Sunday of Lent and her feast day on November 22—are discussed in more detail in chapter 2. For an excellent general introduction to the Roman stational liturgy, see Baldovin, *Urban Character of Christian Worship,* 143–66; also Willis, "Roman Stational Liturgy."

30. "Ad te levavi animam meam. Deus meus, in te confido, non erubescam." This psalm text is also used as the gradual and offertory for the first Sunday of Advent, which thus uses the same psalm for introit, offertory, and gradual. It inculcates humble repentance as the basic Christian attitude at the beginning of each year.

31. "Domine ne in furore tuo arguas me, neque in ira tua corripias me."

32. This argument, which is the basis of my answer to the question "Who was Cecilia?" and thus the foundation on which this whole study is built, is merely summarized here. It will be treated in detail in the next chapter.

33. "Exaudi deprecationem meam, et propitius esto sorti et funiculo tuo, et converte luctum nostrum in gaudium, ut viventes laudemus nomen tuum Domine, et ne claudas ora te canentium."

34. One such sign is discerned in his reference to Ps. 136:2, "in the willows in its [Babylon's] midst, there we hung up our instruments [*in salicibus in medio eius: suspendimus organa nostra*]." This psalm, which tells of Israel's unwillingness to sing her own songs in Babylon, the alien land of her captivity, became a prime source for the opposition, in medieval mystical thinking, of the city of God, the heavenly Jerusalem, and the city of this world's sin and vanity, the city of Babylon. Babylon, it should be noted, is always translated as "confusion" by the mystical and spiritual writers of the Middle Ages, a fact that at once suggests Cecilia's interior song, the song she "sang in her heart to God alone: May my heart and my body be kept immaculate that I not be case into confusion [*ut non confundar*]." The avoidance of this *confusio,* which a medieval spiritual director would instantly have equated with all that Babylon, the city of vanities, represented, is a central concern of Cecilia's liturgy, for its texts refer to it again and again. In addition, Cecilia's legend, and later discussions of her spiritual significance, dwell heavily on her possessing *claritas,* the contrary of confusion.

That Banchieri was in touch with this tradition is firmly established by his opposing the song of joy and the song of sadness, *carmen laetitiae* and *carmen tristitiae,* for these are known, in the same tradition of medieval mysticism, as the song of Jerusalem and the song of Babylon. The passage from joy to mourning, and the conversion of mourning back to joy, thus carry a far more specific significance than they at first seem to.

1. Delehaye, *Etude sur le légendier romain,* 74.

2. The Canon's definitive form, with the names of "Felicity, Perpetua, Lucy, Agatha, Lucy, Agnes, Cecilia, Anastasia," is known from the seventh century, in Frankish copies of the Roman sacramentary. Its earliest known form, which does not include the names of Cecilia and the other saints, is in the *De sacramentis* of St. Ambrose, from about 350. The names were undoubtedly added in Rome, and not by the Franks, but when this happened is not known.

3. For the dating, see Erbes, "Die heilige Cäcilia." Erbes showed that certain central events of the *Passio* were based on the History of the Vandal Persecutions, written by Victor of Vita in 488 to 489, and that the *Passio* is quoted in a section of the *Liber pontificalis* (edited by L. Duchesne) that deals with Pope Urban I (the pope of the *Passio*) and that is known to have been composed in about 535. The *Passio* must then be dated between 488 and 535, with a strong likelihood that it was earlier rather than later in that period. On the many borrowings in the *Passio,* see Quentin, "Cécile," 2717–21.

4. Styger, *Römische Märtyrergrüfte,* 1:83–86. See also Testini, *Le catacombe,* 132–35.

5. Delehaye's study was published the year after Styger's *Römische Märtyrergrüfte.* Styger's conclusion that the crypt was built in its entirety after the persecutions was indeed the key piece of evidence Delehaye needed for his argument. On donors of Roman *tituli* who became saints, and on the introduction of historical saints of the same name as a donor (as was the case with, e.g., the *titulus Anastasiae*), see Delehaye, *Etude,* 85, and Willis, "Roman Stational Liturgy," 61, 64. *Tituli* were roughly the equivalent of parish churches, but did not have territorial limitations as do modern parishes. Rather their origin was in the need to maintain the unity of disparate, and potentially separatist, communities. With the Constantinian settlement, the great basilicas, and eventually a number of other nontitular basilicas, were added to the stational scheme. But the determining factors were liturgical rather than territorial. See Baldovin, *Urban Character of Christian Worship,* 108ff., and Willis, op. cit., 4–9, 58–73.

6. Delehaye, *Etude,* 86. "Let us not complicate the case by asking if the St. Cecilia venerated in the cemetery of Callistus, in the chamber next to the crypt of the popes, was indeed the same person whose anniversary was celebrated on November 22. Since the fifth century there was never any doubt about the identity, and that is all there is to say about it [*Ne la compliquons pas en demandant si la Ste. Cécile, vénérée au cimetière de Calliste, dans la chambre voisine de la crypte des papes, est bien réellement celle dont l'anniversaire se célébrait le 22 novembre. Depuis le Ve siècle, on n'a jamais douté l'identité, nous n'en pouvons dire davantage.*"

7. In support of this thesis, there is the list of signatories to the Roman Synod of 499, where in some sources we find the name of the priest of the *titulus Caeciliae,* "the title of Cecilia" and not "the title of St. Cecilia." See *Acta synodorum habitarum Romae,* 411. It seems, then, that the epithet *saint* may not, as a matter of course, have been put before this Cecilia's name even in this year, which was about the same time the *Passio* was written. Forty-six years later, however, when Pope Vigilius was abducted by the Byzantines, the church was clearly described as dedicated to St. Cecilia. And in 595, in another Roman synod under Gregory the Great, the signatories included the priest of

the "title of St. Cecilia." See St. Gregory, *Registrum* 1:367. Note that De Rossi claimed to have found a fragment of a tablet from the late fourth century in the floor of the basilica that mentioned *S. Cecilia*. But his reconstruction of the fragment is highly conjectural. See Rossi, *Inscriptiones* 1:359, no. 816.

8. Delehaye, *Etude*, 84–85, citing P. Franchi, *Recenti studi intorno a S. Cecilia*, 10, as having held this same view.

9. *Commentarius perpetuus*, 435, 512, 604, 613.

10. Delehaye, *Etude*, 87.

11. Rossi, *Roma sotterranea*, 2:153–54.

12. Delehaye, *Etude*, 87.

13. *SacVer*, 147–50. An oddity, and perhaps a significant one, of the situating of Cecilia's feast at this point, November 17 or 22, is that these two dates are frequently noted in medieval calendars as the days on which winter begins. Given Cecilia's connections with light-giving, to be discussed below, one wonders if there was some symbolic intent in the assignment of her feast to this part of the calendar. This would hardly seem worth noting were it not that the feast of St. Urban, the pope of the *Passio*, is May 25, the beginning of summer in these same calendars. Jean Gerson, the mystical theologian whose writings are steeped in devotion to St. Cecilia, makes this observation in connection with St. Urban, but not with her. See below, chap. 5.

   The Verona Sacramentary is a somewhat haphazard collection of diverse individual mass formulas, and not a compilation intended for official liturgical use within a given Christian community. It often gives several sets of texts for a particular feast, five such sets for St. Cecilia's day, for example. See Vogel, *Medieval Liturgy*, 38–46. These liturgical formulations for St. Cecilia, it should be noted, share certain passages with the *Passio*.

14. Hertling and Kirschbaum, *Roman Catacombs*, 2–17, give a clear and concise overview of the exploration of the Roman cemeteries.

15. Fig. 2.1 is the crypt of the popes as De Rossi found it. His imagined restoration of it is seen in fig. 2.2.

16. Rossi, *Roma sotterranea*, 1:175–83, publishes the various itineraries of Rome, including the *Topographia Einsiedelnensis*, along with the *Index oleorum* and *Pittacia ampullarum*, the lists used by Abbot John.

17. One of these was a small painting of the saint in the posture of an orant, beside the burial niche. This is the uppermost of the three figures in that position in fig. 2.3, above images of Christ and St. Urban. The other was a large painting, in the same posture, in the light shaft of the chamber. Its lower part can be seen in fig. 2.3, above the two sheep standing about the cross. The three images beside the niche have recently been restored, but the one in the light shaft has completely faded. Given Cecilia's links to light-giving, to be discussed in this and in the next chapters, it is possible that the latter painting may have been placed in this position for symbolic reasons. Near the painting of St. Urban, De Rossi found a few letters which he restored as "deCORO caEC(iliae) mAR(tyris)."

18. There has been much disagreement on the date of the paintings in the crypt of Cecilia, but no doubt at all that they are medieval. They are thus witness only to a cult of Cecilia at this spot several centuries at least after the *Passio*. See Wilpert, *La cripta dei papi*; Bar-

bier de Montault, "Iconographie"; Leclercq, "Cécile"; and Quentin, "Cécile." Quentin and Leclercq declared that, except for the orant figure in the light shaft, the paintings in the chamber were all executed much later in the Middle Ages. But I have found no dating of these images that seems at all reliable, and nothing at all in recent scholarship. It does seem fair to say that all the images were painted long after the construction of the chamber and the deposition of the dead that it housed.

The crypt was clearly not intended for someone recently martyred. But could it have been built to receive the body of a martyr translated from elsewhere? This seems most unlikely. The construction of the crypt in stages, the digging first of a space just large enough for a sarcophagus and only later its enlargement and decoration, suggests that it was meant for someone who had just died, when there was need for rapid work to ensure prompt burial. If it had been decided to honor a martyr by translation, there would have been no need for such haste. And even if such a translation did take place, the body must surely have been that of a highly venerated martyr indeed, to merit re-burial in this, the most hallowed of all Roman Christian burial places. Yet no martyr named Cecilia—certainly no highly venerated martyr of this name—was known to the Romans of the fourth century, or, it seems, of the greater part of the fifth century.

19. Testini, *Le catacombe,* 135.

20. A useful summary of these architectural changes and excavations may be found in Caraffa and Massone, *Santa Cecilia martire romana,* 151–94.

21. For a detailed discussion of the significance of the scene, see Schumacher, "Dominus Legem dat"; Davis-Weyer, "Das Traditio-Legis Bild"; and Sotomayor, *S. Pedro,* 126–33. While the composition as a whole has little bearing on our argument, the detail of the phoenix in the palm tree at Christ's right assuredly does, for there are grounds for attributing to it a musical significance. Since the mythical bird figures in an interesting way in Cecilia's *Passio,* the case may yield some evidence for the saint's musical character at the very beginning of her cult. This will be discussed in chapters 3 and 7. See also Connolly, "Legend of St. Cecilia, I," 24–27.

22. A copy of this statue has been placed in the presumed burial niche of St. Cecilia in the crypt in St. Callistus. Cardinal Paolo Sfondrati's restructuring of the basilica (to be discussed shortly) included the removal of the two medieval ambos, or pulpits, "because they served no purpose," according to Bosio, but also, most likely, because Sfondrati wanted to open up the view of Maderno's statue. See Bosio, *Historia passionis,* 171. The same reason lay behind the removal of the old presbyterium, or choir area, before the sanctuary.

23. Bosio, ibid., 155ff., 170. Baronio, *Annales,* 9:507, 604 (cited by Caraffa and Massone, *Santa Cecilia martire romana,* 96 n. 1), also left an account. With the sarcophagus containing the supposed body of Cecilia were others containing the remains of Sts. Valerian and Tiburtius, St. Maximus (their jailer, who was converted and suffered with them; see below, chap. 3), and Popes Sts. Urban and Lucius.

24. Yet Sfondrati is reported to have placed the remains in a new sarcophagus. This obviously took place on another and unrecorded occasion. The body was found in a wooden coffin within the ancient sarcophagus. Sfondrati substituted a coffin of cypress for the old one, placed this in a silver case, and enclosed all within a new sarcophagus of marble.

25. The account of the rebuilding and of Paschal's invention of Cecilia's remains is found in Duchesne, ed., *Liber pontificalis* 2:56–58.

26. "Quod tribuente deo, dum sollicite quaereret, repperit in cimiterio Praetextati, sitim foris portam Appiam, aureis illud vestitum indumentis, cum corpore venerabilis sponsi Valeriani, pariterque et linteamina martirii illius sanguine plena, quando ab impio percussa carnifice Christi domini martyr est regnantis in saecula consecrata. . . . Quae cuncta suis pertractans manibus collegit et cum magno honore infra muros huius Romana urbis in ecclesia nomine ipsius sanctae martyris dedicata, ad laudem et gloriam omnipotentis Dei, eiusdem virginis corpus, cum carissimo Valeriano sponso atque Tyburtio et Maximo martyribus necnon Urbano et Lucio pontificibus sub sacrosancto altare collocavit."

27. See Delehaye, *Etude,* 80–81.

28. These studies include principally Crostarosa, "Scoperte in S. Cecilia" (the Rampolla excavations); Giovenale, "Recherches architectoniques" and "Les sarcophages"; Krautheimer, *Corpus basilicarum* 1:95–112; Matthiae, *S. Cecilia;* Cantino, "Roma sotterranea"; Meli, "Intervento"; Breccia Fratadocchi, "Considerazioni"; and Romano, "Alcuni fatti."

29. *Passio,* 219, cap. 31. The Roman bath here envisioned was a *calidarium,* a chamber warmed or heated by hot air flowing through pipes in the floor and ducts in the walls, all fed from a fire below. Such baths are commonly thought of in their grander public versions, but they were often found in private houses, too. See Anderson, Spiers, and Ashby, *Architecture of Ancient Rome,* chap. 6.

30. Sfondrati decorated the chapel richly, commissioning paintings of scenes from the *Passio* by Cristoforo Roncalli (Il Pomerancio) and two major works by Guido Reni, *The Beheading of Saint Cecilia* and *St. Cecilia and St. Valerian Crowned by an Angel.*

31. Breccia Fratadocchi, "Considerazioni." This investigation concludes that the area was part of a complex of baths around the first century A.D. and was transformed about three hundred years later for purposes of Christian worship.

32. My thanks go to my colleague Professor Norman Smith, who saw this inscription on his first visit to Trastevere. I had not known that any of the inscriptions had been preserved, much less been aware of their whereabouts.

33. This and the succeeding four inscriptions are cited by their numbers in *CIL,* vol. 6. For further information about the shrine, see Platner, *Topographical Dictionary of Ancient Rome,* s.v. "Bona Dea" and "Bona Dea Subsaxana, Aedes." This may well be the same Bolanus who had some interest in Roman baths in Region I (ibid., s.v. "Balineum Bolani"). These four inscriptions have recently been discussed at considerable length by Brouwer, *Bona Dea,* 24–29. On p. 304, Brouwer doubts that the inscriptions found at S. Maria dell'Orto (see *CIL* 6:75, below) are from the same site as those from the Insula Bolani. But he seems not to appreciate the significance of the epithet *Restitut[a]* or *Restitut[rici]* at the latter site. This epithet, whichever supplement is correct, is the equivalent of the *oclata* found beneath S. Maria dell'Orto.

34. Cicero, *De haruspicum responsis,* 17.37.

35. See the discussion in Latte, *Römische Religionsgeschichte,* 228ff. Damia derives from Demeter; her priestess was called *damiatrix,* her sacrifice *damium.* See Festus, exc. 68M. 178L.

36. Thus Arnobius, *Adversus nationes,* 1.36 and 5.18; Macrobius, *Saturnalia,* 1.12.24. Plutarch, *Caesar,* 9.3, says that the Roman θεόϑ ἀγαϑή (Theos Agathe) was identical with the Greek θεόϑ γυναικεῖα (Theos Gynaikeia), and that the Romans said she was the wife of Faunus. The Greek name of the Good Goddess, Theos Agathe, stimulates some interesting speculation about the early cult of Cecilia. For no discernible reason, the convent or monastery that was attached to S. Cecilia in Trastevere in the early Middle Ages, the origins of which are obscure, was dedicated to St. Cecilia and St. Agatha. It may be that the mention of Agatha in this dedication is, like the name of Cecilia herself, a distant echo of the cult of the Theos Agathe. Cecilia and Agatha are linked in other medieval dedications—one in Verona, for instance—and they are represented together in art, as in the apsidal mosaic of the Trastevere basilica and in the fifth vault of the cathedral at Albi. But these can perhaps be adequately explained by the simple and well-known fact that the two virgins shared a dedication in Trastevere.

37. For versions of the legend see Arnobius, 5 18; Macrobius, loc. cit.; Plutarch, loc. cit.; Valerius Maximus, *Factorum ac dictorum memorabilium,* 6.3.9; Servius, *In Vergilii carmina,* Aeneid 1.737; Tertullian, *Apologeticum,* 6.4.

Much will be said below about the most famous passage of Cecilia's *Passio,* the *cantantibus organis* passage. Its text is an undoubted reference to the Pauline injunction to the Ephesians (Eph. 5:19) to "sing in their hearts to the Lord." It may be significant that this command of St. Paul occurs in the context of his command not to become drunk on wine, which is to be equated with *luxuria,* but to be inebriated with the Holy Spirit.

38. Plutarch, loc. cit., and *Cicero,* 19.3; Macrobius, loc. cit.; Propertius, 4.9.25.

39. Detailed accounts are given by Plutarch, *Caesar,* 9–10, and *Cicero,* 28–29; and by Seneca, *Epistulae,* 97.2.

40. Propertius, loc. cit., tells how Hercules, while driving the cattle of Geryon through Italy, became thirsty and sought a drink of water from a priestess of Bona Dea while her rites were being celebrated in a sacred grove. She warned him of the penalty for intruding (*parce oculos, hospes*) and reminded him of the punishment Tiresias had suffered for daring to look upon Athena while she was bathing. See also Cicero, *De domo,* 40, and *De haruspicum responsis,* 18; and Pausanias, *Arcadia,* 5.5.

41. Juvenal, *Satires,* 6.314–41.

42. Ibid., 5.18; also 1.36. "Fenta, Fatua, Fauni uxor, Bona Dea quae dicitur sed in vini melior et laudabilior potu."

43. Tibullus, 1.6.21–22; Ovid, *Ars amatoria,* 3.631–37.

44. Plutarch, *Cicero,* 20.1–2.

45. Juvenal, *Satires,* 2.86–87; also Macrobius, *Saturnalia,* I.12.23.

46. Macrobius, op. cit., 1.12.20.

47. There is ample evidence for the healing aspects of the cult of Bona Dea in other places besides her Roman temple. Serpents, sacred to Aesculapius, were carved on some of her altars. On others, such as the famous altar at Arles (*CIL* 12:654) and another nearby at Glanum (see fig. 2.8), there were ears, with the title *Auribus Bonae Deae.* This title is parallel in meaning to *Bona Dea Oclata,* "the Good Goddess with the Eye": that is, it means *Bonae Deae Auritae,* "to the Good Goddess with the Ear," and not (as Emile Mâle suggested) "to the ears of the Good Goddess." Cf. the inscription *Auribus Aescu-*

lapi et Hygiae, in *CIL* 3:896, which was given *pro salute,* out of concern for healing. At one of the two temples of Bona Dea at Ostia—the later of the two, from the Julio-Claudian period—there was found a marble representation of a serpent coiled round a phallus. See Meiggs, *Roman Ostia,* 352. *Ministrae* are mentioned on the altars at Arles and Glanum, and in an explicitly healing role in an inscription from Trastevere, cited below.

48. Platner, *Topographical Dictionary,* 85.

49. Ovid, *Fasti,* 5.157–58.

50. *CIL* 6:68.

51. This could have been September 16 or November 17 at an earlier stage in the development of the liturgical calendar, as discussed above in this chapter. But by the time of Pope Vigilius's arrest by the Byzantines, the feast was firmly established on November 22.

52. Until the later Middle Ages the texts of the Roman liturgy were divided among several kinds of books, as demanded by the several functions of those who took part. The sacramentary was the celebrant's book and contained the prayers of the Canon of the Mass, and more especially the solemn orations—"collect" prayer, "secret" prayer, "post-communion" prayer, and prayer "over the people"—that varied for each day and whose utterance was an important sacerdotal duty and prerogative. Lectionaries were of two kinds. The epistle lectionary contained those passages of the Old and New Testaments (other than the Gospels) that were appointed to be read on different days in the service of readings and prayers that began the Mass, while the gospel lectionary contained the appointed passages of the Gospels. The texts that the choir sang—introits, graduals, tracts, offertories, communion antiphons—were contained in the gradual, a book that appeared later than the others, first in versions without musical notation, around the eighth and ninth centuries, then in versions with music. The earliest copies of any of these books are from places other than Rome itself, but their Roman origins and general fidelity to the Roman model are well established. Only much later, around the thirteenth century, did books become common in which all of these texts were to be found. These books, of course, are known as missals.

53. They are cited here by their numbers in the editions represented by the abbreviations *Ha* (*Hadrianum,* one of the principal forms of the Gregorian Sacramentary) and *Ge* (*Gelasian*). See the List of Abbreviations.

54. "Deus innocentiae restitutor et amator, dirige ad te tuorum corda servorum, ut spiritus tui fervore concepto, et in fide inveniantur stabiles et in opere efficaces" (*Ha* 216).

55. "Gratia tua nos, quaesumus, domine, non relinquat, quae et sacre nos deditos faciat servituti et tuam nobis opem semper adquirat" (*Ge* 181).

56. "Adesto, domine, famulis tuis et opem tuam largire poscentibus, ut his qui te auctore et gubernatore gloriantur, et grata restaures et restaurata conserves" (*Ge* 182).

57. "Deus innocentiae restitutor et amator, dirige ad te tuorum corda fidelium, ut quos de infidelitatis tenebris liberasti, numquam a tuae veritatis luce discedant" (*Ge* 495).

58. The Gelasian Sacramentary has, as the first of six prayers for vespers during the Pentecost octave, a formula which uses the concluding words of *Ha* 216, "et in fide inveniantur stabiles et in opere efficaces." The same prayer occurs in the Paduan source of the Gregorian Sacramentary [= *Pa*] among a group of six alternative prayers for Pen-

tecost itself: "Deus, qui discipulis tuis spiritum sanctum paraclytum in ignis fervore tui amoris mittere dignatus es, da populis tuis in unitate fidei esse ferventes, ut in tua semper dilectione inveniantur stabiles et in opere efficaces" [*Ge* 646 = *Pa* 479].

The sharing of imagery, here especially the imagery of fire, among the Bona Dea, Cecilia, and the Pentecost liturgy is striking. It leads one to speculate that the intent of the writer of the *Passio* was primarily symbolic when he wrote his story of the virgin unharmed in the fire.

59. Frei, ed., *Corpus Ambrosianum-liturgicum,* 182 n. 110.

60. The verb used here is *restaurare* rather than *restituere,* perhaps suggesting that true, Christian restoration is found through the cross (*stauros*). *Auctor,* with its fundamental sense of "the one who gives increase," was a significant term in the religious usage of pagan Rome. Both *auctor* and *restitutor* may represent pagan religious terms that were adopted as Christian expressions.

61. A study of all the prayers in the Gelasian Sacramentary that use the word *ops* confirms its correspondence with the cult concerns of Bona Dea. See Connolly, "Some Early Orations," 40–44. Bona Dea was the giver of increase in women, the bestower of fertility; and *ops* is prayed for in an oration before the nuptial blessing in the Gelasian Sacramentary, *Ge* 1450. Again, it is interesting to observe the flow of this symbolism into the Cecilia legend. The author of the *Passio* carefully depicts the saint as one who gives increase, who produces offspring, though in the spiritual realm. This will be evident in the discussion of the *Passio* in chapter 3, and again in the discussion of Chaucer's treatment of Cecilia, in chapter 6.

62. The first Christian commentary on Esther was written by Hrabanus Maurus in the ninth century, *Expositio in librum Esther* (PL 109:635–70). See the discussion of the patristic use of Esther in *DTC* 5:870.

63. Morin, ed., "Le plus ancien 'comes,'" 50. "In diebus illis oravit ester d[omi]n[u]m dicens d[omi]ne deus rex omnipotens *usq.* et ne perdas ora canentium te d[omi]ne deus noster." This lectionary, Würzburg, Universitätsbibliothek, MS M.p.th.f. 62, is a northern manuscript, dating from about A.D. 700, but it is purely Roman in its content. See Vogel, *Medieval Liturgy,* 316–17.

64. Most sermons listed in J. B. Schneyer's *Repertorium* (see *RepSerm* in the List of Abbreviations) on texts drawn from the epistle of this day seem to let the attribution pass without comment. At times the attribution to Esther is explicit. Thus the thirteenth-century Dominican Nicholas de Gorran, at St. Jacques in Paris, declares that "these are the words of Esther [*verba sunt Esther*]" (see *RepSerm* 4:275, no. 305). About the same time the Minorite bishop of Tregnier, Johannes Rigaldi, declares in a sermon that "in this epistle is contained the prayer of Esther [*in ista epistola continetur oratio Esther*]" (see *RepSerm* 3:686, no. 104). At times the words are attributed to Mordecai, as in sermons by the fourteenth-century provincial of the Minorites' province of Aquitaine, Bertrandus de Turre (see *RepSerm* 1:516, no. 135) or the contemporary Dominican John of San Gimignano (see *RepSerm* 3:742, no. 260). Only once does Schneyer advert to the problem of the attribution with an editorial correction, in *RepSerm* 9:26, no. 98.

65. The text of the antiphon is "Confundantur superbi, quia injuste iniquitatem fecerunt in me, ego autem in mandatis tuis exercebor, in tuis justificationibus, ut non confundar."

66. Ps. 118:46. "Loquebar de testimoniis tuis in conspectu regum et non confundebar."

67. ". . . etenim universi qui te expectant non confundentur."

68. ". . . non confundar quoniam invocavi te."

69. Thus Einsiedeln, MS 121, facsimile ed. in *Palmus* 4, plates 1 and 2; Laon, Bibl. de la ville, MS 239, facsimile ed. in *Palmus* 10, fol. 3v; and Benevento, Bibl. cap., MS VI.34, facsimile ed. in *Palmus* 15, fols. 1v–2. This is not meant to assert that the offertory chant was sung in this way at the inception, or even in the early stages, of the liturgical cult of St. Cecilia. It does show the continuation of a tradition that made much of her interior song by alluding to it so frequently.

70. See the discussion in chapter 6. At its deepest level, *claritas* would come to signify the richest insight into divine truths achieved by the great mystics in their close union with God. Thus the confessor and biographer of St. Catherine of Siena marvels that one so lacking in natural advantage as was Catherine should yet have "reached the highest degree of virtue and should have acquired such clarity and such perfection of doctrine [*raggiunge il più alto grado delle virtù perfette e acquista tanta chiarezza e tanta perfezione in dottrina*]." See Raimondo da Capua, *S. Caterina da Siena,* 20 [*Prologo* I.5].

71. The legend of St. Clair is found in Saussay, ed., *Martyrologium Gallicanum,* s.v. "Kalendas Iunii." See also Duchesne, *Fastes* 2:128–30. The texts cited are from a medieval hymn to St. Clair, "Martyr, beate, summe Clare Pontifex," in *AH* 11:96. He is hailed as "aegris salutis saepe mirus artifex. / Caecis habendi promptus auctor luminis, / Cujusque demum restitutor debilis." A conscious linking of Cecilia with blindness in the Middle Ages is suggested by the legend of St. Geoberga of Remiremont, whose intercession was sought against diseases of vision, and who was as a consequence known also by the names Cecilia and Clara. See *BibSanc* 3:1080. The hymn "Concentus omnis virginum," found at Moissac in the tenth century (*AH* 2:69) and in a noted hymnal from Albi (Albi, Bibl. Rochegude, MS 46, fol. 27v), describes her as a minister of light, *cunctis ministrans lumina.* (*AH* 2:69 reads *junctis* for *cunctis,* but this is probably a mistake.)

72. Baldovin, *Urban Character of Christian Worship,* 113, discusses the theory of Denis-Boulet, "Titres urbains," that the twenty Roman *tituli* that existed before the mid-fourth century represented ten pairs of Jewish and Gentile Christian congregations. Curiously, Baldovin points out, only one of these suggested pairs certainly existed prior to the Constantinian settlement, and that was the pair of S. Crisogono and S. Cecilia in Trastevere.

73. This episode was popular with later painters. See, for instance, the depiction of the episode in the anonymous fourteenth-century cycle of frescoes in S. Maria del Carmine, Florence (fig. 7.4); or Il Pomerancio's *Predica di Santa Cecilia,* in the *cappella 'del bagno'* at S. Cecilia in Trastevere.

74. Trastevere seems to have been the home of a large Jewish community in late imperial times. And the evidence for the existence of this group shows them to have been the most conservative of such groups in Rome, using a greater number of Hebrew (as opposed to Greek and Latin) names than did their brethren elsewhere in the city. See the cautious conclusions in Leon, *Jews of Ancient Rome,* 75–92, 138–39, 243–44.

75. Delehaye, *Etude,* 78: ". . . un thème intéressant, éclairé de lueurs mystiques."

1. Delehaye's edition, abbreviated as *Passio* throughout this study, is the only modern one. The variants in the story are few, and the agreement among sources is rather greater than is the case with most hagiographical documents. The text is also available in the edition of Mombritius, *Sanctuarium* 1:332–41.

2. *Passio,* 194, cap. 1. "Laus Dei est cum ista leguntur . . . infidelibus nascitur maeror, incredulis livor, indisciplinatis angustia, et sanctis omnibus cum Christo gaudentibus laetitia."

3. *Passio,* 195. "Patulum enim sui pectoris sui praebet auditum." The phrase *ears of the heart* is strongly reminiscent of an important phrase used by St. Paul at the beginning of his letter to the Ephesians, a document that echoes throughout the *Passio.* In Eph. 1:18, Paul prays that "the eyes of your heart may be enlightened, in order that you may know the hope to which he has called you, the riches of his glorious inheritance."

4. *Ge* 182.

5. *Passio,* 196, cap. 3. "Huius vocem audiens sancta Caecilia, virgo clarissima, absconditum semper evangelium Christi gerebat in pectore suo et non diebus, non noctibus a colloquiis divinis et oratione cessabat."

6. I translate the word as "illustrious" so as to maintain its connotations of "light-bearing," though *inlustris* is a conventional title of nobility in its own right. On *claritas,* see Ellebracht, *Remarks,* 24, and Mohrmann, "Note sur doxa."

7. See the remarks in Bugge, *Virginitas,* 30–35, and Colombas, *Paradiso.*

8. Ps. 44:5, 11, 12. "Audi, filia, et vide, et inclina aurem tuam." Although this text is common to many virgin-saints in later sources, it is used for Cecilia alone in the earliest *gradualia* of the Roman liturgy. See *Antiphonale missarum sextuplex,* no. 165.

9. *Passio,* 196, cap. 3. "Quid multa? Venit dies in quo thalamus collocatus est et cantantibus organis illa in corde suo soli Domino decantabat dicens: 'Fiat cor meum et corpus meum immaculatum ut non confundar.'"

10. Thus, for instance, the spelling of her name in the mosiac in the triumphal arch of the Basilica Eufrasina, in Poreč, Istria (see fig. 7.3). The same spelling is encountered occasionally in documents also. A little drama about the saint's legend, entitled *Rappresentazione di S. Cecilia vergine e martyre,* which was published in Florence in 1517, spells the name thus in an escutcheon on its title page.

   In the Middle Ages at least one preacher would make oblique reference to this passage by using the example of asbestos, a "stone" that gives to cloth that is rubbed against it the power to resist fire. Cecilia, who stood upon a stone to preach and wore the garment of penitence, was thus well able to withstand the flames of her intended martyrdom as well as the flames of lust. See below, chapter 6, at n. 82.

11. Ezek. 18:31, 36:26–27, and Ps. 50:12 provide a scriptural basis for the phenomenon. See Cabassut, "Couers (Echange de)."

12. Cited by Cabassut, op. cit., 1050.

13. Ps. 50:12, "Cor mundum crea in me, deus, et spiritum rectum innova in visceribus meis." Ps. 50:19, "Sacrificium Deo spiritus contribulatus; cor contritum et humiliatum, deus, non despicies."

14. "Proiicite a vobis omnes praevaricationes vestras in quibus praevaricati estis, et facite vobis cor novum et spiritum novum."

15. Ezek. 36:26–27. "Et dabo vobis cor novum, et spiritum novum ponam in medio vestri; et auferam cor lapideum de carne vestra, et dabo vobis cor carneum. Et spiritum meum ponam in medio vestri; et faciam ut in praeceptis meis ambuletis, et iudicia mea custodiatis et operemini."

16. See John 14:15–26; 1 John 3:16–24, 4:12–16.

17. Eph. 5:18–19. "Et nolite inebriari vino, in quo est luxuria: sed implemini Spiritu sancto, loquentes vobismetipsis in psalmis, et hymnis, et canticis spiritualibus, cantantes et psallentes in cordibus vestris Domino." The same thought is expressed in almost the same language in Col. 3:16.

18. Eph. 1:18. "Illuminatos oculos cordis vestri, ut sciatis quae sit spes vocationis eius, et quae divitiae gloriae haereditatis eius in sanctis."

19. *Passio,* 198, cap. 7. "One God, one faith, one baptism, one God and Father of all, who is over all things and dwells in us all." (Eph. 4:5–6. "Unus deus, una fides, unum baptisma, unus deus et pater omnium, qui super omnia et in omnibus nobis.") Paul's chief concern in Ephesians was the nature of the Church as the Mystical Body of Christ. See Prat, *Theology of St. Paul* 2:275–83. While stressing, within this metaphor, that it was one, holy, apostolic, and universal, all of which characteristics are described in the *Passio,* he was most especially concerned with the nature of the mystical relationship between Christ and the faithful. This in turn led him to describe this relationship in terms of light-giving and of activity in the heart—two central metaphors of the *Passio.*

He prays for his readers "that the eyes of your hearts may be enlightened, so that you may know the hope to which you have been called [*illuminatos oculos cordis vestri, ut sciatis quae sit spes vocationis eius*]" (Eph. 1:18). He prays that they may be "strengthened through the Spirit unto the inner man," and that Christ may "dwell through faith in your hearts [*virtute corroborari per Spiritum eius in interiorem hominem, Christum habitare per fidem in cordibus vestris*]" (Eph. 3:16–17). He begs them "not to walk like those who walk in the vanity of their senses, their understanding darkened, separated from the life of God through the ignorance which is in them because of the blindness of their hearts [*Hoc igitur dico . . . ut iam non ambuletis, sicut et gentes ambulant in vanitate sensus sui, tenebris obscuratum habentes intellectum, alienati a vita Dei per ignorantiam, quae est in illis propter caecitatem cordis ipsorum*]" (Eph. 4:17–18). This leads to the invitation to put off the old man and put on the new (Eph. 4:22–24). Clearly it is the new man who sees with the eyes of the heart and whose mind is enlightened with the light of Christ. Paul exhorts them to live this new life: "You wre once darkness, you are now light. Walk as children of the light [*Eratis enim aliquando tenebrae: nunc autem lux in Domino*]" (Eph. 5:8). From this there flows directly, and as a consequence, his urging them to lay aside their old ways, not to become drunk on wine (which is *luxuria*), but to know the joy of their new life, to be filled with the Holy Spirit, and to sing and psalm in their hearts to the Lord (Eph 5:18–19).

20. Babylon was interpreted as "confusion" by medieval writers, following probably St. Jerome, *Liber interpretationum,* 119. For the same interpretation by an influential medieval writer, see Richard of St. Victor, *Adnotatio in Psalmum CXXXVI,* in PL 196:371: "Recte ergo huiusmodi salicia Babylonica dicta sunt, quae semper confusionem adducunt; Babylonia namque confusio interpretatur, unde et recte ad illam spectare videntur quae confusionem operantur." Ladner, *The Idea of Reform,* 242 n. 11, traces this

interpretation to Augustine, who translates the names Jerusalem and Babylon as *visio pacis* and *confusio*, respectively, in *De catechizandis rudibus*, 20, 36f. Ladner finds this interpretation of the name Jerusalem even earlier than Augustine, in Philo and Origen.

21. Thus the parable of the wedding banquet, the marriage of the mystic lamb, Hosea, and perhaps especially the Song of Songs. This last is particularly interesting in our context, for it combines the ideas of music and nuptial union. Louth, *Origins of the Christian Mystical Tradition*, 52–74, points out that the doctrine of the three ways of spiritual progress, so closely linked to St. Bonaventure, is in fact found in Origen in the third century. Origen ties the three steps of spiritual progress to three books of the Bible: Proverbs, which is the equivalent of purgation; Ecclesiastes, the equivalent of illumination; and the Song of Songs, the equivalent of union. Thus at the very formation of Christian teaching on the three ways, the way of union, the summit of mystical experience, already bore overtones of musical symbolism.

22. "Quoniam vir caput est mulieris sicut Christus caput est ecclesiae." But it has other and complex roots as well, in the Song of Songs, for instance, and the parable of the bridegroom.

23. One of the most vivid paintings in the Cecilian catalogue takes this celibate espousal as its topic. This is Anton Woensam's *Mystical Betrothal of Sts. Cecilia and Valerian* (early sixteenth century; plate 7), perhaps the most allusive of all representations of the saint. Especially remarkable is the complete reversal and inversion of the natural order that is symbolized musically in the organ resting on the ground just behind Cecilia. Not only are its pipes in the "wrong" order, as are those in Raphael's painting, but they are upside down as well, the mouths (sound-openings) of the pipes being at the top instead of the bottom.

    Celibate marriage, whether actually practiced or simply aspired to, surfaces as an ideal in the lives of numerous medieval mystics. See, for instance, the cases of Marie d'Oignies, Angela of Foligno, Margery Kempe, St. Brigid of Sweden, St. Catherine of Sweden, St. Frances of Rome, Queen Edith (the wife of St. Edward the Confessor), and others. Some commentators claim to find the practice of celibate marriage approved by St. Paul, in 1 Cor. 7:35–38. But such a reading is highly controversial.

24. Note the discussion of this point in chapter 2. Faunus and Fauna were said to be husband and wife, yet she refused his sexual advances and was beaten to death by him with myrtle rods. See also Juvenal's odd references to the cult of the Good Goddess, in Juvenal 6:314–41; and Connolly, "The Legend of St. Cecilia, I," 13 n. 32.

25. *Passio,* 197, cap. 5. "Et quis erit qui me purificet ut ego angelum videam?"

26. "Est senior qui novit purificare homines ut mereantur videre angelum."

27. "Et dum te purificaverit, induet te vestibus novis et candidis cum quibus mox ut ingressus fueris istum cubiculum, videbis angelum sanctum etiam tui amatorem effectum et omnia quae ab eo poposceris impetrabis."

28. *Passio,* 198, cap. 6. "Domine Jesu Christe, seminator casti consilii, suscipe seminum fructus quos in Caecilia seminasti. Domine Jesu Christe, pastor bone, Caecilia famula tua quasi ovis tibi argumentosa deservit. Nam sponsum, quem quasi leonem ferocem accepit, ad te quasi agnum mansuetissimum destinavit. Iste huc, nisi crederet, non venisset. Aperi ergo, Domine, cordis eius ianuam sermonibus tuis: ut te creatorem suum esse cognoscens, renuntiet diabolo et pompis eius et idolis eius."

This little prayer of St. Urban is the source of one of the more celebrated literary images of Cecilia, yet it is an image that was surely not present in the original version of the *Passio*. A common variant of the text has Urban refer to Cecilia not as "a disputatious sheep" (*ovis argumentosa*), but as "a disputatious bee" (*apis argumentosa*). This is the version known to students of Chaucer, who in translating Jacque de Voragine's abbreviation of the *Passio* wrote that Cecilia, "lyk a bisy bee, wyth-outen gyle, / Thee serveth." It is also the version known to the Roman liturgy, which has the passage as an antiphon at vespers and lauds. That the word was originally *ovis* seems evident from the context, for Christ has just been addressed as a "good shepherd" who is attended by Cecilia, and Valerian has been changed from lion to lamb—all rather more in keeping with the activity of a sheep than a bee. Of the two manuscripts used by Delehaye for his edition, the earlier (Paris, Bibliothèque nationale, MS lat. 10861, 8th century) reads *ovis* while the later (Chartres, Bibliothèque municipale, MS 144, 10th century) has corrected *ovis* to *apis*.

The matter is of some importance to my argument, for much weight is to be put upon what Chaucer called Cecilia's "leveful bisynesse," of which the image of the "busy bee" is one of the best-known symbols. Note Prov. 6:6–11, on the ant as busy. The Septuagint here has a parallel passage on the bee.

29. *Passio,* 199, cap. 8. "Istas coronas immaculato corde et mundo corpore custodite, quia de paradiso Dei eas ad vos attuli; et hoc vobis signum erit: numquam marcidum aspectus sui adhibent florem, numquam sui minuunt suavitatem odoris nec ab ullo alio videri poterunt, nisi ab eis quibus castitas placuerit sicut et vobis probata est placuisse. Et quia tu, Valeriane, consensisti consilio castitatis misit me Christus filius Dei ad te ut quam volueris petitionem insinues."

30. It is possible that the healing carried on by Bona Dea in Trastevere involved the practice of incubation. The suppliant would sleep at the shrine for a night and would receive the advice of the goddess in a dream. This passage of the *Passio* may refer to such a pagan practice in Trastevere. See, for example, Deubner, *De incubatione.*

31. *Passio,* 201, cap. 10. "Sicut enim amor Dei mihi fratrem tuum coniugem fecit, ita te mihi cognatum contemptus faciet idolorum.

32. St. Bernard of Clairvaux, *Steps of Humility* 2.3 (*Opera* 3:18), has a similar passage. He speaks of Christ at the top of the ladder of humility (the Ten Commandments also lead up to him), crying out to those who seek him, "Come to me." And Bernard quotes several passages that begin thus (cf. 2 Tim. 2:19, John 10:14, Sirach 24:26, and Matt. 11:28).

Christ-as-Lamb on the holy mountain is the image that Pope Paschal I, drawing on the well-established tradition of the *Adventus in gloria,* caused to be depicted in the apsidal mosaic in the new basilica of St. Cecilia that he built at the Trastevere site in the ninth century. The image of penance accepted, of true humility as the only beginning of the spiritual journey, is expressed visually by the image of the mountain that forms one of the common motifs in medieval miniatures of David Repentant. The kneeling king is beginning the journey that will lead him to this spiritual height. See, for example, the elaboration of this idea in the miniatures of David in the Sforza Hours, discussed below in chapter 4 and summarized in appendix 2, no. 7.

33. *Passio,* 207, cap. 17. "Turcius Almachius, urbis praefectus, sanctos Dei fortiter laniabat

et inhumata iubebat eorum corpora derelinqui." His names appear in slightly different forms in some manuscripts—Turgius, Turbidus, Amachius, Amatius, etc. But the forms given in Delehaye's edition are by far the most common.

Though no *urbis praefectus* of this name is known to history, a Turcius Rufius Apronianus Asterius was consul in 494, and was remembered as a former prefect of Rome. (See Erbes, "Die heilige Cäcilia," 11.) This official is mentioned in the consular listing (*Asterio et Praesidio*) of the memorial inscription of a Caecilia, found in the pavement of S. Paolo fuori le Mura, and of course belonging to the year 494, which is approximately the year of composition of the *Passio*. (See Rossi, *Inscriptiones Christianae* 1:405 n. 906.) Does some event now lost to history's gaze, but involving the people commemorated by this tablet, lie behind the narrative we are studying?

Another suggestion of a possible influence on the author's choice of names for his story concerns the name Valerian. There was in Trastevere a street or neighborhood called the *Vicus statuae Valerianae,* most likely because some member of the *gens Valeriana* had been honored by the erection of a statue there. Nothing further is known of the statue or of the person it represents. See Valentini and Zuchetti, *Codice topografico* 1:46, 145. Local folklore, or the hagiographer himself, might have absorbed the name into the legend and thus brought about the presence in the story of a Tiburtius and a Maximus as well, since these names were linked with a Valerian in the catacomb of Praetextatus and in the Hieronymian Martyrology on April 14.

34. *Passio,* 208, cap. 17. "qui contempserunt quod videtur esse et non est et invenerunt illud quod videtur non esse et est."

35. Ibid. "Almachius dixit: 'quid est quod videtur esse et non est?' Tiburtius dixit: 'Omnia quae in isto mundo sunt quae invitant animos ad mortem perpetuam per laetitiam temporalem.' Almachius dixit: 'Et quid est quae non videtur esse et est?' Tiburtius dixit: 'Vita quae debetur iustis et poena quae debetur iniustis ex omni parte novimus esse quod veniat infelici dissimulatione quod oculis cordis nostri scimus videre, oculis corporis nostri subducimus ut, contra conscientiam nostram, quae bona sunt malis sermonibus obumbremus et quae mala sunt bonis sermonibus adornemus.'"

36. 1 Cor. 2:14. "Quia animalis homo non percipit quae sunt spiritus dei. Spiritalis autem iudicat omnia; ipse autem a nemine iudicatur." Gerson's use of the passage will be discussed in chapter 5.

37. *Passio,* 209, cap. 18. "Nullus sic errat sicut et vos erratis, qui relictis rebus necessariis et utilibus ineptiam sectatis et otium, respuentes gaudia et execrantes laetitiam atque contempnentes omne quod vitae blandimento concessum est illud tota mentis aviditate suscipitis quod saluti contrarium est et gaudiis inimicum."

38. *Passio,* 209, cap. 18. "Iocantes et ridentes et variis deliciis affluentes vidi glaciali tempore transire per campos, in quibus campis stabant rustici pastinantes et cum omni studio sarmenta pangentes atque spinosa surcula rosarum animose et cautissime componentes. Alii quoque taleas inserebant, alii radicitus noxia quaeque truncabant cunctaque ruris opera labore nimio excolentes. Tunc illi qui deliciabantur coeperunt laborantes irridere ac dicere: 'Infelices et miseri istum superfluum laborem abicite et nobiscum gaudentes deliciis vos ac voluptatibus exhibete. Quare sicut insani duro labore deficitis vos ac voluptatibus exhibete. Quare sicut insani duro labore deficitis et vitae vestrae tempora tristissimis occupationibus fatigatis?' Et haec dicentes solve-

bantur super eos risu et dabant plausum manibus, multis increpationibus insultantes. Haec illis agentibus imbriferis atque algidis mensibus serena tempora successerunt. Et ecce floribus roseis vernantes campi, nemoribus pampineis ornabantur et crispas butronum sertas exhibebant suo partu sarmenta et vario genere talium arborum melliflua poma gignebant in quibus vidimus usque hodie abundare et gratiam et fructum pariter et decorem. Tunc gaudentibus illis qui putabantur vani, coeperunt flere qui videbantur urbani; et qui in sua fuerant sapientia gloriati in nimia pestilentia perierunt et sera paenitudine mugitum sui otii gemitumque reddentes sibi invicem loquebantur: 'Isti sunt quos habuimus in derisum; laborem ipsorum putabamus opprobrium, vitam eorum execrabamus ut miseram, personam eorum iudicabamus indignam et conventum eorum sine honore. Isti autem sapientes et nos probamur miseri tunc fuisse et insipientes et vani quando nec ipsi laboravimus nec laborantibus auxilium pro labore praestitimus. Quinimo eos in deliciis positi risimus et credidimus dementes esse quos fulgentes nunc aspicimus et florentes.'"

39. *Passio,* 210–11, cap. 19. "Veniet tempus in quo fructus huius nostrae tristitiae colligamus et nobis gaudentibus lugeant hii qui in suis nunc gaudiis extolluntur. Tempus enim seminandi modo est; qui in ista vita seminaverint gaudia, in illa vita luctum et gemitum metent. Qui autem nunc seminaverint lacrimas temporales, in illa vita gaudia sunt sempiterna messuri." Clearly the author has in mind Psalm 125, with its contrast of joy and sorrow, Jerusalem and Babylon, freedom and captivity. God's love for his chosen ones is shown by his changing one to the other for them. This psalm also expresses its ideas in the symbolism of song: "When the Lord brought back captive Sion, we were made like people consoled; then our mouth was filled with joy, our tongue with exultation."

40. *Passio,* 213, cap. 23. "Igitur cum aurora noctis finem daret, facto magno silentio, Caecilia dixit: 'Eia, milites Christi, abicite opera tenebrarum et induimini arma lucis. Certamen bonum certati estis, cursum consummastis, fidem servastis, ite ad coronam vitae, quam dabit vobis Deus iustus iudex, non solum vobis sed et omnibus qui diligunt adventum eius.'"

This little sermon is a conflation of Rom. 13:12 and 2 Tim. 4:7–8. The Advent theme of approaching light is unmistakable, and indeed this passage of Romans is a principal text for that season. Cecilia, this suggests, had an Advent character, as a herald of the approaching light. Such heralding of the Christmas light, situated as the feast was at the winter solstice, is the underlying poetic of Advent, a conspicuous strain in its liturgical utterance. Other characteristics of Cecilia's early liturgy support this. I have already pointed out the curious fact that her feast marks the beginning of winter in many medieval calendars, while Pope Urban's, on May 25, marks the beginning of summer. There is perhaps a further link here with the cult of Bona Dea, whose principal rites were carried out at the beginning of December and thus stood very close to the beginning of the Christian Advent season. Her other feast was May 1, the traditional date of the founding of her temple on the Aventine, and close enough to the beginning of summer and the later feast of St. Urban.

41. Thus Hubaux and Leroy, *Le mythe du phénix,* 148–50, 159–60.

42. Van den Broek, *The Myth of the Phoenix,* 285 n 1.

43. See ibid., 261–304 and esp. 282–84; and Guarducci, *Cristo e San Pietro,* 30, 70–71.

44. There is a phoenix on the tomb uncovered in S. Cecilia in Trastevere during the excavations of 1599, but this tomb is believed to have been provided by Pope Paschal I at his supposed invention of the remains early in the ninth century.

45. *Passio*, 216, cap. 27. ". . . promiscui sexus et conditionis et aetatis." There may be a faint resonance here, in the reference to "both sexes," of the sexual exclusivity of the rites of Bona Dea.

46. *Passio*, 218, cap. 30. "Nescio ubi tu oculos amiseris. Nam quos tu deos dicis et ego et omnes qui oculos sanos habent saxa videmus esse et aeramentum et plumbum. . . . Ex quo os aperuisti, non fuit sermo quem non probarem iniustum, stultum et vanum. Sed ne quid deesset etian exterioribus oculis te caecatum ostendis, cum quod omnes lapidem videmus esse et saxum inutile hoc tu deum esse testaris. . . . Mitte manum tuam et tangendo disce hoc saxum esse, si videndo non nosti."

47. This is seen in the special music and ritual for this chant laid out in two liturgical manuscripts from S. Cecilia in Trastevere. One is the *graduale* from the basilica, copied in 1071, and now deposited in Cologny-Genève, Biblioteca Bodmeriana, MS 74. The second is a lectionary of about the same date in a private collection in London. They will be discussed in chapter 7.

48. *Passio*, 219, cap. 31. "Cumque fuisset in calore sui balnei inclusa et subter incendia nimia lignorum pabulum ministrarent, die integro et nocte tota quasi in loco frigido inlibata perstitit sanitate, ita ut nec una pars membrorum eius saltim sudoris signo lassasset."

49. See chapter 7, and fig. 7.6. Cf. Dan. 3:91–92, "did we not cast three men into yonder furnace? . . . here were four men . . . walking to and fro in the heat of the fire . . . and such an aspect he wore, the fourth of them, as it had been a son of God."

50. The best sources—including both of those used by Delehaye—say no more of the attempted beheading than that the executioner still did not succeed in beheading her even at the third blow. The improbability seems to have been pretty apparent even in the Middle Ages, for many manuscripts of the *Passio* have an interpolation stating that Roman law forbade the executioner to strike a fourth time in such a case. The interpolation found its way into Jacques de Voragine's *Golden Legend* and, with some further embroidering, into Chaucer's version of the story.

51. "Non cessavit omnes quos nutrierat et quos docuerat in fide dominica confortare."

52. *Passio*, 220, cap. 36. "In qua beneficia dei exuberant usque in hodiernum diem."

Four   The Discarded Harp

1. Fisher, *Treatise*, ed. 1876.

2. Royal MS 2.A.16. Henry's annotations, difficult to read in the original and unpublished to my knowledge, have been transcribed into a printed psalter, dated 1542 and also listed among the king's books, and now deposited in the Library's Department of Printed Books with the shelf number C.25.b.4(2).

3. Royal MS 2.A.16, fol. 79r. Henry appears as David also on fol. 3r, before Psalm 1; on fol. 30r, before Psalm 26, where he carries a sling and faces Goliath armed with helmet, shield, and spear; on fol. 63v, before Psalm 52, where he sits and plays his harp to the fool who stands nearby; and on fol. 98v, before Psalm 80, where he plays a pipe and tabor as one of four musicians seated about a table.

An illustration on fol. 1v of Henry VIII's printed psalter, mentioned in the previous note, furnishes an interesting variant on the crown-laid-aside in the David-in-Penitence. A woodcut of David's messenger addressing Bathsheba when David, after observing her bathing, sends to have her brought to his palace shows the servant's left hand raised to his hat, either to touch it or remove it, in a gesture that might be interpreted as a sign of respect, but more probably is to be equated with the casting down of the crown (fig. 4.2).

In discussing the iconographic detail of the crown cast on the ground, I shall focus entirely on its occurrence in images of David. It should be noted, however, that the detail appears in many other contexts as well. See, e.g., Francesco Francia's painting *St. Augustine and the Crucifixion* in the Pinacoteca Nazionale, Bologna. Here St. Augustine stands beside the cross, his mitre and crozier resting on the ground before him. The crown-cast-down occurs commonly in images of St. Jerome. See, e.g., *St. Jerome* by the youthful Perugino in the Pinacoteca at Perugia. (Like Raphael's *St. Cecilia,* it has been transferred from its original surface to canvas.) In the same gallery is a *Madonna and Child* by Domenico Alfani, which is contemporary with Raphael's Bologna altarpiece. Here the principal figures are situated between St. Gregory the Great and St. Nicholas of Bari, whose tiara and mitre rest on the ground nearby. Examples are indeed legion, and their study in a wider context than is possible here would be a fruitful one.

4. Buchtal, "The Exaltation of David," examines a miniature of David in Paris BN MS grec.139 and a related miniature in Vat. MS gr.1, the "Leo Bible." This Paris psalter is a copy of a lost manuscript made in the imperial scriptorium in Byzantium and given by Constantine Porphyrogenitus to his son in 952. Buchtal identifies the David as the emperor. Similar cases are discussed by Jacobsen, "Sforza Miniature," and by Jaynie Anderson, "Giorgionesque Portrait," in reference to a self-portrait by Giorgione. Jacobsen discusses a detached illumination, in the Wallace Collection, of Duke Galeazzo Sforza in prayer and shows it to derive its iconography from images of King David-in-Penitence. God's promise to David, through Nathan, that his dynasty would last forever (see 2 Sam. 7:8–16), must have had great appeal to medieval and Renaissance dynasties, who saw the promises of the Old Testament as having been transferred to the New.

At the beginning of the sumptuous Psalter and New Testament of King Matthias Corvinus (Florence, Laurentian Library, MS Plut. 15.17, fol. 2v), painted by Gherardo and Monte di Giovanni in the late fifteenth century, is a magnificent David-in-Penitence that includes a discarded psaltery and crown. In the middle ground, just beyond the kneeling king, are seen Louis IX of France, Matthias Corvinus himself, and the young Charles VIII. They are gazing at a battle raging outside the walls of Jerusalem, near which can be seen David's victory over Goliath. This battle is surely allegorical, depicting the defeat of pride and the consequent pursuit of and victory over the other vices, and thus forms a kind of *Psychomachia*. The conquering of pride by humility was the primary lesson of David's victory over the Philistine giant, and must pervade the whole of this scene, given the powerful significance of the king kneeling in penitence.

To such cases of royal or noble identification with David, one can compare instances of wealthy patrons of lesser status who wished to associate themselves with the repentant king in the works they commissioned. See, e.g., the two sides of a triptych by Jan Provoost (1465–1529) in the Groeningen Museum, Bruges (identified as Q.216–217). These were originally in the Dominican monastery of the city. The left panel depicts the donor kneeling at a prie-dieu, beside St. Nicholas (fig. 4.3); in the panel to the right is seen his wife, with St. Godelieve. Resting on the prie-dieu before the donor is a book open at a miniature of the David-in-Penitence. Though small, the miniature has enough detail so that one can make out a harp on the ground beside the Psalmist. Other conventional details—a walled city and a flowing stream—are also visible. An equally clear example is found in a triptych of the Virgin and Child with Sts. Catherine and Barbara and the donors, which was acquired by the Groeningen Museum only in 1991 and is exhibited alongside Provoost's painting. By the Master of the Precious Blood, an anonymous contemporary of Provoost, it depicts St. Barbara and the female donor reading from books both of which are open at miniatures of David-in-Penitence.

A similar case is observed in the central panel of a triptych entitled *La Lignie de Ste. Anne,* painted by Quinten Massys (1460–1530) and exhibited in the Musée des Beaux Arts, Brussels. The left panel shows the angel foretelling the birth of Mary to Joachim, while the right panel shows the death of St. Anne. Mary, with the child Jesus, and St. Anne are the principal figures in the center panel, but two other women and six children are grouped around them. These women are probably to be identified with Mary Cleophas (the figure to the left) and Mary Salome (to the right), who by legend were stepsisters of the Virgin Mary and daughters of St. Anne by other marriages. See the excellent discussion of the painting and of these figures in Silver, *Paintings of Quentin Massys,* 35ff. The four children grouped about Mary Cleophas would thus be St. James the Less, St. Simon, St. Jude, and St. Joseph the Just, while the two children with Mary Salome would be St. James the Greater and St. John the Evangelist. The small child in the left front corner, Joseph the Just, holds a book opened at a miniature of David-in-Penitence. One can see also the letter *D,* most likely intended to be the beginning of Psalm 6, *Domine ne in furore tuo arguas me.* This is the first of the penitential psalms, and it would indicate that the book is a book of hours.

5. Huttar, "Frail Grass and Firm Tree," suggests several promising avenues of research concerning the legend of David in the Renaissance. Steger, *David Rex et Propheta,* has a narrower focus, and is limited to the eighth to the twelfth century. Owens's "Image of King David" is an excellent study but does not range widely beyond the fifteenth century.

6. St. Benedict, *Rule,* cap. 18.

7. 2 Sam. 11 and 12.

8. *Paradiso* 32:11–12. ". . . al cantor che per doglia/del fallo disse 'miserere mei.'"

9. Augustine on Psalm 37, PL 36:396–412. Trans. *Expositions,* Library of the Fathers, 25:68–94.

10. John 16:16–24.

11. Cassiodorus, *Expositio Psalmorum,* 342. "Hic enim psalmus (ut quidem voluerunt) totus ad beati Job vivacissimam pertinet passionem, qui superator fuit vitae mortalis, carnis suae debellator, triumphator ingentium supplicium; scilicet ut paenitentibus onera sua reddantur levia, dum gravissimae tentationis referuntur exempla. Con-

suetudo est enim scripturae divinae, ut cum exercitatissimus miles Christi afflictus dicitur, tironis inde animus efficacius imbuatur. Quapropter in afflictionibus asperis gaudeamus, in carnis nostri cruciatione laetemur: quoniam hoc nos ab aeterna poena liberat, quod hic propter Dominum momentanea celeritate discruciat. Considerandum est etiam quod in his psalmis paenitentium nullus tanta legatur esse perpessus, ut merito ad mensuram malorum recipi credatur qualitas gaudiorum. . . . Post haec provenit quae semper paenitentibus datur exsultativa conclusio: ubi iam a cladibus omnibus liberatus, salutis suae Deum profitetur auctorem; ut manifeste doceatur in spe certissima collocatus, qui tantae laetitiae participatione ditatus est."

12. PL 191:531. "Quarto, exsultativa conclusio de salute ponitur, ut certa sit spes imitantibus. Sic est in omnibus paenitentialibus, ibi, ne derelinquas me, Domine, Deus meus, ne etc."

13. *Rituale Romanum,* Tit. 4, cap. 6, and Tit. 6, cap. 6.

14. Oxford, Bodl. MS Douce 131, fol. 126r. The manuscript is a psalter from about 1325–35. See Sandler, *Gothic Manuscripts,* 1:117ff. Sandler relates this book to the Douai Psalter, the St. Omer Psalter, and sections of the Luttrell, Ormesby, and Gorleston Psalters, all of which she regards as "Italianate" and "innovative" English books. That the innovative forces she describes are largely Franciscan supports the idea about to be advanced, that the influences behind the popularizing of the theme of mourning and joy and of the iconography related to it are those of popular piety and popular preaching following the Gregorian Reform.

15. See, e.g., Wenzel, *Verses in Sermons,* 84, 89–90.

16. Schneyer's inventory of sermons (*RepSerm*), which covers the period from 1150 to 1350, lists a dozen sermons on this precise text for this day. An even greater number take as their thema one of the neighbouring verses of the lesson from Esther, or its first words. Note the discussion below, in chapter 6, of Siegfried Wenzel's reference to Lam. 5:15–16 as a commonplace of the medieval pulpit.

It should be noted that the gospel of the Trastevere station day (Matt. 20:17–28) was throughout the Middle Ages the subject of many sermons on humility, the virtue that underlies repentance and the David-in-Penitence. When they selected this passage, the compilers of this liturgy no doubt had in mind Valerian and Tiburtius, who were so assiduous in ministering to others. Typical of later reference to this gospel is a sermon by Landulphus Caracioli of Naples, a fourteenth-century bishop of Amalfi (see *RepSerm* 4:5, no. 72), which takes as theme Matt. 20:20, "Filius hominis non venit ministrari sed ministrare," and begins with a citation from Bernard's *De gradibus humilitatis.*

17. Deshman, "Exalted Servant," 396 and nn. 43, 44, in which he refers to Buchtal, *Miniatures of the Paris Psalter,* and Omont, *Miniatures.* On pp. 399–400 Deshman understands the fact that the king is uncrowned in various ninth-century representations of Carolingian and Byzantine royalty, and of David, to derive from "devotional usage." This may be true, but one must suspect that the application of scripture texts about fallen crowns, such as Job 19:9 ("he has stripped me of my glory, and taken away the crown from my head") and Lam. 5:15–16 ("the crown is fallen from our head; woe unto us, for we have sinned"), was already in effect.

18. See fig. 4.4, and Morgan, *Early Gothic Manuscripts,* 119, no. 73. Since Morgan's com-

ment, this important manuscript, London, BL MS 49999, has been studied thoroughly in Donovan, *de Brailes Hours*. Remarkably for so early a book, it belongs to a group of quite rare books of hours that have a miniature before each of the seven penitential psalms. See appendix 2 and the discussion of this rare feature later in this chapter.

19. Douai, Bibl. munic. MS 171, fol. 163v. The first of the gradual psalms, Psalm 119 represents another beginning, just as did the more common loci of the David-in-Penitence. The book is one of the stylistically related group of East Anglian books (referred to above, n. 14) that have certain innovative Italianate influences. It was considered one of the most beautiful of all Gothic manuscripts before its tragic deterioration during the First World War. Fortunately, the under-drawing of many of the miniatures, including this one of David with harp at his side, remains perfectly clear. See Sandler, *Gothic Manuscripts,* 2:115, no. 105, and 1:ill. 272.

20. An earlier instance of the discarded harp is seen in a manuscript of the third quarter of the thirteenth century, a choir psalter from a convent of Augustinian nuns at St. Mary and St. Bernard's, Lacock, Wiltshire. But it is a seated, not a kneeling David, and cannot be listed as a David-in-Penitence. See Oxford, Bodleian Library, MS Laud. lat. 114, fol. 7v (fig. 4.5). Here, before Psalm 1, is a seated David, crowned, holding a closed book in his right hand, his left hand raised, and with a harp beside him on the ground. At the head of Psalm 1 in a French Bible of about the same date there is a miniature of David playing the harp while a fiddle stands upright beside him. See New York, Pierpont Morgan Library, MS 110, fol. 54. These instances of unplayed instruments seem to predate slightly the earliest occurrences of the motif in the David-in-Penitence miniature.

21. Laon, Bibl. mun., MS 243[4], fol. 87.

22. Vatican Library, MS Vat. lat. 7792, fol. 8.

23. This detail could be a sign of the complete readiness and absolute guarantee of God to bestow his grace on those who place their hope in him. Thus John Fisher, in his sermon on Psalm 37, at v. 15; see Fisher, *Treatise,* ed. 1876, 82: "He may no more withdraw from them the beams of his grace, if their souls be made open by steadfast hope to receive it, than the sun may withstand his beams out of windows when they be open."

24. An interesting example occurs in the Bedford Hours (London, BL Add. MS 18850, fol. 96r), where the penitential psalms are headed by a single miniature outlining the story of Bathsheba and Uriah, including an image of David-in-Penitence, with the virtues and vices depicted in the border. A beautiful, little-known example is in Naples, Bibl. naz. MS I.B.27, fol. 125r. Three roundels in the border of a miniature of David-in-Penitence depict the sin of David and Bathsheba, the dispatch of the messenger to Joab, and the death of Uriah. David and Bathsheba are shown together in a bath, both naked except for their conspicuous crown and headdress. Of neither can it yet be said, in the words of Lam. 5:16, "the crown is fallen from my head."

25. Many texts could be brought to bear on this image. None has more force than Luke 1:52, from the Magnificat, "he has cast down the mighty from their throne."

26. Saint Augustine rejected the term, as applied to Christ, in *Retractationes* 1.19.8, on the grounds that it is incorrect to identify the single Mediator between God and mankind, the one who is both God and Man, by a phrase that should be applied to any righteous person. There is disagreement about applying the phrase to Christ. Aquinas has an

article on the title (see *Summa theologiae* 3, q.16, a.3. Essentially, he asks whether it is legitimate to use the adjective *dominicus* of him who is *Dominus*.

27. See plate 3. The painting is in MS Urb. lat. 2, fol. 5.

28. "At te, Domine, levavi animam meam; Deus meus, in te confido, non erubescam. Neque irrideant me inimici mei; etenim universi qui sustinent te non confundentur." The introit text differs at two points from the Vulgate, first by omitting the word *Domine,* and then by its reading of *qui te exspectant* in place of *qui sustinent te.* The second variant is of more significance, since the implication of waiting for the Lord in *exspectant* reinforces the Advent character of the text and brings it more in line with the kind of preaching Cecilia engages in in the *Passio.* The sermon she preaches in the house of Maximus the night before the martyrdom of Valerian and Tiburtius is based on the passage from Rom. 13:11–14 that forms the epistle of this first Sunday of Advent: "Now is the time for us to rise from sleep, for our salvation is closer than when we first believed. The night is passing, daylight approaches. Let us cast away the works of darkness and put on the armour of light."

29. See the discussion by Bernardini, "Problemi di fortuna postuma." A common enough variant of the figure of David at this place shows him offering his soul, in the shape of a homunculus, with his raised hands. See, e.g., the beautiful example in the late-fifteenth-century Missal of Laurentia de Castilione Aretino Sforza, London, BL, Add. MS 15814, fol. 7 (plate 5).

The text *Ad te levavi animam meam* occurs also in the seventh penitential psalm, Ps. 142:8, where it is joined to the idea of seeking the way of the Lord: "Make known to me your way, for to thee I have lifted up my soul." On this, there is an interesting discussion by Heribert of Reggio Emilia, in a "Commentary on the Penitential Psalms" formerly ascribed to Gregory the Great, and for that reason of considerable influence. See PL 79:651–52. Heribert sees the elevation of the soul that these words describe as the goal of humility and repentance in the seven psalms. This idea is illustrated vividly by the miniature before Ps. 142 in the Sforza Hours, to be discussed shortly (plate 4b).

A passage of Prudentius (*Psychomachia,* lines 300ff.) shows how deeply embedded in Christian tradition was this notion of David as the one who "raised up his soul." Prudentius describes the death of Pride, who falls headlong with her horse into the pit dug by Deceit and is there slain by Humble Mind. Hope upbraids the dead Vice. She describes David's victory over Goliath and adds: "That day the lad, in the ripening of his valour, followed me; as his spirit came to its bloom he lifted it up towards my kingdom; because for me is kept a sure home at the feet of the all-powerful Lord, and when I call men on high the victors who have cut down the sins that stain them reach after me."

30. *Second Nun's Tale,* line 111.

31. "Vide humilitatem meam et laborem meum, et dimitte universa delicta mea."

32. In earlier medieval times the entrance chant, or introit, consisted of an antiphon, essentially a refrain, which was sung between the individual verses of the psalm; only later, about the thirteenth century, was this reduced to the pattern of a single psalm verse plus the lesser doxology as psalmic hosts for the antiphon. The offertory may never have been a complete psalm, but in earlier times it certainly employed more psalm verses than were customary in later printed mass books. The case of the gradual is

more difficult. All the forms of it that have survived give it in its later form of just a few verses. Yet descriptions like those of Augustine suggest that in some places in the early Church the whole psalm was sung at this point.

33. The fifteenth verse of Psalm 24 occupies an interesting place in later spirituality—interesting especially to those curious about the links between music, spirituality, and St. Cecilia. "My eyes are always on the Lord [*oculi mei semper ad dominum*]," it reads, recalling again the upturned gazes of David and Cecilia. The great fifteenth-century theologian and mystic, Denis Rickel, or Denis the Carthusian, wrote a work on the doctrine of the Mystical Body of Christ called *Sonus Epulantis*. He begins from several texts of Scripture, the chief among them being Ps. 41:5, "I shall go back to the place of the Lord's majestic tabernacle, to God's house, amid the cry of rejoicing and thanksgiving, the sound of one making banquet [*transibo in locum tabernaculi admirabilis, usque ad domum dei, in voce exsultationis, sonus epulantis*]." (Augustine's consideration of Psalm 41 is perhaps his most important and influential statement on the mystical and the contemplative. It also uses musical symbolism extensively. See Butler, *Western Mysticism*, 26–36; and below, chapter 5.) The other texts are Acts 2:44ff., which describes the life-in-common of the infant church: "Omnes etiam qui credebant erant pariter . . . sumebant cibum cum exsultatione, et simplicitate cordis, collaudantes deum et habentes gratiam ad omnem plebem [All those who believed were together as equals and held all things in common . . . they took food together with rejoicing and in simplicity of heart, praising God and giving thanks before all the people]"; and Ps. 67:4: "Et iusti epulentur; et exsultent in conspectu dei, et delectentur in laetitia [The just shall hold banquet; they shall exult in the Lord's sight and shall delight in joy]."

It is this last phrase, "the sound of one making banquet" (*sonus epulantis*), that is Denis's concern. He expounds it in the four traditional modes of exegesis: literal, allegorical, tropological, and anagogical. In his allegorical interpretation he understands the banquet, as it was so often understood, as the union of the grace-filled soul with God in Christ; and he states that the *sonus epulantis,* the sound of the banqueter, is the cry of rejoicing and thanksgiving that the soul experiences in this union. In his next interpretation, the anagogical, he identifies the "sound of the banqueter" with Ps. 24:15, "my eyes are always on the Lord." "In these words," he writes, "there sounds the voice of every banqueter." We have here a strain of mystical thought that identifies mystical vision (the soul's vision of, or union with, God) with the soul's expression of joy at that vision. Succinctly put, it tells us that "the sound of joy is the vision of God."

34. An excellent survey of French miniatures of the period, including a number of examples of the David-in-Penitence, will be found in Plummer, *Last Flowering*.

35. The legend's outline is traced in Huttar, "Frail Grass and Firm Tree," and Owens, "Image of King David."

36. Fisher, *Treatise,* ed. 1876, 70–71. St. John Fisher preached two sermons on this psalm within the same series of sermons, evidently because of the occurrence of the feast of the Blessed Virgin, which led him to weave a Marian interpretation around the text. Later he preached a more straightforward sermon. It is interesting, however, that his Marian version is just as full of the oppositions and polarities expressed in this citation from the second sermon.

37. See the discussion in chapter 3. That Cecilia represents "bisyness," as in Chaucer, who opposes her to Idleness (see below, chap. 6), is on the most obvious level due to her great work of converting, and perhaps especially the episode in her legend which has her preach to an assembly at the house of Maximus the night before Valerian and Tiburtius are to be put to death. Maximus, too, is converted, and dies with them. Cecilia, at dawn, *facto magno silentio,* calls on them to rouse themselves, to put off darkness and put on light. She is preaching on Romans 13, which is the epistle for the first Sunday of Advent and the Church's Advent-call to Christians to accept the coming light, to transform themselves completely.

38. See Bloomfield, *The Seven Deadly Sins,* 69ff., on Cassian's and Gregory's influential lists of the capital sins, and the equation of sloth (*acedia*) with sadness (*tristitia*). Cassian, in the earliest list of the vices, of which he counted eight, had included both *tristitia* and *acedia* separately; Gregory the Great then combined them under the former name in a list of seven. He also added envy, *invidia,* but separated pride, *superbia,* from the others as being in an all-embracing category of its own, the root of all sins. Gregory thus listed pride and the seven vices of vainglory, wrath, envy, avarice, sloth, gluttony, and lust (*vana gloria, ira, invidia, avaritia, tristitia* [=*acedia*], *gula, luxuria.*) Later on *superbia* merged with *vana gloria,* becoming the first of the established list of seven sins.

39. Excellent examples may be found in Mirimonde, *Astrologie et Musique;* Leppert, *The Theme of Music* (see the index under "Still Life, Musical: Vanitas"); and Sterling, *Still Life Painting,* 5–8.

40. For example, Cambridge, Corpus Christi College Library, MS 23, fol. 25v. Prudentius, one notes, has the Virtues look away from the vanities at their feet—another similarity to Raphael's Cecilia.

41. *Psychomachia,* 417ff. *Luxuria* here is more than sexual indulgence, or Lust, and has been appropriately translated as "Indulgence."

Five   Raphael's Commissioners

1. Pope-Hennessy, *Raphael: The Wrightsman Lectures,* 230 n. 15, citing C. Malvasia, *Felsina pittrice, vite de' pittori bolognesi,* (Bologna, 1841), 2:164. The original edition of Malvasia was 1678. *DocTemp,* 258, reprints the passage.

2. See Vasari, *Le vite,* 349–50, for his description of the commission and the painting. Materials for the life of Beata Elena are found in a number of manuscripts in Bologna, of varying worth. The chief sources are Bologna, Biblioteca comunale dell'Archiginnasio, MS B 4314 ("Leggenda anonima di Elena Duglioli"); MS Gozzadini 292 (a collection of miracles and revelations of Beata Elena entitled "Del cuore di Helena vergine dal Signore realmente tolto . . ."); and MS B 4216 (*non schedato*), fols. 1–47r. This last—a compendium of the fuller vita entitled "Compendio della vita della Beata Elena Duglioli dall'Olio"—attributes the vita to Bonifazio Collina, a Camaldolese monk.

3. Melloni, *Atti o memorie,* 300–386.

4. See the ample documentation of Zarri, "L'altra Cecilia," 89 n. 22.

5. Ibid., 96–97.

6. See Mazza, "L'ancona lignea." Though Raphael's work is now in the Pinacoteca, a copy by Clemente Alberi is to be seen in the original location and in the original frame.

7. Thus Mossakowski, "Raphael's 'St. Cecilia,'" 1 n. 6, citing G. Bolognini, "Dario delle cose di Bologna . . . dal 1494 fino al 1513" (Bologna, Biblioteca comunale dell'Archiginnasio, MS B.1108), 202–3. Beata Elena's feast is celebrated on September 23. On that day the chapel in her house, at 33 via Farini, is opened by its present owners to the public for the celebration of Mass.

8. Zarri, "L'altra Cecilia," 92–93 nn. 35–37, documents these relationships. Julius died on February 21, 1513. The Bentivoglio were forced to flee Bologna after the defeat of the French at the Battle of Novara the same year, at which point Bologna returned to church rule and remained there until the French Revolution. Giovanni dei Medici, legate of Bologna, was elected Pope on March 11, 1513.

9. Zarri, "L'altra Cecilia," 99 n. 60, cites the "Leggenda anonima," fol. 101v–102, on the payment; and refers to O. Pucci, "La Santa Cecilia," 6, which states that a document in the Pucci Archives confirms this.

10. A similarly curious circumstance is the foundation, within their diocese of Pistoia, of a great shrine to the Madonna of Humility, which was so named by decree of Leo X in 1515 when Lorenzo was the coadjutor bishop. It was built on the site of an earlier church, S. Maria Foris Portae, in which a fourteenth-century fresco of the Madonna dell'Umiltà was reported to have bled miraculously in 1490. In the great display of devotion that followed, and which had much to do with the general desire to end the city's bitter, centuries-old civil strife, Bishop Niccolò Pandolfini decided to build a much bigger church. It was designed by Ventura Vitoni, but building was suspended at Vitoni's death in 1522 and was not resumed until Vasari undertook to complete it. It was finally consecrated in 1583. Lorenzo succeeded to the diocese in 1519, on Pandolfini's death, but resigned at once, whereupon he was succeeded by his nephew, Antonio. See Beani, *Santa Maria deU'Umiltà,* and Chiti, *Il Santuario.*

    While there are no particular grounds for believing that the founding of the shrine had anything to do with any personal devotion of the Pucci, it is certainly possible that Lorenzo's formation in a diocese with a strong devotion to the Madonna of Humility gave his spirituality a penitential cast.

11. See Arasse, "Exstases et visions"; Chastel, *Art et humanisme;* Mossakowski, "Raphael's 'St. Cecilia'"; and Gurlitt, "Die Musik." Such critics see the Neoplatonic intellectual fashions of the papal court as another influence on Raphael's iconography.

12. See Paschini, "Amour (Compagnie du Divin)," for an overview. It is curious that a church in the Campo Marzio, considered in late medieval legend to have been the site of the house of Valerian, should have become known as the Oratorio di Divino Amore. Caraffa and Massone, *Santa Cecilia martire romana,* 21, declare that it acquired the "Divino Amore" title only in the nineteenth century. Yet they also report that Cardinal Paolo Sfondrati, the titular of S. Cecilia in Trastevere who exhumed her remains in 1599, had connections with it. A twelfth-century tablet there bears the words: "Haec est domus in qua orabat S. Cecilia."

13. Daniel Arasse has introduced another confusion by applying to Cecilia's ecstasy in the painting, as well as to the notion of ecstasy in general (because Beata Elena was a mystic and an ecstatic, this point is of particular relevance) and to ecstasy in other paintings of the period, ideas drawn from a study of "beatific vision" in theologians and in papal pronouncements. See Arasse, "Exstases et visions." The problem with this approach is

that "beatific vision" is a quite specific theological term for the vision of God enjoyed by the souls of the saved. It is not at all correct to equate it with the visions claimed by living mystics, and one can quarrel with the suggestion that Raphael, or any other painter of ecstasy, was trying to depict the state of the blessed after death.

14. Zarri, "L'altra Cecilia," 100 n. 63, citing Pucci, *De corporis et sanguinis D.N. Jesu Christi sacrificio,* 46r–46v.

15. See fig. 5.1. This anonymous sixteenth-century painting depicts her with her son-in-law, Andrea Bentivoglio. Zarri, "L'altra Cecilia," 114, reproduces another early portrait.

16. The Oratory of St. Cecilia was originally a separate, and ancient, Romanesque church, built right against the city's medieval walls. It was incorporated into the complex of buildings around S. Giacomo Maggiore during the construction of the portico along the via Zamboni, immediately to its north; it actually lies directly behind the Bentivoglio Chapel at the northeast curve of the ambulatory. The cycle of ten frescoes of the life of Cecilia, painted on commission of Giovanni II Bentivoglio shortly before his defeat by Pope Julius II, includes work by Francesco Francia, Lorenzo Costa, Amico Aspertini, and perhaps Giovanni Chiodarolo. There is no overt musical reference in the cycle. But one notes that in 1805, at the time of the Napoleonic wars and the suppression of religious orders, the convent of the Augustinians attached to S. Giacomo became the site of one of Europe's most famous conservatories of music, the Conservatorio G. B. Martini.

17. Except for the brief return of the Signoria between 1511 and 1513. It was during this interlude that the citizens destroyed Michelangelo's great statue of Pope Julius II, commissioned by the pope to celebrate his victory of 1506.

18. Silvestro da Prierio was one of the earliest opponents of Martin Luther. He went on to an important curial appointment, that of Master of the Sacred Palace, and confessor to the pope.

19. Zarri, "L'altra Cecilia," 86–87 n. 12, disagrees with Melloni, *Atti o memorie,* 321, over the date. The date is based on a report that the couple had lived eighteen years of virginal marriage, a number which, when added to the year of marriage, 1487, led Melloni to accept 1505 as the date when the story became public knowledge. Zarri prefers to accept the evidence of the "Leggenda anonima" that no revelations about Elena were made before 1506. This was, of course, the year of transition from the rule of the Bentivoglio to the rule of Julius II.

20. See Zarri, "L'altra Cecilia," 95–96. The first revelation of her birth in Constantinople was said to be in January 1512. It was in October of the following year that she conceived the idea of constructing the chapel to Cecilia in S. Giovanni.

21. Ibid., 112–13.

22. Zarri, "L'altra Cecilia," 111 n. 96, points to a report of this in the chronicle of Filene delle Tuate, Bologna, Biblioteca comunale dell'Archiginnasio, MS B 100, vol. 2, fol. 291. The chronicler mentions that such preaching was forbidden to Fra Pietro and adopts an undecided attitude toward the truth of what he said: "Iddio sa il tutto o bene o male che sia."

23. Milk-filled breasts are a common mystical symbol, based on the Song of Songs. See Butler, *Western Mysticism,* 251–52, citing Bernard of Clairvaux, *Sermons on the Song of Songs* ix.7,8. The story may also owe something to Elena's known devotion to Mary

Magdalene. Magdalene's legend tells of a dead mother in a desert place whose breasts continued to nourish her child miraculously, due to the influence of the saint.

24. "Et fu ritrovato detto corpo esser marzo et puzzolento et quella mamiella piena di marza benché detti canonici dicessero esser late tal marza." Cited by Zarri, "L'altra Cecilia," 112, from the fourth volume of Leandro Alberti's chronicle, Bologna, Biblioteca Universitaria, MS Ital. 97, fol. 156.

25. ". . . un certo stato di incorruzione." Zarri, "L'altra Cecilia," 112 n. 100, citing the "Leggenda anonima," fols. 191v–193.

26. Zarri, "L'altra Cecilia," 113 n. 105.

27. St. Catherine was highly cultivated—a writer, a painter, a musician. Her first biographer notes that when she played, she looked toward heaven like David. The remark demonstrates that Raphael's contemporaries would associate a musician's upward gaze, such as he painted in the St. Cecilia, with the gaze of the penitent David. See Sabadino, Gynevra, 229.

28. See Connolly, "Legend of St. Cecilia, I," 33–34. These parallels seemed evident to me after a thorough reading of the passages from Esther and the Passio, long before my study of St. Cecilia had extended to the case of Elena dall'Olio and Raphael's painting. I wrote then: "The most noticeable of these parallels is the singular access they both have to the royal presence. Esther enters the king's presence unbidden, against strict court protocol, and is assured that she need not fear, that the law was made for others, not for her; Cecilia, the virgo clarissima, lives in the vision of angels and enjoys constant communion with God, already as it were in the courts of heaven. Esther fasts for three days when she hears of the danger to her people, then puts on her regal vesture to approach the king; Cecilia wears sackcloth, and fasts likewise, but she also wears golden vesture befitting her noble birth. Esther complains that she was unwillingly wed, that she hates the court, its banquets, her crown, the royal bed; Cecilia, unwilling to wed, turns away from the earthly marriage feast."

29. Rome, Archivio Fratrum Praedicatorum (S. Sabina), MS 14.32, fol. 89v. "The station is at S. Cecilia. On this day pilgrims gather beseeching this glorious virgin St. Cecilia just as Mordecai besought Esther to implore the revocation [of the edict against the Jews] [Statio ad sanctam ceciliam ad quam tali die conveniunt peregrini instantes erga gloriosam virginem sanctam ceciliam sicut mardochaeus institit erga hester ut impetraret revocationem]." In the following sermon in the same manuscript (fol. 90), preached "to the choir of Paris" on the same lesson, Eudes described the various classes of musicians, singers, instrumentalists, actors, jugglers, jesters, and others who are to be found in royal courts and compared their duties to what is required of singers in the heavenly courts and in the Lord's house.

30. The story of Elena's descent from the Paleologi would not, in any event, have been as startling to the Bolognese in the years that followed the fall of Constantinople as it is to us today. The Monferrato family, for instance, were members of the deposed ruling family of Byzantium, the Paleologi. There was, in addition, a Bolognese family named "Turco" or "Turchi," with whom Elena was acquainted. Zarri mentions them, and the name is still encountered in Bologna.

31. A catalogue of books in the convent of Ss. Vitale and Agricola in 1559, for instance, lists his Regula della vita spirituale, published in Bologna in 1504. It is listed next-but-

one to the *Imitation of Christ,* which is attributed (as it often was) to Jean Gerson. See ASB Demaniale 83/3232 (Ss. Vitale ed Agricola). My thanks to Professor Craig Monson for bringing this to my attention.

32. Zarri, "L'altra Cecilia," 88–89 n. 19, cites *Regule de la vita spirituale . . .* (Venice, 1526), fol. 6v: "la quale appresso de sancti e diversamente nominata: cioè sapientia abscondita, mistica theologia, oratione perfecta, carità o vero amore caritativo per la quale la rational creatura ardentemente se unisce con il suo creatore e saporosamente quanto in questo mundo possibile e el gusta et tanto eleva l'intelletto humano che in quelli excessi mentali l'huomo quasi diventa divino: in quanto lascia le operazione delli humani sensi: niuna altra cosa gustando se non il suo amoroso creatore; allora non vede non ode non sa dove si sia, non teme infernal pene ne ancho dimanda la gloria del paradiso, ma solamente abbraccia el summo bene et quello fruisce et gode."

33. I presume Pietro to mean that those who stand upright support their head, or perhaps their weight, on their left hand. In Raphael's painting Paul rests his head on his right, not his left, hand. See discussion in chapter 8.

34. I have seen three editions of the *Fundamento della vita cristiana cioè tractato utillissima della humilità . . .* , dated 1505 (when Pietro was still in Lucca), 1515 (by Girolamo dei Benedetti, Bologna), and 1523 (also at Bologna). The edition of 1515 has a woodcut of another important image of humility, the Annunciation, at its incipit, but in the 1523 print this has become a David-in-Penitence. The Annunciation is one of the great images of humility, supported theologically by Mary's words in the Magnificat (Luke 2:46–55): "he has looked on the humility of his handmaid . . . he has scattered the proud in the conceit of their heart. He has put down the mighty from their throne and raised up the lowly." The Word is born in the utterly humble, the soul perfectly in tune with the divine will. Mary's "Be it done unto me according to thy word" in response to Gabriel's announcement that she would be the mother of God-made-man is the quintessential act of humility. Dante expresses the point in *Purgatorio,* canto 10.

An equally important and influential passage is that of Phil. 2:8–9, "[Christ] humbled himself, becoming obedient unto death, even to death on a cross. For this reason God has raised him up and has given him a name which is above every other name." One should note the context of this passage, which became a central chant of the Holy Week liturgy, both a gradual-responsory and an office-responsory on Holy Thursday, Good Friday, and Holy Saturday. In vv. 1–4, St. Paul has been speaking of the solace, the consolation, the joy of true charity, which can be had only in perfect humility; humility is the complete abandonment of self-will to the will of God, and it leads to perfect solace, which is perfect love. Of this, the eternal example is Christ himself. Here is one of the basic theological foundations of the complex of thought that made up the later medieval plea to "turn our mourning into joy."

35. Zarri, "L'altra Cecilia," 88 n. 16, discusses Pietro's literary activity and gives references to more recent discussions of his writing. She cites Lucchesini, *Della storia letteraria,* 219–20; Berengo, *Nobili e mercanti,* 368–69; and Tenenti, *Il senso della morte,* 310–15 (on *La dottrina del ben morire*).

36. Fischel, *Raphael,* 245, with no knowledge of Pietro's and Gerson's threefold divisions but relying solely on an acutely sensitive vision, discerns the three zones in a superb passage: "But for Raphael also the tones of the organ formed the transition between

this world and the next. . . . We pass from the obtrusively earthbound, through the zone of agitation and effort, to the soaring transfiguration of light."

37. The reader should be aware of the sometimes conflicting labels given by different authorities to the three ways of spiritual progress and (as here with Pietro da Lucca) the three operations of the mind that characterize them. I have in general called them by their usual names: purgation, illumination, and union. Pietro's "cogitation" does not correspond to "purgation." Purgation implies a beginning of spiritual progress, whereas for Pietro "cogitation" is a thoroughly worldly mental act, devoid of all trace of prayerful attitude. A particular difficulty is the conflict between "contemplation," applied here by Pietro to the third and highest kind of operation, and "contemplation" in a wider sense, used of higher forms of mental prayer in general.

38. Ps. 93:11. Pietro definies cogitation as "uno improvido vano e inutile pensare senza faticha le cose corporee sensibile e mundane: si come le nostri corporei ochii vedono e guardano facilmente le corporee substantie."

39. Ritta, *Regule,* fol. 4r–4v. "In questa meditatione cum l'aiuto divino sta nascosta la perfectione del christiano: cioè la sancta charita o vero amore di dio: perche cosi come dalla dura pietra cum forte e dura percussione dell'acciaio si causa el scintillante fuocho: Cosi dalla sancta meditatione delle cose divine si trahe uno ardente fuocho di amore divino."

40. Ibid. "Uno perspicace, libero, facile et expedito vedere, o vero considerare della mente, o anima nostra nelle cose che debbano essere vedute o considerate al tutto diffuso: et nelle celeste cose al tutto suspenso."

41. Ibid., fol. 5v–6r. "una improvida et vagabunda: et inutile affectione: la quale dimandare si può Cupidità, o libidine, o vera concupiscentia: et quelli che sequitano tale cogitatione sono homo animali e sensuali. . . . Questi sono quelli che tutti si danno a piaceri carnali: Alli honori mundan': All'avaritia delle terreni substantie: niente alzando l'intellecto loro al considerare el creatore de tutto el mundo."

42. Ibid., fol. 6r–6v. "Dalla meditatione . . . sequita nellanima ben disposta una provida et fructuosa affectione dalla prima molto differente laquale si dimanda compunctione o devotione o vera oratione cioè un affecto pio et humile che sempre si forza ad amare la divina bonta: E questa meditatione e quella che fa li homini devoti humili et benigni: et falli fugire li peccati et il pernicioso consorzio del mondo li quali se per qualche disgratia caschano. ad un tracto si rilevano e cum affluente lachryme li perpetrati delicti piangono, e questi tengano la via dimezo. perho buoni et divoti da noi chiamati sono."

43. Ibid., fol. 7r–7v.

44. Ibid., fol. 7v. "Questi sono li piu excellenti: li piu savii: li piu docti: li piu degni e profundi uomini che si trovino."

45. Gerson makes the comparison in his commentary on the Song of Songs, acknowledging his own indebtedness to Hugh of St. Victor. See Gerson, *Oeuvres* 8:581.

46. ". . . si come anchora si legge di sancta cecilia: e questo modo similmente tenne sancta Bonaventura."

47. The story of David's dancing and Michol's reproof is in 2 Sam. 6:12–23. Note that Michol's punishment for ridiculing and rejecting humility was childlessness. From this the lesson would be reinforced that humility is fruitful, generative, while pride is barren. Cf. especially the text of the Magnificat, Luke 1:46–55, Mary's canticle of joy at

being chosen, though so lowly, as the mother of God-made-man. This motif, the generative power of humility, could explain the fact that the patron kneeling in the corner of a Flemish painting has his prayerbook open to a David-in-Prayer. He is humble, he hopes for increase. See, e.g., the donor with St. Nicholas in a panel from a triptych by Jan Provoost in the Groeningen Museum, Bruges (fig. 4.3).

48. In Ritta, *Doctrina,* cap. 2. The work is divided into three chapters, each dealing with a different phase of preparation for death. First there is the state of health, then illness, then the last hours. The distinction between perfect and imperfect contrition is an important one. Perfect contrition is sorrow for sin from the motive of charity, because sin offends God's infinite goodness. Imperfect contrition is sorrow for sin for lesser motives, such as the fear of divine punishment. Perfect contrition is considered sufficient in itself to obtain God's forgiveness for mortal sin, even before receiving the sacrament of penance and confessing the sin (though the intention of confessing the sin is implicit in the act of perfect contrition), while imperfect contrition is considered to bring forgiveness only in conjunction with the sacrament.

49. Ritta, *Fundamento,* fol. 141r.

50. See fig. 5.1. Pietro has three columns on custody of the eyes as essential to humility, in the *Fundamento,* at fol. 124r.

51. Ritta, *Arte,* 15.

52. Luke 7:36–50.

53. They were, for instance, quite commonly held to have been the bridal couple at the wedding at Cana (John 2:1–11). John, in this story, was called from the wedding feast to follow Christ. Mary's subsequent fall into sin was by some ascribed to this desertion.

54. Gerson, *Oeuvres* 4:137. "Vocibus Ecclesiae pater Augustine, fateris / Motum te lacrimis ora rigasse piis / Felix cujus erant peccata retecta, o Maria / Quae totiens voces coelitus aure capis / Organa dum cantant sibi soli corde canentem / Corde Deo pleno Ceciliam legimus. / Cordibus ut nostris psallamus, Paule, monebas, / Actio nam talis jure beat duplici. / Inchoat hic et nunc coelum vitaeque beatae / Moribus et ritu degit in exilio / Mors venit interea quae carnis vincla resolvit / Cantantem in psalmis victor in alta vehit."

55. See St. Augustine, *Confessions* 9.6.14 and 10.33.49–50. Gerson refers to the second of these passages in the *De canticis* (see Gerson, *Oeuvres* 9:460). Mary Magdalene was as closely associated with the ideals of contemplation as she was with penitence. Her legend tells of her going to Provence with her brother Lazarus, elected bishop of Marseilles, and there retiring to solitude for thirty years, during which she was daily lifted to heaven at the time of the canonical hours and heard the chanting of the heavenly hosts. The reference to Paul is to Eph. 5:19–20, a passage of central importance to the relation of musical language to mysticism.

56. These ten volumes are those of the modern edition by P. Glorieux. See Gerson, *Oeuvres,* in the bibliography.

57. Irwin, "Mystical Music of Jean Gerson," 187–88.

58. See the biographical note in Gerson, *Oeuvres,* vol. 1, and the biography by J. Connolly, *John Gerson: Reformer and Mystic.* Note that the Gersonites were one of the families of singers in the Temple in Jerusalem. Cf. 1 Chron. 6 and 25. Asaph, in 25:1, represents the sons of Gerson, or Gersom (see 6:39–43). Jean Gerson does not, to my knowledge,

advance this explanation for his choice of name. But he could hardly have been unaware of it. This play on the Hebrew suggests that he pronounced his name with a hard rather than a soft g.

59. J. Connolly, *John Gerson*, 210–11. Connolly states here that the manuscripts are beautifully illuminated. I have not had the opportunity to examine them.

60. Gerson, *Oeuvres* 9:569.

61. In *Super cantica canticorum*. See Gerson, *Oeuvres* 8:585.

62. Gerson, *Oeuvres* 7:113. "Je te responds que tu, cuer mondain ne puez veoir ou appercevoir ce qui me delitte par dedens, quia animalis homo non percipit ea que sunt spiritus . . . dy pour quoy je ne le puis veoir. Reputes tu que je soye ung aveugle sans yeulz, ou une teste sote sans sens? Pour quoy me juges tu tel? On me repute ung saige mondain, et toy a tout dire ung fol triste, melancolieux, secundum illud: tota die contristatus ingrediebar."

63. *Passio*, 208, cap. 17. "Utinam dignarentur nos ut servos suos computare, quorum tu nos aestimas esse collegas, qui contempserunt quod videtur esse et non est et invenerunt illud quod videtur non esse et est!"

64. *Passio*, 209, cap. 18. "Quoniam non est sani capitis frater tuus, tu saltem poteris sapienter dare responsum."

65. *Passio*, 218, cap. 30. "Nescio ubi tu oculos amiseris. Nam quos tu deos dicis et ego et omnes qui oculos sanos habent saxa videmus esse et aeramentum et plumbum."

66. Gerson, *Oeuvres* 9:525.

67. See Connolly, "Legend of St. Cecilia, I," 14–17.

68. Gerson probably uses the word *tonus* here not in the sense of a musical sound or pitch—the usual modern sense of the word *tone*—but in its common medieval meaning of a model-melody for the singing of psalm verses.

69. The title, a not uncommon one in the fifteenth century, is probably taken from an early Neoplatonic work that was mistakenly attributed to Ptolemy, the *Centiloquium*. See *Pauly-Wissowa*, s.v. "centiloquium."

70. Thus, in the second "tone" of the third volume of the *De canticis*, in Gerson, *Oeuvres* 9:596, nos. 37–39:

37. Canticum purae laetitiae reperitur apud Deum gloriosum suo modo et apud angelum bonum et apud hominem beatum.

38. Canticum purae tristitiae vel quasi, reperitur in daemonibus, in damnatis hominibus, in desperatis viatoribus.

39. Canticum mixtum est viatorum, spei scilicet et timoris; diversificatur secundum tres status incipientium qui purgantur, proficientium qui illuminantur, approximantium qui perficiuntur; in quibus experimur quandoque lamenta gaudiosa esse et gaudia luctuosa pro diversitate finium vel objectorum, sicut mater complacet cum filius cum lacrimis quaerat eam, aut dominus in catuli clamorem post absentem condelectatur.

71. Gerson, *Oeuvres* 9:602, "Solatium Christi sequitur suo modo qui Christum induit, hoc est qui sibi sicut exemplari vivendo conformatur. Neque enim tali deerit angelus de coelo confortans eum, dum factus erit in agonia. Quisquis ergo tristatur, aspiciat hoc exemplar, et psallat bono animo exsultans ad gaudentem Christum, et cum lamen-

tante plangens. Quod docuit sub parabola puerorum sedentium in foro et clamantium coaequalibus: cecinimus vobis et non saltastis, lamentavimus et non planxistis."

72. There are many references to this in Gerson. It is fully stated three times in the *Tractatus de canticis,* in Gerson, *Oeuvres* 9:542, 580–81, and 4:1, summarized each time in a couplet: "A sit amor gaudens, E spes, compassio Iota, / O timet, U que dolens odit, et ista notes." It is explained at some length, and in rather simpler style, in the tract intended for the less learned, the *Canticordum du pélerin;* see Gerson, *Oeuvres* 7:112–39.

73. The text of Boethius includes the lines "*Gaudia pelle, / Pelle timorem / Spemque fugato / Nec dolor adsit* [Drive joys away, and fear, flee hope, let sorrow not be present]." Thus the Loeb edition, p. 168. See Gerson, *Oeuvres* 9:581, no.8. Virgil's lines are "hinc metuunt cupiuntque, dolent gaudentque, neque auras / dispiciunt clausae tenebris et carcere caeco." Gerson cites the liturgical text—the source eludes me—when referring to this text of Virgil in a sermon on the subject of errors concerning the commandment "Thou shalt not kill." See Gerson, *Oeuvres* 5:29, "Hinc 'metuunt, cupiunt gaudentque timentque,' conformiter ad illud prosaicum: 'Confusa sunt haec omnia, spes, metus, moeror gaudium.'"

St. Thomas Aquinas, *Summa,* 1a–2ae, q.25, a.4, in justifying the reduction of the passions to four, cites the same passage of Boethius. The thought behind this reduction can be properly understood only in the context of the Aristotelian-Scholastic doctrine of the passions of the soul. The following seems a fair summary:

(a) The sensitive appetite is twofold, concupiscible and irascible. As concupiscible, it tends toward the good and away from the bad. As irascible, it tends to resist those things that hinder the good or induce the bad.

(b) There are six passions under the heading of the concupiscible appetite. Love and Hate tend toward the good as attractive, away from the bad as repugnant; Desire and Aversion tend toward the good and away from the evil insofar as it is absent; Joy and Sadness tend toward the good and away from the bad insofar as it is present and possessed.

(c) There are five passions under the heading of the irascible appetite. The irascible appetite tends toward the good that is difficult of attainment (*bonum ut arduum*) and away from the corresponding *malum arduum* (the evil that is difficult to avoid) in two ways. In regard to the good that is difficult of attainment and is not yet present, there are two passions, Hope and Despair. In regard to the evil that is difficult to avoid and that is not yet present, there are Boldness and Fear. In regard to evil that is difficult to avoid and that is present, *malum arduum praesens,* there is Anger; there is no corresponding passion for *bonum arduum praesens,* for if it were present it would not be *arduum.*

74. Gerson, *Oeuvres* 9:578.

75. Ibid., 580. "Hoc plane est signaculum quod Maria posuit supra cor suum in meditationibus, et super brachium in operationibus." He is here citing Song of Songs 8:6.

76. Gal. 6:14. The mystical gamma symbolizes the cross, among other things; and it is the cross, says Paul, that changes and mutates the soul, indeed the whole of creation. Gerson's states that Paul "sings" this passage, which is indeed hymnlike.

77. Eph. 3:18, but see the surrounding verses also. Paul prays for the Ephesians, that Christ may dwell by faith in their hearts, "ut possitis comprehendere cum omnibus sanctis

quae sit latitudo, et longitudo, et sublimitas, et profundum: scire etiam supereminentem scientiae charitatem Christi." See below, chapter 8, for this text in the context of Raphael's painting.

78. Four miniatures in an astronomical treatise in the British Library, MS Sloane 3983, fols. 41v–43v, combine the elements of Gerson's gamma in an instructive way. They show Venus in *exaltatio,* in her *domus* (house), in *declinatio,* and in *casus* (fall). These correspond to the four states of Fortune. In her *casus* and *declinatio* (fol. 43; see fig. 5.5), the crown falls from her head and the musical instruments from her hand, just as is the case with David.

79. Gerson, *Oeuvres* 9:584–92.

80. Ibid., 9:528, no. 9.

81. Ibid., 9:532. He is commenting on Ps. 150:3, "laudate eum in psalterio et cithara." This idea of reversal, conversion, is the same one that underlies the symbolism of the reversed pipes of Cecilia's organ in the Bologna altarpiece, and of many other representations of organs in the Renaissance. See, e.g., the painting of St. Cecilia and Valerian by Anton Woensam (plate 7) and the discussion of this in chapters 7 and 8. See especially the passage by Richard Rolle, cited below toward the end of chapter 8.

82. See the *Tractatus de canticis,* in Gerson, *Oeuvres* 9:591. "Reducuntur ad .U. tristitia contritio, dolor, odium bonum, detestatio, invidia bona, cruciatus, torsio, planctus seu plangor, lamentum, rugitus, gemitus, ululatus, languor." The reductions of the other letters, A, E, I, and O, are found in the same place. *Tristitia* has already been associated with the cult of Cecilia through the explanations, deriving principally from Augustine, of the text of Psalm 37, and from the listing of the deadly sins by Gregory the Great, who equated *tristitia* with sloth. The association will be further developed in chapter 6, particularly in discussing Chaucer's *Second Nun's Tale.*

83. Gerson, *Oeuvres* 7:121–22.

84. "Nunc gaudeo; non quia contristati estis, sed quia contristati estis ad poenitentiam. Contristati enim estis secundum Deum. . . . Quae enim secundum Deum tristitia est, poenitentiam in salutem stabilem operatur; saeculi autem tristitia mortem operatur."

85. See Matt. 5:4 and John 16:20–22.

86. He cites *mutatio dextere excelsi* ("the change of the right hand of the Most High"), from Ps. 76:11. This may signify a mutation, an inversion, of right and left, the equivalent of the fear of the thief, on the right hand of the cross, turning to hope, of hatred turning to love, and sadness to joy.

87. "De bonne tristesse le cuer saulte en bonne joye, comme de ut en la; et de bonne paour en bonne espoir, comme de re en sol; et pitié generalement se joint puis a l'une voix puis a l'autre, puis a toutes ensembles en maintes guises et modulacions."

88. "Si avons parlé du chant qui appartient a creature raisonnable pour ce mortel pelerinage en tant que son chant approuche plus a cely de paradis en pardurable eternité; lequel chant du cuer nous disons Canticordum de la haulte game, qui appartient au cuer depuis qu'il a esté sensuel, puis espirituel est devenu celestial, c'est assavoir de devocion a speculacion, puis a contemplacion. Dieu chant nouvel te chanteray, de tout mon cuer te louveray."

1. Prudentius, *Psychomachia,* 163–66. ". . . nam proximus Job / haeserat invictae dura inter bella magistrae / fronte severus adhuc et multo funere anhelus, / sed iam clausa truci subridens ulcera vultu."

2. Dante's journey is at one level (and this has been long recognized) an allegory of the soul's traversing of Bonaventure's three ways—purgation, illumination, and union. See Gardner, *Dante and the Mystics,* 87–91, and esp. 90, with its reference to the *Celestial Hierarchy* 3.2, as the Dionysian source of the idea. Dante was of course influenced by Pseudo-Dionysius. But in fact, the idea of the three ways is much older, originating with Origen in his commentary on the Song of Songs. See Louth, *Origins of the Christian Mystical Tradition,* 57ff. It is significant that Origen, in inventing (or deducing) this doctrine, associated the summit of the spiritual journey with music, with song. In his scheme, the three ways parallel three books of the Old Testament. The soul begins at Proverbs, which is equated with the defeat of the vanities, with purgation. It proceeds through Sirach to receive increasing illumination. And it achieves union with God as expressed in the Song of Songs. Here it arrives at the supreme song, the song of truest joy.

3. Thus at *Paradiso* 2:52, in the sphere of the moon, Beatrice smiles a little; at 3:24–25, still at the moon, she continues to smile; at 5:97, Mercury itself smiles with the increase of Beatrice's joy; at 7:17–18, still in the sphere of Mercury, Beatrice bestows a smile "that would make a man happy in the fire"; at 8:15, arriving at Venus, Beatrice becomes more beautiful. And so it continues throughout the other spheres. In canto 23:46–48, Beatrice tells Dante that his strength has grown as they have progressed, enabling him to withstand her increasing beauty and her more ardent smile—all this as they pass to the starry sphere and have looked back at the earth and the planets, passing finally from the region of Saturn. "Open thine eyes and look at me as I am," she says, "thou hast seen such things that thou hast gained strength to bear my smile [*Apri li occhi e riguarda qual son io, / tu hai vedute cose, che possente / se' fatto a sostener lo riso mio*]."

4. *Paradiso* 21:61–63. " 'Tu hai l'udir mortal sì come il viso;' / rispuose a me 'onde qui non si canta / per quel che Beatrice non ha riso. . . .' "

5. *Confessions* 9.10. This is the luminous passage in which Augustine describes the evening at Ostia when he and St. Monica sat overlooking the garden and spoke together of the Beatific Vision. Its relevance to Dante is discussed in Gardner, *Dante and the Mystics,* 47–48.

6. See the discussion in Gardner, *Dante and the Mystics,* 265ff., in his chapter titled "Dante and the Two Mechthilds." Note the excerpt from Mechthild of Magdeburg on p. 274, which can be read as purification in sorrow being succeeded by joy represented as music.

7. *Purgatorio* 28:91–96. "Lo sommo bene, che solo esso a sè piace, / fece l'uom buono e a bene, e questo loco / diede per arra a lui d'etterna pace. / Per sua difalta qui dimorò poco; / per sua difalta in pianto ed in affanno / cambiò onesto riso e dolce gioco." It should be noted that Dante uses *riso* and *ridere* both for the laughter, the happiness, of the Earthly Paradise, and generally for the smile or laughter of Matilda, Beatrice, and

others. It is *riso* that was changed into *pianto* by the Fall; it is *riso,* growing ever more intense, that marks the poet's progress from purgation to the source of blessedness in the Empyrean.

8. *Paradiso* 22:10–12. "Come t'avrebbe trasmutato il canto, / e io ridendo, mo pensar lo puoi, / poscia che 'l grido t'ha mosso cotanto."

9. Wenzel, *Verses in Sermons,* 89–90. At n. 134, he cites Woolf, *English Religious Lyric.*

10. I am grateful to Professor Wenzel for his observation, in a private communication, that Lam. 5:15–16 "is one of the most common texts in English verse sermons, and no one seems to know why."

11. Lotario dei Segni, *De miseria,* 128–31.

12. Rome, Archivio Fratrum Praedicatorum (S. Sabina), MS xiv.32, fol. 89v. Eudes' sermon, however, was on the latter part of v. 17, "do not close the mouths of those who sing your praises," not on the words "turn our mourning into joy."

13. Oxford, Bodleian Library, MS Hatton 101 (*RepSerm* 9:26, no. 98).

14. For Aldobrandinus (d. 1314), see *RepSerm* 1:163, no. 190; 1:200, no. 680; 1:217, no. 916. For Thomas Aquinas (d. 1274), see *RepSerm* 5:623, no. 604; 5:614, no. 480. For Nicholas (d. ca. 1250), see *RepSerm* 4:225, no. 245. For John (d. after 1333), see *RepSerm* 3:742, no. 260. The sermon of Eudes de Chateauroux was considered earlier in this chapter.

15. *RepSerm* 8:3, no. 34.

16. See *RepSerm* 8:248, no. 9, and 8:682, no. 55.

17. *RepSerm* 8:290, no. 34. See in this same series such incipits as no. 25, *humilitas est torcular cordis,* and no. 26, *humilitas est luna in moerore.*

18. *RepSerm* 8:381, no. 21, and 9:299, no. 66.

19. *RepSerm* 9:761, no. 127.

20. Thomas à Kempis, *Imitation of Christ* 2.9.5. This chapter is a remarkable one. It uses several excerpts from Psalm 29 to describe the alternating sense of desolation and consolation of the contemplative, and to put him on guard against being carried away by spiritual consolation. It may be worth quoting (here, in the translation by Michael Oakley, finishing the work that Ronald Knox had carried only to book 2:4 when he died): "It was this that made someone say, when grace was with him: 'I said in time of ease, Nothing can shake me now [v. 7]'; but when grace had left him, he tells us how he felt when he adds: 'Then you turned your face away from me, and I was at peace no more [v. 8].' Yet amid this distress he doesn't by any means despair, but begs the Lord all the more earnestly, saying: 'I will cry to you, Lord, and call upon my God [v. 9].' Finally, he has his prayer answered, and gives witness to that answer, when he says: 'The Lord listened and had pity on me; the Lord became my helper [v. 11].' In what way, though? 'You have turned my mourning into joy,' he says; 'and with gladness surrounded me [v. 12].' If that is the way God dealt with the great Saints, we poor weaklings are not to give up hope if our hearts are sometimes afire and sometimes cold; that is because the will of God comes and goes according as it pleases his will. It was this that made the holy Job say: 'Never a day dawns but you will surprise him at his post; never a moment when you are not making proof of him [Job 7:18].'" In the next verse, the author of the *Imitation* mentions "sweet-sounding chants and hymns" among the "consolations" that it is dangerous to become dependent on.

21. *Leggenda di Santa Chiara,* in *FontFran* 2, no. 3168. "Il padre Francesco le ordina che il giorno della festa, adorna e elegante, vada a prendere la palma in mezzo alla folla, e la notte seguente, uscendo dall'accampamento, converta la gioia mondana nel pianto della passione del Signore." The chapter title underlines the radical change of life—the interior, spiritual change—that was involved: "Come per opera del beato Francesco mutò vita e passò dal mondo alla vita religiosa." Conversion and mutation are aspects of the theme that assume some primacy in its later development, particularly in its iconography.

22. The sojourn at Urbino, and her family's closeness to the Montefeltro court when it was at its height, are not her only ties to the milieu of Raphael's early years. There is reason also to suspect some intellectual proximity to the circle around Elena dall'Olio. Thus, she knew the writings of St. Catherine dei Vigri of Bologna, a mystic who undoubtedly influenced Elena's spiritual development, and with whom Camilla Battista had much in common: both were noblewomen with continuing bonds with important courts, both were imbued with Franciscan spirituality, both were highly educated in the humanist tradition. Among her writings one finds correspondence with a physician named Battista Pucci, who may well have been a member of the Florentine family of Antonio Pucci. See Camilla Battista da Varano, *Le opere spirituali,* 351.

23. *La vita spirituale,* cap. 6.

24. Ibid., cap. 15. "Et ideo 'versa est in luctum cithara fiduciae meae.'"

25. Ibid., cap. 16.

26. The fourteenth-century English mystic, Richard Rolle, makes a similar allusion to the *cantantibus organis* passage by his use of the phrase *intonantibus simphonaicis,* in *Le chant d'amour,* cap. 44. In cap. 9 of the *Vita spirituale,* discussing the relation of *timor domini* to *amor domini,* Battista cites Lam. 5:16, "Heu mihi, cecidit corona capitis mei."

27. Raimondo, *S. Caterina da Siena* 1.4. "Era una preghiera continua al Signore, perchè custodisse la sua verginità, e cantava con santa Cecilia il verso di David: 'Sia, O Signore, il mio cuore e il mio corpo immacolato.'"

28. The relation between the two versions of the text is a complex and difficult question. The Short Text is undoubtedly by Julian, but the case for asserting that the so-called Long Text is also her own work is somewhat weaker. I have used the translation by the editors of the critical text: Julian of Norwich, *Showings,* trans. E. Colledge and J. Walsh (Classics of Western Spirituality, New York: Paulist Press, 1978). Colledge and Walsh assert Julian's authorship of the Long Text, pp. 19–23. This view may be stated as follows: The Short Text was written immediately after the revelations took place, in 1373. Julian pondered them, and the many perplexities they presented, for the next twenty years, during which time she wrote the longer, more reflective text, the conclusion of which was being written in 1393. Since Julian's reference to Cecilia is in the Short Text, the question of her authorship of the Long Text is of slight concern here.

29. Julian, *Showings,* 127. One needs to be attentive to the distinction between Julian's three desires and the three "wounds" she asked to suffer. The three wounds were the object of her third "desire," and were themselves three further desires, in effect.

30. Julian, *Showings,* 179–81 (Long Text) and 127–29 (Short Text). She understood this sickness to the point of death as God's granting the second grace she had prayed for. Was she prompted to make such as petition by the text of the lesson for the feast of

St. Cecilia, from Sirach 51:13–17? It is often suggested that this lesson was selected because its opening words seem so apt for a saint whose house became one of Rome's most venerated churches: "Lord my God, you have raised up my house over the earth." But the immediate continuation of the text is most suggestive, given Julian's prayer for an illness near to death: "and I have prayed for a death passing away [*Domine Deus meus exaltasti super terram habitationem meam, et pro morte defluente deprecata sum*]."

31. This is a sign of Franciscan influence in Julian's early piety. See Julian, *Showings*, 27 (introduction): "The editors have remarked in the Introduction to the critical text on the 'Franciscan' influences in Julian's early piety, and especially on that of popular devotions to the Passion."

32. Julian, *Showings*, 180.

33. This precise association of Cecilia with reflection on the Scriptures was made by a famous mystic, St. Catherine of Bologna. Caterina Vagri, or dei Vigri, was a Poor Clare of cultivated background, like Camilla Battista da Varano, who emphasized Cecilia as a model of the "seventh weapon" in the mystic's armory, the remembrance of Scripture, keeping God's word in the heart. She was not without influence on Beata Elena and Pietro da Lucca. See St. Catherine, *Le sette armi*, 123: "La settima arma con la qualle possiamo vincere li nostri nemici si è la memoria della santa scriptura, la qualle dovemo portare nel core nostro e da essa, sì commo la fidellissima madre, prendere consilgio [sic] in tute le cosse nue abiamo a ffare, sì como se leze della prudentissima e sacrata vergine santa Cecilia, dove dice: Absconditum semper evangelium Christi gerebat in pectore suo."

34. Julian, *Showings*, 204–5. This is chapter 15 of the Long Text. It corresponds closely with chapter 9 of the Short Text, pp. 139–40.

35. Julian, *Showings*, 231–33.

36. See B. A. Windeatt's comments in Kempe, *Book of Margery Kempe*, 15–22. On Angela, see Atkinson, *Mystic and Pilgrim*, 157–94. Atkinson compares Angela to Margery Kempe. Both were married, had children, were great weepers. On Gherardesca, see the vita in Petroff, *Consolation of the Blessed*, 87. At chapter 5, there is a lengthy discussion of the joy Gherardesca showed in her religious state after seeming always sad in the secular condition. At pp. 87–88, in chapter 7, she, too, hears angelic music; and for her, too, as for St. Cecilia at Bologna, there is an association with John the Evangelist.

37. Petroff, *Consolation of the Blessed*, iii. The force and tragedy of such familial determination is movingly captured by Dante in *Paradiso*, canto 3, where he describes the case of Piccarda Donati and discusses the problem of violence and the failure of the will.

38. The early chapters, on Margery's conversion, echo uncannily the beginning of the *Passio*. (a) Her conversion begins when, lying in bed beside her husband (she wishes to begin celibate life), she hears heavenly melody. "One night, as this creature lay in bed with her husband, she heard a melodious sound so sweet and delectable that she thought she had been in paradise. And immediately she jumped out of bed and said, 'Alas that ever I sinned! It is full merry in heaven.' This melody was so sweet that it surpassed all the melody that might be heard in this world . . . when she was in company with any people she would often say, 'It is full merry in heaven'" (Kempe, *The Book of Margery Kempe*, 46, chap. 3). (b) "And also, after this creature heard this heavenly melody, she did great bodily penance. She was sometimes shriven two or three

times on the same day. . . . She gave herself up to much fasting" (p. 47). (*c*) She wore a hair shirt made from the fabric that the malt was dried on (p. 47). (*d*) She mingled tears and joy in abundance (pp. 46–48). (*e*) She "often prayed to Our Lord that he should preserve her and keep her so that she should not fall into temptation" (p. 49). This echoes the prayer Cecilia sang in her heart: "May my heart and my body be kept spotless so that I not be cast into confusion." In Margery's case, the prayer was uttered during a time of repeated temptation to lechery, given her, she believed, as an antidote to her vainglory. (*f*) Christ promises to "slay her husband" (p. 56; chap. 9, n. 10). This is interpreted by an annotation in the manuscript to mean that he would extinguish her husband's sexual desire. But in the note, on p. 304, Windeatt (the editor of this [Penguin] edition) suggests, in view of Margery's later remarks to her husband in chapter 11, that she really did believe that if her husband did not refrain from touching her he would be killed by God. Such a threat is found in the *Passio*, 197, when Cecilia warns Valerian that her angel lover will kill him if he loves her with a tainted love: "hic si vel leviter senserit quod tu me polluto amore contingas, statim suum furorem circa te exagitat et amittis florem tuae gratissimae iuventutis." (*g*) Margery heard celestial music daily (p. 124, chap. 35). "Sometimes she heard with her bodily ears such sounds and melodies that she could not hear what anyone said to her at that time unless he spoke louder. These sounds and melodies she had heard nearly every day for twenty-five years when this book was written, and especially when she was in devout prayer, also many times while she was at Rome, and in England too." (*h*) She deeply regrets the loss of her virginity, noting that virgins dance in heaven (p. 86, chap. 22). "As this creature lay in contemplation, weeping bitterly in the spirit, she said to our Lord Jesus Christ, 'Ah, Lord, maidens are now dancing merrily in heaven. Shall I not do so? Because I am no virgin, lack of virginity is now great sorrow to me. I think I wish I had been killed as soon as I was taken from the font, so that I should never have displeased you, and then, blessed Lord, you would have had my virginity without end.'" Jesus comforts her and, among other things, promises her a happy and consoled death. At this point, his words include the following: "with my own hands . . . I shall take your soul from your body with great joy and melody." Jesus goes on to console her for the loss of her virginity and to assure her that she shall have a great and singular reward: "and because you are a maiden in your soul, I shall take you by the one hand in heaven, and my mother by the other, and so you shall dance in heaven with other holy maidens and virgins" (p. 88). On p. 84, chap. 21, Christ assures her that he loves wives also, "and especially those wives who would live chaste if they might have their will."

39. Ibid., 65; chap. 14.
40. An unpublished paper entitled "From Woe to Weal and Weal to Woe: The Structure of the Book of Margery Kempe," by Timea K. Szell and read at the Twenty-fourth International Congress on Medieval Studies at Western Michigan University, Kalamazoo, Mich., on May 6, 1989, analyzed Margery's narrative from this viewpoint. It should be noted that Margery in later life traveled to Gdansk, where she undoubtedly came in contact with the cult of Dorothea of Montau, a mystic whose spirituality is tinged with Cecilian themes, though she does not mention Cecilia directly: celibate marriage, texts of mourning and joy, hearing the angels sing, and so forth. See Kempe, *Book of Margery Kempe*, 275–77.

41. Fra Nicholas Philipp, cited by Jeffrey, *Early English Lyric,* 175, sang a song at the end of an Easter sermon. He introduced it thus: "sic secure domino clames dicens sibi sic. Et cantes devote in corde."

42. A modern editor of Jacopone, F. Mancini, expresses beautifully this tension of joy and sorrow in the genius of the singers of *laude:* "The inspiration of the singer of *laude* is encountered in the joyfilled mystery of the Incarnation, and—most especially—in the sorrowful mystery of the Passion, which has its beginning in that which the world labels foolishness. From meditation on these mysteries [cf. Cecilia's "gospel in heart"] there derives on the one hand the implacable judgment of the ascetic [cf. Cecilia's ceaseless fasting, her hair shirt], which reveals itself in preaching [Cecilia preached constantly] or outward demonstration; and on the other hand the burning love of the mystic, which by reason of its unutterableness is revealed in silence, in muttering, in crying out or in whispering [cf. Cecilia's "singing in her heart"] [*L'ispirazione del laudario s'incontra nel mistero gaudioso dell'incarnazione e—prevalentemente—in quello doloroso della passione del Cristo, che assurge a divino Prototipo di quella che il mondo giudica e chiama stoltezza. Della meditazione di questi misteri deriva da un lato il giudizio implacabile dell'asceta—che può tradursi in predica o in dimostrazione—dall'altro l'amore ardentissimo del mistico, che per sua ineffabilità, si rivela nel silenzio, nel balbettio, nel grido o nel sibilo*]." See Jacopone, *Laude,* 350.

43. Suor Cecilia, *Miracula,* 316–19. Laderchi, *S. Caeciliae* 2:31–33, repeats the story. He attributes it to *The Life of St. Dominic* by Theodoric of Appoldia, bk. 2, chap. 11.

44. The story is recounted in *AaSs,* April 3:689; cap. 1, num. 6. The passage is cited by Laderchi, *S. Caeciliae* 2:44ff. It is from the Vita by Thomas de Lensino.

45. Thus, a sermon for St. Cecilia's feast day attributed to St. Thomas Aquinas by Laderchi, *S. Caeciliae* 2:50. "Gloriosa fuit propter tria: In rationabili, propter aureolam praedicationis: In irascibili, propter aureolam Martyrii. In concupiscibili, propter aureolam Virginitatis. Fuit enim Praedicatrix, Martyr, & Virgo. Patent haec in Legenda sua." At 2:56 Laderchi cites a sermon by St. Bonaventure to the same effect: "Haec enim Virgo sacra sapientia mirâ resplenduit, Christum aliis praedicavit, adversarios fidei confutavit, multos ad fidem convertit, ita ut tradatur a multis, quod sicut habuit aureolam virginitatis, & effusionis sanguinis, sic habuit, & praedicationis."

    For the triple aureole of St. Peter, see *AaSs,* April 3:694; and Jacques de Voragine, *Golden Legend,* at April 29. On Cecilia as a model for preachers, see the discussion of the Umiliati, below.

46. See *FontFran* 2, nos. 3024–40, for the canonization testimony.

47. Thus, Aliati, *La chiesa,* writing about the church of St. Cecilia in Como, which had for a long time belonged to the female branch of this order. Aliati refers to an article by the eminent historian and archbishop of Milan, Cardinal Schuster in *L'Italia* (January 19, 1938).

48. Thus the Church of St. Cecilia in Bologna, later absorbed into S. Giacomo Maggiore and now forming a chapel behind, but attached to, the larger church. This is the chapel in which Francia and others painted the beautiful series of frescoes on the saint's life for the Bentivoglio family. For a church similarly situated in Modena, see Soli, *Chiese* 1:273–93, and especially the map on p. 281.

49. This is learned from the study of the scanty archival materials from the basilica that

have survived (Loevinson, "Documenti"). The order founded by St. Brigid of Sweden was in possession from 1419 to 1438, and the female Umiliati were reinstalled after 1527. Saint Brigid is said to have had a strong devotion to Cecilia. She called a daughter Cecilia.

At about this time, and in the environs of the Trastevere basilica, there lived another great mystic with an ardent devotion to St. Cecilia. That most Roman of saints, Francesca Buzzi in Ponziani, better known simply as S. Francesca Romana, lived much of her life close to S. Cecilia in Trastevere. Indeed, the basilica was the site of many of her visions and mystical experiences. One of its chapels, the Capella Ponziani, still bears the name of her family. It stands directly next to the chapel containing the remnants of the ancient *calidarium* that is believed to be the site of Cecilia's martyrdom. There seems to have been a hospital attached to the basilica at that time—the Umiliati were noted for their work in founding and administering hospitals—which St. Frances used to visit as a work of charity. See the two contemporary lives of S. Francesca, by J. Matteotti (her confessor) and Maria Anguillaria, in *AaSs,* March 2:92, 179. The pertinent passages, relating to the saint's deeds and revelations at S. Cecilia, appear also in Laderchi, *S. Caeciliae* 2:129ff.

50. See Aquinas, *Commentary on Aristotle's "Physics"* 1.1 (par. 3).

51. Pseudo-Dionysius, *Divine Names* 4.8–9 (704D–705C); 9.9 (916C–D). Aristotle describes these three motions as the only possible local motions in *Physics* 8. For Aquinas on this passage, see *Commentary* 8.16 (par. 1105).

52. See the discussion of Gardner, *Dante and the Mystics,* 77–110. And note that Dante attributes to Love, in the *Vita Nuova* 12.4, the words: "I am the center of the circle."

53. See Aquinas, *Commentary* 5.2 (par. 649), to justify this strict sense of the two terms in Aristotle and Aquinas. See par. 659 for the exclusion of generation and corruption as motion, though they are mutation; they are also contradictories. Motion deals in contraries and privations, and privation can be understood also as a contrary, because it can be stated affirmatively (e.g., "naked"). Next, in *Commentary* 5.3 (par. 660), Aquinas states that Aristotle has divided mutation into generation, corruption, and motion. Motion can only be in some genus of the categories. He has already shown in 3.5 (par. 324) that it is in action and passion. Now he goes on to demonstrate that it is restricted to the three categories of quantity, quality, and place. "Action and passion do not differ from motion in subject. Rather they add an intelligibility [*ratio*], as was said in book 3 [3.5 (pars. 317–18)]. Hence to say that there is motion in action and passion is the same as to say that there is motion in motion." Thus 5.3 (par. 668).

54. Any manual of Scholastic philosophy will offer a concise explanation. See, e.g., Boyer, *Cursus philosophiae* 1:111ff. Such exclusion means simply that contraries cannot both be present in the same subject at the same time, as in the two propositions "I am hot" and "I am cold." Contraries cannot both be true at the same time, though they can both be false at the same time. Contradictories, on the other hand, cannot both be true or both false at the same time, as with the statements "No man is just" and "Some man is just." One of the contradictories necessarily excludes the other.

55. Wrath was the one passion that had no contrary. Since the irascible appetite tends toward the good that is difficult to attain, *bonum arduum,* and away from the evil that is difficult to avoid, *malum arduum,* and since wrath is the passion that by definition

tends to avoid such evil when it is present, there is an obvious contradiction in the concept of its contrary. For if the good difficult to attain were present, it would not be difficult to attain.

56. Aquinas, *Summa theologiae*, 1a–2ae, q.25, a.4, citing Aristotle 2 *Ethics*, cap. 5.

57. The principal scriptural conduit for this teaching is Paul's Letter to the Ephesians, and especially the third chapter. It was this chapter that the old man who appeared to Valerian summarized by the title of the book he held in his hands: "One Lord, One Faith, One Baptism, One God and Father of All, who is above all things, pervades all things, and who dwells within us." (Eph. 3:5–6).

58. Compassion is an important element in the numerous medieval images of St. Francis receiving the stigmata on Mount Alverna. The five rays that descend from the seraph and imprint the wounds of Christ on Francis's body indicate that Francis "suffers with" Christ in both the devotional-emotional sense and the metaphysical sense (i.e., he "undergoes" the Passion of Christ, is *patiens* with Christ.) Gerson's mystical gamma can, of course, represent the five wounds. In Gerson's scheme, the center of his figure, the *I* that symbolizes *compassio*, would be the wound of the heart, the mark of the lance in Christ's side. The musical implications of "sympathy," the Greek equivalent of *compassio*, hardly need spelling out in this context. By compassion the music of Christ is mirrored in the compassionate soul, just as a vibrating string will set vibrating any nearby string that is tuned to the same frequency as itself. Such vibration is known as "sympathetic vibration."

59. Matt. 5:5. See Gerson, *Oeuvres* 5:91–107.

60. Plato, *Republic* 10.616b–617d; *Timaeus* 47B–C.

61. Cassiodorus, *Institutiones* 2.5.2, 9.

62. Aldhelm, *De virginitate*, 292–93, 424–25.

63. "*Columba inter .LX. reginas et bis quadragenas pelices.*" The song of the Sirens that he has described at the wedding is equated with the concubines, the *pelices*, and it is this that has led Aldhelm to declare that the Sirens "would allure the unwary into the dangers of life [*inexpertos quosque ad vitae pericula pellexerint*]," punning on the relationship of *pelices*, "concubines" (in his discussion of Mary), and *pellicere*, "to allure" (in his opposing Cecilia to the Sirens).

64. Flodoard, *De Christi triumphis apud Italiam* 4.10, in PL 135:661. "Accelerat taedas superatus amore petitor / Invitans laetus epulis gaudere choreas / Organici psallente melos achromate festi, / Illa deo mentis cithara sua festa canebat, / Cor mundum casto tribui sibi corpore poscens."

65. *AH* 27:140. "Noctis horas et dies / Mentis implens cantico."

66. The first half of the story follows the *Golden Legend* closely, then the narrative suddenly becomes little more than an outline of the full legend. Kolve, "Chaucer's *Second Nun's Tale*," 138, comments that "in the second half he follows an expanded *Passio* of her martyrdom, the precise exemplar of which has not yet been discovered." Chaucer's narrative may be an expansion of the *Golden Legend*, but it is much shorter than the *Passio* itself. In fact, there is very little difference in the various versions of the *Passio Caeciliae*. See the remarks of Delehaye, *Etude sur le légendier romain*, 77–78. Sherry L. Reames, who has made a thorough study of the sources, has succeeded in identifying the exact version—and, it seems, the exact manuscript—used by Chaucer.

67. See Grennen, "Chaucer and the Commonplaces of Alchemy" and "St. Cecilia's 'chemical wedding' "; Rosenberg, "Contrary Tales"; and Kolve, "Chaucer's *Second Nun's Tale*." One of the more piquant details is Chaucer's listing valerian among the materials needed by the alchemist. Valerian is the name of a plant and of a substance derived from it; it is also the name of Cecilia's husband.

68. Kolve, "Chaucer's *Second Nun's Tale*," 139.

69. Ibid., 154–55.

70. Lines 1402–3. "Lo! swich a lucre is in this lusty game, / A mannes mirthe it wol torne unto grame."

71. On Cecilia's "working," see the discussions later in this chapter of the *opus mulierum* of alchemy and of the "busyness" ascribed to Cecilia by Chaucer.

72. Lines 1400–1401: "A man may lightly lerne, if he have aught, / To multiplye, and bringe his good to naught!"

73. *Passio*, 215, cap. 25–26. "Et rogabant eam dicentes ne tale decus omitteret, ne tantam pulchritudinem versaret in mortem. Quibus flentibus atque animos eius revocare cupientibus ita dixit: 'Hoc non est iuventutem perdere sed mutare; dare lutum et accipere aurum; dare habitaculum vile et parvum et accipere domum magnam et amplissimam ex lapidibus pretiosis et auro constructam; dare angulum brevem et oppressum et accipere forum lucidum et margaritis caelestibus coruscantem; dare rem perituram et accipere quae finem nescit et mortem ignorat; dare lapidem vilem, qui pedibus conculcatur et accipere pretiosum qui in diademate regio vibrante resplendet aspectu.' "

74. *Passio*, 216, cap. 26. " 'Creditis haec quae dixi?' At illi omnes una voce dixerunt: 'Credimus Christum, filium Dei, verum Deum esse. . . .' Dicit eis Caecilia: 'Ite ergo et dicite infelici Almachio quod ego inducias petam ut non urgeat passionem meam. Et huc intra domum meam faciam venire qui vos omnes faciat vitae aeternae participes.' "

75. In her discussion of Chaucer's conversion scenes, Reames, "Cecilia Legend," 52, proposes that his "description does not suggest that the brothers' preaching simply calls forth belief, as in the *Passio*, but that it works rather violent changes in the minds of passive subjects." She quotes lines 375–78, "And with hir prechyng, ere that it were eve . . . ."

76. Other preachers did the same. See, for instance, the sermon on St. Cecilia by Roberto Carraciolo, *Sermones de sanctis* (Venice, 1490), s.v. "S. Cecilia."

77. For the parable, see Matt. 11:16–19 (and Luke 7:31–35). Especially suggestive are Christ's opening words, "To what shall I compare this generation? It is like children sitting in the marketplace [*Cui autem similem aestimabo generationem istam? Similis est pueris sedentibus in foro*]," for generation was one of the principal forms of mutation, of motion less strictly considered, in Aristotelian-Scholastic thought, and was one of the alchemist's principal goals. Christ answered his question with one of the musical texts of mourning and joy: "This generation is like children sitting in the marketplace; they call out to their friends, 'We piped to you and you would not dance, we sang dirges to you and you would not mourn' [*Similis est pueris sedentibus in foro, qui clamantes coaequalibus dicunt: Cecinimus vobis, et non saltastis, lamentavimus, et non planxistis*]." It is not primarily about the *conversion* of mourning to joy, but of *resistance* to this conversion, and as such seems to fit the sense of the alchemical tag. Though the parable itself does not speak of children *playing*, this seems to have been a common gloss of the

passage in copies of the Vulgate. John Bromyard, in his popular handbook for preachers, begins his discussion of the word *game* with this parable. See Bromyard, *Summam
predicantium*, s.v. "ludus."

A present-day reader is likely to translate the titles *opus mulierum* and *ludus puerorum* as the familiar expressions "women's work" and "child's play," and indeed in some
alchemical texts they seem to have the meaning of easy, or undependable. But the
names, whatever their precise meanings, constitute an ancient alchemical topos with
roots in the Alexandrine alchemy of late antiquity. (See the discussion in Pseudo-
Thomas Aquinas, *Alchemistische Traktat*, 70–71.) Their origin and significance are obscure, but they seem to have become increasingly common in later medieval use. I want
to suggest that the terms at least became associated with the scripture passages I have
cited, if they were not always so associated. Both passages are explanations of commerce, of *commutatio*, of change and mutation. Both would have been entirely familiar
to any medieval Christian thinker, and their contents would have fitted perfectly the
tags *opus mulierum* and *ludus puerorum*. Both fit admirably two principal themes of
Cecilian cult, her "working" and her "converting." One of them, the parable of the children playing in the marketplace, suggests the flux of the passions of sadness and joy;
the other at least makes reference to it, with its declaration that the valiant woman
"will smile in the latter day." And the terms are explained thus quite explicitly in at
least one treatise: "for the work of women, as in many things, goes sometimes well,
sometimes badly, and scarcely ever leads to perfection; while the game of children is
at times laughter, at times tears. Our work is just like that, for a worker will sometimes
succeed, sometimes fail . . . and so he rejoices sometimes, weeps sometimes, like a
woman, and like a child he sometimes succeeds, sometimes fails [*quia opus mulieribus,
ut in pluribus, modo bene, modo male se habet, et vix ad perfectum deducitur, et ludus puerorum est modo risus, modo fletus: Ita est opus nostrum, nam guidam artifex modo bene agit et
sine errore, modo male agit et cum errore. . . . Et sic modo gaudet, modo flet sicut mulier, et
sicut puer, modo bene, modo male operatur*]." (*Theatrum chimicum* 3 [1659]: 39, cited in
Pseudo-Thomas Aquinas, *Alchemistische Traktat*, 72 n. 187.) The reversing of the terms
of the comparison is peculiar, but not unexpected in alchemy. Why is the "women's
work" explained first as flux of success and failure, the "child's play" as flux of tears
and laughter? And why is application then made to an actual practitioner of alchemy,
who is now said to rejoice and weep like a woman, to succeed or fail like a child?

78. Rome, Vatican Library, MS Burgh. lat. 24 ("Sermones ad clerum"), fol. 220vb.
Johannes's name appears in the convent's archives as early as 1307 and as late as
1338. See Creytens, "Les écrivains dominicains," 253 n. 112, and 280; Bock, "Der
Este-Prozess," 100; D'Amato, "Atti del capitolo," 140, 142.

79. "Fallax gratia, et vana est pulchritudo: mulier timens dominum, ipsa laudabitur."

80. See the discussion of Chaucer's Prologue, esp.; and chapter 8 for Raphael, the armlet,
the sandals, and the reference to music.

81. Matt. 9:24. "Non est enim mortua puella, sed dormit." For the sermon, see Rome,
Vatican Library, MS Vat. lat. 1259, fols. 248r–249v.

82. "Non est mortua puella etc. Secundum Augustinum deus dat anime vivere per gratiam
sicut corpori per naturam. Et ideo sicut nunquam moritur corpus quamdiu habet animam coniunctam sic nec anima moritur per peccatum quamdiu Xto unitur per fervo-

rem caritatis. Exemplum in natura. Dicunt philosophi quod est quidam lapis preciosus amates nomine qui est tante virtutis quod incantacionibus magorum obviat et resisitit et plus quia vestis isto lapide bene contacta et confricata non consumitur nec comburitur. Sic de lapide nostro precioso scilicet Hiesu Christo. Isto lapide fuit bene contacta et confricata beata cecilia quia perfecta fuit sibi et coniuncta per ferventem caritatem et ideo virtute eius cantoribus inferni in tantum obviavit et resistit quot plus quam quadringentas personas ab eorum potestate eripuit et ad fidem Xti convertit et plus quia unitate illius lapide cui erat perfecte unita ab igne tribulationibus et adversitatis consumi non potuit."

83. Pliny, *Natural History* 36.31: "Amiantus alumini similis nihil igni deperdit. Hic veneficiis resistit omnibus, privatim Magorum." Isidore, *Isidori Hispalensis Episcopi Etymologiarum* 16.4.19: "Amiantos appelatus a veteribus eo quod, si ex ipso vestis fuerit contexta, contra ignem resistat et igni inposita non ardeat, sed splendore accepto nitescat; et est scissi aluminis similis, veneficiis resistens omnibus, specialiter magorum."

84. In his self-memoir the monk Guibert of Nogent, who died about 1125, says of his mother, when she underwent temptations against chastity, that "placed in the fire, she did not burn [*In igne posita non ardebat*]." See Guibert, *Self and Society*, 65. In his n. 2, the editor says, "Variations of this idea and phrase . . . are common in the twelfth century, appearing in the works of the Archpoet, Andreas Capellanus, and Jean of Haute-Seille. The phrase echoes Proverbs 6:27–28." Proverbs 6:27–28 asks, "Can a man hide fire in his bosom, so that his garments will not catch fire? or walk upon coals, so that his feet will not burn? [*Numquid potest homo abscondere ignem in sinu suo, ut vestimenta sua non ardeant? Aut ambulare super prunas, ut non comburantur plantae ejus?*]" The phrase also reflects the legend of Cecilia, and certain aspects of it that interested Chaucer, such as her preservation in the burning bath. Cecilia, placed in the fire of the bath, did not burn. There are alchemical overtones to this, and Chaucer's awareness of them is reflected in his joining the *Second Nun's Tale* and the *Canon's Yeoman's Tale*.

85. Ashmole, *Theatrum chimicum*, A4vff.

86. The image of the bee was probably substituted for that of the sheep at some point. Many manuscripts of the *Passio*, however, maintained the reading "sheep." See the remarks above, in chapter 2, concerning the variant readings *ovis argumentosa* and *apis argumentosa*. The former fits the general context of the *Passio* much better. Christ is shepherd; Valerian is a "roaring lion" turned by Cecilia into a gentle lamb—a much more suitable metamorphosis.

The "busy bee" could also suggest fecundity in the Middle Ages. Thus the confessor and biographer of St. Catherine of Siena, describes her mother, Lapa Benincasa, as filling the house with sons and daughters "like a fruitful bee" (*come un' ape fruttuosa*). See Raimondo, *S. Caterina*, 38 (cap. 2, 26).

87. *Moralia* 6.56. Cited by Butler, *Western Mysticism*, 96.

88. See Bloomfield, *The Seven Deadly Sins*, 69ff.

89. Aquinas, *Summa*, 2a-2ae, q. 35, a.1 and a.3.

90. See Aquinas, *Summa*, 2a-2ae, q. 28, on *gaudium* as an effect of charity.

91. Ibid., 2a-2ae, q. 35, a.1, *ad primum* and *respondeo*. "Ita deprimit animum hominis, ut nihil ei agere libeat; sicuti ea, quae sunt acida, etiam frigida sunt."

92. See Multhauf, "Science of Matter," 381.

93. *Summa,* 2a-2ae, q. 35, a.1. "Maxime acedia circa horam sextam monachum inquietat, ut quaedam febris ingruens tempore praestituto, ardentissimos aestus accensionum suarum solitis ac statutis horis animae inferens aegrotanti."

94. Ibid. "Quanto magis cogitamus de bonis spiritualibus, tanto magis nobis placentia redduntur; ex quo cessat accidia."

95. Ibid., 2a-2ae, q. 35, a.2. "Tristari de bono divino, de quo charitas gaudet, pertinet ad speciale vitium, quod accidia vocatur."

96. Ibid., 2a-2ae, q. 35, a.3. "Accidia contrariatur praecepto de sanctificatione Sabbati; in quo, secundum quod est praeceptum morale, praecipitur quies mentis in Deo; cui etim contrariatur tristitia mentis de bono divino."

97. Ibid., 2a-2ae, q. 35, a.1. "Passiones appetitus sensitivi et in se possunt esse peccata venialia, et inclinant animam ad peccatum mortale: et quia appetitus sensitivus habet organum corporale, sequitur quod per aliquam corporalem transmutationem homo fit habilior ad aliquod peccatum; et ideo potest contingere, quod secundum aliquas transmutationes corporales certis temporibus provenientes, aliqua peccata nos magis impugnent: omnis autem corporalis defectus de se ad tristitiam disponit; et ideo jejunantes circa meridiem, quando jam incipiunt sentire defectum cibi, et urgeri ab aestibus solis, magis ab accidia impugnantur."

98. Paris, Bibliothèque nationale, MS lat. 12412, fol. 157r. "Cantantibus organis cecilia virgo in corde suo domino decantabat dicens: Fiat domine cor meum et corpus meum immaculatum ut non confundar. Sicut ait beatus Gregorius in electis et reprobis divisi sunt impetus. Nam electi impetum spiritus sebsecuntur; reprobis autem carnis impetu dominantur. Impetus autem spiritus ad spiritualia, impetus carnalis ad carnalia. Hic ad interiora dona, ille ad exteriora."

99. *Paradiso* 2:121–23. "Questi organi del mondo così vanno, / come tu vedi omai, di grado in grado, / che di su prendono e di sotto fanno."

100. *Summa,* 2a-2ae, q. 35, a.2.

101. The crucifix itself is eighteenth-century, but replaced an earlier work destroyed in the Revolution. The wooden figures of Mary and John, and the Adam and Eve in polychrome stone, are from the fifteenth century.

102. Chaucer, *Second Nun's Tale,* 22–23.

103. See Aquinas, *Summa,* 1a, q. 66, a.2.

104. Johannes de Biblia, Rome, Vatican Library, MS Burgh. lat. 24, fol. 223rb. "Nam sequitur procul et de ultimis finibus pretium eius. gratia eius omne rarum carum immo omnis ponderatio terrenorum bonorum non est condigna ad huius fortitudinis pretium. procul igitur et de ultimis finibus pretium eius. in corpore spherico circulus quanto maior fuerit tanto magis distat a centro. cum igitur mundus figuram habet sphericam a centro terre in quo nos sumus celum empyreum quod est maxime capacitatis magis procul est et ibi sunt ultimi fines huius tocius sphere. i. mundialis machine. ibi haec fortis mulier suum habet pretium."

105. Rola, *Alchemy,* 14–15.

106. Ibid. The circle with center is sometimes found as a curious paleographic detail in medieval liturgical manuscripts in places that suggest the scribe intended this same symbolism—of the sun, and perhaps even of alchemical mutation. A famous antiphoner from Verona, Biblioteca capitolare MS 94, the celebrated *Carpsum,* provides a good example; see fols. 13ff. (A modern edition by G. Meerseman, E. Adda, and J. De-

shusses appeared in 1974.) The letter *O* at the beginning of certain chants has been decorated with a point at its center. What is striking is that the texts of the chants in question sometimes contain a solar symbolism, and even express the kind of radical remaking of human nature that is consistent with alchemical comparison. The famous series of *O*-antiphons sung on the days preceding Christmas are a good example. Like other texts of the Christmas season, these make much of the idea of the approaching light, the return of the sun following the winter solstice. The best example is the antiphon *O Oriens:* "O rising splendor of eternal light, O sun of justice, come and enlighten those who are sitting in darkness, and in the shadow of death."

107. *Moralia* 20.41.78.

Seven   St. Cecilia before Raphael

1. See Bernardini, "Problemi di fortuna postuma," for a discussion of the painting's influence, with considerable attention to Cecilia's upward glance.

2. On the shrine of Bona Dea, see the discussion in chapter 2. How enduring was the influence of St. Cecilia's origin in light-giving? Did Chaucer's and Jacques de Voragine's explanation of Cecilia's name as "way to the blind" (because of her teaching) or as "lacking blindness" (because of the light of wisdom in her) result from an unbroken tradition, or simply from a late medieval observation of the similarity of the saint's name to the Latin word for "blind"? There are indications—like the occurrence of the cult language of Bona Dea in the legend of St. Clair of Albi, where devotion to Cecilia also took root—that the idea was an enduring one, but they are no more than indications.

3. See fig. 7.1. See Ricci, *Tavole storiche* tables H and 44. Cecilia differs from the other virgins in the group in one respect, which I cannot explain: the others wear a jewel around the neck, she does not.

4. For a more detailed treatment of this idea, see Connolly, "Legend of St. Cecilia, II," 14–15.

5. Of the two, Macrobius is by far the more accessible for modern readers. The universe, he says, is governed, knit together, by the proportions of music established in the world-soul and in the harmony of the spheres. Souls in their pristine state dwell in the outermost realm; they are only drawn down to bodies as they let themselves lose sight of their divine origin, and be attracted to, and defiled by, the impurities of physical bodies. As they descend they gather physical accretions, and once established in the world they undergo debasing transmigrations. Their only way back is by directing their inner gaze to their former high estate. Every soul in the world is allured by music, because it remembers the music it once knew in the sky; all souls have life from the World-Soul, which is itself knit together by harmony, and is the cause of all harmony in the universe. Thus music and the memory of the celestial music have the strongest ethical influence. Souls can even regain the celestial habitation through music. The fixing of the soul's gaze upon its celestial origin means for Macrobius the cultivating of the memory of the celestial music. Indeed, the wise and virtuous souls (of wise rulers and heroes) may be said never to have left the heavenly realm, but to carry it with them, since they keep their origin always in mind, fixing their inner gaze upon it. See Macrobius, *Commentary on the Dream of Scipio* 1.9.6.

Macrobius emphasizes one element of these Neoplatonic ideas that is especially pertinent to understanding the links among light, virginity, and music. He goes to some pains to explain that although there are eight moving spheres, two of them (Mercury and Venus) move at the same speed, so that only seven tones result, not eight, as Plato has it (ibid. 2.4.9). Seven, he points out, quoting Cicero, is a number of special significance—one might almost say it is the key to the universe. For seven, in Neoplatonic numerology, was the virgin number; it was even called Pallas, for the virgin goddess born from the head of Zeus (and identified commonly with Minerva), whose attributes included wisdom and music (ibid. 1.6). This connection of seven with virginity made a deep impression upon the ancients, and was attributed to the position of seven within the decad: it was said neither to be begotten (it is a prime number) nor to beget (as a factor it does not yield a number within the decad). For further discussion, see Connolly, "Legend of St. Cecilia, II," 16–17, and "Legend of St. Cecilia, I," 25 n. 66.

6. The *Adventus in gloria* itself derives from the *Traditio legis,* a similar and important early Christian composition that originated in fourth-century sculptured sarcophagi. For a fuller discussion, see Sotomayor, *S. Pedro,* Schumacher, "Dominus legem dat," and especially Davis-Weyer, "Das Traditio-Legis Bild." See also Connolly, "Legend of St. Cecilia, I," 25–26.

7. And on its other bank from the worshipers. This is where Dante saw Matilda, and heard her sing, as discussed above in chapter 6.

8. MS Barb. lat. 4402.

9. See Offner, *Florentine Painting* 3:1, pl. 5a. Kolve, "Chaucer's *Second Nun's Tale,*" 143, cites Robert Pratt's suggestion that Chaucer may have seen this painting on his visit to Florence in 1373. This unknown artist was a painter of great power, a contemporary and perhaps an associate of Giotto. A much disputed view holds that he painted the last three frescoes of the cycle on the life of St. Francis, which some attribute to Giotto, in the upper basilica at Assisi.

10. Offner and others are plainly mistaken in describing the fifth panel as the baptism of Tiburtius. There are two nimbed figures standing beside Cecilia, who can only be the two brothers, after their baptisms. The kneeling figure is one of those converted by the activity of the three saints, perhaps Maximus.

11. See Pseudo-Bonaventure, *Meditations,* 1.

12. Eph. 5:25–26. "Viri, diligite uxores vestras, sicut et Christus dilexit ecclesiam, et seipsum tradidit pro ea, ut illam sanctificaret, mundans lavacro aquae in verbo vitae."

13. Rev. 3:15–23. "Scio opera tua: quia neque frigidus es, neque calidus: utinam frigidus esses, aut calidus: sed quia tepidus es, et nec frigidus, nec calidus, incipiam te evomere ex ore meo: quia dicis: Quod dives sum, et locupletatus, et nullius egeo: et nescis quia tu es miser, et miserabilis, et pauper, et caecus, et nudus. Suadeo tibi emere a me aurum ignitum probatum, ut locuples fias, et vestimentis albis induaris, et non appareat confusio nuditatis tuae, et collyrio inunge oculos tuos ut videas. Ego quos amo, arguo, et castigo. Aemulare ergo, et poenitentiam age. Ecce sto ad ostium, et pulso: si quis audierit vocem meam, et aperuerit mihi ianuam, intrabo ad illum, et coenabo cum illo, et ipse mecum. Qui vicerit, dabo ei sedere mecum in throno meo: sicut et ego vici, et sedi cum patre meo in throno eius. Qui habet aurem, audiat quid Spiritus dicat Ecclesiis."

14. *Passio,* 213, cap. 22; 214, cap. 24. The first of these passages is Tiburtius's assertion to

Maximus that the body, reduced to dust, will rise like the phoenix "at the appearance of the light that will come." The second tells of Cecilia's having a phoenix carved on Maximus's tomb, in token of his faith in the Resurrection. The phoenix appears in the apsidal mosaic of S. Cecilia in Trastevere (fig. 2.5); on the sarcophagus of Maximus in the crypt of the Trastevere basilica, as discussed in chapter 2; and in the series of frescoes formerly in St. Cecilia, Cologne.

15. See the example in Mirimonde, *Sainte-Cécile,* 42.

16. See Cambridge, Fitzwilliam Museum, MS 368. This is a single leaf from a manuscript of *Somme le roi* copied for Philip le Bel in 1296. The rest of the manuscript is in the British Library, Add. MS 54180. Chastity holds a globe, which contains the bird, in her hand, and tramples a pig underfoot. For a reproduction, see *Treasures from the Fitzwilliam,* 33.

17. See Van den Broek, *Myth of the Phoenix,* esp. pp. 261–304.

18. On the phoenix as symbol of virginity, see ibid., 357–89, and especially his defense, on pp. 382ff., of the thesis that "Lactantius was concerned in the first place with the eschatological Paradise that the *virgo* brought to realization in his earthly life." I have accepted Van den Broek's justification of Lactantius's description of the phoenix's daily song to the sun, which renders unnecessary and gratuitous the transfer of this passage (*De ave phoenice,* 43–50) by Hubaux and Leroy, *Le mythe du phénix,* 148–50, 159–60, to the scene of the bird's death. They did so because Lactantius's poem seemed to be the only one of many sources of the legend to describe this daily song welcoming the sun, and this led them to conclude that the text was faulty. Van den Broek's demonstration that there is ample evidence for the story just as Lactantius has it seems decisive.

19. *Passio,* 213, cap. 22. "Et corpus quidem quod terrenum semen per libidinem dedit terreno ventri redditur, ut in pulverem redactum sicut phoenix futuri aspectu luminis resurgat."

20. *Passio,* 213, cap. 23. Romans 13:12. "Nox praecessit, dies autem appropinquavit. Abiiciamus ergo opera tenebrarum et induamur arma salutis."

21. Guarducci, *Cristo e San Pietro,* 30, 70–71. And see the discussion of Van den Broek, *The Myth of the Phoenix,* 159–61, 284. Though Guarducci's findings were received with serious reservations, her reading of the *graffiti* relating to the bird's singing seems corroborated by its agreement with the conclusions of Van den Broek (that the bird sang daily, not just at its death), which were reached independently and were evidently unknown to her.

22. Van den Broek, *Myth of the Phoenix,* 160–61. His conclusion simply states that "it may therefore be considered probable that the drawing in the tomb of the *Valerii* reflects the conception of the resurrection of Christ as promising the resurrection of mankind."

23. An excellent summary, with scriptural and patristic texts, will be found in Bethune-Baker, *Early History of Christian Doctrine,* 23, 357 n. 1, 358, 365, 370 n. 3.

24. The linking of the phoenix heads to the head of Christ seems to rule out any interpretation of this phoenix as a purely abstract symbol of resurrection. The interpretation I suggest, following Van den Broek, can be supported in other ways. For instance Lactantius's phoenix, upon waking each morning and immediately before greeting the rising light, immerses itself several times in the paradisal spring and drinks some of its

water of life. Thus lines 35–38, cited by Van den Broek, *Myth of the Phoenix,* 282 n. 1. The liturgical, sacramental tone of this image, if one accepts Van den Broek's powerful arguments for the Christian character of the poem, is unmistakable. The bird's daily drinking of the water of life would recall to the Christian mind texts like John 4:13–14. "Whoever shall drink of the water I shall give him shall not thirst for ever; and the water I shall give shall become for him a fountain of living water springing forth to life eternal." Similarly, Lactantius's description of the singing of the phoenix at fixed hours of the day is probably a reference to some forerunner of the liturgical hours.

25. The *Traditio legis* (the Giving of the Law) typically shows Christ on the mountain of the four rivers—paradise is intended—flanked by Peter and Paul. In his hand is a scroll bearing the legend "The Lord is the Law-giver" (*Dominus legem dat*), while to the left of the scene a phoenix sits on a tree branch. Van den Broek's researches show that this bird signifies not just "resurrection," but something much more sharply defined. It can indeed represent the Christian departed, who has changed an old life for a new, and hails the Law-giver and Light-bearer who brings this about.

26. St. Gregory, *Dialogues* 4:58.

27. See Platner, *Topographical Dictionary of Ancient Rome,* s.v. "Sts. Cosmas and Damian."

28. Van den Broek, *Myth of the Phoenix,* 388; plate 34.

29. Rev. 14:1–5.

30. Cecilia's virginal status is thus grounds for her to be considered a musician, a singer. But it does not of itself explain why she, rather than Agnes or Agatha or Lucy, should have been singled out as a preeminently musical figure.

31. *Hali Meidenhad,* 19.

32. The Pythagoreans opposed cremation "because they did not wish something mortal to receive a share of the divine (i.e., fire)." Thus Van den Broek, *Myth of the Phoenix,* 413 n. 1, where he cites Iamblichus, *De Vita Pythagorica,* 154. Fire and burning could thus be perceived as transmitting divinity.

33. London, British Library, Add. MS 29704-05, fol. 160v. This miniature is from an English Carmelite missal of the late fourteenth century. Dismembered and mutilated, its remnants, preserved in the two manuscripts cited along with Add. MS 44892, are now grouped in six volumes. The miniature of St. Cecilia is in vol. 3. For the missal, see Rickert, *Reconstructed Carmelite Missal.* The miniature is discussed by Kolve, "Chaucer's *Second Nun's Tale,*" 172.

34. This manuscript is in the collection of Mr. B. S. Cron of Kew Gardens, in London. Formerly in the collection of Sir Sidney Cockerell, it was noticed by Lowe, *Beneventan Script,* 267 n. 2, and by Frere, *Studies in Early Roman Liturgy, III,* 270. Its interesting rubrics for the Holy Saturday chanting of the Hymn of the Three Young Men should be compared with the different, but equally interesting and singular, rubrics for the same canticle as given following the fifth lesson of Ember Saturday in Advent in the *graduale* from S. Cecilia in Trastevere, now at Cologny-Genève, Biblioteca Bodmeriana, MS 74. Such rubrics as *hic partitur, hic dividitur, hic mutetur sonus in cantu,* and *hic incipiant cantare cum organis* indicate most certainly a highly dramatic presentation of the text, and very possibly an early instance of polyphonic performance with the use of the organ. The *graduale* is dated 1071, the lectionary is contemporary, perhaps a little later.

35. On this church, see Biancolini, *Notizie storiche* 2:629–30, and the memoir of Barto-

lomeo Campagnola, a late-eighteenth-century archpriest of the church, entitled "Della chiesa parrochiale di S. Cecilia in Verona," Verona, Bibl. civ., MS 1726.

The St. Anastasia Master is so named from his work on the architrave of the front door of the great church of St. Anastasia in Verona. His statue of Cecilia is not without complications, due to its having suffered more damage over the years than other works in the group. Such damage is of course consistent with its having been in an exposed position, the object of a high degree of veneration. The most recent research shows that the face was restored in the eighteenth century, and that the arm and hand supporting the organ, but not the organ itself, are of a different stone from the rest of the work and seem to have been added later. Thus Marinelli, *Castelvecchio a Verona*, 15–16. In spite of Marinelli's caution, however, none of these repairs affects the highly probable identification of the statue. The hair has the same quite singular style of braids as the St. Libera in the same group, and everything else in the unrestored parts places it firmly in the works of the St. Anastasia Master. The *organetto* itself is part of the original work. Thus I conclude that this statue, of a female figure with portative organ belonging stylistically to an early-fourteenth-century group of female saints, all deriving from closed churches one of which was dedicated to St. Cecilia, can be classified with a high degree of probability as a statue of music's patroness.

36. See Quintavalle, "Appunti di pittura." The identification is made in a number of tourist publications, but I have not been able to verify it from historical records.

37. Thus Casanova, *Arte a Gaetà*, 28.

38. Ibid. "Questi 'Angeli' appartengono invece ad un ambito chiaramente fiorentino, come del resto aveva già affermato il Toesca." The same doubt appears in the catalogue of musical subjects in trecento painting by so careful an observer as the late Howard Mayer Brown (see Brown, *Catalogus* 5:230), who lists the frescoes as "St. Cecilia and Angel Musicians," yet describes the performers only as angels: "At least five angels play two shawms, portative organ, fiddle, and lute. In the other panel (b) [= 665b], at least five angels play two double recorders, psaltery, portative organ, and rebec."

39. *Kunst und Kultur* 2:356, no. 46.

40. Cambridge, Fitzwilliam Museum, MS McClean 201, fol. 26. This is an especially eloquent example of a common image of the saint, made clear by the association of picture and text.

41. The center ground of this panel is of the wedding banquet, which takes place beneath an architectural canopy. There is a strong visual contrast between the far right and left of the panel, which are set outside the canopy. To the left the musician with the portative organ plays the wedding music; to the right, within the bridal chamber, is seen the colloquy of Cecilia with Valerian while a protecting angel hovers over her. The panel is reproduced by Mirimonde, *Sainte-Cécile*, 15 (planche 1).

42. Chantilly, Musée Condé, MS 1887, fol. 419v.

43. The text is the same as the beginning of the narrative portion of the *Passio*: "Cecilia, virgo clarissima, absconditum semper evangelium Christi gerebat in pectore suo." The serpent can always represent Satan, but it is an important symbol of sin cast off at baptism, as in the often-repeated legend of the stag and the serpents in the mosaics of the baptistery at St. John Lateran. The stag was believed to kill serpents, and then to develop a great thirst, which led it to the running stream of water. Saint Augus-

tine developed the idea in his Sermon on Psalm 41, "As the hart pants for running streams," pointing out that this was the text the Church sang at the public rite of baptism. This passage of Augustine has been considered his clearest and most important statement on mysticism (see Butler, *Western Mysticism*, 26–36). And in it, as Abbot Butler points out, he employs musical imagery to describe the mystical experience of union with God.

44. London, British Library, Add. MS 29902, fol. 6.

45. Mirimonde, *Sainte-Cécile*, 17. Does one enter this door into a paradisal garden? Or is the garden image here taken from the biblical and patristic analogies for the soul? Is Cecilia here the portress of the interior garden?

46. It is surprising how often the illustrations of Cecilia playing the organ in sixteenth-century pictures show an angel working the bellows. See Mirimonde, *Sainte-Cécile*, planches 74–78, 80–82, 86–88.

47. Brussels, Bibliothèque royale, MS 5648, fol. 262r. There is a similar miniature in another gradual from Gembloux, copied by Jean Massy in the same year. See Brussels, Bibliothèque royale, MS 5646, fol. 264r. On the books and the miniatures, see Hottois, *Musiekiconographie*, 13, catalogue no. 23, illus. no. 64.

48. Their chief was a Francesco Donnella (he signed his name to some of the frescoes) from Carpi, just north of Modena, who is probably to be identified with a Francesco da Carpi who worked at S. Maria della Vita in Bologna in 1508. See E. Mâle, *La cathédrale d'Albi*, 144–46.

49. Bécamel, *A la découverte*, 126–29, and E. Mâle, *La cathédrale d'Albi*, 149.

50. See E. Mâle, *La cathédrale d'Albi*, 146. Raphael worked with Pinturicchio on the frescoes in the Piccolomini Library in the Duomo at Siena; see Pope-Hennessy, *Raphael: The Wrightsman Lectures*, 131. Tradition has it that he was the model for one of the youths in the fresco of the canonization of St. Catherine of Siena, painted in 1503, when Raphael was twenty. Jones and Penny, *Raphael*, 20, date the fresco to 1502. They state that Raphael drew cartoons for Pinturicchio, and that he went to Siena with Perugino, to whom he was apprenticed. They point out that this was a good time to be away from Urbino and its environs, for this was the time when all went in terror of Cesare Borgia. Pinturicchio, too, had been a pupil of Perugino. It is quite possible, at any rate, that Donnella knew Raphael.

51. Bécamel, *A la découverte*, 126.

52. "Angelus dedit coronam Ceciliae" and "Et alteram dedit angelus ad Valeriano [sic]."

53. *De Christi triumphis* 4.10 (PL 135:662): "Atque viam pandens apprime informat alumnum, / Uberibusque fovet geminos et lacte Sophiae. / Vix una tantum quae credita nocte marita, / Nubere namque putata, suum parit ipsa maritum."

54. *Paradiso* 33:1.

55. *Paradiso* 33:2. ". . . umile e alto, più che creatura."

56. Luke 1:46–48. "Magnificat anima mea dominum et exsultavit spiritus meus in deo salutari meo. Quia respexit humilitatem ancillae suae; ecce enim ex hoc beatam me dicent omnes generationes."

57. London, British Library, MS Harley 2897, fol. 440v.

58. See Jones and Penny, *Raphael*, 49–57.

Eight   Raphael and St. Cecilia

1. The complex question of the dating and attribution of this engraving, and more particularly of its relation to the painting, is surveyed by Marzia Faietti, *DocTemp,* 187–204. What changes, it has been asked, did Marcantonio introduce into his work? How faithfully does it reflect the now-lost sketch by Raphael from which he worked? One opinion has it that the engraving represents a "conventionalizing" by the engraver of the painter's early ideas. Since the question of possible changes by Marcantonio is so speculative, I have chosen to treat his engraving as a faithful rendering of Raphael's early thoughts about the composition, with a caveat that there is some doubt about this. The identification of Jean Gerson as the source for the musical-spiritual thinking of the circle around Pietro da Lucca and Elena dall'Olio, always considered to have influenced Raphael, introduces a new element into this question. The comparison of engraving and painting presents a valuable, albeit speculative, opportunity to see how the artist's thinking may have developed.

2. On Augustine's mysticism, and his dependence on St. John, see Butler, *Western Mysticism,* 23–88.

3. Attention has recently been drawn to the legend's possible influence on Raphael by Stefaniak, "Raphael's *Santa Cecilia,*" though her conclusions have little in common with the speculations here set forth.

    In his letter to Peacock, Shelley declared that John "with a tender yet impassioned gesture bends his countenance towards her [Cecilia] languid with the depth of his emotion." It is easier to agree with the poet about the character of John's gaze than about its direction: tender and impassioned it assuredly is, but it is not bent toward Cecilia. The first impression of most viewers is that John looks at Augustine. Augustine certainly looks at John, they are standing side by side, and John's head is turned and bent slightly to his left, in Augustine's direction. But since John and Augustine are placed in the same plane, toward the back of the painting, in order for John to look at Augustine, his face would have to be in virtually complete profile, just as Augustine's is so that he looks at John. John's face, by contrast, is turned in a three-quarters view toward the foreground of the painting. The case is complicated by the fact that his eyes are turned slightly to his left, making it difficult to be sure whether he is looking at Augustine or Magdalene.

    If it can be sustained that John's "tender yet impassioned" look is indeed turned to Mary Magdalene in Raphael's painting, one could interpret it as a reference to this legend, which associated them as the couple called by Christ from their own love to a singular love for him, and to the transformation of their onetime earthly love into a shared, divine love. The story would have an obvious resonance with the wedding-story of Cecilia and Valerian and would give a particular reason for the inclusion of John and Magdalene in Raphael's picture.

    The identification of John as the groom was more common than that of Magdalene as the bride, but versions of the story in which they formed a couple were not rare, and colorful details grew around their supposed relationship. Some held that Jesus had called John at the wedding feast to leave all and follow him, and thus desert his bride on their wedding day. Some declared that it was Magdalene's distress at John's desertion that caused her to abandon herself to the life of carnal pleasure that tradition held she led before her conversion. Jacques de Voragine tells the story, but only to deny it, calling it "false and frivolous" and pointing to St. Albert's discussion of it in his comments on St. John's Gospel. A writer close to the commissioning of the painting who likewise tells the story while denying it is the Bolognese Dominican Fra Silvestro da Prierio, who for a time acted as a spiritual counselor to Elena dall'Olio. Silvestro published a life of Mary Magdalene in 1501, at about the time he was close to Elena. Though he denies that Magdalene was the bride, he accepts that John was the groom. The bride, he says, whoever she was, went to live either with the virgins in the temple or with Mary the mother of Jesus. Other writers and preachers had no compunction about repeating the story as true. Very often such stories of Magdalene are found not on her feast day (July 22), but on the Thursday after Passion Sunday. Both days had the same gospel reading, from Luke 7:36–50, which told the story of the sinful woman, identified as Magdalene in the Middle Ages, whose sins Jesus forgave after she anointed his feet. This Lenten gospel was the occasion for many sermons on repentance and divine love in medieval preaching, particularly in the Lenten series of sermons known as the *Quadragesimale*.

Often these sermons offer insight into other beliefs about John and the Magdalene. Some held that John was assumed, body and soul, into heaven just as Mary had been— thus the Dominican Gabriele de Bareleta, *Sermones de sanctis,* fols. 49r-51r. Some discussed the effect of John's betrothal on his state of virginity. J. Herolt, for instance, describes this in great detail in a sermon "Concerning Virgins" (Sermon 157 in his *Sermones de tempore et de sanctis . . .* , p. 587). Responding to the question of whether the aureole of virginity is received by one who is betrothed to be married but dies before the wedding, he answers in the negative, but alleges that the right to the aureole can in this case be regained, and appeals to St. Thomas Aquinas in support (*Summa,* 2a-2ae, q. 152, a.3). John the Evangelist, he says, is a case in point. When Christ called him from the wedding at Cana, John had already lost his virginity not by sexual act, but by consent. By following Christ's call, John was able to regain the aureole of virginity. In a sermon for the feast of Magdalene, the Dominican Leonardo da Udine, *Sermones de sanctis,* fols. 199v–216v, states flatly that, though a sinner, she recovered her virginity.

Both John and Mary Magdalene stood out in the ranks of the saints as figures especially loved by Christ and called by him in a particular and quite personal way. John's position as the "beloved disciple," who laid his head on Jesus' breast at the Last Supper, is well known and has strong scriptural support. So, too, does the position of Magdalene, though the legend that grew up around her was of an even more fantastic kind than that surrounding John. Great significance was attached to the fact that Christ appeared to her before anyone else after his resurrection. She was thus among the last to see him in his earthly life, for she was present on Calvary, and was the first to see him in his risen, immortal life.

It is possible, too, that Raphael intended one of those intensely personal references that are not unknown in his painting. For the year before he completed the *St. Cecilia* was the year in which Cardinal Bibbiena proposed that his niece should become the artist's wife. See Golzio, *Raffaello nei documenti,* 31–32, cited in Jones and Penny, *Raphael,* 132. On July 1, 1514, Raphael wrote to his uncle Simone Ciarla in Urbino, telling him how rich and powerful he was becoming, and informing him that Cardinal Bibbiena "wishes to give me his niece as a wife." The niece died and the marriage did not take place, but the arrangement must surely have represented a calling-away of the artist from his alliance with the baker's daughter who was his mistress and often his model, and whose features some have seen in the face of the Magdalene of the Bologna altarpiece.

Mossakowski, "Raphael's 'St. Cecilia,'" at n. 136, says, "The fact of giving Mary Magdalene the features of the artist's beloved becomes fully understandable only in the light of the neoplatonic idea that human love, as the desire of visual beauty which is the reflex of divine beauty, forms the first stage leading to the love of God. This view, widespread at that time [since Dante and Petrarch] . . . is commonly found in contemporary authors, especially in *Il cortegiano*." Mossakowski quotes M. Ficino, *Sopra l'amore,* 2:6–9 and 6:19, and various others, including Castiglione, *Il cortegiano* 4:62, 67–68. He adds: "For the spreading of this opinion in poetry under the influence of *Gli Asolani,* by Pietro Bembo, see L. Torrelli, *L'amore nella poesia e nel pensiero del Rinascimento,* 1933, pp. 67–107."

4. Gerson, *Oeuvres* 9:578. "Whoever wishes to hear or to know the gamma of the heart's song must put off the old man and put on the new, as if to become a child—indeed, a fool—in Christ. . . . Such was John in old age when, renewed like the eagle, he could utter scarcely anything except the new speech of the new love, sighing constantly: 'Children, love one another.' Is it to be wondered that the beloved of the beloved, the guardian of the woman most loved through that love of Christ than which no one had greater love, fashioned this saying about love's yoke [*Gamma canticordi quiquis desiderat vel audire vel cognoscere debet exuere veterem hominem et novum induere, quatenus in Christo puer immo et stultus fiat. . . . Talis erat Joannis senectus ut aquilae renovata, cum nihil aliud pene loqueretur quam amoris novi vocem novam: filii diligite alterutrum, semper ingeminans. Quid mirum si dilectus de dilecto, si custos dilectissimae et amicae per amorem Christi quo nemo majorem habuit caritatem, fecit de dilectione juge verbum*]."

5. It is described in three places by St. Luke: in Acts 9:3–19, 22:6–16, and 26:12–18. Paul himself refers to it in his letters, but only in passing. See, for example, 1 Cor. 9:1, 15:8; 2 Cor. 4:6; Gal. 1:13; Eph. 3:7–8; Phil. 3:12.

6. In eventually bending John's head to the right, to give him the look that so enthralled Shelley, Raphael had to change the bend of Cecilia's head also, from left to right. At the same time he inclined her gaze even more heavenward than it appeared in Raimondi's version.

7. Zarri, "L'altra Cecilia," 88–89, suggests that Paul's pose, head on hand, reflects Pietro's recommendations for the best bodily position to pray in. But in fact Pietro recommends that the head rest on the other hand, the left, since this will allow the heart to rest. The pose Raphael has chosen is thus rather a contradiction of Pietro. In any case, the pose of head on hand is only one of several that Pietro recommends.

8. 1 Cor. 13:1.

9. Gerson, *Oeuvres* 4:137. "Vocibus Ecclesiae pater Augustine, fateris / Motum te lacrimis ora rigasse piis."

10. PL 36:464–76; transl. in *Expositions,* Library of the Fathers 25:187–89. And see Butler, *Western Mysticism,* 25ff.

11. See 1 Chron. 6:37. Psalm 41 is the first of a group that bear this title. Others are Psalms 43 through 48 (Psalm 41 and 42 are really two parts of one psalm, so they are strictly consecutive). These complex genealogical divisions include a principal division of the Levites, who were the tribe responsible for the Temple ritual, into the sons of Gerson (or Gersom), of Caath, and of Merari. See 1 Chron. 6:1, 16–17. Here was yet another reason for Jean Charlier's adoption of the name of his village as his surname.

12. Gerson, *Oeuvres* 4:137.

13. Mark 16:9; Luke 8:2.

14. Antonius de Bitonto, *Sermones quadragesimales*, fol. 195.

15. Ibid. "Septimo et ultimo maria magdalena plorat magistrum suum cum musica di[cens]: O musici mutate modum vestrum et flete: quoniam verus cantor et musicus hodie in cruce mortuus est." Mary also calls on the other arts to mourn.

16. Kempe, *Book of Margery Kempe,* 67–71 [chap. 15].

17. For example, Mossakowski, "Raphael's 'St. Cecilia,'" 14; and Stefaniak, "Raphael's *Santa Cecilia,*" 355.

18. See Bober and Rubenstein, *Renaissance Artists* 55, and ill. 7a. I am indebted to Professor John Shearman for pointing this out to me.

19. Luke 7:36–50.

20. Bernard, *Sermons on Song of Songs,* in *Sancti Bernardi opera* 1:14ff.

21. Kempe, *Book of Margery Kempe,* 234 [chap. 80].

22. Raphael painted a similar inviting look in the face of John the Baptist, another of the great icons of repentance, in the *Madonna di Foligno.*

23. Gerson developed the idea of the flesh and the spirit being at war within the heart through their opposed senses in various diagrams of the chessboard. Virtues and vices were represented by the opposing pieces, the senses through which these virtues and vices operate were represented by the corresponding pawns. In one of these diagrams, for example (Gerson, *Oeuvres* 9:708), the king on the side of the spirit is labeled "humility under God" and is opposed by the king of the flesh, who is "pride against God." The spirit's queen is "loving charity," that of the flesh is "libidinous cupidity." The spirit's bishops (called counselors at that time) are wisdom and prudence, opposed by folly and craftiness. The pawn that stands before each piece, and serves it, is labeled as one of the senses through which that virtue or vice finds particular expression. Thus the king's pawn, on each side, is "the obedient ear." The queen's pawn of the spirit is "the chaste eye with [corresponding] touch," that of the flesh is "the unchaste eye with [corresponding] touch." Wisdom and prudence, the bishops of the spirit, are served respectively by "the sweet taste and smell of heavenly things" and "the eloquent mouth," while the opposing bishops, folly and craftiness, are served by "the shameful taste and smell of fleshly things" and "the insolent mouth."

What is most striking about Gerson's scheme (which is in the well-known tradition of moralized chess) is that the operations, the moves, of spirit and flesh through the virtues and vices by way of the senses, are carried out by music. At the bottom of the diagram cited, e.g., is a sentence which labels all pieces and pawns as being the keys of an instrument: "The keys of the interior chessboard which, when struck by the fingers of meditation give forth the pitches of each affection [*Claves interioris scacordi que percusse digitis meditationis reddunt voces cujuslibet affectionis*]." The diagram in fact bears the heading: "Diagram of the musical chessboard of the heart . . ." [*Figura scacordi musicalis . . .*]." The game is played within the heart, as is evidenced by another of Gerson's curious, punning titles, for *scacordum* is a composite word, combining the notions of chess (*scacarium*), heart (*cor*), and string (*corda*). He himself explains it thus, *quasi scacarium cordis vel cordarum* (*Oeuvres* 9:709). It is possible that Gerson was referring to an actual instrument, the mysterious stringed keyboard instrument of the fourteenth to sixteenth centuries known as the chekker. See Marcuse, *Musical Instruments,* s.v. "Chekker."

24. *Paradiso* 33:22 27. "Or questi, che dall'infima lacuna / dell'universo infin qui ha vedute / le vite spiritali ad una ad una / supplica a te, per grazia, di virtute / tanto, che possa con li occhi levarsi / più alto verso l'ultima salute." The beginning of the prayer was partly incorporated by Chaucer in the Prologue to the *Second Nun's Tale.*

25. Zarri, "L'altra Cecilia," 104–9, discusses the identifications previously suggested, with the sanctuary of the Madonna of San Luca and with that of S. Maria del Monte. Her reasons for rejecting them in favor of S. Giovanni in Monte seem sound. Neither had, at that time, the round shape of the church in the painting. Neither did S. Giovanni in Monte, but Zarri reasons that the artist and the commissioners wished to suggest a primitive shape for S. Giovanni, thus making it accord with a building that the legend of St. Petronius, founder and patron of the Bolognese Church, declares he built. The scaffolding Raphael painted around it suggests the rebuilding carried out under Elena's patronage, and thus fortifies the comparison of Elena with Cecilia, who left her house, destined to become a great basilica, to the Church of Rome.

26. See Butler, *Western Mysticism,* 96, citing St. Gregory the Great, *Moralia* 6.56.

27. Cited in Gardiner, *Dante and the Mystics,* 274.

28. Rolle, *Chant d'amour* 1:294 [cap. 25]. "Demum hoc dicet doloribus dampnatus [nunc] mugiens in mundo ut magnus magister: 'Conversa est in luctum cithara mea et organum meum in vocem flencium.' Utique iam ego assumptus amori, laudando Levantem me lubricum qui lavit, carmen captivi in contra converto, doloris dono melodie mutato. Audeo asserere talem tenorem: conversus est luctus meus in citharam et vox flebilis mea in organum."

29. Gerson, *Oeuvres* 9:532–33.

30. Representations of reversed organs are known as early as the thirteenth century. See, e.g., the French psalter dated 1260 in Philadelphia, Free Library, Lewis MS 185, fol. 1v; also the Psalter-Hours of Yolande of Soissons, ca. 1290, in New York, Pierpont Morgan Library, MS 729, fol. 16. Both examples occur within a historiated B of *Beatus,* at Psalm 1. In the Lewis Manuscript, the instrument is played by one of the secondary psalmists, but in the Morgan Psalter-Hours it is David himself who plays the reversed instrument. A number of later examples are found in Mirimonde, *Sainte-Cécile,* and Marshall, *Iconographical Evidence.*

31. The passage is from Judith 10:3, and Johannes's text in Vatican Library, MS Burgh. lat. 24, fol. 224vb, reads: "Imposuit mitram ca[piti] supei caput suum et induit se vestimentis iocunditatis sue induitque sandalia pedibus suis assumpsitque dextrariola et lilia et inaures et anulos et omnibus ornamentis suis ornavit se." The context of the passage is suggestive, for Judith has just laid aside the sackcloth in which she had prayed and fasted, beseeching God's help in delivering her people from the encircling Assyrian

army. In her finery, she will go forth to meet Holofernes, and will return undefiled, bearing the head of their enemy.

32. Chastel, *Art et humanisme,* 492.

33. Johannes de Biblia, Vatican Library, MS Burgh. lat. 24, fol. 224vb. "Haec imposuit mitram capiti super caput suum. per q[uo]d intelligitur spes eterne retributionis. mitra quidem quae super caput est significat spem quae de supernis est. et induit se vestimentis iocunditatis sue. h[aec] est vestis nuptialis divine scilicet fraterne dilectionis. induitque sandalia pedibus suis per quod accipitur elevatio sue affectionis. q[uae] significatur in hoc quod sandalia in superiori parte discooperta sunt. assumpsit dextrariola. in quibus intelligitur operationis fortitudo. dextrariola quippe sunt armilla quae sunt ornamenta brachiorum."

34. See Aquinas, *Summa,* 1a, q. 18, a.1 and a.3. "Motus proprie significat actum imperfectum mobilis; sed, secundum similitudinem, praedicatur de omni operatione."

35. "Comparatio musicorum scilicet instrumentorum est proportio sonorum secundum grave et acutum. Cum enim corde comparantur, id est proportionantur ut reddant gravem sonum et acutum, ex hoc suavis melodia redditur. Tales sonos sic proportionatos secundum grave et acutum reddidit haec sancta mulier in convivio ecclesiae. Quasi corda gravis fuit eius difficultas ad malum, corda vero acuta eius celeritas ad bonum. Ex hac duplici corda in convivio ecclesie suavis sonuit melodia."

Bibliography

Acta synodorum habitarum Romae. In *Cassiodori Senatoris Variae,* edited by T. Mommsen, 393–455. Monumenta Germaniae historica, Auctores antiquissimi, 12. Berlin: Weidmann, 1894. Reprint, 1970.

Alan of Lille. *The Plaint of Nature.* Translated by J. J. Sheridan. Mediaeval sources in translation, 26. Toronto: Pontifical Institute of Mediaeval Studies, 1980.

Aldhelm. *De virginitate.* Edited by R. Ehwald. In Monumenta Germaniae historica, Auctores antiquissimi, 15:226–323, 350–471.

Aliati, G. *La chiesa e il monastero di Santa Cecilia in Como.* Como: E. Cavalleri, 1939. [Reprinted from *Periodico storico comense,* vol. 3 fasc. 1–2, Maggio 1939–XVII.]

Amalarius of Metz. *Liber officialis.* Vol. 2 of *Amalarii episcopi opera liturgica omnia,* edited by I. M. Hanssens. Studi e testi, 139. Vatican City: Biblioteca apostolica vaticana, 1948. Reprint, 1968.

Anderson, Jaynie. "The Giorgionesque Portrait: From Likeness to Allegory." In *Giorgione: Atti del Convegno Internazionale di studio per il 5° centenario della nascità, 29–31 Maggio 1978,* 153–58. Castelfranco Veneto, 1978.

Anderson, W. J., R. P. Spiers, and T. Ashby. *The Architecture of Ancient Rome.* London: Batsford, 1927.

Andrieu, Michel. *Les Ordines romani du haut moyen âge.* . . . 5 vols. Spicilegium sacrum lovaniense, 11, 23–24, 28–29. Louvain: Spicilegium sacrum lovaniense administration, 1931–61.

Antiphonale missarum sextuplex. Edited by J. Hesbert. Brussels: Vromant, 1935. Reprint. Rome: Herder, 1967.

Antonius de Bitonto. *Sermones fratris Antonii de Bitonto ordinis fratrum minorum de observantia super epistolas dominicales per totum annum. Et super ep[istu]las q[ua]dragesimales.* Frankfordia: Joannes Herzog, 1496.

———. *Sermones Quadragesimales de Vitiis Reverendi Patris Fratris Antonii Bitontini: Per modum dyalogi* ad Illustrem et religiosissimum principe[m] Guidantoniu[m] Urbini ac Dura[n]tis Comitem prae-celle[n]tissimu[m]. . . . 1499.

Aquinas, St. Thomas. *Commentary on Aristotle's "Physics."* Translated by R. J. Blackwell, R. J. Spath, and W. E. Thirlkel. New Haven: Yale University Press, 1963.

———. *Summa theologiae.*

Arasse, Daniel. "Extases et visions béatifiques à l'apogée de la Renaissance." *Mélanges de l'Ecole Française de Rome* 84 (1972): 403–92.

Aristotle. *Aristotle's Physics, Books I and II.* Translated by W. Charlton. Clarendon Aristotle Series. Oxford: Clarendon Press, 1970.

Arnobius. *Arnobii adversus nationes libri VII.* Edited by C. Marchesi. 2d ed. Corpus scriptorum latinorum Paravianum. Turin: I. B. Paravia, [1953].

Ashmole, Elias. *Theatrum Chimicum Brittanicum containing Severall Poeticall Pieces of our Famous English Philosophers, who have written the Hermetique Mysteries in their owne Ancient Language.* London: Nathaniel Brooks, 1652.

Atkinson, Clarissa W. *Mystic and Pilgrim: The Book and the World of Margery Kempe.* Ithaca: Cornell University Press, 1983.

[Attavanti] Paulo Fiorentino [dell'ordine di sancto spirito]. *Cominciamo sette psalmi peniten-tiale secondo la sententia de theologi I quali divotamente chi ciaschuno giorno: dice: puo essere certo come David intese: e la chiesa representa: non dovere morire senza penitenza. Alla illus-trissima Madona Bona ducesa di Milano.* . . . [1480].

Augustine, St. *Aurelii Augustini De musica.* A. c. di G. Marzi. Collana di classici della filosofia cristiana, 1. Florence: Sansoni, 1969.

———. *Confessions.* Translated by R. S. Pine-Coffin. Penguin Classics. New York: Penguin, 1961.

———. *Expositions on the Book of Psalms.* Translation of *Enarrationes in Psalmos* [PL 36], with notes and indices by C. Marriot and E. B. Pusey. 6 vols. Library of the Fathers, 24–25, 30, 32, 37, 39. Oxford: Parker, 1847–57. [*Enarrationes in Psalmos.* 3 vols. Corpus christianorum series latina, 38–40. Turnhout: Brépols, 1956.]

Aurigemma, S., and A. De Santis. *Gaetà, Formia, Minturno.* Itinerari dei musei, gallerie e monumenti d'Italia, no. 92. 2d ed. Rome: Libreria stato, 1955.

Backhouse, Janet. *The Bedford Hours.* London: British Library, 1990.

———. *Books of Hours.* London: British Library, 1985.

———. *The Isabella Breviary.* London: British Library, 1993.

Bailly, Paul. "Flagellants." In *DSAM* 5:392–408.

Baldovin, John. *The Urban Character of Christian Worship: The Origins, Development, and Mean-ing of Stational Liturgy.* Orientalia christiana analecta, 228. Rome: Pontificale institutum studiorum orientalium, 1987.

Banchieri, Adriano. *Conclusioni nel suono dell'organo.* Bologna: Heredi di G. Rossi, 1609. Re-print. Bibliotheca musica bononiensis 2:24. Bologna: Forni, 1968.

Bandmann, Günther. *Melancholie und Musik: Ikonographische Studien.* Wissenschaftliche Ab-handlungen der Arbeitsgemeinschaft für Forschung des Landes Nordrhein-Westfalen, 12. Cologne: Westdeutscher Verlag, 1960.

Barbier de Montault, X. "Iconographie de Sainte Cécile." In *Revue de l'art chrétien,* n.s., 5 (1887): 426–47; 6 (1888): 23–50.

Baronio, Caesare. *Annales ecclesiastici*. . . . Novissima editio, postremum ab auctore aucta et recognita. Antwerp: Ex officina Plantiniana, 1601–24.

Battista da Varano, Camilla. *La vita spirituale*. 1621.

———. *Le opere spirituali*. Edited by G. Boccanera. Iesi: Scuola tipografica francescana, 1958.

Beani, Gaetano. *Santa Maria dell'Umiltà: Notizie storiche della sua immagine e del suo tempio in Pistoia*. Pistoia: Bracali, 1885.

Bécamel, Marcel. *A la découverte de la cathédrale d'Albi: Les trente chapelles, les peintures de la voûte, le Jugement dernier*. Albi: Gilbert Assémat, 1976.

Beck, James H. *Raphael*. New York: Abrams, 1976.

Benati, Pino. *Santa Cecilia nella leggenda e nell'arte*. Milan: Alfieri, 1928.

Benedict, St. *The Rule of Saint Benedict in Latin and English with Notes*. Translated by T. Fry. Collegeville, Minn.: Liturgical Press, 1981.

Bentivoglio, Carlo e Costante. *Compendio della vita della B. Elena Dall'Olio Vergine, Maritata, e Vedova*. Epilogato dal Co. Carlo del Co. Costante Bentivogli. 2d ed. Bologna, 1693. [1st ed. 1651.]

Berengo, M. *Nobili e mercanti nella Lucca del Cinquecento*. Turin: Einaudi, 1965.

Berenson, Bernard. *Italian Painters of the Renaissance: Central Italian and North Italian Schools*. 2 vols. London: Phaidon, 1968.

Bernardini, Carla. "Problemi di fortuna postuma: Fra maniera e accademia, pittura senza tempo e ideale classico." In *Indagini*, 141–79.

Bernardino dei Busti, OM. *Rosarium sermonum*. Venice, 1498.

Bernard [of Clairvaux], St. *Sancti Bernardi opera*. Edited by J. Leclercq, C. H. Talbot, and H. M. Rochais. Rome: Editiones cistercienses, 1957–.

Bernards, Matthäus. *Speculum Virginum: Geistigkeit und Seelenleben der Frau im Hochmittelalter*. 2d ed. Beihefte zum Archiv für Kulturgeschichte, 16. Cologne: Böhlau Verlag, 1982.

Berton, Charles. *Dictionnaire des Cardinaux* . . . . Paris: J.-P. Migne, 1857. Reprint. Farnborough: Gregg, 1969.

Bethune-Baker, J. F. *An Introduction to the Early History of Christian Doctrine to the Time of Chalcedon*. London: Methuen, 1903.

Biancolini, Giambatista. *Notizie storiche delle chiese di Verona*. 9 vols. Verona: Alessandro Scolari al Ponte dalle Navi, 1749–71. Reprint. Bologna: Forni, 1977.

Biget, Jean-Louis. "Un problème d'historiographie et d'histoire: La dédicace de la cathédrale d'Albi." In *Gaillac et Pays Tarnais: Actes du XXXIᵉ Congrès de la Fédération tenu à Gaillac les 21–23 mai 1976*, 259–85. Albi: Ateliers professionels de l'Orphelinat Saint-Jean, 1977.

Biget, Jean-Louis, ed. *Histoire d'Albi*. Pays et villes de France. Toulouse: Privat, 1983.

Birgitta, St. *The Revelations of Saint Birgitta*. Edited from Princeton University Library, Garrett MS 1397, by W. P. Cumming. Early English Text Society, Original Series, 178. London: Oxford University Press, 1929.

Black, Christopher F. *Italian Confraternities in the Sixteenth Century*. Cambridge: Cambridge University Press, 1989.

Bloomfield, Morton. *The Seven Deadly Sins: An Introduction to the History of a Religious Concept, with Special Reference to Medieval English Literature*. [East Lansing]: Michigan State University Press, 1952.

Bober, Phyllis Pray, and Ruth Rubinstein. *Renaissance Artists and Antique Sculpture: A Hand-*

book of Sources. With contributions by S. Woodford. London: H. Miller, Oxford University Press, 1986.

Bock, Friedrich. "Der Este-Prozess von 1321." *AFP* 7 (1937): 41–111.

Bokenham, Osbern. *Legendys of Hooly Wummen.* Edited from MS Arundel 327 by M. S. Serjeantson. Early English Text Society, Original Series, 206. London: Humphrey Milford, Oxford University Press, 1938.

Bologna, Ferdinando. *I pittori alla Corte Angioina di Napoli, 1266–1414.* . . . Saggi e studi della storia dell'arte, 2. Rome: Bozzi, 1969.

Bömer, Franz. *Untersuchungen über die Religion der Sklaven in Griechenland und Rom.* 4 vols. Abhandlungen der Geistes- und Sozialwissenschaftlicher Klasse. Mainz: Akademie der Wissenschaften und der Literatur, 1958.

Bonardi, Piergiovanni, and Tiburzio Lupo. *L'imitazione di Cristo e il suo autore.* 2 vols. Turin: Società editrice internazionale, 1964.

Bonaventure, St. *De triplici via alias incendium amoris.* In *Doctoris Seraphici S. Bonaventurae Opera omnia,* 8: 3–27. Ad Claras Aquas: ex typographia collegii S. Bonaventurae, 1898.

Borghini, Raffaello. *Il riposo.* . . . Florence: Giorgio Marescotti, 1584.

Bosio, Antonio. *Historia passionis B. Caeciliae virginis . . . Accedit relatio eorundem sanctorum corporum novae inventionis et repositionis.* . . . Rome, 1600.

Boyer, Carolus. *Cursus philosophiae.* 2 vols. Paris: Desclée, 1937.

Breccia Fratadocchi, Margarita Maria, Sandra Ricci, and Bianca Maria Sarlo. "Considerazioni su un nuovo ambiente sottostante la basilica di Santa Cecilia in Trastevere." *Bolletino d'arte* 61/3–4 (July–December 1976): 217–28.

Brentano, Robert. *Rome before Avignon: A Social History of Thirteenth-Century Rome.* New York: Basic Books, 1974.

Brévart, Francis B. "The German *Volkskalender* of the Fifteenth Century." *Speculum* 63 (1988): 312–42.

Brizio, Anna Maria. "La Santa Cecilia di Raffaello." *Arte lombarda* 10 (1965): 99–104.

Bromyard, Johannes de. . . . *in Summam predicantium.* Nuremberg: A. Koberger, 1485.

Brouwer, H. H. J. *Bona Dea: The Sources and a Description of the Cult.* Etudes préliminaires aux religions orientales dans l'Empire romain, 110. Leiden: E. J. Brill, 1989.

Brown, D. Catherine. *Pastor and Laity in the Theology of Jean Gerson.* Cambridge: Cambridge University Press, 1987.

Brown, Howard Mayer. "Catalogus: A Corpus of Trecento Pictures with Musical Subject Matter." *Imago musicae* 1 (1984): 189–243; 2 (1985): 179–281; 3 (1986): 103–87; 5 (1988): 167–241. [Only Part 1, Installments 1–4, was published.]

Brownlee, Kevin. "Ovid's Semele and Dante's Metamorphosis: Paradiso XXI–XXIII." *Modern Language Notes* 101 (1986): 147–56.

Brumana, Biancamaria. "Iconografia della S. Cecilia ed accademie musicali: Nuovi contributi." In *Musica e immagine, tra iconografia e mondo dell'Opera: Studi in onore de Massimo Bogianckino,* edited by B. Brumana and G. Ciliberti, 115–36. "Historiae musicae cultores" biblioteca, 70. Florence: Olschki, 1993.

Buchtal, Hugo. "The Exaltation of David." *Journal of the Warburg and Courtauld Institutes* 37 (1974): 330–34.

———. *The Miniatures of the Paris Psalter.* Studies of the Warburg Institute, 2. London: Warburg Institute, 1938.

Bugge, John. *Virginitas: An Essay in the History of a Medieval Idea.* International Archives of the History of Ideas, Series minor, 17. The Hague: Martinus Nijhoff, 1975.

Burney, Sir Charles. *The Present State of Music in France and Italy.* 2d rev. ed. London: T. Becket, J. Robson, and G. Robinson, 1773. Reprint. New York: AMS, 1976.

Butler, Dom Cuthbert. *Western Mysticism: The Teaching of Sts. Augustine, Gregory and Bernard on Contemplation and the Contemplative Life; Neglected Chapters in the History of Religion.* New York: Dutton, 1924.

Cabassut, André. "Couers (Echange de)." In *DSAM* 2:1046–51.

Cantino, Gisella Wataghin. "Roma sotterranea: Appunti sulle origini dell'archeologia cristiana." *Ricerche di storia dell'arte* 10 (1980): 5–14.

Caraffa, Filippo, and Antonio Massone. *Santa Cecilia martire romana: Passione e culto.* Rome: Titulus Caeciliae, Centro di spiritualità liturgica, n.d. [Cardinal Poletti's letter is dated 1983.]

Carraciolo, Roberto. *Sermones de sanctis.* Venice, 1490.

Casanova, Maria Letizia, ed. *Arte a Gaetà: Dipinti dal XII al XVII secolo.* Exhibition catalogue, Gaetà, Palazzo De Vio, August–October 1976.

Cassiodorus Senator, Flavius Magnus Aurelius. *Cassiodori Senatoris institutiones.* Edited by R. A. B. Mynors. Oxford: Clarendon Press, 1963.

———. *Expositio Psalmorum.* Cassiodori Opera Pars II, 1. Corpus christianorum series latina, 97. Turnhout: Brépols, 1958.

Catherine of Bologna, St. *Le sette armi spirituali.* Edited by C. Foletti. Medioevo e umanesimo, 56. Padua: Editrice Antenore, 1985.

Cecilia, Suor. *Miracula Beati Dominici.* Edited with introduction by A. Walz. In "Die 'Miracula Beati Dominici' der Schwester Cäcilia," *Miscellanea Pio Paschini: Studi di storia ecclesiastica,* 1:293–326. Rome: Facultas Theologica Pontificii Athenaei Lateranensis, 1948.

Celletti, Maria Chiara. "Cecilia di Roma: Iconografia." In *BibSanc* 3:1081–86.

———. "Domenico: Iconografia." In *Bibsanc* 4:727–34.

Cellini, Antonia Nava. "Stefano Maderna, Francesco Vanni e Guido Reni a Santa Cecilia in Trastevere." *Paragone* 227 (January 1969): 18–41.

Chamberlain, David. "Musical Signs and Symbols in Chaucer: Convention and Originality." In *Signs and Symbols in Chaucer's Poetry,* edited by J. P. Herman and J. J. Burke, Jr., 43–80. University: University of Alabama Press, 1981.

Chastel, André. *Art et humanisme à Florence au temps de Laurence le magnifique: Etudes sur la Renaissance et l'humanisme platonicien.* Publications de l'Institut d'Art et d'Archéologie de l'Université de Paris, 4. Paris: Presses universitaires de France, 1961.

Chaucer, Geoffrey. *The Canon's Yeoman's Tale.* In *Chaucer's Major Poetry,* edited by A. C. Baugh, 510–25. New York: Appleton-Century-Crofts, 1963.

———. *The Second Nun's Tale.* In *Chaucer's Major Poetry,* edited by A. C. Baugh, 501–10. New York: Appleton-Century-Crofts, 1963.

Chiti, Alfredo. *Il Santuario della Madonna dell'Umiltà in Pistoia: Ricordi e notizie.* Pistoia: Tipografia pistoiese, 1952.

Christie, A. *English Medieval Embroidery: A Brief Survey of English Embroidery Dating from the Beginning of the Tenth Century until the End of the Fourteenth: Together with a Descriptive Catalogue of Surviving Examples.* . . . Oxford: Clarendon Press, 1938.

————. "A Reconstructed Embroidered Cope at Anagni." *Burlington Magazine* 48, no. 245 (1926): 65–77.

Ciaceri, Emanuele. "La festa di Sant'Agata e l'antico culto di Iside in Catania." *Archivio storico per la Sicilia orientale* 2 (1905): 265–98.

Cicero, Marcus Tullius. *De haruspicum responsis.* In *Cicero: The Speeches,* translated by N. H. Watts, 312–401. Loeb Classical Library. London: Heinemann, 1923.

————. *M. Tulli Ciceronis De domo sua ad pontifices oratio.* Edited by R. G. Nisbet. Latin texts and commentaries. Oxford: Clarendon Press, 1939. Reprint. New York: Arno Press, 1979.

Colombas, G. M. *Paradiso y vida angelica: Sentido escatalógico de la vocación cristiana.* Biblioteca vida cristiana, 3. Montserrat: Abadia, 1958.

Commentarius perpetuus in Martyrologium Hieronymianum ad recensionem Enrici Quentin O.S.B. Edited by H. Delehaye. In *AaSs* Novembris, vol. 2, Pars posterior. Brussels: [Society of Bollandists], 1931.

Connolly, James L. *John Gerson: Reformer and Mystic.* Louvain: Librairie universitaire, 1928.

Connolly, Thomas H. "The Cult and Iconography of St. Cecilia before Raphael." In *Indagini,* 119–39.

————. "The Legend of St. Cecilia: I, The Origins of the Cult." *Studi musicali* 7 (1978): 3–37.

————. "The Legend of St. Cecilia: II, Music and the Symbols of Virginity." *Studi musicali* 9 (1980): 3–44.

————. "L'iconografia di S. Cecilia prima di Raffaello." In *DocTemp,* 228–34.

————. "Some Early Orations from S. Cecilia in Trastevere." *Benedictina* 25 (1978): 31–46.

Craven, Wayne. "The Iconography of the David and Bathsheba Cycle at the Cathedral of Auxerre." *Journal of the Society of Architectural Historians* 34 (1975): 226–37.

Creytens, Raymond, OP. "Les écrivains dominicains dans la chronique d'Albert de Castello (1516)." *AFP* 30 (1960): 227–313.

Crostarosa, P. "Scoperte in S. Cecilia in Trastevere." *Nuovo bulletino di archeologia cristiana* 5 (1899): 261–78; 6 (1900): 143–60, 265–70.

Crozes, Hippolyte. *Monographie de la cathédrale d'Albi.* Paris: V. Didron, 1850.

D'Amato, Alfonso, OP. "Atti del Capitolo Provinciale della Lombardia Inferiore celebrato a Vicenza nel 1307." *AFP* 13 (1943): 138–48.

Dante. *The Divine Comedy of Dante Alighieri.* With translation and comment by J. D. Sinclair. Vol. 1, *The Inferno.* Vol. 2, *The Purgatorio.* Vol. 3, *The Paradiso.* Oxford: Oxford University Press, 1939.

————. *Vita nuova.* Edited by M. Colomba. Universale economica Feltrinelli, i classici, 2072. Milan: Feltrinelli, 1993.

Davis-Weyer, Cecilia. "Das Traditio-Legis Bild und seine Nachfolge." *Münchener Jahrbuch der bildenden Kunst* 12 (1961): 7–45.

Delcorno, Carlo. *La predicazione nell'età comunale.* Scuola aperta, 57. Florence: Sansoni, 1974.

Delehaye, Hippolyte. *Etude sur le légendier romain: Les saints de novembre et de décembre.* Subsidia hagiographica, 23. Brussels, 1936.

Denis-Boulet, N. M. "Titres urbains et communautés dans la Rome chrétienne." *La maison-dieu* 36 (1953): 14–32.

Denis the Carthusian [Denis Rickel]. *Sonus epulantis.* In *Doctoris ecstatici D. Dionysii cartusiani opera omnia in unum corpus digesta,* edited by the Carthusians, 41:291–314. 42 vols. in 44. Montreuil, Tournai, and Parkminster, 1896–1935.

Denyse, Nicolaus [fratr. minorum de observantia . . . Provincial of French province]. *Gemma predicantium.* . . . Paris: François Regnault, 1508.

————. *Sermones limpidissimi [de tempore et de sanctis].* Rothmagi [Rouen]: Martin Morin, 1507.

Deshman, Robert. "The Exalted Servant: The Ruler Theology of the Prayerbook of Charles the Bald." *Viator* 11 (1980): 385–417.

Deubner, Ludovicus. *De incubatione, capita quattuor.* . . . Leipzig: B. G. Teubner, 1900.

Dictionarius pauperum omnibus predicatoribus verbi divini p[er]necessarius . . . de tempore et de sanctis. Paris: Andreas Bocard, 1498.

Dogaer, Georges. *Flemish Miniature Painting in the Fifteenth and Sixteenth Centuries.* Translated from the French by A. E. C. Simoni et al. Amsterdam: B. M. Israel, 1987.

Dolce, L. *Dialogo della pittura.* Venice: Gabriel Giolito de' Ferrari, 1557.

Donovan, Claire. *The de Brailes Hours: Shaping the Book of Hours in Thirteenth-Century Oxford.* London: British Library, 1991.

Duchesne, Louis. *Fastes épiscopaux de l'ancienne Gaule.* 3 vols. Paris: A. Fontemoing, 1900–1915.

Duchesne, Louis, ed. *Le 'Liber pontificalis': Texte, introduction et commentaire.* [2d ed. revised by C. Vogel.] 3 vols. Paris: Boccard, 1955.

Dussler, Luitpold. *Raphael: A Critical Catalog of His Pictures, Wall-Paintings and Tapestries.* Translated from the German by S. Craft. London: Phaidon, 1971.

Eco, Umberto. *Art and Beauty in the Middle Ages.* Translated by H. Bredin. New Haven: Yale University Press, 1986.

Ellebracht, M. M. P. *Remarks on the Vocabulary of the Ancient Orations in the Missale Romanum.* Latinitas christianorum primaeva, 18. Nijmegen: Dekker and Van de Vegt, 1963.

Elliott, Dyan. *Spiritual Marriage: Sexual Abstinence in Medieval Wedlock.* Princeton: Princeton University Press, 1993.

Epstein, Marcy J. "*Ludovicus Decus Regnantium*: Perspectives on the Rhymed Office." *Speculum* 53 (1978): 283–334.

Erbes, C. "Die heilige Cäcilia im Zusammenhang mit der Papstcrypta sowie der ältesten Kirche Roms." In *Zeitschrift für Kirchengeschichte* 9 (1887): 1–66.

Evans, Mark. *The Sforza Hours.* London: British Library, 1992.

Festus, Sextus Pompeius. *Sexti Pompeii Festi De verborum significatu quae supersunt cum Pauli epitome.* Edited by W. M. Lindsay. Bibliotheca scriptorum graecorum et romanorum Teubneriana. Leipzig: Teubner, 1913.

Finney, Gretchen L. " 'Organickal Musick' and Ecstasy." *Journal of the History of Ideas* 7 (1947): 273–92.

Fischel, Oskar. *Raphael.* Translated from the German by B. Rackham. 1948. Reprint. London: Spring Books, 1964.

Fisher, St. John. *A treatise concernynge the fruytfull saynges of Davyd the kynge & prophete in the seven penytencyall psalmes.* London: Wynkyn de Worde, 1509. [Modern edition in *The English Works of John Fisher,* edited by J. E. B. Mayor, vol. 1, 1–267. Early English Text Society, Extra Series, no. 27. London, 1876. Reprint, 1935.]

Foster, Genette. "The Iconology of Musical Instruments and Musical Performance in Thirteenth-Century Manuscript Illuminations." Ph.D. diss., New York University, 1977.

Franchi de' Cavalieri, P. "Recenti studi intorno a S. Cecilia." *Note agiografiche* 4 (1912): 3–38.

Freedberg, S. J. *Painting of the High Renaissance in Rome and Florence.* Rev. ed. New York: Hacker, 1985.

Frei, Judith, ed. *Corpus Ambrosianum-liturgicum herausgegeben von Odilo Heiming, III: Das Ambrosianische Sakramentar D3-3 aus dem Mailändischen Metropolitankapitel.* Liturgiewissenschaftliche Quellen und Forschungen, 56. Münster in Westfalen: Aschendorff, c. 1974.

Frere, Walter H. *Studies in Early Roman Liturgy, III: The Roman Epistle Lectionary.* Alcuin Club Collections, 32. Oxford: Oxford University Press, 1935.

Gabriele de Bareleta [Barletta]. *Sermones de sanctis.* Brescia: Jacobus Brittanicus, 1498.

Gardner, Edmund G. *Dante and the Mystics: A Study of the Mystical Aspect of the* Divina Commedia *and Its Relations with Some of Its Mediaeval Sources.* London: J. M. Dent, 1913. Reprint, 1968.

Gerson, Jean. *Oeuvres complètes.* Edited by Msgr. [P.] Glorieux. 10 vols. Paris, Tournai: Desclée, 1961–73.

Giesel, Helmut. *Studien zur Symbolik der Musikinstrumente im Schrifttum der Alten und Mittelalterlichen Kirche (von den Anfängen bis zum 13. Jahrhundert).* Kölner Beitrage zur Musikforschung, 94. Regensburg: Gustav Bosse Verlag, 1978.

Giovenale, G. B. "Recherches architectoniques sur la basilique." *Cosmos catholicus* 4 (1902): 648–61.

———. "Les sarcophages des saints martyrs." *Cosmos catholicus* 4 (1902): 662–69.

Golzio, V. *Raffaello nei documenti, nelle testimonianze dei contemporanei, e nella letteratura del suo secolo.* Vatican City: Arti grafiche Panetto e Petrelli, 1936. Reprint. Farnborough: Gregg, 1971.

———. "The Sonnets." In *The Complete Work of Raphael,* 603–6. New York: Reynal, [1969].

Grabes, Herbert. *The Mutable Glass: Mirror-Imagery in Titles and Texts of the Middle Ages and English Renaissance.* Translated from the German by G. Collier. Cambridge: Cambridge University Press, 1982.

Gregory the Great, St. *Dialogues* [French and Latin]. Translated by A. de Vogue. 3 vols. Sources chrétiennes, 251, 260, 265. Paris: Editions du Cerf, 1978–80. [*Dialogi de vita et miraculis patrum italicorum.*]

———. *Gregorii I papae registrum.* Edited by P. Ewald. Monumenta Germaniae historica, Epistolarum 1.1. Berlin, 1887.

———. *Moralia in Job.* 3 vols. Edited by M. Adriaen. Corpus christianorum series latina, 143, 143A–B. Turnhout: Brépols, 1979–85.

Grennen, Joseph E. "The Canon's Yeoman's Alchemical Mass." *Studies in Philology* 62 (1965): 546–60.

———. "The Canon's Yeoman and the Cosmic Furnace: Language and Meaning in the *Canon's Yeoman's Tale.*" *Criticism* 4 (1962): 225–40.

———. "Chaucer and the Commonplaces of Alchemy." *Classica et mediaevalia* 26 (1965): 306–33.

———. "Jargon Transmuted: Alchemy in Chaucer's *Canon's Yeoman's Tale.*" Ph.D diss., Fordham University, 1960.

———. "Saint Cecilia's 'chemical wedding': The Unity of the Canterbury Tales, Fragment VIII." *Journal of English and Germanic Philology* 65 (1966): 466–81.

Grisar, Hartmann. *Das Missale im Lichte römischer Stadtgeschichte: Stationen, Perikopen, Gebrauche.* Freiburg: Herder, 1925.

Guarducci, Margherita. *Cristo e San Pietro in un documento preconstantiniano della Necropoli Vaticana.* Rome: "L'Erma" di Bretschneider, 1953.

Guéranger, Dom [Prosper]. *Sainte Cécile et la Société romaine aux deux premiers siècles.* Paris: Firmin Didot Frères, 1874.

Guibert, Joseph de. *Theologia spiritualis, ascetica et mystica: Quaestiones selectae in praelectionum usu.* 4th ed. Rome: Gregorian University, 1952.

Guibert of Nogent. *Self and Society in Medieval France: The Memoirs of Abbot Guibert of Nogent.* Translated by C. C. Swinton; revised and edited by J. F. Benton. New York: Harper and Row, 1970.

Gurlitt, Walter. "Die Musik in Raffaels Heiliger Cäcilia." *Jahrbuch der Musikbibliothek Peters* 14 (1938): 84–97.

Hali Meidenhad. Edited by O. Cockayne. Early English Text Society, Original Series, 18. London: Trubner, 1866.

Hammerstein, Reinhold. *Die Musik der Engel: Untersuchungen zur Musikanschauung des Mittelalters.* Bern: Francke Verlag, 1962.

Hansen, Bert. "Science and Magic." In *Science in the Middle Ages,* edited by D. C. Lindberg, 483–506. Chicago History of Science and Medicine. Chicago: University of Chicago Press, 1978.

Harthian, John. *The Book of Hours.* New York: Crowell, 1977.

Haseloff, G. S. *Die Psalterillustration im 13 Jahrhundert: Studien zur Geschichte der Buchmalerei im England, Frankenreich und den Niederlanden.* Kiel, 1938.

Heninger, S. K., Jr. *Touches of Sweet Harmony: Pythagorean Cosmology and Renaissance Poetics.* San Marino, Calif.: Huntington Library, 1974.

Herolt, J. *Sermones de tempore et de sanctis.* Venice, 1606.

Hertling, Ludwig, and Engelbert Kirschbaum. *The Roman Catacombs and Their Martyrs.* Translated from the German by M. J. Costelloe. Rev. ed. London: Darton, Longman and Todd, 1960.

Hollander, John. *The Untuning of the Sky: Ideas of Music in English Poetry, 1500–1700.* Princeton: Princeton University Press, 1961. Reprint. New York: W. W. Norton, 1970.

Hottois, Isabelle. *De Musiekiconographie in de handschriften van de Koninklijke Bibliotheek Albert I.* Exhibition catalogue, July 7–August 21, 1982. Brussels: Koninklijke Bibliotheek Albert I, 1982.

Hubaux, Jean, and Maxime Leroy. *Le mythe du phénix dans les littératures grecque et latine.* Bibliothèque de la Faculté de Philosophie et Lettres de l'Université de Liège, 82. Liège: Faculté de Philosophie et Lettres, 1939.

Huelsen, C. *Le chiese di Roma nel medioevo.* Florence: L. Olschki, 1927.

Huttar, Charles A. "Frail Grass and Firm Tree: David as a Model of Repentance in the Middle Ages and Early Renaissance." In *The David Myth in Western Literature,* edited by R. J. Frontain and J. Wojcik, 38–54. West Lafayette, Ind.: Purdue University Press, 1980.

Irwin, Joyce L. "The Mystical Music of Jean Gerson." In *Early Music History: Studies in Medieval and Early Modern Music,* edited by I. Fenlon, 1:187–201. Cambridge: Cambridge University Press, 1981–.

Isidore of Seville. *Isidori Hispalensis Episcopi Etymologiarum sive Originum Libri XX. . . .* Edited by W. M. Lindsay. 2 vols. Oxford: Clarendon Press, 1911. Reprint, 1966.

Jacobsen, Michael A. "A Sforza Miniature by Cristoforo da Preda." *Burlington Magazine* 116, no. 851 (1974): 91–96.

Jacopone da Todi. *Laude.* Edited by F. Mancini. Scrittori d'Italia 257. Rome: Laterza, 1974.

Jacques de Voragine. *The Golden Legend.* Translated and adapted by G. Ryan and H. Ripperger [from the Latin ed. of Graesse, Leipzig, 1850, but altered after other editions to correct 'obvious' flaws]. London: Longmans, 1941.

———. *Sermones pulcherrimi variis scripturarum doctrinis referti de sanctis per anni totius circulum concurrentibus.* N.p, n.d.

Jean-Nesmy, Dom Claude. *Albi: La cathédrale et l'histoire, le décor sculpté et peint.* Pierre-qui-vire: Zodiaque, 1976.

Jeffrey, David L. *The Early English Lyric and Franciscan Spirituality.* Lincoln: University of Nebraska Press, 1975.

Jerome, St. *Liber interpretationum hebraicorum nominum.* In *S. Hieronymi presbyteri opera.* Corpus christianorum series latina, 72. Pars I [opera exegetica], 1. Turnhout: Brépols, 1959.

Johnston, William. *Silent Music.* New York: Harper and Row, 1974.

Jones, Roger, and Nicholas Penny. *Raphael.* New Haven: Yale University Press, 1983.

Jørgensen, Johannes. *Saint Bridget of Sweden.* Translated by Ingeborg Lund. 2 vols. London: Longmans, 1954.

Josi, Enrico. "Cecilia di Roma." In *BibSanc* 3 (1963): 1064–81.

Julian of Norwich. *Showings.* Translated by E. Colledge and J. Walsh. Classics of Western Spirituality. New York: Paulist Press, 1978.

Justi, Karl. "Raphaels heilige Cäcilia." *Zeitschrift für christliche Kunst* 17 (1904): 129–44.

Juvenal. *Satires.* In *Juvenal and Persius,* rev. ed., 1–307. Loeb Classical Library. 1940.

Katzenellenbogen, Adolf. *Allegories of the Virtues and Vices in Medieval Art from Early Christian Times to the Thirteenth Century.* Translated by A. Crick. Studies of the Warburg Institute, 10. London: Warburg Institute, 1939. Reprint. Medieval Academy Reprints for Teaching, 14. Toronto: University of Toronto Press, 1989.

Kelber, Wilhelm. *Raphael von Urbino.* Stuttgart: Urachhaus, 1979.

Kempe, Margery. *The Book of Margery Kempe.* Translated by B. A. Windeatt. London: Penguin, 1985.

Kennedy, V. L. *The Saints of the Canon of the Mass.* 2d rev. ed. Studi di antichità cristiana, 14. Vatican City: Pontificio istituto di archeologia cristiana, 1963.

King, Catherine. "The Liturgical and Commemorative Allusions in Raphael's *Transfiguration and Failure to Heal.*" *Journal of the Warburg and Cortauld Institutes* 45 (1982): 145–89.

Kirsch, J. P. *Die heilige Caecilia in der römischen Kirche.* Studien zur Geschichte und Kultur des Altertums, 4. Paderborn: F. Schoningh, 1910.

Klene, Jean, C.S.C. "Chaucer's Contributions to a Popular Topos: The World Upside-Down." *Viator* 11 (1980): 321–34.

Knight, F. Jackson. *St. Augustine's De Musica: A Synopsis.* London: Orthological Institute, 1949. Reprint. Westport, Conn.: Hyperion Press, 1979.

Kolve, V. A. "Chaucer's *Second Nun's Tale* and the Iconography of St. Cecilia." In *New Perspectives in Chaucer Criticism,* edited by D. M. Rose, 137–74. Norman, Okla.: Pilgrim Books, 1981.

Koudelka, Vladimir J. "Domenico, fondatore dell'ordine dei Frati Predicatori." In *BibSanc* 4:692–727.

Kraus, Franz X. *Geschichte der Christlichen Kunst*. Edited by J. Sauer. 2 vols. Freiburg im Breisgau: Herder, 1908.

Krautheimer, Richard. *Corpus basilicarum christianarum Romae: Le basiliche cristiane antiche di Roma (sec. IV–IX)*. 5 vols. Monumenti di antichità cristiana, II serie, 2. Vatican City: Pontificio istituto di archeologia cristiana, 1937–77.

Kunst und Kultur im Weserraum, 800–1600: Ausstellung des Landes Nordrhein-Westfalen, Corvey, 1966. 3d ed. 2 vols. Münster: Aschendorff, 1967.

Lacoste, Jean-Yves. "Les anges musiciens: Considérations sur l'éternité à partir de thèmes iconographiques et musicologiques." *Revue des sciences philosophiques et théologiques* 68 (1984): 549–75.

Laderchi, Giacomo. *S. Caeciliae virginis et martyris acta et transtyberina basilica*. . . . 2 vols. Rome: ex typographis Rocchi Bernabò, 1722–23.

Ladner, Gerhart B. *Handbuch der frühchristlichen Symbolik: Gott, Kosmos, Mensch*. Stuttgart: Belser, 1992.

――――. *The Idea of Reform: Its Impact on Christian Thought and Action in the Age of the Fathers*. Cambridge, Mass.: Harvard University Press, 1959.

――――. *Images and Ideas in the Middle Ages: Selected Studies in History and Art*. 2 vols. Rome: Edizioni di storia e letteratura, 1983.

Latte, K. *Römische Religionsgeschichte*. Handbuch der Altertumswissenschaft Abt. 5, t. 4. Munich: C. H. Beck, 1960.

Leclercq, Henri. "Cécile (crypte et basilique de Sainte-)." In *DACL* 2 (1910): 2738–79.

Leonardo da Udine. *Sermones de Sanctis*. Venice: Johannes de Colonia, 1475.

Leon, Harry J. *The Jews of Ancient Rome*. Philadelphia: Jewish Publication Society of America, 1960.

Leppert, Richard D. *The Theme of Music in Flemish Paintings of the Seventeenth Century*. 2 vols. Musik und Musiker im Bild, Ikonologische Studien 1. Munich: Emil Katzbichler, 1977.

Leroquais, V. *Les Livres d'heures manuscrits de la Bibliothèque nationale*. 3 vols. Paris: [Protat Frères], 1927; with supplement, Mâcon, 1943.

Loevinson, Ermanno. "Documenti del monastero di S. Cecilia in Trastevere." *Archivio della R[eale] Società Romana di Storia Patria* 49 (1926): 355–404.

Lomazzo, G. P. *Trattato dell'arte della pittura*. . . . Milan: Paolo Gottardo Pontio, 1584.

Loomis, Roger Sherman. *A Mirror of Chaucer's World*. Princeton: Princeton University Press, 1965.

Lotario dei Segni [Pope Innocent III]. *De miseria condicionis humane*. Edited and translated into English by R. E. Lewis. The Chaucer Library. Athens: University of Georgia Press, 1978.

Louth, Andrew. *The Origins of the Christian Mystical Tradition: From Plato to Denis*. Oxford: Clarendon Press, 1981.

Lowe, E. A. *The Beneventan Script*. Oxford: Oxford University Press, 1914.

Lucchesini, C. *Della storia letteraria del ducato lucchese*. Vol. 1. Lucca, 1825.

Luckett, Richard. "St. Cecilia and Music." *Proceedings of the Royal Musical Association* 99 (1972–73): 15–30.

Machabey, A. "Remarques sur le lexique musical du *De Canticis* de Gerson." *Romania* 79 (1958): 175–236.

Macrobius, Ambrosius Aurelius Theodosius. *Ambrosii Theodorii Macrobii Saturnalia apparatu critico instruxit, In Somnium Scipionis commentarios selecta varietate lectioni ornavit, Iacobus Willis.* Edited by J. Willis. 2 vols. Bibliotheca scriptorum graecorum et romanorum Teubneriana. Leipzig: Teubner, 1963.

———. *Commentary on the Dream of Scipio.* Translated and with an introduction and notets by W. H. Stahl. Records of Civilization, Sources and Studies 48. New York: Columbia University Press, 1952.

Mâle, Emile. *La cathédrale d'Albi.* 2d ed. Les points cardinaux, 23. Pierre-qui-vire: Zodiaque, 1974.

Mâle, Gilberte Emile. "Le transport, le séjour et la restauration à Paris de la Sainte Cécile de Raphael 1796–1815." In *Indagini,* 217–34.

Malvasia, Carlo Cesare. *Felsina pittrice.* 2 vols. Bologna, 1678.

Marcocchi, Massimo. *La Riforma cattolica: Documenti e testimonianze, figure ed istituzioni dal secolo XV alla metà del secolo XVII.* Introduction by M. Bendiscioli. 2 vols. Brescia: Morcelliana, 1967–70.

Marcuse, Sybil. *Musical Instruments: A Comprehensive Dictionary.* Rev. ed. New York: W. W. Norton, 1975.

Marienwerder, Joannes. *Vita prima B. Dorotheae* [Short Vita of Dorothy of Montau]. In *AaSs* Octobris, 13:493–98.

———. *Vita B. Dorotheae Lindana* [Long Vita of Dorothy of Montau]. In *AaSs* Octobris, 13:499–588.

Marinelli, Sergio. "Il castello, le collezioni." In *Carlo Scarpa a Castelvecchio,* exhibition catalogue, edited by L. Magagnato, 133–48. Milan: Edizioni di comunità, 1982.

———. *Castelvecchio a Verona.* Milan: Electa, 1991.

Marshall, Kimberley. *Iconographical Evidence for the Late Medieval Organ in French, Flemish and English Manuscripts.* 2 vols. New York: Garland, 1989.

Matter, E. Ann. *The Voice of My Beloved: The Song of Songs in Medieval Christianity.* Philadelphia: University of Pennsylvania Press, 1990.

Matthiae, Guglielmo. *S. Cecilia in Trastevere.* Le chiese di Roma illustrata, 113. Rome: Marietti, 1970.

Mazza, Angelo. "Arduino Arriguzzi e la Capella della beata Elena." In *DocTemp,* 50–55, 67–80.

———. "L'ancona lignea e Andrea da Formigine." In *DocTemp,* 57–62, 81–90.

———. "Le vicende storiche della Santa Cecilia." In *DocTemp,* 63–66, 91–103.

McGinn, Bernard, John Meyendorff, and Jean Leclercq, eds. *Christian Spirituality: Origins to the Twelfth Century.* 2 vols. New York: SCM Press, 1988.

McKinnon, James. *Music in Early Christian Literature.* Cambridge Readings in the Literature of Music. Cambridge: Cambridge University Press, 1987.

Meiggs, R. *Roman Ostia.* 2d ed. Oxford: Clarendon Press, 1973.

Meli, Bernardo. "Intervento di risanamento, consolidamento e restauro." In *Tre interventi di restauro,* 79–89. Rome: Ministero per i beni culturali e ambientali, 1981.

Melloni, G. B. *Atti o memorie degli uomini illustri nati o morti in Bologna.* Classe II, vol. 3. Bologna: Lelio della Volpe, 1780.

Mercati, Angelo. "L'autore della 'expositio in septem Psalmos poenitentiales.'" *Revue bénédictine* 31 (1914–19): 250–57.

Meyer, Hans G. *Eine Sabbatampel im Erfurter Dom.* Studien zur Kunstgeschichte, 16. Hildesheim: G. Olms, 1982.

Meyer-Baer, Kathi. "Music in Dante's *Divina Commedia.*" In *Aspects of Medieval and Renaissance Music: A Birthday Offering to Gustave Reese,* edited by J. LaRue, 614–27. New York: W. W. Norton, 1966.

Mirimonde, Albert P de. *Astrologie et musique.* Iconographie musicale, 5. Geneva: Minkoff, 1977.

———. *Sainte-Cécile: Métamorphoses d'un thème musical.* Iconographie musicale, 3. Geneva: Minkoff, 1974.

Mogan, Joseph J., Jr. *Chaucer and the Theme of Mutability.* De proprietatibus litterarum, Series practica, 3. The Hague: Mouton, 1969.

Mohr, Joseph. "Beiträge zu einer kritischen Bearbeitung der Martyrakten der heiligen Cäcilia." *Römische Quartalschrift* 3 (1889): 1–14.

Mohrmann, C. "Note sur doxa." In *Etudes sur le latin des chrétiens,* 277–86. Storia e letteratura: Raccolta di studi e testi, 65. Rome, 1958.

Mombritius, Boninus. *Sanctuarium seu vite sanctorum.* [1st ed. before 1480.] Edited by the monks of Solesmes. 2 vols. Paris: A. Fontemoing, 1910.

Moore, Carey A., ed. and trans. *Daniel, Esther and Jeremiah: The Additions.* A new translation with introduction and commentary. Anchor Bible 44. New York: Doubleday, 1977.

Morgan, Nigel. *Early Gothic Manuscripts.* 2 vols. A Survey of Manuscripts Illuminated in the British Isles, 4. London: Harvey Miller, [c. 1982–c. 1988].

Morin, G., ed. "Le plus ancien 'comes' ou lectionnaire de l'Eglise romaine." *Revue bénédictine* 27 (1910): 41–74.

Moroni, G., ed. *Dizionario di erudizione storico-ecclesiastica da S. Pietro fino ai nostri giorni.* 103 vols. Venice, 1840–61. With 6 vols. of indexes. Venice, 1878–89.

Mossakowski, Stanislaw. "Raphael's 'St. Cecilia': An Iconographical Study." *Zeitschrift für Kunstgeschichte* 31 (1968): 1–26.

Multhauf, Robert P. "The Science of Matter." In *Science in the Middle Ages,* edited by D. C. Lindberg, 369–90. Chicago History of Science and Medicine. Chicago: University of Chicago Press, 1978.

Murdoch, John E., and Edith D. Sylla. "The Science of Motion." In *Science in the Middle Ages,* edited by D. C. Lindberg, 206–64. Chicago History of Science and Medicine. Chicago: University of Chicago Press, 1978.

Negri, Giulio. *Istoria degli scrittori fiorentini.* Ferrara: Bernardino Pomatelli, 1722.

The New Penguin Dictionary of Music. Edited by A. Jacobs. 4th ed. London: Penguin, 1986.

The Norton/Grove Concise Encyclopedia of Music. Edited by S. Sadie and A. Latham. New York: Norton, 1988.

Offner, Richard. *A Critical and Historical Corpus of Florentine Painting.* New York: College of Fine Arts, New York University, 1931–.

Omont, Henri A. *Miniatures des plus anciens manuscrits grecs de la Bibliothèque nationale du VIe au XIVe siècle.* Paris: H. Champion, 1929.

O'Reilly, Jennifer. *Studies in the Iconography of the Virtues and Vices in the Middle Ages.* New York: Garland, 1988.

Ortolani, Sergio. *Raffaello.* Reprint of 1st ed. of 1942, with a new introduction by C. Gentili. Bergamo: Istituto italiano d'arti grafiche, 1983.

Osthoff, Wolfgang. "Raffael und die Musik." In *Raffael in seiner Zeit,* edited by V. Hoffman, 155–88. Nuremberg: Verlag Hans Carl, 1987.

Ovid [Publius Ovidius Naso]. *Ars amatoria: Cum appendice ad Remedia pertinente.* Edited by F. W. Lenz. Corpus scriptorum latinorum Paravianum. Turin: I. B. Paravia, [1969].

————. *Fasti* [English and Latin]. Translated by J. G. Fraser. 2d ed. rev. by G. P. Goold. Loeb Classical Library. London: Heinemann, 1989.

Owens, Margareth Boyer. "The Image of King David in Prayer in Fifteenth-Century Books of Hours." *Imago musicae* 6 (1989): 23–38.

————. "Musical Subjects in the Illumination of Books of Hours from Fifteenth-Century France and Flanders." Ph.D. diss., University of Chicago, 1987.

Pagden, Sylvia Ferino. "From Cult Images to the Cult of Images: The Case of Raphael's Altarpieces." In *The Altarpiece in the Renaissance,* edited by P. Humfrey and M. Kemp, 165–89. Cambridge: Cambridge University Press, 1990.

Paschini, Pio. "Amour (Compagnie du Divin)." In *DSAM* 1 (1937): 531–33.

Passio Sanctae Caeciliae. Edited by H. Delehaye. In *Etudes sur le légendier romain: Les saints de novembre et décembre,* 194–220. Subsidia hagiographica, 23. Brussels, 1936.

Pastor, Ludwig Freiherr von. *Storia dei papi dalla fine del medio evo.* 17 vols. in 21. Translated from German into Italian [by A. Mercati et al.]. Rome: Desclée, 1942–64.

Pausanias. *Description of Greece* [English and Greek]. Translated by W. H. S. Jones and H. A. Ormerod. 5 vols. Loeb Classical Library. London: Heinemann, 1918–35.

Pelbartus de Themeswar [OFM; d. 1504]. *Pomeriu[m] sermonu[m] de S[an]ctis Hyemales et Estivales editi per Fratre[m] Pelbartu[m] de Themeswar divi Ordinis sancti Francisci.* N.p., n.d.

Peregrinus [Frater Peregrinus, Provincial of the Dominicans]. . . . *sermones de tempore et sanctis.* . . . N.p., 1487.

Petroff, Elizabeth. *Consolation of the Blessed.* New York: Alta Gaia Society, 1979.

Petrus de Alliaco [Pierre d'Ailly]. *La vraye penitance.* . . . 1480.

Pfeiffer, Heinrich, S.J. "Raffael und die Theologie." In *Raffael in seiner Zeit,* edited by V. Hoffman, 99–117. Nuremberg: Verlag Hans Carl, 1987.

Platner, S. B. *A Topographical Dictionary of Ancient Rome.* Revised by T. Ashby. London: Oxford University Press, H. Milford, 1929.

Plato. *Plato's Timaeus.* Translated by F. M. Cornford. Library of Liberal Arts, 106. Indianapolis: Bobbs-Merrill, [c. 1959].

————. *The Republic of Plato.* Translated by F. M. Cornford. New York: Oxford University Press, 1945.

Pliny the Elder. *Natural History.* Translated by H. Rackham. 10 vols. Loeb Classical Library. London: Heinemann, 1938–63.

Plummer, John. *The Last Flowering: French Painting in Manuscripts, 1420–1530, from American Collections.* New York: Pierpont Morgan Library, 1982.

————. "Looking at Art: Jean Fouquet's *King David in Prayer.*" *Art News,* February 1984, 98–99.

Plutarch. *Plutarch's Lives.* Translated by B. Perrin. 11 vols. Loeb Classical Library. London: Heinemann, 1948–59.

Pope-Hennessy, John. *Raphael: The Wrightsman Lectures Delivered under the Auspices of the New York University Institute of Fine Arts.* New York: Harper and Row, 1970.

Poque, Suzanne. *Le langage symbolique dans la prédication d'Augustin d'Hippone.* 2 vols. Paris: Etudes augustiniennes, 1984.

Prat, F. J. *The Theology of Saint Paul.* Translated from the French by J. L. Stoddard. 2 vols. London: Burns Oates and Washbourne, 1926. 6th impression revised, 1957.

Propertius, Sextus. *Propertius* [English and Latin]. Translated by H. E. Butler. Loeb Classical Library. London: Heinemann, 1962.

Prudentius Clemens, Aurelius. *Hamartigenia.* In *Prudentius,* edited and translated by H. J. Thomson, 1:200–273. Loeb Classical Library. London: Heinemann, 1949.

———. *Psychomachia.* In *Prudentius,* edited and translated by H. J. Thomson, 1:274–343. Loeb Classical Library. London: Heinemann, 1949.

Pseudo-Bonaventure. *Meditations on the Life of Christ: An Illustrated Manuscript of the Four-teenth Century, Paris, Bibliothèque nationale, MS. Ital. 115.* Translated by I. Ragusa; edited by I. Ragusa and R. Green. Princeton Monographs in Art and Archaeology, 35. Princeton: Princeton University Press, 1961. Reprint, 1977.

Pseudo-Dionysius the Areopagite. *The Celestial Hierarchy.* In *The Complete Works,* translated by C. Luibheid, 145–91. Classics of Western Spirituality. New York: Paulist Press, c. 1987.

———. *The Divine Names and Mystical Theology.* Translated from the Greek by J. D. Jones. Mediaeval Philosophical Texts in Translation, 21. Milwaukee: Marquette University Press, 1980.

Pseudo-Thomas Aquinas. *Der Alchemistische Traktat "Von der Multiplikation" von Pseudo-Thomas von Aquin.* Edited by D. Goltz, J. Telle, and H. J. Vermeer. Sudhoffs Archiv Zeitschrift für Wissenschaftsgeschichte, 19. Wiesbaden: Franz Steiner Verlag, 1977.

Pucci, A. *De corporis et sanguinis D.N. Jesu Christi sacrificio: Homiliae XIIII.* Bologna: A. Giaccarelli, 1551.

Pucci, O. "La Santa Cecilia di Raffaello d'Urbino." *Rivista fiorentina* 1 (June 1908): 6ff.

Quentin, Henri. "Cécile (Sainte)." In *DACL* (1910) 2:2712–38.

Quintavalle, Armando O. "Appunti di pittura napoletana nell'Annunziata di Minturno." *Bolletino d'arte* 29 (1936): 470–87.

Raffaello: Elementi di un mito. Le fonti, la letteratura artistica, la pittura di genere storico. Exhibition catalogue. Florence: Centro Di, 1984.

Raimondo da Capua, Beato. *S. Caterina da Siena.* Translated from Latin into Italian by G. Tinagli, OP. 5th rev. ed. Reprint. Siena: Cantagalli, 1991.

Randall, Lilian M. C. *Medieval and Renaissance Books of Hours in the Walters Art Gallery.* 3 vols. in 2. Baltimore: Johns Hopkins University Press in association with Walters Art Gallery, 1989–92.

Randall, Richard H. "In Honor of Janet Wurtzburger." *Walters Art Gallery Bulletin* 28, no. 6 (March 1976): 1–2, 4.

Raphael Urbinas: Il mito della Fornarina. Exhibition catalogue. Milan: Electa, 1983.

Rappresentazione di S. Cecilia Vergine e Martyre. [Florence]: Francesco di Giovanni Benvenuto, 1517. Reprint. Florence: Leo Olschki, 1969.

Reames, Sherry L. "The Cecilia Legend as Chaucer Inherited It and Retold It." *Speculum* 55 (1980): 38–57.

————. "A Recent Discovery Concerning the Sources of Chaucer's *Second Nun's Tale.*" *Modern Philology* 87 (1990): 337–61.

————. "The Sources of Chaucer's 'Second Nun's Tale.'" *Modern Philology* 76 (1978–79): 111–35.

Ricci, C. *Tavole storiche dei musaici di Ravenna,* vol. 5. Rome: Istituto poligrafico dello stato, 1934.

Rickert, Margaret J. *The Reconstructed Carmelite Missal: An English Manuscript of the Late XIV Century in the British Museum.* London: Faber and Faber, 1952.

Riehle, Wolfgang. *The Middle English Mystics.* Translated by B. Strandring. London: Routledge and Kegan Paul, 1981.

Ritta, Pietro [da Lucca]. *Arte nova del ben pensare e contemplare la passione del nostro Signore Giesu Cristo benedetto.* Bologna: Girolamo di Benedetti, 1523.

————. *Doctrina del ben morire con molte utili resolutioni di alchuni belli dubii Theologici.* Bologna: Hier. de Benedetti, 1518. [The second part of a single volume with *Opusculo.*]

————. *Fundamento della vita cristiana cioè tractato utilissimo della humilità: novamente composto.* Bologna: Girolamo de' Benedetti, 1515.

————. *Opusculo di trenta Documenti. Per le persone che desiderano esser spirituali.* Bologna: Hier. de Benedetti, 1518.

————. *Regule della vita spirituale et secreta Theologia.* Bologna: Per Joannem Antonium de Benedictis, 1504.

Rituale Romanum Pauli V Pont. Maximi jussu editum . . . Ss.mi. D. N. Pii Papae XII auctoritate ordinatum et auctum. Turin: Marietti, 1953.

Robertson, D. W., Jr. *A Preface to Chaucer: Studies in Medieval Perspectives.* Princeton: Princeton University Press, 1962.

Rola, Stanislas Klossowski de. *Alchemy: The Secret Art.* London: Thames and Hudson, 1973.

Rolle, Richard. *Le chant d'amour: Melos amoris.* Latin text by E. J. F. Arnould. Introduction and notes by F. Vandenbroucke. Translated by the nuns of Wisque. 2 vols. Sources chrétiennes, 168–69. Paris: Editions du Cerf, 1971.

Romanini, Angiola Maria. "Il restauro di S. Cecilia a Roma e la storia della pittura architettonica di età gotica." In *Tre interventi di restauro,* 75–78. Rome: Ministero per i beni culturali e ambientali, 1981.

Romano, Serena. "Alcuni fatti e qualche ipotesi su S. Cecilia in Trastevere." *Arte medievale: Periodico internazionale di critica dell'arte medievale,* 2d ser., 2, no. 1 (1988): 105–19.

Rondeau, Marie-Josephe. *Les commentaires patristiques du Psautier (3e–5e siècles).* 2 vols. Orientalia christiana analecta, 219–20. Rome: Pontificale institutum studiorum orientalium, 1982–85.

Rosati, Antonio M. *Memorie per servire alla storia dei vescovi di Pistoia.* Pistoia: Atto Bracali, 1766.

Rosenberg, Bruce A. "The Contrary Tales of the Second Nun and the Canon's Yeoman." *Chaucer Review* 2 (1968): 278–91.

Rossi, G. B. de. *Inscriptiones Christianae urbis Romae septimo saeculo antiquiores.* 2 vols. Rome: Ex officina libraria pontificia, 1857–88.

————. *La Roma sotterranea cristiana. . . .* 3 vols. Rome: Cromo-litografia pontificia, 1864–77.

Ruskin, John. *Modern Painters.* 5 vols. New York: Thomas Crowell, 1873.

Sabadino de li Arienti, Joanne. *Gynevra de le clare donne*. A. c. de C. Ricci e A. Bacchi della Lega. Bologna: Presso Romagnoli dall'Acqua, 1888. Reprint, 1968.

Salmi, Mario. *Italian Miniatures*. New York: Abrams, 1954.

Sandler, Lucy. *Gothic Manuscripts, 1285–1385*. 2 vols. London: Oxford University Press, 1986.

Santi, A. de. "S. Cecilia e la musica." *La civiltà cattolica* 4 (1921): 318–33.

Saussay, A. du, ed. *Martyrologium gallicanum*. 2 vols. Paris: S. Cramoisy, 1637.

Scanelli, F. *Il microcosmo della pittura*. Cesena: Neri, 1657. Reprint. Milan: Labor, 1966.

Schneyer, J. B. *Geschichte der Katholischen Predigt*. Freiburg: Seelsorge Verlag, 1969.

Schramm, Albert. *Der Bilderschmuck der Frühdrucke*. . . . 23 vols. in 19. Leipzig: Deutsches Museum für Druck und Schrift, 1920–43.

Schueller, Herbert M. *The Idea of Music: An Introduction to Musical Aesthetics in Antiquity and the Middle Ages*. Early Drama, Art, and Music Monograph Series, 9. Kalamazoo, Mich.: Medieval Institute Publications, 1988.

Schumacher, W. N. "Dominus legem dat." *Römische Quartalschrift* 54 (1959): 1–39.

Seebass, Tilman. *Musikdarstellung und Psalterillustration im früheren Mittelalter: Studien ausgehend von einer Ikonologie der Handschrift Paris, Bibliothèque Nationale, fonds latin 1118*. 2 vols. Bern: Francke, [1973].

Seneca, Lucius Annaeus. *Ad Lucilium epistulae morales*. 3 vols. Translated by R. M. Gummere. Loeb Classical Library. London: Heinemann, 1917–25.

Servius. *Servii grammatici qui feruntur in Vergilii carmina comentarii*. Edited by G. Thilo and H. Hagen. 3 vols. Leipzig: Teubner, 1881–1902. Reprint. Hildesheim: G. Olms, 1961.

Shearman, John. *Mannerism*. Harmondsworth: Penguin, 1967.

———. "Le seizième siècle européen." *Burlington Magazine* 108, no. 755 (1966): 59–67.

Shelley, Percy Bysshe. *The Letters of Percy Bysshe Shelley*. Edited by F. L. Jones. 2 vols. Oxford: Clarendon Press, 1964.

Silver, Larry. *The Paintings of Quinten Massys, with catalogue raisonné*. Montclair, N.J.: Allanheld and Schram, 1984.

Silvestro [Mazzolini] da Prierio, Fra. *Quadragesimale*. Venice: Lazzarus de Scandii, 1515.

———. *Vita di Sancta Maria Madalena*. Bologna: Caligola de Bazalieri, 1501.

Smits van Waesberghe, Joseph. *Musikerziehung: Lehre und Theorie der Musik im Mittelalter*. Edited by H. Besseler and W. Bachmann. Musikgeschichte in Bildern 3, Lfg. 3. Leipzig: VEB Deutscher Verlag für Musik, 1969.

Soli, Gusmano. *Chiese di Modena*. A. c. di G. Bertuzzi. 3 vols. Modena: Aedes Muratoriana, 1974.

Sotomayor, M. *S. Pedro en la iconografía paleocristiana*. Granada, 1962.

Spearing, A. C. *Medieval Dream-Poetry*. Cambridge: Cambridge University Press, 1976.

Spiera Tarvisinus, Ambrosius. [*Sermons*.] Venice: Antonius de Valentina et Jacobus Brittanicus et socii, 1481.

Spitzer, Leo. *Classical and Christian Ideas of World Harmony*. Baltimore: Johns Hopkins University Press, 1963.

Stefani, Gino. "Miti barocchi: Santa Cecilia." *Nuova rivista musicale italiana* 7 (1973): 176–84.

Stefaniak, Regina. "Raphael's *Santa Cecilia*: A Fine and Private Vision of Virginity." *Art History* 14 (1991): 345–71.

Steger, Hugo. *David Rex et Propheta: König David als vorbildliche Verkörperung des Herrschers und Dichters im Mittelalter, nach Bilddarstellung des achten bis zwölften Jahrhunderts.* Erlanger Beiträge zur Sprach- und Kunstwissenschaft, 6. Nuremberg: Verlag Hans Carl, 1961.

Steiner, George. *Real Presences.* Chicago: University of Chicago Press, 1989.

Steiner, Ruth. "The Canticle of the Three Children as a Chant of the Roman Mass." *Schweizer Jahrbuch für Musikwissenschaft,* n.s., 2 (1982): 81–90.

Sterling, Charles. *Still Life Painting: From Antiquity to the Twentieth Century.* 2d rev. ed. New York: Harper and Row, [c. 1981].

Strumwaner, Gina. "Heroes, Heroines and Heroic Tales from the Old Testament: An Iconographic Analysis of the Most Frequently Repeated Old Testament Subjects in Netherlandish Painting, ca. 1430–1570." Ph.D. diss., UCLA, 1979.

Styger, P. *Die römischen Katakomben.* Berlin: Verlag für Kunstwissenschaft, 1933.

———. *Römische Märtyrergrüfte.* 2 vols. Berlin: Verlag für Kunstwissenschaft, 1935.

Surtees, Virginia. *The Paintings and Drawings of Dante-Gabriel Rossetti (1828–1882): A Catalogue Raisonnée.* 2 vols. Oxford: Clarendon Press, 1971.

Tenenti, A. *Il senso della morte e l'amore della vita nel Rinascimento (Francia e Italia).* Turin: Einaudi, 1957.

Tertullian [Quintus Septimius Florens Tertullianus]. *Apologeticum.* Edited by P. Frassinetti. Corpus scriptorum latinorum Paravianum. Turin: I. B. Paravia, [c. 1965].

Tester, S. J. *A History of Western Astrology.* Woodbridge: Boydell, 1987.

Testini, Pasquale. *Le catacombe e gli antichi cimiteri cristiani in Roma.* Roma cristiana, 2. Bologna: Cappelli, 1966.

Thomas à Kempis. *The Imitation of Christ.* Translated by R. Knox and M. Oakley. New York: Sheed and Ward, 1962.

Tibullus, Albius. In *Catullus, Tibullus and Pervigilium Veneris* [Latin and English]. Loeb Classical Library. London: Heinemann, 1968.

Tiraboschi, H. *Vetera Humiliatorum monumenta.* 3 vols. Milan, 1766–68.

Toesca, Pietro. *Monumenti e studi per la storia della miniatura italiana, I: La collezione di Ulrico Hoepli.* Milan: Hoepli, 1930.

———. *Il Trecento.* Turin: Unione tipografico-editrice torinese, 1951.

Treasures of the Fitzwilliam Museum: An Illustrated Souvenir of the Collections. Cambridge: Pevensey Press for Fitzwilliam Museum Enterprises, [1982].

Tuve, Rosemond. *Allegorical Imagery: Some Medieval Books and Their Posterity.* Princeton: Princeton University Press, 1966.

Underhill, Evelyn. *Mysticism: A Study in the Nature and Development of Man's Spiritual Consciousness.* Rev. ed. New York: Dutton, 1961.

Valentini, Roberto, and Giuseppe Zuchetti. *Codice topografico della città di Roma.* 4 vols. Fonti per la storia d'Italia, 81, 88, 90–91. Rome: Tipografia del Senato, 1940–53.

Valeri, F. Malaguzzi. "La Santa Cecilia di Raffaello." *Archivio storico dell'arte* 7 (1894): 367–68.

Valerius Maximus. *Valerii Maximi Factorum ac dictorum memorabilium libri IX. Cum Iulii Paridis et Ianuarii Nepotiani epitomis.* Edited by C. Kempf. Bibliotheca scriptorum graecorum et romanorum Teubneriana. Stuttgart: Teubner, 1966.

Van den Broek, R. *The Myth of the Phoenix according to Classical and Early Christian Traditions.* Translated from the Dutch by I. Seeger. Etudes préliminaires aux religions orientales dans l'Empire romain, 24. Leiden: Brill, 1972.

Vasari, Giorgio. *Le vite de' più eccellenti pittori scultori ed architettori. . . .* Con nuove annotazioni e commenti di G. Milanesi. 9 vols. Florence: Sansoni, 1906. Reprinted as *Le opere di Giorgio Vasari*, 1981.

Viller, Marcel. "Catherine de Gènes (Sainte)." In *DSAM* 2:290–324.

Vincent Ferrer, St. *Oeuvres*. Edited by Père H. D. Fages, OP. 2 vols. Paris, 1909.

Voelkle, William M. *Masterpieces of Medieval Painting: The Art of Illumination*. Chicago: University of Chicago Press, 1980.

———. "Morgan Manuscript M.1001: The Seven Deadly Sins and the Seven Evil Ones." In *Monsters and Demons in the Ancient and Medieval Worlds: Papers presented in Honor of Edith Parada,* edited by A. B. Farkas, P. O. Harper, and E. B. Harrison, 101–14. Mainz: Verlag Philipp von Zabern, 1987.

Vogel, Cyrille. *Medieval Liturgy: An Introduction to the Sources*. Revised and translated from the French by W. G. Storey and N. Krogh Rasmussen. Washington, D.C.: Pastoral Press, 1986.

Walker, D. P. "Orpheus the Theologian and Renaissance Platonists." *Journal of the Warburg and Courtauld Institutes* 16 (1953): 100–120.

Watson, Arthur. "The *Speculum Virginum* with Special Reference to the Tree of Jesse." *Speculum* 3:445–69.

Wenzel, Siegfried. *Verses in Sermons: "Fasciculus morum" and Its Middle English Poems*. Medieval Academy of America Publications, 87. Cambridge, Mass.: Medieval Academy, 1978.

Whiting, B. J. *Proverbs, Sentences, and Proverbial Phrases from English Writings Mainly before 1500*. Cambridge, Mass.: Belknap Press, 1968.

Wieck, Roger S. *Time Sanctified: The Book of Hours in Medieval Art and Life*. New York: George Braziller, 1988.

Williams, E. *The Rose-Garden Game: A Tradition of Beads and Flowers*. New York: Herder and Herder, 1969.

Willis, G. G. "Roman Stational Liturgy." In *Further Essays in Early Roman Liturgy,* 1–87. Alcuin Club Collections, 50. London: SPCK, 1968.

Wilpert, G. *La cripta dei papi e la cappella di Santa Cecilia nel cimitero di Callisto*. Translated from German into Italian by E. Josi. Rome: Desclée, 1910.

Winternitz, Emanuel. *Musical Instruments and Their Symbolism in Western Art: Studies in Musical Iconology*. 2d ed. New Haven: Yale University Press, 1979.

Wolf, Edwin, II. *A Descriptive Catalogue of the John Frederick Lewis Collection of European Manuscripts in the Free Library of Philadelphia*. Philadelphia: Free Library, 1937.

Woodruff, Helen. *The Illustrated Manuscripts of Prudentius*. Cambridge, Mass.: Harvard University Press, 1930.

Woolf, Rosemary. *The English Religious Lyric in the Middle Ages*. Oxford: Clarendon Press, 1968.

Zanoni, L. *Gli Umiliati nel loro rapporti con l'eresia, l'industria della lana ed i comuni nei secoli XII e XIII*. Bibliotheca historica italiana, 2d ser., vol. 2. Milan: Hoepli, 1911.

Zarri, Gabriella. "L'altra Cecilia: Elena Duglioli dall'Olio (1472–1520)." In *Indagini,* 81–118.

Zazzaretta, A. "I sonetti di Raffaello." *L'Arte* 32 (1929): 77–88, 97–106.

Index

Numbers in boldface refer to illustrations

Clare of Assisi, St.: mourning and joy in legend of, 159–60

Clarity, 62, 65–66

Compassion: renders passions concordant, 148; importance of to Julian of Norwich, 162–63; in Franciscan spirituality, 174–75, 249, 320n58; equivalent of Greek *sympathia,* suggesting sympathetic vibration, 175, 320n58

Conca, Sebastiano: *Apotheosis of St. Cecilia,* 34

Confusion: Cecilia prays against, 52–53; in *Ps. 24,* 97. *See also* Babylon

Contemplation: silence or concord symbolizes, 127; banishes *acedia,* 187

Contrariety: distinguishes motion, 173

Contrary musics of sorrow and joy, 258

Costa, Lorenzo: *Madonna Enthroned,* 112; frescoes at oratory of St. Cecilia, Bologna, 201

Crown: discarded, **82,** 297n3; on David's hands in Sforza Hours, 101, 104

Crowns of flowers, 68–69

Crypt of popes. *See* Catacomb of St. Callistus

Dall'Olio, Ser Benedetto: husband of Elena dall'Olio, 116

Damasus, Pope, 30–31

Dante: bases cosmography on mourning and joy, 152–55; perfection of the circle, 173; impulse and *organi del mondo,* 190; on seeing and hearing in heaven, 254–55. *See also* Beatrice

David: early catechesis on, 84; composition of *Ps. 37* arose from sin of sloth, 99; plays harp at *Ps. 37,* 102; with harp in Albi vaults, 237; raises soul to God, pl. 5, 301n29

David-in-Penitence, miniature of: congruence with Raphael's *St. Cecilia,* 79, 246, 261; patrons identify with, 80–82, 297–98n4; earliest examples, 87–88; iconography of, 89–95; place in early books, 96–98; in *Fundamento* of Pietro

da Lucca, 128; development parallels musical representation of Cecilia, 219–20

De Brailes Hours: earliest English book of hours, 88; captions in, 101

Denis the Carthusian: on *sonus epulantis,* 245–46, 302n33

Discarded instruments: in Raphael's *St. Cecilia,* 12, 261, 277n6; harp, 18, 81, 88–89, 90–91, 99; organ, 90–91; lute, **91,** 92; viol, **91,** 92; symbolize vice defeated, vanities abandoned, 108–9; in miniature of Venus, 312n78; and reversal of mourning and joy, 109, 110

Donkey illustrating sloth: 99, 102

Donnella, Francesco (da Carpi): chief painter of Albi vaults, 229

Doria Pamphili, Cardinal G., 34

Duglioli, Ser Silvestro, 116

Ears of the heart. *See* Spiritual senses

Easter Vigil: deacon as phoenix, 209

Ecstasy: described by Pietro da Lucca, 126

Ecstasy of St. Cecilia: Shelley on, 11–12; description of, 12–13; significance of music in, 149–50; choice of saints, 242–43; St. Paul in, 243–44; St. John Evangelist in, 244–45; St. Augustine in, 245–47; St. Mary Magdalene in, 247–53; St. Cecilia in, 253–61; influence of, 301n29, 325n1

Elena Duglioli dall'Olio, Beata: work at S. Giovanni in Monte, 112; legendary aspects of life, 115, 117–21; charitable works, 117; sources for life of, 303n2, 304n7, 305n22, 306n24

Emblems. *See* Cecilia, St.

Esther: Hebrew name Hadassah, "myrtle," 51, 55

Eudes de Chateauroux: sermon on Cecilia to the choir of Paris, 120–21, 157

Eyck, H. and J. van: St. Bavo altarpiece, Gand, 214

Eyes of the heart. *See* Spiritual senses

59; compares Cecilia to correct tuning, 259–60

John of S. Gimignano: preaches on *Esther* 13:17, 159

John the Evangelist, St.: influence on Pietro da Lucca, 131–32; and command to love, 145; Gerson describes musical character of, 244–45. See also *Ecstasy of St. Cecilia*

Joy: passion of the blessed, 153. *See also* Gerson, Jean

Jubal: with hammers in Albi vaults, 237

Julian of Norwich: revelations founded on Cecilia's three wounds, 161–62; spiritual life is flux of mourning and joy, 161–66

Juvenal: on Bona Dea, 43

Kempe, Margery: parallels with Cecilia, 167, 316–17n38; narrative strategy of mourning and joy, 168, 317n40; white dress of, 249

Kempis, Thomas à: mourning and joy in *Imitation of Christ*, 159

Lactantius: and legend of the phoenix, 75–76, 206

Liturgical books: nature of, 287n52

Macrobius, Ambrosius Aurelius Theodosius: on Bona Dea, 44–45; music and virginity, 197

Maderno, Stefano: statue of St. Cecilia, 35–36, **36**

Malvasia, C.: calls Raphael *boccalaio urbinate*, 13; on Raphael's commissioners, 111

Manuscripts cited:
—*Albi, Bibliothèque Rochegude, MS 46,* 289n71
—*Baltimore, Walters Art Gallery Library, MS W.245,* 98, 102, 104; *MS W.430,* 98, 102, 104
—*Benevento, Biblioteca capitolare, MS VI.34,* 289n69
—*Bologna, Biblioteca comunale dell'Archi-*

ginnasio, MS B.100, 305n22, *MS B.1108,* 304n7, *MS B.4216, MS B.4314, MS Gozzadini* 292, 303n2; *Biblioteca universitaria, MS Ital. 97,* 306n24
—*Brussels, Bibliothèque Albert Ier, MS 5648,* 226; *MS 5646,* 330n47
—*Cambridge, Corpus Christi College Library, MS 23,* 303n40; *Fitzwilliam Museum, MS McClean 201,* 329n40, *MS 368,* 327n16
—*Chantilly, Musée Condé, MS 1887,* 223n42
—*Chartres, Bibliothèque municipale, MS 144,* 292–93n28
—*Cologny-Genève, Bibliotheca Bodmeriana, MS 74,* 296n47, 328n34
—*Douai, Bibl. mun., MS 171,* 88, 300n19
—*Einsiedeln, Stadtbibliothek, MS 121,* 289n69
—*Florence, Biblioteca Laurenziana, MS Plut. 15.17,* 297n4
—*Kew Gardens, Collection of B. S. Cron, lectionary from S. Cecilia in Trastevere,* 328n24
—*Laon, Bibliothèque municipale, MS 239,* 289n69; *MS 243*[4], 90, 281n28, 300n21
—*London, British Library, MS 29902,* 224; *MS 49999,* 98, 99, 100–101, 103, 104, 299–300n18; *Add. MS 15814,* 301n29; *Add. MS 18850,* 300n24; *Add. MS 29704–05,* 328n33; *Add. MS 29902,* 330n44; *Add. MS 34294,* 98, 100, 101–2, 103, 104; *Add. MS 54180,* 327n16; *MS Harley 2897,* 330n57, *MS Sloane 3983,* 312n78; *Royal MS 2.A.16,* 296nn2,3; *Yates Thompson MS 3,* 98, 99, 101
—*Naples, Bibl. naz., MS I.B.27,* 300n24
—*New York, Pierpont Morgan Library, MS M.110,* 300n28; *MS M.677,* 98, 100; *MS M.729,* 335n30; *MS M.1001,* 98, 99
—*Oxford, Bodleian Library, MS Douce 219–20,* 98, 100, 104; *MS Douce 131,* 299n14; *MS Hatton 101,* 314n13; *MS Laud lat. 114,* 300n20
—*Paris, Bibliothèque nationale, MS grec. 139,* 297n4; *MS lat. 10861,* 292–93n28; *MS lat. 12412,* 324n98

Penitential psalms: origin of, 84; and story of David, 85, 103; illustrated by individual miniatures, 99–104; *Ps. 37* the most musical, 100–109

Perugino: *St. Jerome*, 297n3

Peter Damian, St.: 153

Peter Lombard: on *Ps. 37*, 85; music and motion from sadness to joy, 109

Peter the Martyr, St.: 169

Phoenix: in *Passio Ceciliae*, 71, 75–76; significance in Cecilia's cult, 205–11

Pietro de Lucca: and Elena dall'Olio, 119–22; teaching of, 123–32

Pinturicchio: teacher of Francesco Donnella, 229, 330n50; similarities to figures in Albi vaults, 236

Preaching and mourning-into-joy, 155–59, 168

Provoost, Jan (1465–1529): *St. Nicholas with Donor*, **83**, 297–98n4

Pucci, Cardinal Antonio: co-commissioner of Raphael's *St. Cecilia*, 111–15

Quadrigesimale, 157

Quartararo, Riccardo: *St. Cecilia Listens to an Angel Lutenist*, 223–25

Raphael: and commissioners of *St. Cecilia*, 111–14, 149–50; *Portrait of Bindo Altoviti*, 252; *Madonna di Foligno*, 334n22. See also *Ecstasy of St. Cecilia*

Reversed organ: in Verona statue, 216–17; due to woodcut, 277n4; significance of, 257–58; further illustrations of, 335n30

Ritta, Pietro. *See* Pietro da Lucca

Rolle, Richard, 257

Rossi, Giovanni Battista de: and rediscovery of catacombs, 28–29

Sadness: song of, 142–43; in mystical gamma, 148; passion of the damned, 153; equated with sloth, 186

S. Giovanni in Monte, church of, 111–12

S. Cecilia in Trastevere, Basilica of: de-

scription, 33–35; *cappella del bagno*, 39; apsidal mosaic, 199–200

Saturn and contemplation, 153, 154–55

Scripture references:

—*1 Sam. 17:34*, 93, *18:6–7*, **107**

—*2 Sam. 6:12–23*, 308n47, *7:8–16*, 297n4, *11–12*, 298n7

—*2 Kings 2:23*, 247

—*1 Chron. 6*, 309n58, *6:1, 16–17*, 334n11, *6:7*, 334n11, *25*, 309n58

—*Jth. 10:3*, 258, 335n31

—*Esther 2:7*, 51, *13:9–17*, 21, 50, *13:17*, 4, 22, 87, 110, 152, 157, 158, 159, 258, *14:1–19*, 50

—*Job 7:8*, 314n20, *21:12–13*, 156–57, *30:31*, 4, 16, 19, 22, 54, 85, 86, 101, 152, 156, 157, 160, 194, 257, 258, 279n20

—*Ps. 1*, 93, *1:4–18*, 97, *6*, 101, 102, 103, 280n24, 298n4, *24*, 93, *24:1*, 109, *24:1–3*, 96–97, *24:15*, 109, 131, 245, 246, 261, 302n33, *29*, 314n20, *29:12*, 159, *31*, 101, 102, *37*, 101, 102, 103, 104, **106, 107**, 109, 188, 280n24, 312n82, *37:7*, 137, *38:4*, 124, *41*, 245, 247, 330n43, *41:5*, 245, 302n33, *44:5,11,12*, 290n8, *50*, **107**, *50:12*, 290nn11,13, *67:4*, 302n33, *76:11*, 312n86, *91*, 154, *93:11*, 308n38, *101*, 102, *119:1*, 88, *125*, 295n39, *129*, 102, *136:2*, 279n20, *281n34*, *142*, 102, *142:8*, 109, 301n29, *150:3*, 312n81

—*Prov. 14:13*, 159, *31:10–31*, 182, 183, 258

—*Sg. 6:7*, 177, *8:6*, 311n75

—*Sir. 5:13–17*, 316n30, *32:7*, 259–60, *51:13–17*, 48, 182

—*Isa. 12:1*, 86, *61:2–3*, 159

—*Jer. 31:13*, 159

—*Lam. 5:15–16*, 4, 19, 54, 85, 87, 101, 110, 128, 152, 280n27, 300n24, 314n10

—*Ezek. 18:31*, 65, 290n11, *36:26–27*, 290n11, 291n15

—*Dan. 3:94*, 78

—*Matt. 1:1*, 84, *5:4*, 149, 159, *5:5*, 175, *9:24*, 322n81, *11:16–19*, 143, 321n77,